"With the release of *Good Spirits*, there's nothing left to do but drink. Rathbun has left no spirit unturned. It's a great companion in the search for **a truly well-made cocktail**."

STEVE MAKO, owner, BalMar cocktail lounge, Seattle, Washington

"This is not just a drink recipe book. A.J. has managed to combine his extensive **bar know-how with wonderfully entertaining prose**. After years of hanging out on both sides of the bar, A.J. has created a great bar book—perfect for pros and amateurs alike. I have been bartending for 15 years and I was amazed at the things I learned from this book."

JEFF DENNEY, owner, Auntie Mae's Parlor, Manhattan, Kansas

"For all who have dinner parties, *Good Spirits* is the **must-have** book for setting up a home bar and delving into the art of mixology."

DAVE JEMILO, owner, Green Mill Cocktail Lounge, Chicago, Illinois

"Finally, a top-shelf spirits guide that captures the essence of mixology culture. A.J. Rathbun not only teaches the basics but also provides **a hip, informed roadmap** to both the classics and the newest innovations."

JASON LAGARENNE, General Manager/Mixologist, The Anchor, New York City

"My praise! In an era when the term 'martini' is used so loosely, it is refreshing to see that **imaginative drinks are still being created**, aptly titled, and cleverly selected and archived by Rathbun. *Good Spirits* provides an excellent companion to *The Bartender's Bible* and *Mr. Boston*."

JEREMY REH SIDENER, Mixologist/Manager, Eighth Street Tap Room, Lawrence, Kansas

"A great combination of history and instruction that all new bartenders should have to read and **recipes that every customer would love to know.** *Good Spirits* should be a staple behind every bar."

DAVID A. PARATORE, Esq., owner, Vintage Lounge and Who's on First, Boston, and North West Restaurant, New York City

"A.J. Rathbun's humorously informative approach to the subject is truly an enjoyable and pleasurable experience. The home mixologist will want to refer back to *Good Spirits* again and again. Like a well-made cocktail, this book **appeals to the senses, quenches the soul, and finishes with a smooth aftertaste** that the reader will savor long after the last word is read."

ANDREW ORTH, FMP, Director of Food and Beverage, The Court of Two Sisters, New Orleans, Louisiana

Good
Spirits

Recipes, Revelations,
Refreshments, and
Romance, Shaken and
Served with a Twist

A.J. Rathbun

The Harvard Common Press
Boston, Massachusetts

The
Harvard
Common
Press
5 3 5
Albany
Street
Boston
Massachusetts
0 2 1 1 8

www.harvardcommonpress.com

Printed in China | Printed on acid-free paper

Library of Congress Cataloging-in-Publication Data
···· Rathbun, A. J. (Arthur John), 1969– ····
Good spirits : recipes, revelations, refreshments,
and romance, shaken and served with a twist /
··········· A.J. Rathbun ···········
······ p. cm. Includes index. ······
ISBN 978-1-55832-336-0 (hardcover : alk. paper)
1. Cocktails. I. Title. TX951.R1685 2007
641.8'74—dc22 2007002511

Special bulk-order discounts are available on this and
other Harvard Common Press books. Companies and
organizations may purchase books for premiums or
resale, or may arrange a custom edition, by contacting
the Marketing Director at the address above.

······· Book design by Vivian Ghazarian ·······
······· Photography by Melissa Punch ·······
···· Drink styling by Brian Preston-Campbell ····
Production/prop styling by Antoinette Douglas-Hall

2 4 6 8 10 9 7 5 3

For all of those friends

who have bought—or who will buy—me a drink.

Thanks.

The next round's on me.

Contents

Acknowledgments

It took a full bar to put together this book. Since I probably won't have all those folks who helped me along the way together at one time in a bar to buy them all drinks, I'd like to instead send out some big thanks. The thanks start with Valerie Cimino, my editor at The Harvard Common Press. Valerie is like the Champagne in a French 75, adding levels of elegance and class to any mix, elevating it to a plane unthought-of originally. This book wouldn't have happened without her help at every level.

And speaking of the folks at The Harvard Common Press, well, they're a fantastic bunch, a family of book- and drink-loving people that I'm exceptionally blessed to have been able to work with, as their energy and ideas and artistry turn normal books into treasures. *Salute!*

Of course, not even one page of this book would have happened without the indefatigable efforts of my superhero agent, Michael Bourret (who hangs his tankard at the offices of Dystel & Goderich in New York). He's as important to this author as a well-made Manhattan, which may be the highest praise I feel I can give. Thanks, MB, for always being able to listen to questions about everything from contracts to rooftop bars, and for always having a quick reply and gracious words of encouragement (but really, go home—you're working too much). The number of drinks I owe you has reached stratospheric proportions.

There have been many, many other dedicated imbibers and cocktail slingers who have helped me, starting with two who sit on the top shelf for their ability to slip tasty recipes and advice my way, generally providing big shoulders that I leaned upon any time I needed a reliable human resource: Joel Meister and Jeremy (Husky Boy) Holt. Gentleman, start your bar tabs. And for Jon Sholly, Ed Skoog, and Michael Mahlin (and their wives, Nicole, Jill, and Sara), who pitched in beyond the last call of duty with their expertise on bars and drinks and how they relate to a variety of historical and modern media, thanks a liquid ton. Also pitching in (sometimes by the pitcherful) with their creative, catchy, and clever imbibable ideas were Maile and Matt Bohlmann and Rebecca Staffel. You are all bon vivants of the very best variety, and I appreciate the help.

It's been one of the luckier aspects of my life that I've had the pleasure of knowing a number of great bartenders, beyond those already mentioned, and I'd like to thank them for the drinks they've made me (and taught me to make), for the conversations we've had, and for the many friendships that have developed on both sides of the bar, with special mention going out to Kenny P., Jeremy S., Jeff Denny, and Markie Mark Miller.

It's not much fun hanging out at the bar without good conversation with fellow patrons, and I'd like to shout out to those whose jawing with me while sipping on a cold beverage led to much of the talk in this book, including Seattleites Megan, Ean and Reba, Mark (a chronicler of odd alcohol favorites) and Leslie, Erin and Tom, D-Rock, Shane, Brad and Christy, Andy and Deena, Christy S., Petey, Bob, Brett, Eric B., the Kitchen team at work (especially the editors), Brad P., Dish It Up, Kerika, and Kyla; Portlanders Katie and Eddie; Chicagoans Lisa and Dave, and Jim and Lora; New Yorkers Nate and Laura; NYC/New Orleanians EVH and Laura; Ithacans John and Rhian; Haysians Eric and Tami, and Christie; and the international Steph S.

Every party or bar needs a good soundtrack to keep things popping, and mine during the writing of this book starts with the Withholders (thanks Valbert and Aubrey), and shakes into songs by the Malinks, Truck Stop Love, God's Favorite Band, UFB and DGRE, Arthur Dodge and the Horsefeathers, National Trust, and Tom Waits.

There have been many, many books and columns and essays written by drink historians, cocktailians, and mixologists that have influenced and taught me. I want to highlight two erudite beverage balladeers—Gary and Mardee Haidin Regan. Not too many years ago they started writing a column for Amazon.com, which I coordinated, and through their columns and their friendliness I discovered an incredible amount about the world of drinks.

I picked up what I know about the fine art of throwing fun parties first and foremost from my parents (who threw amazing parties for me from the beginning), Trudy James and Arthur Rathbun, and my stepmom, Theresa, and then later picked up more hints from my sisters, Holly and Jill, who both know how to set up a successful shindig with the best of them (usually with the help of my brothers-in-law, Al and JD). Thanks, family, including my in-laws, the Fullers, for being supportive and helpful throughout this process. In addition, a special thanks goes to my incredible nephews Kaiser and Coen, who promise to enjoy this book even more once they've passed 21 years of age; and to Sookie, who won't read this book at all but who helped keep me sane while I wrote it.

Finally, and most important, the largest thanks of all go to my wife, Natalie Fuller, who I was fortunate enough to meet one historic summer when she was bartending at Auntie Mae's Parlor, in Manhattan, Kansas. Thanks, darling, for pouring me such good drinks and for cutting me a little slack on that one weekend's tab, and for being willing to listen to sidebar ideas, test innumerable drink variations, and run to the liquor store after work when the cabinet needed restocking. It wouldn't be fun in the least to write this book, or to have drinks in the backyard on a sunny summer afternoon, if you weren't there with me.

Introduction

The world revolves around conversation. Whether it's a conference call among colleagues or a simple hello between friends, everyone communicates for the majority of their lives, in a variety of conversational styles. E-mail and instant messaging have made it even easier to talk with one another frequently. And yet, in my experience, many of the finest and most enjoyable conversations I've had have come either after or before a toast made with a lovely cocktail. Maybe it's precisely because of the impersonal or rushed communication that exists in cyberspace, but more than ever before, a good drink or two with friends or relatives, new or old, leads to great conversations (some that continue over days). Whether people are out at a local watering hole, sitting on their back deck as the sun slips behind the horizon, or having dinner under chandeliers in an upscale eatery, they love to have a cocktail along with their conversations—either an erstwhile favorite or a mix recently introduced by friend or bartender.

This love of cocktails and conversation abounds today more than at any time since Prohibition. Folks are trying drinks they've never heard of, delving into blends long forgotten, and ordering up time-honored classics, as well as buying the hottest liquors to experiment with at home. People are having fun with their cocktailing, always looking for cutting-edge recipes they have not yet imbibed (and those their friends haven't tried—everyone wants to be the shining star introducing a sparkling drink to pals). This drive to expand one's drink knowledge and repertoire while having a good time is the stirrer behind today's cocktail revolution, and it is the base liquor this book is built upon as it strives to introduce you to an array of enjoyable drinks, both young and old.

This modern cocktail love has also spilled into a renewed love of hosting parties, soirées, and other festive revelries. Of course, serving the same drinks time after time at these gatherings does get a bit old (much like a cocktail cherry that's sat behind the bar far too long) and happens a bit too often. And, while there are many restaurants and bars boasting potent (and sometimes bizarre) potions, it can be a bit daunting trying to figure out what to try, which leads to ordering the same mix night after night.

Friends, this book is here to help. If you're looking to add a signature new cocktail to ensure your party stands out in guests' minds and stands the tests of time, making its way into party legend, this compendium has got you covered. If you desire a new favorite to have when hitting the bars, or want to take a potential new favorite for a test drive before ordering it while out, or want to have an idea of a smooth drink to order on a first date, it's got you covered. From the classics that have been around for a century or more to the freshest shaken, stirred, and blended beverages, this book will start you on a sparkling cocktail conversation that lasts until closing time—and beyond.

How to Use This Book

Unlike books that contain a variety of cocktails broken down by type of liquor (vodka, bourbon, etc.) or by alphabetical order, *Good Spirits* is divided into 12 thematic chapters.

Some themes are seasonal, meaning they contain drinks grouped to match a party that would take place at a certain time of year (such as Cool It Down and Turning Up the Heat) or parties that would have a certain number of people (such as Pacifying a Crowd and Dinner for Two). Some themes are more "time in history" related (such as Fresh Faces and Unburied Treasures), some are more "time in life" related (such as Collegiate Classics), some are related to specific bar equipment (such as The Blender's Whirr and Shooting the Moon), and some are more subject related (such as A Multitude of Martinis, An Obscure Reliquary, and The Gold Standards). Within each chapter, the drinks are alphabetized, to make it easier to find particular drinks. Unless otherwise noted, each recipe makes one drink. In addition, there are two indexes at the back: one that categorizes each drink according to its primary, or base, liquor, and a general comprehensive index.

Overall, breaking drinks out by theme makes it less of a hassle for you to track down a recipe for a particular type of gathering, or to track down a particular type of old or newer drink, or just to browse and do a little liquid research on a specific genre of drinks. It also helps to make it a breeze to match up a couple of different drinks if, for example, you want to host a party highlighted by one or two signature beverages—always a cool idea and one that makes your party stand out from the party pack. Finally, breaking it down by theme adds an extra dash of fun and creativity. I hope that this book reflects the conversations and merriment of a great party, or of being out with friends in a good bar. Because that, pals, is—finally—what having drinks together is all about.

STOCKING THE BAR

Would an acrobat try to swing from tent-corner to tent-corner of the circus tent without a rope? It would be impossible, and not only would the crowd be dismayed, but injuries might occur. Would a quarterback try to connect on a game-winning pass without a ball? It would look silly, and the crowd would boo and the game would be lost. Would a guitar hero break into that rocking mid-song solo without a guitar? Unless it was an air guitar contest, the silence would be deadly, and the crowd would walk away disappointed. In the same way, you have to have the right materials and tools to have a successful home bar. Without them, your guests will drift away, and you won't ascend into the party-thrower pantheon.

This is why preparation is the first ingredient for any party. While throwing together a last-minute late-night dance-a-thon is (or can be) a pretty sweet event, having a little bit of basic preparation at all times makes such events even sweeter. If you want to have a more planned-out soirée, with signature drinks to delineate your party from other, more mundane affairs, then proper prior planning is a must. Having the right tools and ingredients on hand also makes your job as host or hostess much easier, because you won't be spending the whole evening stressing about how the drinks possibly can be constructed when you've run out of ice and limes and there are only plastic cups left. Luckily, you in no way have to take out a loan to install the right basics in a home establishment.

The First Round: Liquors

There are six liquors that fall into the "base" liquor category. That doesn't mean that every one of the many drinks in this book relies on these "bases," but they do show up in a large percentage of the drinks, and in cocktails 'round the world in general. These base liquors are: gin, rum, whiskey/bourbon, vodka, tequila, and Champagne. Being stocked up on three of those bases establishes a solid home-bar foundation to build upon. Having an additional three should make it easier to cover a variety of tastes, which allows you to whip up a dandy drink outside of what was originally planned if a particular guest doesn't enjoy tequila, for example.

The individual histories of each of these six base liquors could fill up a large book, so I'm not going to delve too deeply into them (because I wouldn't want to keep you so busy you didn't get to the drink recipes). But it is good to at least touch on each, just so you can feel you've become acquainted at more than a passing level. Our first base, gin, is a juniper berry–flavored grain spirit, which picked up its name from an English shortening of *genever*, the Dutch word for juniper, after British troops began drinking a juniper-flavored spirit during the Dutch War of Independence (to provide themselves with "Dutch courage" before battle). Gin usage in the United States dates back to Colonial times, but the gin highpoint was in the years leading up to, and the years after, Prohibition (the term "bathtub gin" actually dates to Prohibition, when bootleggers would mix raw alcohol with juniper berry extract in the bathtub before selling it to speakeasies), when gin was atop most imbibers' cocktail lists. You don't find flavored gins, in the way you do flavored vodkas, but there are a range of subtle differences between gins from different companies, especially as there are now a number of small gin makers, such as Hendrick's, bringing more individual gins to the market.

Although no one can pinpoint the moment of its birth and christening, rum's name probably originates from the Latin word for sugarcane, *saccarum*, or the old Gypsy *rum*, which means "grand" or "potent." Rum's worn other colorful monikers, too, most a reflection of its once-thought-dangerous nature: *kill-devil, hydra-monster, rumbowling, cursed liquor, rhum,* and, of course, *that demon rum.* Mainly derived from molasses, a byproduct of the sugar-refining process, rum in the seventeenth century was an inexpensive import from the West Indies, making it the most popular liquor in the British colonies at the time. At one point in the 1700s, there were 30 rum distillers around Boston and Rhode Island. But, by the early 1800s, rum's moment was past. When the Revolutionary War broke out, the British blockaded many Atlantic ports, making it hard, if not impossible, to import molasses and export rum, and this started the decline. There are both white or light rums (which are clear) and dark rums (which tend toward an amber color, but are sometimes a very dark brown). The former have a lighter taste, and are used a bit more in cocktails, while the latter have a fuller, rich taste, which tends to evoke the molasses more. There are also flavored rums now available, usually found in coconut and other tropical styles.

There are whiskies or whiskey-style liquors available almost everywhere grains are harvested. The actual ingredients and method of construction depend a lot on geography. For example, American straight whiskies are made of a grain mash that contains at least 51 percent of a single grain (corn for bourbon, rye for rye), but no more that 79 percent, and must be aged in charred barrels of oak; Scotch whisky (spelled without an e) must be made in a distillery in Scotland and must contain water and barley (to which other grains may be added) and be aged in oak casks for at least three years. Beyond having a slightly different spelling, Irish whiskeys come in three forms: single malt (which is pure malted barley), pot still (a combination of malted and unmalted barley), and blended (which may have corn or other grains in with the barley). All are aged for three years in oak casks. "Whiskey" comes most likely from the Celtic for "water of life," *usquebaugh,* which may very well come from the Latin *aqua vitae.* Whiskies have seen a little explosion of popularity (not that they haven't been popular for a long while) in the past 20 years, as more and more are being made and consumed, especially those of the higher-end variety. This pattern of drinking straight whiskey leads many people away from thinking of whiskey as being a good base for cocktails, but don't fall into this trap.

What most people today think is a good base for cocktails is vodka, which may be said to currently sit atop the cocktail and bar liquor ladder. Vodka was developed in a northern European region, either Poland or Russia (depending on whom you ask). The word itself, "vodka," is a diminutive of the Russian word for water, *voda*. Vodka first made a splash on the United States drinking scene in the 1950s via an advertising plan involving the drink the Moscow Mule (page 222). Through this advertising campaign, the American public learned more about this usually colorless liquor, which is made from potatoes, soybeans, grapes, molasses, or grains (including corn, rye, wheat, and sorghum). There is an amazing array of flavored vodkas available, including citrus vodkas, spicy pepper vodkas, sweet vodkas (such as chocolate and vanilla), herbal vodkas, and more. While flavored vodkas taking over the shelves of liquor stores and bars may seem a recent trend, flavoring vodkas with herbs, spices, and fruit has long been a traditional practice in Eastern European countries, both for health reasons and for taste.

Though vodkas are now created worldwide, all true tequila is made around the town of the same name in Jalisco, Mexico (it's about 50 kilometers from Guadalajara), and all tequilas are made from the agave plant. This means that tequila is a type of mescal (which is the name for any distilled spirit made from the agave), but to be listed as tequila it has to follow certain rules set up by the Tequila Regulatory Council. The guidelines restrict tequila to being made only in the area mentioned, and require that it is made from at least 51 percent blue agave (a specific type of the plant), though there are premium varieties made from 100 percent blue agave. Tequila traces its history back to the sixteenth century, when the Spanish conquerors overtaking the area ran out of the brandy they had brought on their trip. Of course they couldn't go without, and so, taking a cue from the Aztec natives who drank a fermented beverage made from agave, the Spanish created a distilled liquor using the same ingredients. Today, you usually see four categories of tequila: silver, which is aged only a few months; gold, which is basically silver tequila colored to look aged; *reposado* (which means "rested"), which is aged usually a year in oak casks; and *añejo*, which is also aged in oak, usually from one to three years.

The final of the six bases, Champagne, isn't usually considered in the same grouping as the above, as it's not a liquor, but instead a wine. I tend to think of it in the same way as the others due to the fact that I revel in Champagne-based cocktails (as you should, too). Champagne is attractive to most sippers because of its bubbly nature, which is produced via a second fermentation of the wine used, a fermentation that happens in the bottle. While only wines actually made in the Champagne region of France are supposed to use the uppercase "Champagne" on the bottle (due to the Treaty of Madrid, 1891), you do occasionally see it listed incorrectly on wines from other areas (shame, shame). There are, naturally, many other sparkling wines not made in that particular French region that are lovely, and it may be that when mixing a cocktail that calls for Champagne you end up using a sparkling wine instead. This is fine, and probably isn't a bad idea, as you may not want to lay down a large amount of money for a wine you'll be mixing with other ingredients.

Even though it runs contrary to legend, the French monk Dom Perignon didn't invent Champagne or sparkling wine, though he did do much to advance production techniques. From the reports I've read, the first commercial sparkling wine came out of the Limoux area of the Languedoc region of France in 1535, though the process was invented somewhere yet to be pinned down. Wherever it originated, Champagne and sparkling wines have continued to enjoy immense popularity since the 1700s, and the bubbly has long been thought to add a little elegance to any evening. There are five types of Champagne: brut, extra-dry, sec, demi-sec, and doux, ranging in sweetness from the driest, brut, to the sweetest, doux.

So, after you have decided on your base liquors and have them in place, try a little experimenting to start filling in your home liquor assortment nicely. It's as simple as picking a cocktail or two for an upcoming event or a particular evening solely because they look tasty and you want to try them. Make an ingredient list, and then head to the local liquor store (or online if the time, inclination, and ability are in place) and purchase the needed nonbase liquors and liqueurs. After following this procedure a couple of times, you will discover that you have well more than three bottles, making possible a wide range of beautiful beverages without any trouble at all.

If you'd like to get a jump on stocking the bar, there are a couple of specific bottles worth picking up, because you'll find them in a goodly number of drinks. The first, which I almost put with the six bases above, is brandy. Brandy isn't used as often in the modern cocktail arena (which is a disgrace, really). I think brandy usage declined because many started to think of it as more of an upper-class drink, and as prohibitively expensive to mix—which isn't true, as affordable brandies abound. The word "brandy" comes from *brandewijn*, which is Dutch for "burnt wine," and it's now made in Spain, Portugal, Australia, Italy, South Africa, the United States, and France—France being where the most famous brandies, Cognac and Armagnac, are made (in their respective regions). There are flavored brandies that can be handy to have around, too, including apricot and blackberry.

Some other good bottles to add right away to your bar selection include sweet and dry vermouths (more on the vermouth varieties on page 26), orange curaçao (which is an orange-flavored liqueur, crisp in taste and originally clear in color, though available today in blue and other colored versions), and an absinthe substitute—as absinthe is no longer available in the United States. The absinthe substitutes include Pernod, Ricard, Herbsaint, and Absente.

As far as storage rules, many home bartenders have opinions (some fierce, some friendly) on whether certain items must be stored in the freezer or in a dark place, or buried underground. My take is that Champagne should be chilled, but that the other base liquors don't need chilling if they will be added to drinks. If you're someone who is fond of a little vodka, gin, or tequila straight up, or drizzled lightly over a handful of ice cubes, then chilling it in the freezer is a good idea (because shaking adds extra water, and in this case you probably don't need or want it). But in other cases, I think regular shelf or home-bar storage is fine, though I wouldn't keep items anywhere where direct hot sunlight would hit them for long.

A Little Bit of This and That: Mixers

Though there are drinks constructed only with liquors (and sometimes ice, which is detailed below), scores of them use some type of nonalcoholic mixer. I see the mixer category as very broad, crossing from natural mixers like fruit to man-made mixers like ginger ale. There is one constant in the mixer equation, however, with two exceptions mentioned below, and that's the rule of freshness. The rule of freshness means that the aim should always be to have ginger ale or club soda opened just before it is used, and that the bottle should open with a mighty hiss of carbonation and not the barely audible breath of a bottle that's sat in the fridge for a month. The fresh rule leads to squeezing the lemon juice out of the lemon minutes before adding it to the shaker, to keep its tartness alive and well. The fresh rule says that if you want to woo a date with a smooth after-dinner treat, always use cream that hasn't been cozying up to the bottle of barbecue sauce for weeks. In short, use the freshest mixers possible and you will sip with supreme confidence.

While staying fresh takes you far along the path to mixer mastery, there are a few other points to keep in mind. When purchasing bottled mixers, remember that if a recipe calls for "club soda," you should utilize a bottle of the same and not bottled seltzer water. Most seltzer doesn't have the coveted pizzazz, and some have a tinny aftertaste that should be avoided. But if you own an old-school CO_2-style seltzer dispenser, use it as much as possible (and not solely because it looks cool; it also dispenses ideal bubbling water). When picking up club soda, ginger ale, or other bottled mixers, don't automatically go for the bottom-shelf bargains, thinking it'll provide more money for liquors. Buy the brand you would drink on its own. If the mixer doesn't have the proper taste, it's a problem, and a number of the bargain brands leave too much taste to the imagination (and while imagination is a fine quality, it's not much help when drinks have a flavor echoing dishwater).

When a recipe calls for fruit juice—especially citrus juice—if possible leave the premade varieties out of the equation altogether. As mentioned above, fresh juice is the best route to take every time. When picking out fruit to juice, or squeeze, or turn into twists or garnishes, look for produce that has unblemished skin, rich colors, and a tiny bit of give. Don't be shy about lifting, touching, or even sniffing fruit in the supermarket. It's better by far to be seen as a little nutty at the store than to come home with badly bruised or rotten fruit.

To get the most juice out of citrus fruit, bring it to room temperature before using, or place it in a damp towel in the microwave on medium for about 20 seconds (if you don't have a microwave, running it under warm water also works). This helps get the juice flowing. In addition, rolling the fruit under your palm while applying steady pressure for a couple of seconds helps to get the juices ready, ensuring that maximum juice extraction occurs.

If you don't have a juicer (yet) to make larger quantities of fresh juice, then using frozen concentrate is acceptable as a last resort. And frozen orange juice, for example, is definitely preferable to orange juice in a carton. I would always have a bit of fresh fruit around though, even if you do go the frozen-juice route. You can use it for garnishing, and also to add at least a touch of fresh juice to the frozen, to bring the frozen up to a slightly higher flavor level.

Another absolutely essential mixer—one that is, to a sad degree, less utilized today—is bitters, which are discussed a bit more on page 139. They are allowed to break the rule of freshness. (That doesn't mean you shouldn't refresh your bitters on occasion, too, however. There's no need to have the same bottle sitting around for centuries. First off, you should be using it more.) Basically, bitters are a secret mix of herbs, spices, roots, and other arcane ingredients in a liquid form. A decent array of bitters can be found in liquor stores, specialty shops, grocery stores, and online, including Angostura, Peychaud's, Regan's Orange Bitters No. 6, and the range of flavored bitters available from Fee Brothers. Don't skip the bitters in any recipe in which they're mentioned, or the drinks won't leave them screaming for more; instead, they'll have guests walking out the door.

The last crucial mixer to mention is the second one allowed to break the rule of freshness: simple syrup. As the name implies, this combination of sugar and water comes together without any undue

Simple Syrup

2½ cups **water**

3 cups **sugar**

1. Add the water and sugar to a medium-size saucepan. Stirring occasionally, bring the mixture to a boil over medium-high heat. Lower the heat a bit, keeping the mixture at a low boil for 5 minutes, stirring occasionally.

2. Turn off the heat, and let the syrup cool completely in the pan. Store in a clean, airtight container in the refrigerator.

Makes 4½ cups (36 ounces)

aggravation (the recipe on page 7 gets you going). This ease of construction means you should always have it around, chilling in a bottle in the refrigerator, where it remains healthy for a good month, providing the bottle has a respectable seal on top. It's used in so many cocktails, though, I can't imagine you'll ever have a bottle around for that long. And *because* it's used in a number of drinks, making it in advance and having a bottle as a permanent resident in the fridge makes sense. That way, you'll be prepared.

The Cold Facts: Ice

Ice is the too-often undervalued key element in most drinks (except for those hot drinks in Turning Up the Heat, of course). Since ice is so significant, give it the same amount of thought as you do other ingredients. Do not use ice that has been sitting in the freezer for months alongside a carp caught on a past boating trip. You *will* taste it if you do. Go with regular 1-inch ice cubes for most drinks made in a cocktail shaker and strained, and drinks served over the rocks. There are times when you'll want to use cracked ice, which is the ice you will find in stores, and which, due to its irregular size (which leads to quicker melting), tends to add more water to drinks. Cracked ice is called for in the drinks where you'll want that instead of cubes. And don't shy away from using cracked ice instead of cubed if your cubed ice has, as in the example above, been sleeping in the freezer with the fishes. There are also drinks in this book that call for crushed ice (the ice found in fountain drinks). Crushed ice adds extra slushiness that makes some drinks dreamy, and the recipes call for it when that slushiness is desired. If you have a crushed ice–maker built into your freezer, lucky you. If not, you can buy bags of crushed ice in liquor stores. You could use shaved ice in these situations, too, if you happen to have an ice shaver. Last, but not least, when making a punch in an honest-to-goodness punch bowl, using a block or ring of ice makes a charming presentation. You can buy blocks of ice, or make ice rings by pouring water into a Bundt cake pan or other ring mold and freezing it. Cubed or cracked ice can work if no blocks are available.

Always Accessorize: Garnishes

You've shaken or stirred the major ingredients, poured them into the appropriate glass, and then immediately served the finished drink to a happily waiting pal (or yourself). Wait, wait, wait: The drink is not finished. You've forgotten one of the key parts of many drinks: the garnish. Not only do they add that extra attractive visual touch, garnishes also often provide important flavor embellishments without which a drink is still naked. The range of garnishes is wide, and goes far beyond just citrus fruit to include strawberries, nutmeg, cinnamon, mint leaves, raspberries, cranberries, coffee beans, and more. Don't let this prospect generate fear, though—the key to garnishing is simple enough. Just remember the rule of freshness from the mixer section above.

While the garnish group is a large one, it's wise to get friendlier with the three top garnishes, due to their significance. These garnishes are citrus fruit twists, wheels, and wedges. Twists may be the most difficult to grasp and sometimes are sadly used solely as ornament, placed in a drink without any actual "twisting." This shortcut fails to utilize the light oils that are released over a drink during the twisting process—oils that are vital to flavor. To make a twist, cut both ends of a citrus fruit off in a straight line, removing only enough so that the remaining fruit has a flat surface. Then, place the flat part of the fruit on your cutting board. Using a garnishing knife or paring knife, cut off ½-inch-wide strips of peel, cutting from top to bottom, getting all of the outer skin and just a hint of the inner white pith. These strips are your twists, and should be sturdy enough to twist over a drink and not break into pieces. The fruit left over after you've made twists should be used for juicing purposes. To actually twist your twist, hold each end of the fruit strip (one side in each hand) about ½ inch above the cocktail or drink it's going in. Then, slowly, rotate your hands in opposite directions, turning the fruit strip into a sort of curlicue. You'll see, if you look closely, the oils bursting out of the skin of the fruit and into the drink, which is what adds the flavor. If you're having a party and want to prepare in advance, you can make a number of twists earlier the same day (but no sooner than that) and store them sealed tightly in the refrigerator. Don't actually twist them, of course, until assembling the drink.

Wheels (and via wheels, slices) are the most self-explanatory of the citrus garnishes. Slice both ends off of your fruit, about ⅛ inch off of each end. Then cut the fruit into uniform wheels about ½ inch thick, notching each wheel not quite all the way through to the center if it's going to perch on the lip of a glass. If you cut the wheels in half, you've got slices. It's as easy as pie (which, coincidentally, sort of looks like a wheel).

Wedges are also comparatively easy. Start as with wheels, by cutting ⅛ inch off of each end of your citrus fruit. Cut the fruit in half lengthwise, and then lay each half, cut side down, on a cutting board. Make three lengthwise cuts through each half, angled toward the center line, ending with three equally sized pieces. Then cut those pieces in half, or in thirds if using a large piece of fruit. (Some call these pieces quarters, and use the term "wedge" for the longer piece. But for this book, let's have "wedge" mean the smaller size.) You will end up with 12 wedges per piece of fruit. If you don't mind your wedges being less uniform and more individual, and want a little less cutting, feel free to skip the first step (cutting the ⅛ inch off the ends) and start by cutting the fruit in half lengthwise.

THE BAR NECESSITIES: TOOLS

Ladies and gentleman, let me introduce in this corner of the home bar the champion of the bar tool assortment, the cocktail shaker. While a cocktail shaker isn't essential for every single alcohol-based mélange in these pages, enough do call for it that not having a cocktail shaker limits you immensely—any solid home bar set-up is substandard without one. This is why the cocktail shaker is the first bar tool to bring into the bar tool conversation, and to bring into your home bar.

There are two cocktail shaker options, both of which are widely available and both of which work well. The first option is the cobbler shaker, which has been used by cocktail lovers since before that failed experiment known as Prohibition. The cobbler shaker has a bigger bottom receptacle covered by a smaller top piece (they should fit together snugly to reduce any spillage potential). The top piece usually has a built-in strainer and a cap, the latter of which often doubles as a measuring device. These shakers are easy to use and can reduce the fear factor for any home bartender. It's a straightforward process: Add ice and ingredients to the bottom piece, then secure the top (make sure it's on there firmly), and then shake, shake, shake. Remove the cap, strain into glasses, garnish, and serve. Cobbler shakers tend toward all-metal construction, but there are some sturdy and attractive glass versions available. If you purchase a metal version, choose one that's 18/10 stainless steel. You don't want to skimp on your shaker.

The second type is called a Boston shaker. This style of shaker has a glass bottom cup and a top cup made of metal. You will need a stand-alone bar strainer if you go the Boston shaker route. Using a Boston shaker is a tad bit more difficult, but not daunting by any means (and it, like the cobbler, delivers lovely and chilly results). Start by adding the ice and ingredients to the bottom glass cup. Next, place the metal top cup over the bottom cup, and carefully, with the palm of your hand, thump the bottom of the metal cup to create a seal between the two pieces. Holding both pieces securely (that means one in each hand), shake, shake, shake. Once the drink has reached the proper level of shaken-ness, place it on a flat surface, with the glass side down. Then, again carefully, strike or nudge the metal piece with your hand to break the seal. Use the bar strainer to strain the drinks into glasses, garnish, and serve.

No matter what your shaker choice, it's a good idea to shake drinks for at least 10 to 15 seconds, to guarantee they reach that properly frothy level of existence. There are drinks in this book that need longer shaking (such as the Ramos Fizz, page 129) or shorter shaking, and those drinks are noted appropriately.

Even if your shaker has a built-in measuring device, and especially if it doesn't, it's crucial to secure a jigger for measuring, or the potential for problematic-tasting drinks rises rapidly. You'll want to invest in one that's sturdy (again, go for 18/10 stainless steel if possible), and one that has a 1-ounce measuring cup on one side and a 1½- or 2-ounce measuring cup on the other side. These sizes should cover most needs and most measuring situations.

Another tool you'll want to pick up, which is used directly with the shaker, is a muddler. The muddler is a wooden or metal tool slightly resembling a miniature baseball bat or an oversized pestle, having a wider end tapering to a smaller end. It's used to macerate and generally beat up ingredients (usually fruits) in the bottom of a shaker or mixing glass. You want one that's sturdy and that fits your hand well. Avoid overly varnished models to avoid varnish in your drinks. You can track down a muddler at most restaurant-supply stores and discover a number of nice models online. If you absolutely can't find a muddler, then a hefty wooden spoon can sub in a pinch.

To make the garnishes described in the "Always Accessorize" section on page 8, a sharp garnishing knife or a thin-bladed paring knife becomes mandatory. As with any time you're working with knives, please be careful, because there are few things that ruin the drink-making experience like a cut finger. Having a large all-purpose knife around is a good idea, too, because there are drinks in this book that use larger fruits (which might be a bit too much for your normal garnishing knife).

Following up on the fresh garnishes idea, don't forget about the fresh juices angle, too. When making a lot of juice-containing drinks, purchasing a handheld juice squeezer, lever-model juicer, or motorized juice extractor becomes one of the finest investments a drink slinger can make.

Useful Math

I'm not suggesting anyone calculate serious equations here, but in case you don't have a jigger or bar measurer, a little conversion knowledge gets you through the night. Remember:

1 fluid ounce = 2 tablespoons
8 fluid ounces = 1 cup
1 cup = ½ pint
2 cups = 1 pint
2 pints = 1 quart
1 quart = 4 cups, or 32 ounces

If you want to (and I hope you do, or your summer will be sorry) flip the switch on the recipes in The Blender's Whirr, picking up an electric blender is imperative. While everybody wants to have a fashionable-looking machine, there are a few blender features that are more important than color. First, find a model that holds at least 27 ounces of liquid—though going to 40 ounces is a better idea (and you might even want to go up to 48 ounces if you roll with larger groups of friends). Also, find a blender that has multiple speed settings and a pulse feature, seals tightly around the top, has stainless steel blades, and comes apart easily for cleaning. When shopping, you'll probably see models with a pouring lip, and this comes in handy (as long as the seal stays tight—spraying blender contents around the kitchen isn't handy one bit), as do the nonslip rubber feet that some models boast.

Finally, while it doesn't live in the "tool" category per se, I think of the pitcher as a type of tool, too, more so than other pieces of glassware, as the pitcher is used to stir up a number of drinks when making them for a crowd. Since there are many nice pitchers out there at reasonable prices, I suggest getting two: an indoor one and an outdoor one. The indoor one can be of the fancier glass variety and the outdoor pitcher can be of the sturdier variety, either glass or thick plastic if you're nervous. Both should share one feature: a pouring lip. This lip makes pouring a breeze, naturally, but helps to hold back ice if straining a drink out of the pitcher. You'll want a pitcher that holds at least 50 ounces (the small size) and might want to invest in a larger one that holds 75 to 100 ounces.

Expand Your Bar Repertoire: More Tools

The above tools are central, to be sure, but there is no reason not to develop your bar implements list past the basics. The home bar experience can be as involved as you want it to be, with as many tools and accoutrements as you want or think are necessary. Other items that you might find helpful on a regular basis (I sure find all of these helpful, by the way) include a user-friendly corkscrew for wine and a brawny bottle-opener for beer and other bottles, a spice grater (one that makes grating nutmeg over a glass a neat affair), a conveniently sized but sturdy cutting board for cutting fruits and garnishes, a long and thin stirring spoon or other dedicated stirring device, more measuring apparatus (especially measuring cups for large parties), an ice bucket and ice scoop (here again, 18/10 stainless keeps things clean and sparkly) for constructing drinks away from the fridge (which is always enjoyable), a bar towel that isn't tattered and torn, toothpicks or short skewers for stacked garnishes, bottle stoppers and pourers, a tray for transporting drinks from room to room, and colorful and creative coasters, cocktail napkins, swizzle sticks, and straws to add that extra shot of style every home bar needs.

LET ME BE CRYSTAL CLEAR: GLASSWARE

The right glassware matches up with a drink like a sunny day matches up with sitting outside with a cool beverage and a good book. Meaning that it makes it all the better, and can be crucial to enjoyment. Certainly if one has to alter the glassware on some occasions, the world won't actually stop (unless the drink is a Martini, or many of the Gold Standards). If you don't have a poco grande glass for your Piña Colada, few curses will descend from waiting mouths. But to ensure that you do have the right glassware in most situations, start by investing in a few important categories, and then expand as you see fit.

Begin with the classic cocktail or martini glass, which boasts a design known worldwide. The cocktail glasses available, however, do have a wide variety of sizes, from around 3 ounces all the way up to 12 ounces. The older glasses, if you're going antique, tend to be smaller, as the drinks served way back when, as well as many of the drinks in this book, hovered around the 3- to 3½-ounce size. A drink this size, it was thought, stayed chilled throughout its consumption, and in addition allowed one to, as the great Harry Craddock said, drink the cocktail "while it's laughing at you." Today, we see much larger cocktail glasses, and often much larger cocktails. There is nothing inherently wrong with this, of course, as long as the cocktails aren't losing their chill before the last drop.

Next, stock up on highball glasses, which are long and somewhat slender, and which should be 10 to 12 ounces in size, and on old-fashioned glasses, which are squatter and thick-bottomed and should hold 6 to 10 ounces. There are also double old-fashioned glasses out there, in the 10- to 15-ounce range, and they come in handy as well (though when a recipe here calls for an old-fashioned glass, it's referring to the regular size, unless otherwise stated).

You'll want to collect a good set of both red and white wine glasses, making sure that the red are in a goblet-style, as well as a set of Champagne flutes. To accommodate extra-large drinks, a 24-ounce "big girl" beer glass is nice, though a pint glass can do in a pinch.

To accommodate the warm and hot drinks found throughout the book (and in life), stock up on some heatproof mugs. Glass mugs, often called Irish coffee glasses, look lovely, but ceramic or others work as well (if using glass, it's a safe idea to run them under warm water before adding a hot drink). Make sure the handles are large enough so that one might sip from the mug without cramping one's fingers.

There are drinks that traditionally have their own special glasses, including the Piña Colada (page 426), which uses a poco grande glass, and the Hurricane (page 337), which uses the creatively named hurricane glass. With these fancy sippers, if you have the traditional glasses, or don't mind ponying up for a set, then by all means use them. If you don't have them, then you'll have to improvise. For a Piña Colada, a large goblet steps in if needed, and for a Hurricane, any 8- to 12-ounce glass will do dandy in a pinch (if it has a little wave in it, all the better). The key is to not get frustrated, or feel that you absolutely can't have a particular drink because you don't have the traditional glass. This doesn't mean that you should forget every rule and start slinging hot whiskey punch in cocktail glasses. Safety, friends, should always be rule number one. Don't stress over glassware to a point where the party's not enjoyable, either. If you have a lovely set of little crystal punch cups to go along with your punch bowl and punch, then use them with a twinkle in your eye at the next wingding. If there aren't any punch cups available and you'll have to use white wine glasses as a substitute, don't let it take away that twinkle.

Once you've assembled this basic array of glittering glassware, you'll be set for many, many drinks. But don't rest on any laurels here, because there are lots of attractive specialty glasses out there in the big bar world that add a superior bit of flash to any evening (or morning or afternoon). A set of charming apéritif glasses or pousse café glasses are so snazzy, and a set of crystal shot glasses brings a distinctive flair to the communal affair of taking shots. A warning, though: Once you've started, glassware collecting tends to get a little dangerous, as there are always more great-looking glasses available, and only so much shelf space at home (at least, that's what my wife keeps telling me).

HERE'S TO YOU: THE LAST TOAST

Now that the glassware is perched on the shelf, the shaker is shining, and the liquor cabinet is stocked, there's only one last ingredient to remember— fun. Drinking with others should always be enjoyable, a hoot, a pleasurable experience. Even if some occasions aren't boisterous, sitting down to a good cocktail with a close friend should be a communal moment that makes the pain or doldrums of the world temporarily drift out of reach. On the majority of occasions, those where you wish the celebration would never stop, a well-mixed drink brings out the best of all those partaking in the revelry. The recipes in each of the 12 chapters of this book follow up on that idea, mixing up a little zaniness, a little history, and a few informative hints, with the end result of nearly 500 drinks for all occasions. The cocktails, punches, highballs, and more in these pages help get any evening rolling, and add a little sparkle wherever it's needed. But what are you sitting here dawdling for? Turn the pages and let the party begin.

Swinger, page 275

"Why don't you get out of that wet coat
and into a **dry Martini**?"

ROBERT BENCHLEY *(attributed to, at least)*

The Gold Standards

The word "classic" gets tossed around a lot, as do the words "ultimate," "first-rate," and "star." Not to get stuffy on you (though meandering bar talk goes with drinking like sunglasses go with a sunny day), but this overuse of certain high-falutin' designations comes from a culture that is too ready to appoint something (or someone) with greatness, a culture that doesn't demand, in many situations, the rigorous test of sustained perfection over time, instead allowing the popular sentiment of the moment to bestow accolade after accolade when nothing substantial has really been achieved. That's a shame, I think, and enough of a shame that it's going to lead me to drink one of the true Gold Standards represented in this chapter. I suggest you do the same.

These drinks have maintained popularity over time (or have, at least in the case of the Mojito, managed to become popular in two different times) for a reason. Merrymaking favorites, they're instantly ready to be any group event's centerpiece, be it a box social or a Memorial Day lost weekend. These classics have resided in the collective drinking public's eye through generations of revelers, both at home and out on the town. These classics shine as beacons, calling out any time one doesn't know what to order. They always deliver.

Why? First, it's because they taste amazing. The alchemists who originally came up with the recipes for these Gold Standards are sometimes known to us, and sometimes guessed at, and sometimes not even thought about, but those first pourers were channeling magic in a cocktail glass, and magic like this lasts and lasts.

But the Gold Standards also have history. The Mai Tai, created by Trader Vic in the 1940s, has been riding high on that tiki craze all the way through to today, when Mai Tais fly at any bar, restaurant, or home that wants to bring a little of the beach into the picture. And who doesn't instantly become transported to the rolling green grasses of Kentucky in May, with flowery big hats on female heads and the rolling sound of horse's hooves in the background, when drinking a Mint Julep? The following recipes are true classics. This doesn't mean, by the way, that they're musty old tomes only to be trotted out because one has to have them in a collection. Don't fall into that trap. Like every true classic (be it book, movie, song, or shoe), these drinks should be used often, and enjoyed. They're ready for any party.

The Alexander

An emperor of alcohol-laced sweet treats, with many pretenders to its throne, the Alexander is too often relegated to grandmother-drink status. I must admit that even I, for years, thought only of the brandy Alexander, and that it was a favorite at late-afternoon bridge games and as an accompaniment to gossip and good times in small Midwestern parlors where doilies ruled the room. Now I know better, and know that while a brandy Alexander is a swell enough mix, the true gin Alexander is a step above, and a **worthy after-dinner drink** for all types (and I have learned to trust those bridge players). Admittedly, the Alexander is a touch too sweet for those who desire to appear always the hard rotgutter, serious swillers wanting to impress all within vocal reach with their disdain of the lighter, creamier side of life. Pay no mind to them while we sip our Alexanders late into the evening.

Ice cubes

1 ounce **gin**

1 ounce **crème de cacao**

1 ounce **heavy cream**

Strawberry slices
for garnish

1. Fill a cocktail shaker halfway full with ice cubes. Add the gin, crème de cacao, and heavy cream. Shake well.

2. Strain into a cocktail glass. Garnish with a strawberry slice, or 2 if waiting on dessert.

A VARIATION: The brandy Alexander is made by just subbing brandy for the gin in the above recipe. If you substitute crème de menthe for crème de cacao in the above recipe, it becomes an Alexander's Sister. Skip the strawberry if going the sister route.

The Bloody Mary

Though seen by many as a modern potion, the Bloody Mary traces its roots back to Paris in the 1920s. The Bloody Mary may just have the distinction of being the drink with the most variations on the recipe. Every home and professional bartender has a singular spin on what makes his or her Bloody Mary the tip top, from the addition of secret "Cajun spice mix" to a dollop of Pickapeppa Sauce, from achingly precise measurements of celery salt to pickled jalapeños. This variety can make for a slightly hazardous experience for those ordering the drink, though most recipes probably at least accomplish the goal of taking the edge off the A.M. Watch out for those identified as "spicy," as they may contain horseradish or other incendiary devices—unless you need waking up badly. Then ask for spicy by name. The recipe below walks a sensible line on the spice question, and, if I can say so without sounding a braggart, tastes darn fine.

Ice cubes

4 ounces **tomato juice**

3 ounces **vodka**

1 ounce **freshly squeezed lemon juice**

1 dash **Louisiana-style hot sauce** (Tabasco or Red Hot works well)

1 dash **Worcestershire sauce**

¼ teaspoon **celery salt**

Salt and **freshly ground black pepper** to taste

Celery stalk, dill pickle spear, or **pickled green bean** for garnish

⬆ **A Note:** *As evidenced, I prefer a vertical garnish with the Bloody Mary. But if a lime or lemon wedge starts your morning brightly, don't be ashamed.*

1. Fill a pint glass three-quarters full with ice cubes. Add the tomato juice, vodka, lemon juice, hot sauce, Worcestershire sauce, celery salt, and salt and pepper. Stir well.

2. Add your choice of garnish (the pickled green bean is my favorite).

A VARIATION: As mentioned, variations abound. Want to kick it up a notch? Add 1 teaspoon prepared horseradish. Want to make a prairie-style Mary? Drop the Worcestershire and substitute liquid smoke, and garnish with a sliver from a tumbleweed.

A VIRGIN VARIATION: Need to wake up without upping the vodka intake? Remove it from the mix and add an extra 2 ounces tomato juice and an extra ¼ ounce lemon juice.

The Bronx

The Bronx *should* be a cocktail that comes automatically to mind when musing over what constitutes an all-time all-star. Who knows why such an ideal mix gets forgotten while others get imbibed from Pittsburgh to Petaluma? Well, here's for bringing it back, and right now. You'll find this beauty meets all requirements, and fits in just fine as an eye-opener (when you need those eyes opened quickly) or as an afternoon special when having pals over to watch any sort of pro athletics (it's a little much for college sports, though). Just remember two things: First, always use freshly squeezed orange juice (you'll thank yourself and be thanked); and, second, that this drink **isn't named for the deserving borough,** but for the Bronx Zoo. If you need to get even more historical when serving it, bring up that it was created by Johnny Solon way back when, when he was the champ behind the Waldorf-Astoria bar in NYC.

Ice cubes

1½ ounces **gin**

1½ ounces **freshly squeezed orange juice**

¾ ounce **sweet vermouth**

¾ ounce **dry vermouth**

Orange slice for garnish

1. Fill a cocktail shaker halfway full with ice cubes. Add the gin, orange juice, sweet vermouth, and dry vermouth. Shake well.

2. Strain the mix into a large cocktail glass, making sure the ice doesn't come along. Garnish with the orange slice and a 1920s smile.

The Champagne Cocktail

There's beauty in the basics (I say, philosophically, in my best greeting-card voice): a roof over one's head, bread and cheese (make mine Parmigiano-Reggiano), warmth in the winter, shade in the summertime, a loyal dog to chase away pesky rodents, comfortable hand-stitched shoes, a reliable Internet connection, loquacious pals around who know when to zip it, and an endless supply of Champagne Cocktails. The simple life has its charms.

1 **sugar cube**

3 dashes **Angostura bitters**

Chilled Champagne

Lemon twist for garnish

1. Add your sugar cube to a Champagne flute. Cover it with the 3 dashes of Angostura bitters.

2. Elegantly fill the flute up with Champagne. Garnish with the lemon twist.

A VARIATION: I've recently become rather addicted to orange bitters with my Champagne—enough so that people are talking. But they can't make me stop, and that's what I use when I make Champagne Cocktails. Neither should I stop you from experimenting with different bitters in this drink. Peychaud's adds a rich loamy touch.

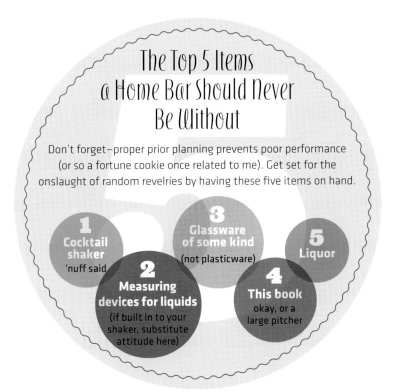

The Top 5 Items a Home Bar Should Never Be Without

Don't forget—proper prior planning prevents poor performance (or so a fortune cookie once related to me). Get set for the onslaught of random revelries by having these five items on hand.

1 Cocktail shaker 'nuff said

2 Measuring devices for liquids (if built in to your shaker, substitute attitude here)

3 Glassware of some kind (not plasticware)

4 This book okay, or a large pitcher

5 Liquor

The Classic Martini

Like the Classic Martini itself, sometimes **keeping it simple** is the safest bet. So, here it is, the lowdown, the scoop, the word, all in four ingredients and two simple steps.

Ice cubes

2½ ounces **gin**

½ ounce **dry vermouth**

Olive or **lemon twist** for garnish (see Note)

1. Fill a cocktail shaker halfway full with ice cubes. Add the gin and vermouth. Shake well.

2. Strain into a cocktail glass (which some call a martini glass). Garnish with an olive (or 2, if you're starving). Enjoy what many others have enjoyed before you.

⬆ **A Note:** *The olive is possibly more popular today than the lemon twist, which is why I listed it first. I think the lemon twist adds that bit of brightness that brings the Martini together, but I also recognize that the olive is beloved by many. And I wouldn't want them not to buy me a drink, so the olive appears here on equal footing with the lemon.*

A VARIATION: Not dry enough for you? Next time, just swirl the vermouth around the glass and then discard. Still shake the gin with the ice, though.

A VODKA VARIATION: Want to join the vodka revolution? Fine with me (but keep mine gin, please).

A LARGER VARIATION: Martinis, like most drinks, are more fun in a crowd. Don't fret a bit about making a pitcher full, and stirring instead of shaking. Things might not get quite as icy, but you'll be having so much fun that you won't notice a bit.

ANOTHER 40 VARIATIONS: See every recipe in A Multitude of Martinis, beginning on page 49.

"The three-Martini lunch is the epitome of American efficiency. Where else can you get **an earful, a bellyful, and a snootful** at the same time?"

GERALD R. FORD

The Daiquiri

A long-standing lime-licious favorite such as the Daiquiri almost makes one nervous—what if I make a Daiquiri and it doesn't taste quite up to legend? Friends, don't sweat it. And I mean that literally, because the Daiquiri is one **wonderful fusion to savor** when the mercury's rising and the sun's striking. But also, you shouldn't sweat making a Daiquiri because it's a favorite, both for its stellar sweet-sour taste and for its ease of creation—especially if you take my advice and eschew the blender. Just shake it up, and you'll be on a second Daiquiri, and happier for it, before the wading pool's even filled. Remember that, sullen famous novelists aside, the Daiquiri is a drink for sharing, so be sure your pool fits at least two.

Crushed ice

3 ounces **white rum**

1 ounce **freshly squeezed lime juice**

½ ounce **Simple Syrup** (page 7)

Lime wedge for garnish

⊕ **A Tip:** I like crushed ice for a Daiquiri, because it really enhances the frosty quotient. But if you have to, use cubed or cracked ice; don't blush about it too much.

1. Fill a cocktail shaker halfway full with crushed ice. Add the rum, lime juice, and simple syrup. Shake it Havana-style.

2. Strain into a cocktail glass. Squeeze the lime wedge over the glass, and then drop it in.

A VARIATION: People sometimes raise an eyebrow about fussing with an old favorite, but I say, *why not* try a watermelon Daiquiri, if watermelon season is upon us? The day before you're drinking, halve a fresh watermelon. Using a small ice cream scoop or melon baller, scoop out a nice number of round pieces of watermelon (1 or 2 for each drink). Put the watermelon rounds in the freezer and the rest of the watermelon in the refrigerator. The next day, scoop out a cup (if you're going to make more than 1 drink, which I hope you are) of the flesh, avoiding any seeds, and run it through the blender until it liquefies. Add 1 ounce of this watermelon "juice" instead of lime juice to the above recipe. Then garnish with the frozen watermelon balls.

A VIRGIN VARIATION: If a virgin Daiquiri is desired, I suggest going with a strawberry model, as the lime just doesn't have enough liquid on its own to really wet those whistles. Just substitute 2 ounces strawberry syrup for the rum. If needed, to thin, add a little cold water.

Unlocking the Vermouth Varieties

Sometimes referred to as an "aromatized" wine, vermouth is wine that has had various items added to modify the flavor, including herbs, spices, roots, flowers, and sugar (all these herbal and other additives once made vermouth a favorite medicinal tonic). This aromatization is unlike a fortified wine, which has a spirit added to up the alcohol ante. While we think of vermouth as being originally from Italy, due to Antonio Benedetto Carpano using the name for a mix of his in the late 1700s, he was actually borrowing from Germany, as the name derives from the German *vermut*, which means "wormwood"—wormwood being the main flavoring ingredient at one time in German aromatized wines. However, people have been adding flavorings to wine almost as long as they've sipped the wine itself.

There are three main types of vermouth: dry, sweet/red, and bianco/white, though the first two are what's seen and used the majority of the time. Dry vermouth, which is white (clear, actually), is sometimes called French vermouth, and it was probably developed in the early 1900s by Joseph Noilly. Dry vermouth is enjoyed by itself as an apéritif, and is used in a host of cocktails, including the Martini. The other popular kind of vermouth, sweet or red vermouth, is sometimes called Italian vermouth (as it mirrors the original vermouth made in Italy), and, like the dry variety, is served as an apéritif and used in cocktails, such as the Manhattan.

The third vermouth variety, bianco, isn't seen as much on bar menus. It is slightly sweeter than the red variety and should be used with a delicate hand. It was supposedly first made by J. Boissiere (Boissiere is a company still making vermouth today). There are other flavors of vermouth, including rosé, orange, and lemon, usually seen when visiting France or Italy, as most are not exported. When you do come across these, don't hesitate to try them, first by themselves and then mixed into drinks.

There are a number of vermouth brands available, and each company has its own secret recipe. When trying a new brand (much like when trying any new flavor that you haven't had before), it's best to sip it straight before mixing it into a favorite cocktail. Some of the more obtainable brands include Martini & Rossi and Cinzano (which has been made since 1796), both of which are made in Turin, Italy, and Noilly Prat, which is made in France. But keep an eye open in your local liquor store (and online), because there are many newer vermouth companies, including makers in the United States such as the Vya vermouth company in California.

The Gibson

Talk about having a famous relative (we could even call it a brother or sister—almost a twin except for that vast difference in hair color). The Gibson must deal with being always referred to as "a Martini with a cocktail onion." This is true, but how must that make the Gibson feel at family reunions, never taken on its own merits? It has had separate listings in many drinks books since at least 1917, which should provide it with some comfort. And, it could be truly said that the Gibson keeps the cocktail onion business **alive and kicking,** being the drink most faithfully accented by this pearly garnish. Maybe the Gibson doesn't have it so bad after all. I mean, the Martini probably picks up the tab when they hit the town together. I'd refuse to refer to it as solely another Martini variant, though, or the drink may just spill itself.

Ice cubes

2½ ounces **gin**

½ ounce **dry vermouth**

Cocktail onion for garnish

1. Fill a cocktail shaker halfway full with ice cubes. Add the gin and dry vermouth. Stir well.

2. Add the cocktail onion to a cocktail glass. Strain the mix over the onion. Give it up y'all, for the Gibson.

A VARIATION: This Gibson recipe rides the middle ground of dryness. If you desire a drier combination, remove a bit of the vermouth and add more gin. But stick with 1 onion.

The Gimlet

In the golden, olden, early evenings in the early part of the last century, the orders would come in waves for Gimlets, with their touch of sour and barest hint of sweet, balancing the flavors like sunset balances between afternoon's brightness and night's dark and shadows. The Gimlet back then was also made with gin, a practice that today has largely fallen out of fashion, putting vodka in as a late twentieth-century surrogate. It's not the first change in the Gimlet, though it's my least favorite—maybe because about 45 years before I had my first Gimlet, it was already seen as out of line to have a Gimlet recipe with orange juice instead of lime, or carbonated in rickey-style (see more on the Rickey on page 391). My first was, though, in the not-too-distant past, when gin still popped out of shakers in Gimlets now and again. Which is why I say go with gin, and a good gin, too, because the Gimlet showcases the natural love generated between gin and lime juice. One thing to be wary of is a too-heavy hand with the sweetener. There are times to be sweet, and times to merely hint at sweetness. The Gimlet is one of the latter occasions.

Ice cubes

2¼ ounces **gin**

½ ounce **freshly squeezed lime juice**

½ ounce **Simple Syrup** (page 7)

Lime twist for garnish

1. Fill a cocktail shaker halfway full with ice cubes. Add the gin, lime juice, and simple syrup. Shake well.

2. Strain into a cocktail glass. Squeeze the twist over the glass, and then drop it in, impassively letting it float slowly, inexorably, to the bottom.

A VARIATION: On occasion, a Gimlet may be made over ice (in the high desert, perhaps). If this extra chill is needed, fill a rocks glass with ice cubes, and then strain the shaken mix over them. Don't forget the twist.

The Mai Tai

Shake those grass skirts, everybody, and light up the tiki torches. Strap a few 4-foot-tall South Sea masks to a nearby fence, set out some pu-pu platters, discard shoes in favor of sandals, and start living and loving the tropical life—or, if nothing else, the faux tropical life circa 1940s America. For that is where the Mai Tai was born.

Specifically, the Mai Tai owes its creation to Mr. Polynesia himself, Victor Bergeron, better known to the world as Trader Vic. Trader Vic's theme restaurants lit up the bar landscape with brightly colored atmosphere, slightly spicy food, and barrels of rum drinks (though never served in actual barrels; Trader Vic's was fond of serving communal drinks in vessels the size of small buckets). And there are still Trader Vics around today. You don't have to travel to one (or back in time to 1944) to taste a good Mai Tai, though. Follow the right rum path, and invest in a little orgeat, which is a sugary almond syrup available in many grocery and gourmet stores, and you'll be halfway there. To get the whole way there? What did I just say about the grass skirts?

Ice cubes

2½ ounces **dark rum**

1 ounce **white rum**

1 ounce **orange curaçao**

1 ounce **freshly squeezed lime juice**

½ ounce **Simple Syrup** (page 7)

¼ ounce **orgeat**

Fresh mint sprig for garnish

Lime wedge for garnish

1. Fill a cocktail shaker halfway full with ice cubes. Add the dark rum, white rum, curaçao, lime juice, simple syrup, and orgeat. Shake well.

2. Fill a highball glass three-quarters full with ice cubes. Strain the mix over the ice. Garnish with the mint sprig and lime wedge. Do you have your grass skirt ready yet?

A VARIATION: If you add 1 ounce of freshly squeezed orange juice, you'll be entertaining a Suffering Bastard. Don't say I didn't warn you.

A Historical Note: *The legend goes that when Trader Vic served the first Mai Tai (which was yet to be named), the recipients, who happened to be from Tahiti, said "Mai tai—ro ae," which translates to "Out of this world—the best."*

"Anybody who says I didn't create this drink is a **dirty rotten stinker**."

TRADER VIC, on the Mai Tai

The Manhattan

The Martini gets many of the accolades and the immeasurable endorsement deals, but the Manhattan should rightly be considered the father (or grandfather) of the cocktail family tree. One of the, if not *the*, first cocktails to use vermouth as its mixing agent, the Manhattan, by many accounts, constitutes proof that there's a benevolent force working for us in the universe. But this nigh-perfect drink didn't randomly appear as is. The recipe in Jerry Thomas's *Bar-Tender's Guide or How to Mix Drinks* from 1862, lists as ingredients: 2 dashes Curaçao or maraschino, 1 pony of rye whiskey, 1 wine glass of vermouth, and 3 dashes of Boker's bitters. Now, that's not exactly what we today know as the Manhattan, with no offense meant to "The Professor," Jerry Thomas, without whom we'd all be a bit sadder, as his was one of the first real cocktail books. I suppose even the greats must change over time.

While the Manhattan seems simple, don't be deceived. **It's a deadly simplicity** (like driving through the Midwest: It seems simple enough, but then you're in the middle of western Nebraska, miles away from a gas station with no way to get the car started). With the right balance of vermouth to the right rye or whiskey, you'll find yourself in the seventh plane of drinker's heaven. If using a forceful whiskey, stick with the ratio below. If going with a smoother, lighter whiskey, don't be shy about cutting back a bit on the vermouth. But don't cut back too much, because the vermouth doesn't like being left out. By the same token, start with the 2 dashes of bitters, and then add a bit more as need and desire demand.

Ice cubes

2½ ounces **bourbon** or **rye**

½ ounce **sweet vermouth**

2 dashes **Angostura bitters**

Maraschino cherry for garnish

1. Fill a cocktail shaker halfway full with ice cubes. Add the bourbon, sweet vermouth, and Angostura bitters. Pause a moment, in honor of all the Manhattans drunk before yours. Then shake well.

2. Strain into a cocktail glass. Garnish with the cherry.

A Note: Here's a bar challenge to throw out when ordering Manhattans. Who knows in what year the now-lost film Manhattan Cocktail was released? I believe only a 1-minute sequence from the film survives today, so this can be a bit of a doozy.

A Tip: I suggest Angostura bitters with a Manhattan, but if you'd like to experiment with Peychaud's or an orange bitters, I surely wouldn't caution against it. And, if you can find Boker's bitters (referenced above), please get in touch with me ASAP, as it's been unseen for many years.

The Margarita

The Margarita, for a period in the late 1980s, owned the cocktail world. Owned it, I tell you, with an iron fist enclosed in a salt-rimmed glove. This wasn't necessarily a bad thing, except that it led to cutting corners when making the drink, as well as awful concoctions like pre-made Margarita mix. This would make the original creator of the Margarita roll over in his or her lime-scented grave. If only we knew who that creator was—but the origins of the Margarita are soaked in mystery. There are three good possibilities. It could have been Margarita Sames, a rich Texan who some say invented the drink in the midst of a series of out-of-hand parties or at one very worthy Christmas party. Or was it the more romantic version, which has California bartender Danny Negrete creating it for his girlfriend, Marjorie? The third option, the working-class version, features a nameless bartender fixing the first Margarita in the 1930s at a local tavern in Mexico. But which local tavern: Bertha's in Taxco? The Caliente Racetrack Bar in Tijuana? The Garci Crespo Hotel in Puebla?

What's a known fact is that Margaritas go great with spicy foods, served up in bunches to a whole flock of friends. Next thing you know, *you'll* be in the midst of a series of out-of-hand parties, and that's not something to shy away from.

Coarse kosher salt

Lime wedge

Ice cubes

2 ounces **silver tequila**

1 ounce **Cointreau** or **triple sec**

½ ounce **freshly squeezed lime juice**

1. Pour a thin layer of salt onto a small plate or saucer. Wet the outside of the rim of a cocktail glass or margarita glass with the lime wedge. Holding the glass by the stem, rotate the rim through the salt. You want to be sure that salt coats only the outside of the rim.

2. Fill a cocktail shaker halfway full with ice cubes. Add the tequila, Cointreau, and lime juice. Shake well, humming "La Cucaracha" quietly.

3. Strain the mix into the cocktail glass. Garnish with the wedge of lime.

The Mint Julep

This revered combination has been sipped honorably for well over a century, if not two centuries or longer. The derivation of the word "julep" goes back to the Arabic *julab*, which has meant "rosewater" for many more centuries. In the early period of the history of the United States, the julep, in some form, usually using mint and sugar in a variable proportion with liquor, was consumed every day. Go back to Jerry Thomas's 1862 *Bar-Tender's Guide* and you'll see the Mint Julep made with brandy instead of bourbon. When you are taking that trip into the past, you'll also see a wider array of the julep family in attendance, unlike today, when the Mint Julep made with bourbon is usually the sole representative. Oh, what happened to the real Georgia Mint Julep (made with Cognac and peach brandy), the Pineapple Julep (made with raspberry syrup, orange juice, gin, sparkling Moselle, and maraschino), and the western-style Mint Julep (made with bourbon and rum and without the sweetener)? They have gone into that big bar in the sky, where all cocktails go when they stop being consumed by plain folks watching the sun go down on a summer's day.

But the Mint Julep won't fade away, as long as there's a Kentucky Derby every year to celebrate this fine, fine creation (I hear there's also a horse race, but the Julep seems more important). Whether you celebrate Derby Day or abstain, try a Mint Julep the first Saturday in May and you'll be not only drinking an ice-cold sip of history, you'll also quickly realize why this particular drink is served most often on this particular day. The Mint Julep is as ideal for spring as large hats are ideal for keeping the Kentucky sun out of one's eyes.

4 or 5 **fresh mint leaves**

1 ounce **Simple Syrup** (page 7)

Crushed ice

3 ounces **Kentucky bourbon**

Fresh mint sprig for garnish

⤴ **A Note:** *To be traditional, you must crush the ice in a cloth bag. But if this is too much work, just start with crushed ice.*

1. Rub 1 mint leaf over the inside of a metal julep cup (if you have one) or a highball glass. Be sure the mint touches each inch of the inside of the cup. Drop the leaf in the cup when done.

2. Add the remaining mint leaves and the simple syrup to the cup. Using a muddler or wooden spoon, muddle the leaves and syrup. You want to be strong, but respectful.

3. Fill the cup halfway full with crushed ice. Add the bourbon. Stir until the cup gets icy.

4. Fill the cup the rest of the way with crushed ice. Stir once. Garnish with the mint sprig.

"A Mint Julep is not the process of a formula. It is a ceremony and must be performed by a gentleman possessing **a true sense of the artistic**, a deep reverence for the ingredients, and a proper appreciation of the occasion."

S.B. BUCKNER, JR., in a letter to General Connor, 1937

Instantly Serve Better Drinks

Want to up your home-bartending cred—and become the home bartender that guests rave about—in the time it takes to sip a Martini? Well, I'm not sure I can help you in that amount of time (I'm guessing y'all are fast sippers), but there are a couple things that might easily make homemade cocktails hum.

1

Always, always use fresh fruit and fruit juice. It's as simple as that.

2

Pick up a soda siphon and use it instead of bottled club soda; you'll get better bubbles.

3

Sniff old ice before using it to ensure no unwanted odors have snuck in (or just use new ice every time).

4

Don't be shy—ask your guests if they're allergic to grapefruit juice before making a Peter Sellers, or any other ingredient in any other drink.

The Mojito

Currently enjoying its second round of popularity (the first being in the 1940s, but not with the fervor seen today), the Mojito has taken hold of bar and restaurant patrons in the past five or ten years, creating an obsession usually reserved for celebrities in embarrassing situations. The parallel isn't as far off as it might seem, since hard-drinking writer Ernest Hemingway, known to get into embarrassing situations, was not only a big Cuba Libre (page 331) and Daiquiri (page 25) fan, but also a Mojito imbiber. Don't let the hype drive you away. The Mojito, with its **refreshing attitude,** is worth the excitement. It makes a great accompaniment to a backyard barbecue or to a chip–and–dip fest around the pool.

7 or 8 **fresh mint leaves**

2 **lime quarters**

1 ounce **Simple Syrup** (page 7)

Crushed ice

2½ ounces **white rum**

Club soda

1. Add the mint leaves, lime quarters, and simple syrup to a highball glass. Muddle well with a muddler or wooden spoon.

2. Fill the glass three-quarters full with crushed ice. Add the rum while reading the Hemingway story "Big Two-Hearted River," if a copy is lying around.

3. Top off with club soda. Stir well (but don't spill on the book).

A VARIATION: If you want to make the Mojito less of an afternoon delight and more of a refined nighttime cocktail, it's no trouble at all. First, remove the club soda. Then, instead of adding the mint leaves, lime, and simple syrup to a highball glass, add them to a cocktail shaker or mixing glass. Muddle well, then add the rum and a healthy amount of ice. Shake well, and strain into a cocktail glass.

"Don't you drink? I notice you speak slightingly of the bottle. I have drunk since I was fifteen and few things have given me more pleasure. When you work hard all day with your head and know you must work again the next day what else can change your ideas and make them **run on a different plane** like whisky? When you are cold and wet what else can warm you? Before an attack who can say anything that gives you the momentary well-being that rum does?"

ERNEST HEMINGWAY, in a letter to Ivan Kashkin, 1935

The Old Fashioned

For a drink that is sadly, oh so sadly, neglected by 96.7 percent of drinkers drinking right now, the Old Fashioned causes approximately 50 percent of all cocktail-related black eyes. Don't let it happen to you by sipping, instead of swearing, when the ruckus starts about whether to use rye or whiskey or bourbon, whether to garnish with a cherry, a cherry and an orange, a cherry and an orange and a lemon twist, or (egad) all of the above and a pineapple, and whether **this venerable mix** was first mixed at the Pendennis Club in New Orleans in the late 1800s or has actually been around as long as the United States itself. You'll enjoy it more without the fussing and the feuding, and when everyone else is standing around with raw steaks held over bruised eyes, you'll already be engaging your second drink.

1 **sugar cube** or 1½ teaspoons **granulated sugar**

2 dashes **Angostura bitters**

Ice cubes

2½ ounces **bourbon** or **rye**

Lemon twist

1 **maraschino cherry** (if absolutely necessary—but I'm not going to argue about it)

1. Add the sugar to an old-fashioned glass (now, isn't that handy, having the glass named after the drink?) or other thick-bottomed, wide-mouthed, short stocky glass. Top it with the Angostura bitters.

2. Using a muddler or wooden spoon, muddle the sugar and bitters until they're well mixed and spread around the bottom of the glass.

3. Add a couple (2 or 3) ice cubes to the glass. Pour the bourbon delicately, gently, over the ice.

4. Squeeze the twist of lemon over the top, and then release it to its fate. Give the drink a quick stir with a stirring rod or spoon. Top with a cherry if you're really lonely.

The Rob Roy

Perhaps not an unquestioned classic like some of the others in this chapter, the Rob Roy nevertheless has a resonance that can still a barroom, and has a cachet that most modern mixes only dream of attaining. It was originally designed to commemorate the play of the same name, said play being based on Sir Walter Scott's novel of the same name, both of which led to the 1995 movie. I think the drink's aura comes from the inspiration for all of the above artistic endeavors, and that is Rob Roy MacGregor himself, a late-1600s, early-1700s Scottish outlaw, family man, and legend—the three simultaneous designations were possible in Scotland at the time. It could also be that the Rob Roy is **an ideal balance** of Scotch and sweet vermouth (and a very close cousin to the Manhattan, page 31). Don't get caught up in theories, though. You might lose your place in the drink-ordering line.

Ice cubes

2½ ounces **Scotch**

½ ounce **sweet vermouth**

2 dashes **Angostura bitters**

Lemon twist

1. Fill a cocktail shaker halfway full with ice cubes. Add the Scotch, sweet vermouth, and Angostura bitters. Shake well.

2. Strain into a cocktail glass. Garnish with the lemon twist.

A VARIATION: If using orange bitters instead of Angostura, this might be called a Highland Cocktail.

⬆ *A Note: To get the Rob Roy spirit, I like mine heavy on the Scotch. If you're looking for a tad sweeter taste, reduce the Scotch and increase the vermouth.*

Big Easy Sazerac Spots

A historically classic and classy cocktail, the Sazerac (opposite) has been around, and has been a part of New Orleans history, since 1870. But when you're in that fair city, where's the best place to go to enjoy a true Sazerac while you sit and soak in the atmosphere? Well, any of these spots will do just fine.

1 Sazerac Bar

2 Commander's Palace

3 The Carousel Bar (in the Hotel Monteleone)

4 The Napoleon House (also a dandy spot for a Pimm's Cup if the weather's warm)

The Sazerac

There are many great cocktails that originated in New Orleans (the Vieux Carré, page 140, for one, and the better-known Hurricane, page 337, for another; not to mention the exerciser's favorite, the Ramos Fizz, page 129), but the **splendid king of Louisiana drinks** is the Sazerac. Its history is aligned with that of cocktail making itself (at least according to one tale), and definitely bound together with Peychaud's bitters. In the early 1800s, apothecary Antoine Amédie Peychaud came to New Orleans from Haiti and began treating a variety of stomach and other ills with a combination of brandy and his own bitters, served in an egg cup. The egg cup at the time was referred to as a "coquetier," a word often pronounced, the story says, as "cocktail." Soon many folks were using the Peychaud's bitters remedy, but the fervor really began when a coffee house in 1853 started mixing the bitters with its imported house Cognac. This hot spot was called the Sazerac Coffee House, and the Cognac was Sazerac de Forge et Fils. Since then, the Sazerac has gone through changes (with rye replacing Cognac, and with absinthe becoming part of the formula, and more recently with bourbon often replacing rye), but its popularity, both in New Orleans and beyond, hasn't waned—at least with those who've had the good fortune to try one. Be sure you're on that list.

¼ ounce **Pernod** or **other absinthe substitute**

Ice cubes

2 ounces **rye** or **bourbon**

½ ounce **Simple Syrup** (page 7)

2 dashes **Peychaud's bitters**

Lemon twist

1. Coat the inside of an old-fashioned or a rocks glass with the Pernod, swirling it around to ensure it meets all sides of the glass. Fill the glass with ice cubes.

2. Fill a cocktail shaker halfway full with ice cubes. Add the rye, simple syrup, and Peychaud's bitters. Shake well.

3. Strain the mix into the glass. Garnish with the lemon twist.

🔂 **A Note:** *While bourbon and rye, when possible, are used primarily in the Sazerac today, if you have a good Cognac, try it. As Kerri McCaffety, author of the exquisite homage to New Orleans bars,* Obituary Cocktail *(Vissi d'Arte Books, 2001), says, "The Cognac version is magnifique."*

The Screwdriver

Okay, let me have it. Tell me (not too violently, I hope) that the Screwdriver is in no way a gold standard, that it's solely created to further spread vodka's insidious reach, that it's favored by delinquent high-schoolers in parking lots stirring up quick fixes to forget about school (at least that's how I remember the introductions). Okay, enough already. I understand your qualms, your qualifiers, and your quizzical looks. But even if all of the above is true, the Screwdriver remains **a delicate and satisfying combination** when made with freshly squeezed orange juice and when consumed in the morning as a less spicy sub for the Bloody Mary (page 21). And maybe, just maybe, the ubiquitous hold it has in the minds of many, young and old (but especially young), makes it a classic in its own right, even if it's a simple merger.

Ice cubes

2 ounces **vodka**

4 ounces **freshly squeezed orange juice**

Orange slice for garnish

1. Fill a highball glass three-quarters full with ice cubes. Add the vodka and orange juice. Stir 5 times.

2. Garnish with the orange slice and pure contentment.

A Bar with a View

There's nothing wrong with traditional bar scenery (all those bottles definitely look pretty), but it's also nice to be perched high on a rooftop, looking out over a panoramic scene while sipping. To find this on-top-of-the-world feeling, step into the elevator and ride up to one of these five spots.

1. Top of the East, Eastland Park Hotel, Portland, Maine
2. The Rooftop, The Vendue Inn, Charleston, South Carolina
3. The Rooftop Bar, Hotel Oregon, McMinnville, Oregon
4. High Bar, Gramercy Park Hotel, New York, New York
5. UpTop Lounge, Madison, Wisconsin

The Sidecar

Numerous accounts mention the number of cocktails created during Prohibition, mixes made to deal with the bathtub gin and rotgut whiskey. Though many of these accounts are false, the one that insists the Sidecar was created during Prohibition is true—though it was created overseas, at a Parisian bar, either by the proprietor of the bar or by a friend of *The Fine Art of Mixing Drinks* author David Embury (who says the name comes from the fact that his friend was an army captain and had a sidecar on the motorcycle he drove to and from the bar). Mr. Embury also states, "This cocktail is the most perfect example I know of **a magnificent drink** gone wrong."

His reasoning is sound, and not related to the fact that the Sidecar now contains three ingredients, as opposed to the six or seven originally involved. The problem comes from the fact that too many Sidecars are made too sweet, with an equal balance of Cognac or brandy and Cointreau, as well as too much lemon juice. My take is that if you order a Sidecar in a bar, take the safe route and request (in your friendliest manner) that the pourer go light on the Cointreau. If you have a frequented spot where you know and trust the bartenders (which I'm hoping you do) or you are at home where you *are* the bartender, then this shouldn't be a problem at all.

Ice cubes

2 ounces **Cognac** or **brandy**

½ ounce **Cointreau**

½ ounce **freshly squeezed lemon juice**

1. Fill a cocktail shaker halfway full with ice cubes. Add the Cognac, Cointreau, and lemon juice. Shake well, putting a little muscle into it.

2. Strain into a cocktail glass and serve.

A VARIATION: Mr. Embury tells us that the Sidecar can be made with applejack as opposed to the Cognac or brandy, at which time it's called a Kiddie Car, Apple Car, or Apple Cart.

🔊 *A Note: Some enjoy their Sidecars with a sparkling, sugared glass rim. I don't tend toward this, but neither would I turn down a Sidecar offered me if it did have this sweet rim (my momma didn't raise me to be a fool). If you'd like yours with sugar, start out by rubbing a lemon wedge around the outside edge of the cocktail glass's rim. Then add some sugar to a saucer or small plate. Rotate the rim of the glass through the sugar, being sure to get sugar only on the outside of the glass.*

The Bourbon Small-Batch Bounty

Since at least the 1800s, and probably even earlier for a good percentage of the population, American citizens have been pretty fond of bourbon. There have been a wide variety of bourbons produced, many but not all made in Kentucky (although Kentucky is the only state allowed to advertise its name on the bottles), and many have been absolutely a gift to the consumer, both when drunk by themselves and when mixed into cocktails. Today, there's a lot of talk about "small-batch bourbons." Don't be thrown off by the name into thinking these are reserved for those able to shell out incredible amounts of dough (even though some particular versions are expensive). Small-batch bourbon, much like regular bourbon, is corn-based and aged in charred oak barrels, but giving it the small-batch designation means the bourbon was blended from a small number of selected barrels (selected by the company's master distiller, usually), as opposed to the regular bourbon, which may come from hundreds or thousands of combined barrels. This more selective mixing does tend to impart a higher quality level and a smoother taste, with tiers of flavors. There are also "single-barrel" bourbons now available, and these are just what the name implies—bourbons made solely from one select barrel. Both small-batch and single-barrel bourbons are usually aged longer than regular bourbons, too.

There are now a number of brands of both available, at varying price ranges, making a single-barrel and small-batch tasting a viable, and enjoyable, affair. A good place to start your small-batch tasting is by trying one of the small-batch samplers, such as the one from Jim Beam, which includes a small bottle each of Baker's, Basil Hayden, Knob Creek, and Booker's. Or, you could start with an introductory-level small-batch bourbon, such as Knob Creek or Elmer T. Lee, and work your way up to a more expensive variety, such as Booker's or Woodford Reserve.

The Stinger

A whippersnapper (as far as Gold Standards go) that dates back at least to August, 1917, the Stinger (like too many drinks, alas) seems to be on the verge of slipping into obscurity. It is not too late, though. If entering any bar where the pourer is of wise years (or an especially wise youth), ordering a Stinger won't cause confusion at all. You, too, can be wise, by "stinging" your guests at home in this liquid manner. They'll enjoy it much more than a traditional stinging (or towel snapping). It goes well after dinner, and is a fine **dress-up party restarter** if revelers are being weighed down by their unaccustomed-to finery.

There have been times, in history, in certain locales, when the Stinger had a bit of fresh lime juice added. It makes some sense, because the Stinger needs to be shaken mightily, and most heavily shaken drinks have eggs, or cream, or fruit juices. I propose abstaining from the juice, and taking this as a pure duet. However, if experimentation is the spice of life at your house, give the lime juice addition a try. At least you won't lie down at the end of the day regretting a missed chance.

Ice cubes

2½ ounces **brandy** or **Cognac**

½ ounce **white crème de menthe**

1. Fill a cocktail shaker halfway full with ice cubes. Add the brandy and crème de menthe. Shake until your arms start to sting slightly.

2. Strain into a cocktail glass and serve.

⬆ *A Note: Be sure to use white crème de menthe. If you use green, I can't be held responsible.*

The Tequila Sunrise

Perhaps not a Gold Standard in the traditional sense (meaning, accepted in at least 10 places as a classic), the Tequila Sunrise does deserve mention as one of the few drinks that boasts a namesake movie (albeit a somewhat forgettable movie) and song (by the Eagles, whose California laid-back-ness seems fitting). Contrary to some reports, the drink wasn't named after the song (while I haven't found a reliable history of the Tequila Sunrise, I have seen it mentioned in books published before 1971, the year the Eagles formed). I believe this tall drink matches up strongly with the scruffy '60s and early '70s beach occupant, who loved **living and loafing near the surf** and under the sun, as it's one of the ideal mixes for kicking back and forgetting about all the rest of the busy world out there. And don't those folks (and those of us who might tarry in that mindset for a while) deserve a classic to call their own?

Ice cubes

2½ ounces **silver tequila**

4 ounces **freshly squeezed orange juice**

¼ ounce **grenadine**

Orange slice for garnish (optional)

1. Fill a highball glass three-quarters full with ice cubes. Add the tequila and orange juice. Stir well.

2. Being very careful, using a spoon if necessary, pour the grenadine around the circumference of the glass (that's around the top inside edge), parsing the grenadine out slowly so you make the full circle. Garnish with the orange slice.

⟳ *A Note: With grenadine, a drink gets sweet quickly. Watch the pouring so you don't add too much.*

The Tom Collins

Here's a combination that's been poured pretty steadily in the past century and a third, except for one monumental change: We no longer have at our drink-holding fingertips Old Tom gin, a sweetened gin that was the preeminent ingredient here and that led to the name Tom Collins. Today, a little sweetener (sugar or simple syrup) is used to make up the difference. The other change is that once there were many Collins drinks available (including the John Collins, exactly the same as the TC but made using the drier Holland gin), but currently others don't pass muster at most establishments. The formula is a fine one, though, so try it at least with other liquors as well as gin: Whiskey and brandy add their own nice touches.

Much heavier with sugar in its early days (as were many drinks at the time), the Tom Collins played well in the top hot spots that allowed ladies and gentlemen both, and had a hip cachet among those in the know. Before long, as other potent potions came around and tastes and styles changed, the Tom Collins shifted its popularity to a more conservative constituency, as it began to be poured more in the middle part of the twentieth century by and for those who favored tightly trimmed hair and neatly pressed trousers. Today, it's had a renaissance of sorts with the young professional type looking to unwind after a long day in the cubicle.

Whoever is drinking it, two things have to be remembered. First, our collective palate has changed, shifting to a love of drier drinks. With that firmly in mind, be careful when sliding in the simple syrup. There's no need to cause tooth decay while drinking a classic. Second, the bubbles here need to be of the energetic variety. If available, use a soda siphon—if not, buy and open the club soda as close to constructing the drink as possible, and chill it beforehand.

Ice cubes

2 ounces **gin**

½ ounce **freshly squeezed lemon juice**

½ ounce **Simple Syrup** (page 7)

Chilled club soda

Lemon slice for garnish

1. Fill a cocktail shaker halfway full with ice cubes. Add the gin, lemon juice, and simple syrup. Shake well.

2. Fill a Collins glass three-quarters full with ice cubes. Strain the mix over the ice. Top off with chilled club soda. Garnish with the lemon slice.

The Whiskey Sour

The Sour family is so large as to almost defy description. Considering that every cocktail constructed of fruit juice and booze could be, and has been, called a "Sour," the list goes on for hours and days and then into longer periods of time—which would keep us away from any actual drinking for too long to contemplate. The Whiskey Sour, along with the basic Gin, Rum, and Brandy Sours, has been around at least as long as citrus juice and the liquors themselves in one raw form or another. More than the other originating Sours, though, the whiskey version has taken a modern foothold, and orders for it echo within collegiate bastions of youthful inebriations as well as village Elks Lodges. In the back bar of any reliable diner, you might hear an order for blackberry pie and a Whiskey Sour; by the same Sour token you might hear an order for one in a metropolitan elegant eatery after the foie gras has been finished. I count this basic beauty as one of my first bar memories, making it for any number of twenty-first birthday parties when they became the first words trickled off the newly legal tongue. A great leveler, the Whiskey Sour is **at heart a favorite** for a reason beyond its easily surfaced nomenclature and boundary-free nature. It's a favorite simply because it tastes so good.

Ice cubes

2 ounces **bourbon**

½ ounce **freshly squeezed lemon juice**

½ ounce **Simple Syrup** (page 7)

Lemon slice for garnish

1. Fill a cocktail shaker halfway full with ice cubes. Add the bourbon, lemon juice, and simple syrup. Shake well.

2. Strain into a cocktail glass. Garnish with the lemon slice.

A Note: I've suggested bourbon here, because that's the way I roll. Other whiskeys are swell, too, including rye, if available. Also, I suggested a single lemon slice here as a garnish because of the way it mirrors the fragile nature of existence, or because too much fruit often gets in the way. There are Sours served with cherries, orange slices, and more. Go that route—if you need a snack.

A Multitude of Martinis

First off, if you are looking for The Classic Martini, flip back to page 24. This chapter is about all those other drinks that carry the Martini moniker. Certainly, the Martini has been talked about and written about by learned men and women in all manner of places, from the walls of bathroom stalls to highbrow literary journals and every type of printed page in between. There are multiple books entirely devoted to this emperor of imbibibles, for gosh sakes. Each time the Martini appears to be on the wane (the 1960s, for example, with its rebellion against everything the 1950s enjoyed), the pendulum swings back as those very people pooh-poohing the drink decide to actually try one. And then the Martini has gained another score of converts.

This Martini-love has only become more fervent in the past 15 years. I would venture to say (without any scientific research at all) that at least a quarter of cocktails ordered in bars are Martinis. Now, you say, is he talking about all those cocktails with Martini monikers (the Chocolate Cherry Martini, for example) or with "ini" names (the Saketini, say)? No, I wasn't even including the newer extensions of the Martini family. Add those in, and the number rises much higher. But within your question lies the rub: Just what about all those variants carrying at least some part of the Martini name? What's the deal with them?

Many (maybe even most) of the cocktail writers through history have been Martini purists. David Embury, in his book *The Fine Art of Mixing Drinks,* says, after listing recipes for a dry Martini (with orange bitters, which was the rage at one time) and a medium and a sweet Martini (both of which boast sweet vermouth), "The above recipes are given merely in order that you may know the difference between the various types of Martinis as set forth in most recipe books and served in most bars. My advice is to forget them all and, in your own home serve . . . [the] Martini De Luxe." Said Martini De Luxe is solely seven parts imported English gin to one part Lillet vermouth. The always entertaining Crosby Gaige follows this up in his *Cocktail Guide and Ladies Companion,* saying, "From my own personal point of view, the only Martini fit for man or beast is made by the dry formula [a slightly more vermouthy version of Embury's] with a touch of lemon zest." What would these two cocktail heroes make of the recipes in this chapter, A Multitude of Martinis? Well, this is just a guess, but I think they'd drink them.

They might be a little shocked at the lack of imagination from those naming these Martini spawn. I mean, there have always been drinks that were cousins, sometimes close cousins (the Gibson, for example, which only changes the Martini's olive to an onion). Embury lists in his book after the Martini a number of near neighbors—but they have different names. (The Gordon is first, which changes the vermouth to sherry. Today, it would be called a "Sherrytini.") In this chapter, there are drinks aplenty, good drinks, interesting drinks (such as the Flirtini or the Brazilian Martini), drinks that you'll be proud to serve at après-ski parties, yacht dances, backyard picnics, bocce tournaments, fishing derbies, and every occasion where a toast might be given. And each has been named after the Martini, when many don't include any type of vermouth (which many historians think is crucial); there might even be a few hiding within that don't have vodka or gin (let's not get started on the vodka versus gin debate right now). Don't, I beg of you, hold this utter lack of originality in naming against these cocktails. They, like us, didn't have a choice about the original name attached to them, and, unlike us, they can't change their names.

So, if you're the type who is usually put off by a cocktail that has a Martini name but isn't that basic beautiful mingling of gin and vermouth, then I appeal to you—give these cocktails a chance. They just want to make you happy, and I can assure you that you won't be sorry.

Appletini

One of the most popular Martini-monikered drinks of the past several years, the Appletini (or Apple Martini if you want some breathing room) is **ideal for late October occasions** where you're toasting the night near a roaring fire. The fire is indoors, naturally, with a very efficient flue and a comfy couch not far away. There's no need to get the eveningwear all smoky.

Ice cubes

1½ ounces **vodka**

1 ounce **sour-apple schnapps**

1 ounce **apple juice**

1 **apple slice** for garnish

1. Fill a cocktail shaker halfway full with ice cubes. Add the vodka, schnapps, and juice. Shake well—away from the fire.

2. Strain into a martini glass. Garnish with the apple slice.

A VARIATION: Using apple juice in the Appletini (as opposed to cider) keeps the color cleaner, but if you're not scared off by a cloudy drink, experiment with pure ciders, as they provide a fuller and woodsier apple taste.

⬆ *A Note: A slice from a tart apple works best as the garnish here, maybe a Granny Smith (if you want to go the green route) or a Cripps Pink (for the red).*

The Classics: Five Classic Cocktail Books Published Before 1950

Many, many entertaining and informative bar, drink, and party guides were published in the late 1800s and early 1900s, and while I haven't read each of them (and haven't by any means seen them all), I have seen a good bar shelf's worth. And I can say with honesty that if you see any of the five classics listed here, you should snap them up, even if you have to wrestle another bookstore patron. It'll be worth the bruises.

1. *Bar-Tender's Guide or How to Mix Drinks* (published 1862), by Jerry Thomas. The venerated Professor was one of the earliest and most inventive bar-scribes.

2. *Applegreen's Bar Book* (published 1899), by John Applegreen. "This little book is intended to serve a useful purpose as a 'vest-pocket' ready reference."

3. *Drinks* (published 1914), by Jacques Straub. There is a whole passel of potions in one little book by the former wine steward of the Blackstone, in Chicago, and the Pendennis Club, in Louisville.

4. *Cocktail Guide and Ladies Companion* (published 1941), by Crosby Gaige. This is more enjoyable than a barrel of soused monkeys. Crosby's parties would have been a kick.

5. *The Fine Art of Mixing Drinks* (published 1948), by David A. Embury. Embury takes no prisoners as he details the whys and wherefores of famous and newer drinks.

Bacontini

The number of cocktails combining pork products and vodka can be counted on one hand. Perhaps even a solo finger, unless the Bacontini has brethren I've yet to hear tell of. All other meat-tinis aside, this is the top of the heap for those who want a sophisticated blend and a little protein served all at once. Created (as told to me by bar maven Mark Butler) at the Streetside in Chicago, the Bacontini was originally chopped and shaken to convince a couple of unfriendly and annoying patrons that their request for an original drink after hours of obnoxious behavior only made the bartender desire their quick exit. Such is the way of genius (the bartender in this situation was such a genius that he couldn't make a poor-tasting drink even when trying), and such is the way of legend, and thus the Bacontini began. Other hot spots nationwide now take the credit, but trust me, there's only one honest hog-and-vodka history.

1½ slices **alder-smoked, black peppercorn–crusted bacon**

¼ ounce **dry vermouth**

Ice cubes

3 ounces **vodka**

1. In a sauté pan over medium heat, cook the bacon until crisp. Drain the cooked slices on a paper towel.

2. Add the vermouth to a martini glass. Swirl around, coating the entire inside of the glass. Pour out any excess.

3. Fill a cocktail shaker halfway full with ice cubes. Add the vodka. Break the full slice of bacon into ½-inch pieces, and add the pieces to the shaker. Shake well (dry your hands before shaking to ensure a steady grip).

4. Strain into the martini glass. Garnish with the remaining half slice of bacon.

Bees Knees Martini

I first sipped this at the Green Zebra restaurant in Chicago, and was entranced by its slightly sweet ways. The combination of **lavender, honey, and gin** adds etherealness to any afternoon—if you don't mind me getting all fluffy for a moment. That fluffy etherealness is what Bees Knees Martinis lead to, which means that stocking up on feather pillows and spreading them around before serving the second round isn't a bad idea.

Ice cubes

2 ounces **gin**

1½ teaspoons **lavender honey**

½ ounce **freshly squeezed lemon juice**

1. Fill a cocktail shaker halfway full with ice cubes. Add the gin, honey, and lemon juice. Shake very well, for 1 minute at least. While the Bees Knees may lead to dreamy contemplation, it does demand a good shaking. Sometimes dreams have their price.

2. Strain into a cocktail glass.

⬆ *A Note: If this seems naked without any garnish, and is making you blush because of it, slip in a single twist of lemon.*

⬆ *Another Note: Lavender honey is key here— resist the urge to use regular honey. The lavender variety is available in specialty stores and gourmet food stores.*

The Best Ways to Have the Bartender Stand You a Drink

Sure, you don't mind paying for them (being a stand-up kind of a person), but having the bartender pick up a round feels darn swell. How do you reach this state of bar nirvana? Try the following and sip that free one with a smile (trying not to look smug).

1. Tip well (this one I'm hoping you already knew).

2. Know what you want when at the bar. Don't stand at the bar waving a twenty and saying "gimme a beer" when there are many kinds of beer available.

3. Mention in casual bar conversation with your bartender that it's a special occasion (birthday, anniversary, engagement, promotion, etc). But avoid being one of those customers who say, "Hey, it's my birthday, shouldn't you give me a free drink?"

4. Be a generous, friendly, accommodating, good-mannered customer for a period of time—at least three rounds' worth of drinks. Good things happen to good customers.

5. Become a friendly regular, or be employed at another bar or restaurant that your bartender frequents (or, if you see your bartender out of the bar, buy him or her a drink).

Bikini Martini

It's a sing-along: She drank an itsy-bitsy teeny-weeny vodka, rum, and juice Martini, that she drank for the first time today. There are two small things wrong with that ditty. The Bikini Martini **isn't itsy-bitsy or teeny-weeny.** And it doesn't have to be consumed solely by thonged ladies. Both sexes should enjoy this beachy beauty, no matter what level of duds they're sporting.

Ice cubes

2 ounces **white rum**

½ ounce **vodka**

½ ounce **freshly squeezed orange juice**

½ ounce **fresh pineapple juice**

1. Fill a cocktail shaker halfway full with ice cubes. Add the rum, vodka, orange juice, and pineapple juice. Shake it up.

2. Strain into a cocktail glass. Garnish with any remaining modesty you might have.

Blood Martini

Eerie, isn't it? Mention the Blood Martini and bats swoop out of a suddenly Transylvanian sky, and in the distance a black horse is seen, galloping up with a somewhat familiar-looking caped rider leaping off, and the low-end strings start playing a haunting melody in the background as clouds shift to reveal a full moon, and then a wolf-like creature starts howling, and then the rider (who bears a remarkable resemblance to Christopher Lee) smiles, shows his lengthy teeth and says, "I am Dracula, and **I welcome you**," and opens those hypnotic eyes wide and leans nearer to your neck, which has veins a-popping. At this moment, reach into your portable bar, whip up the Blood Martini, and save Drac the trouble of unleashing his famous incisors. The Martini was what he really wanted, anyway (hence the "I never drink wine" quote; the second part, "I only drink Blood Martinis," was sadly left on the cutting-room floor). If only all those lonely travelers had known.

Ice cubes

2 ounces **vodka**

¾ ounce **Campari**

½ ounce **freshly squeezed blood orange juice**

Orange twist for garnish

1. Fill a cocktail shaker halfway full with ice cubes. Brush Dracula away from the throat area. Add the vodka, Campari, and juice to the shaker. Shake vigorously, but not in such a rush that it brings the blood to your cheeks.

2. Strain the Blood Martini into a cocktail glass. Garnish with the orange twist.

Brazilian Martini

Don't run from this thinking that the construction involves some scary shaving of body parts best left unmentioned. Making a Brazilian Martini is no more threatening to hair than making any other cocktail—meaning, if you have Crystal Gale–style locks (which went down to hip level, for those not in the know), they should be pinned back when shaking to avoid unnecessary hair-pulling or unwanted hair in the drink.

Sneakily sweet, while still featuring the kick of Brazilian favorite cachaça (see also the Caipirinha, page 205), which is made from sugarcane juice, the Brazilian Martini naturally suits parties near the pool, when the temperature's high and the music's swinging to a samba beat. One warning—for any round past the second, switch to plastic glasses. Because at some point a guest's going to slip, dive, or be pushed into the pool, and there's no call for glass in the water.

Ice cubes

2 ounces **cachaça**

½ ounce **Simple Syrup** (page 7)

½ ounce **passionfruit juice**

½ ounce **freshly squeezed lime juice**

Lime slice for garnish

1. Fill a cocktail shaker halfway full with ice cubes. Add the cachaça, simple syrup, passionfruit juice, and lime juice. Shake, shake, shake.

2. Strain into a cocktail glass. Garnish with the lime slice and an itty-bitty bikini.

Breakfast Martini

For those rapidly unfolding mornings when there's a need to combine breakfast with a waker-upper (though I wouldn't suggest this before work, as I don't want to take the blame for any boss-employee conflicts), this beverage is best served with a fluffy biscuit, or a large side of hash browns.

Ice cubes

2½ ounces **vodka**

½ tablespoon **seedless raspberry jelly**

1. Fill a cocktail shaker halfway full with ice cubes. Add the vodka and jelly. Shake as if you meant it.

2. Strain into a cocktail glass (if your jelly is too chunky for straining, pour the whole mix into a rocks glass).

⬆ *A Note: Substituting other jellies is okay, as long as they're legally meant to be consumed.*

⬆ *A Second Note: If you would like to go the jam route, instead of jelly, then definitely pour the ice and mix into a glass without straining. Jam's thicker consistency tends to leave too much behind in the shaker if you strain it.*

Bubbletini

As if having "tini" at the end didn't make this drink hopping enough, this hip helping doubles it up with another of today's trendy beverages, bubble tea. Bubble tea (or pearl tea or boba or *zhen zhou nai cha* or milk tea or tapioca ball drink or QQ) is as popular with kids of all ages in Taiwan or Hong Kong as soda pop is in the United States, and its popularity is rapidly spreading. Bubble tea is known both for the tapioca balls that populate the bottom of the drink and for the vast variety of possible fruit flavorings. So, guessing that the Bubbletini is fruity and features a special garnish would be an easy, and correct, guess. If you haven't yet had bubble tea, or chewed on a tapioca ball, then go easy on the amount added to the drink. If you're already a fan, go tapioca crazy.

Ice cubes

2 ounces **vodka**

¾ ounce **fresh pineapple juice**

½ ounce **mango-flavored rum**

4 or 5 **tapioca balls** (see Note)

1. Fill a cocktail shaker halfway full with ice cubes. Add the vodka, pineapple juice, and rum. Shake well.

2. Add the tapioca balls to a cocktail glass. Strain the mix into the glass.

A VARIATION: When bubble tea is made as "milk tea," it's milky and fruity instead of just tea-y and fruity. To follow the milk tea route, add ½ ounce of cream and call it a Milkteatini.

⬆ *A Note: If you're hard-pressed to find tapioca balls, check at www.bubbleteasupply.com or your local Asian market.*

Cajun Martini

There are two roads (traveled by bayou boat, because in "Cajun country" the roads are water-based) to take when making a Cajun Martini. This recipe is for those who haven't yet mastered the reflective and patient nature of many bayou residents. **For those who want their gratification quickly,** have at it. If you're one who doesn't mind a little waiting, who enjoys the anticipation as well as the end result, you might try a different tactic (see the variation).

Ice cubes

2½ ounces **gin**

½ ounce **dry vermouth**

2 dashes **Louisiana-style hot sauce** (such as Red Hot or Tabasco)

Small **jalapeño chile** for garnish

1. Fill a cocktail shaker halfway full with ice cubes. Add the gin, vermouth, and hot sauce. Shake well, with a zydeco rhythm.

2. Strain into a cocktail glass. Garnish with the jalapeño and a clean handkerchief (to wipe away any pepper-induced sweating, or perspiring if you're a lady).

A VARIATION: Pour a whole bottle of dry gin into a jar, jug, or bottle that has a tight seal. Add a whole fresh cayenne pepper. Then let those two elements get acquainted over the course of 2 weeks. After the 2 weeks have passed, use the infused gin in this recipe, leaving out the hot sauce.

4 Drinks to Induce Dancing

Looking to shake that rump and get either a friend or a more-than-a-friend to shake that rump at the same time (because taking over the dance floor by yourself bites a bit off the lonely and pathetic cake)? Pick up one of these four shaking combinations and start feeling the groove.

1 Don't Just Stand There (page 298)

2 Eye-Opener (page 107)

3 Tidal Wave (page 194)

4 Brass Monkey (page 328)

Caramel Apple Martini

Perhaps the circus side-show nature of this mix makes it **too sweet for many Martini maniacs?** I think that it's an obvious accompaniment for watching the movie *3 Ring Circus* (from 1954, starring Jerry Lewis and Dean Martin and originally called *Big Top*) or for watching *Big Top Pee-wee* (from 1988, starring Paul Reubens, aka Pee-wee Herman).

Ice cubes

2 ounces **apple-flavored vodka**

½ ounce **butterscotch schnapps**

½ ounce **sour-apple schnapps**

Apple slice for garnish

1 teaspoon **caramel sauce**

1. Fill a cocktail shaker halfway full with ice cubes. Add the vodka, butterscotch schnapps, and sour-apple schnapps. Shake as if you were being shot out of a cannon.

2. Strain the mix into a cocktail glass. Cut a small slit into the apple slice, and perch it on the side of glass.

3. Carefully drizzle the caramel onto the apple slice. Serve with a painted-on smile.

⬆ **A Note:** *If the caramel is too thick for drizzling, heat it slightly (but not so much that it becomes runny).*

Cherry Martini

One thing to remember—if shaking your memorable groove thing to Wild Cherry's "Play That Funky Music" while sipping on a Cherry Martini, be sure the glass isn't too full by the time the line "funking out in every way" comes on, because that combination is an accident waiting to **spill onto the dance floor.** Instead, when starting to high-step in that funky manner, set your drink down near a trusted friend (or wannabe friend). It'll be there to chill you out when the song's over, and happiness is bound to descend.

4 **fresh cherries,** pitted (Bing cherries are nice)

Ice cubes

2½ ounces **vodka**

½ ounce **maraschino liqueur**

1. Add 3 of the cherries to a cocktail shaker or mixing glass. Using a muddler or wooden spoon, muddle the cherries well.

2. Fill the cocktail shaker halfway full with ice cubes. Add the vodka and maraschino liqueur. Shake well and funkily.

3. Strain into a cocktail glass. Garnish with the remaining cherry.

A VARIATION: Want to try a little more disorderly dance step? Instead of straining the mix, just pour it, cherry skins and all, into a large cocktail glass or goblet. Call it a Messy Cherry Martini.

Chocolate Martini

Searching for a way to add something extra to the next Valentine's Day dinner you're stirring up for your main squeeze? Looking for a way to **sweeten an evening** spent with your pleasant paramour? Seeking a way to deliciously raise your profile during a hopeful romantic interlude? Let me introduce you to the Chocolate Martini. Your investigations are over.

Ice cubes

1½ ounces **chocolate-flavored vodka**

½ ounce **chocolate liqueur,** such as Godiva

½ ounce **crème de cacao**

½ ounce **heavy cream**

Chocolate syrup for garnish

1. Fill a cocktail shaker halfway full with ice cubes. Add the vodka, chocolate liqueur, crème de cacao, and heavy cream. Shake well, but charmingly.

2. Strain into a cocktail glass. Swirl a light pattern (a heart if you don't think it's too cheesy and if you have the swirling skills) on the top of the drink with the chocolate syrup.

⊕ *A Note: The chocolate syrup swirl isn't for everyone. Other garnishing options include a chocolate kiss placed in the bottom of the glass, or a chocolate-dipped strawberry set on the edge of the glass (you'll need to make a small slice in the strawberry for balancing purposes).*

Chocolate-Cherry Martini

Not just an offspring of the above Cherry Martini (page 59) but a brightly boozy candy that stands alone, the Chocolate-Cherry Martini (or the CCM) is for those located at the bar who look like they missed out on Valentine's Day, as it covers two of the three big Valentine's basics (the three being chocolates, cherries, and flowers). Of course, buying your very own valentine one of these, served with a dozen roses, isn't a bad idea either. Valentino himself would be proud.

Ice cubes

2 ounces **black cherry-flavored vodka,** such as Effen

¾ ounce **chocolate liqueur,** such as Godiva

¼ ounce **Bailey's Irish Cream**

Chocolate-covered cherry for garnish

1. Fill a cocktail shaker halfway full with ice cubes. Add the vodka, chocolate liqueur, and Bailey's. Shake well.

2. Place the chocolate-covered cherry gently into a cocktail glass. Strain the CCM into the glass. Prepare to be covered in kisses, if giving it away. If keeping it for yourself, maybe just look in the mirror and tell yourself you're amazing.

⬆ *A Note: A trustworthy bartender once told me that this just might be better going half and half with the Godiva and Bailey's. Try it and let me know if he was right.*

Citritini

There are moments when a serious cocktail constructor must go outside of his or her garnish comfort zone to match an occasion or a particular drink. Making the Citritini is one of those times (don't start trembling, though). Whether you serve it with a weekend brunch alongside an asparagus frittata or in the early evening while playing a round of dominoes, the sorbet garnish is essential. Not only does it set this Martini apart from the masses, it also provides a chilly little side dish, too, and assures cocktail frigidity (a good thing, despite frigidity's negative modern connotations). If no orange sorbet is available, raspberry or any other slightly tart berry sorbet can be a palatable substitute.

Ice cubes

2 ounces **citrus-flavored** or **plain vodka**

1 ounce **Citrónge liqueur**

1 scoop (about ¼ cup) **orange sorbet**

1. Fill a cocktail shaker halfway full with ice cubes. Add the vodka and Citrónge. Shake well.

2. Add the sorbet to the bottom of a cocktail glass (you want it to be a nicely round serving). Strain the mélange over the sorbet.

Cranberry Martini

All right, all right, all right, keep the clamoring down. I realize that a Cranberry Martini is close enough to the frenetically popular Cosmo (page 159) that even mentioning it is bound to cause uproar amongst those drinkers who enjoy causing uproar. I, admittedly, think that this delight **stands on its own pure merits,** as it's not identical, and to pass it by at first glance due to similarities is a crying shame. So all uproarious folks in the corner—quiet down!

Ice cubes

2 ounces **cranberry flavored vodka** or **plain vodka**

1 ounce **cranberry juice cocktail**

½ ounce **freshly squeezed lime juice**

3 **frozen cranberries** for garnish

1. Fill a cocktail shaker halfway full with ice cubes. Add the vodka, cranberry juice, and lime juice. Shake rapidly, in the direction of anyone tsk-tsking.

2. Add the 3 frozen cranberries to a cocktail glass (they'll keep everything nice and icy). Strain the mix over the cranberries.

LIQUEUR SPOTLIGHT
Citrónge

Constructed with care by the fine folks at the Patron company (known—so far—mainly for their fine, fine tequilas), Citrónge is the only all-natural orange liqueur imported from Mexico. It is in the same family as Grand Marnier (though not quite as sweet) and Cointreau. Its layers of orange flavors emanate out of its purity, as only sweet Jamaican oranges and bittersweet Haitian oranges are used, blended with pure cane sugar and a high-proof neutral grain spirit. While the oranges come from two lovely countries known for beaches and for locals dabbling in voodoo, the chances of consuming Citrónge in a cocktail, or straight up or on the rocks, and then turning into a zombie are nil. The chances of you being enchanted, however, are very high indeed. Try experimenting with Citrónge in a Margarita or other drinks that use triple sec.

Dirty Martini

The first time someone ordered a "dirty" Martini when I was bartending, I blanked on the proper approach. **Pull a Swayze** (à la *Dirty Dancing*) series of moves behind the bar while making it? A little bump and grind with the shaker subbing for a stripper's pole? Or not going the blue route and instead adding a little honest Midwestern dirt to the mix? Luckily (for me and for the patron), my fellow bartender (I believe it was the famous Ken Pingleton) let me in on the dirty secret. To make a Martini dirty, you must add olive brine to the mix. If you still desire to unveil the dance moves alluded to above while making it, that's your choice.

Ice cubes

2½ ounces **gin**

½ ounce **dry vermouth**

½ ounce **olive brine** (the juice in the olive jar)

Green olive for garnish

1. Fill a cocktail shaker halfway full with ice cubes. Add the gin, vermouth, and brine. Shake well.

2. Add the olive to a cocktail glass. Strain the dirty mix into the glass. Wash your hands.

⬆ A Note: I tend toward a standard green olive in a Martini situation, especially when serving to someone who hasn't expressed a preference. But there are numerous green olive varieties out there, with the greatest taste differential being in what they've been stuffed with. Beyond the more traditional pimento, finding olives stuffed with garlic, jalape-ños, blue cheese, citrus peel, and more is an easy task. I tend to think these stuffings obscure the Martini taste. However, if you like a bit of tang or other flavor mixed with your gin and vermouth, don't hesitate to experiment.

⬆ A Second Note: Worried that you don't have enough brine to make your Dirty Martini dirty enough? You can get bottles full of just olive juice, in various flavors, at an online site called olivejuiceforsale.com. The name notwithstanding, the company also has stuffed olives and other olive accoutrements.

"I am prepared to believe that a dry Martini slightly impairs the palate, but think what it does for **the soul**."

ALEC WAUGH, *In Praise of Wine and Certain Noble Spirits*, 1959

Dragontini

My friends, it is as the great Bruce Lee said in Enter the Dragontini, "Never take your eyes off your Martini . . . even when you bow." And, "Do not concentrate on the finger or you will miss all that heavenly Dragontini glory." Remember these words, and remember that the Dragontini has **a tongue of fire and a mighty kick,** and boundlessly joyful will be your evenings.

Ice cubes

2 ounces **pepper-flavored vodka**

1 ounce **citrus-flavored vodka**

½ ounce **freshly squeezed lime juice**

2 dashes **Louisiana-style hot sauce,** such as Tabasco

1. Fill a cocktail shaker halfway full with ice cubes. Add the pepper and citrus vodkas, lime juice, and hot sauce. Shake masterfully.

2. Strain into a cocktail glass. Serve with speed and catlike balance.

A Note: I took slight liberties with the quotes above. Please toast Bruce Lee every time a Dragontini is consumed to assure my forgiveness.

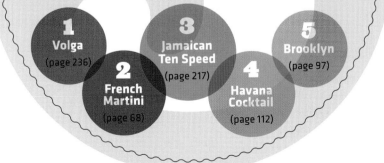

Go 'Round the World without Leaving the Bar

Ah, crappers, why are airline tickets so expensive? Why do jobs take up the majority of hours in a week? Why isn't there a simpler way to traverse the globe's many corners? Friend, there is; with the right ingredients and the right bartender, making that worldwide adventure happen in one night (or a series of nights) isn't an impossibility. The trick is scaling back a bit, and not being insistent on actually touching soil in a variety of far-flung places. Instead, try the following mixes, each of which will transport you, if only for a while, to a different exciting locale.

1 Volga (page 236)

2 French Martini (page 68)

3 Jamaican Ten Speed (page 217)

4 Havana Cocktail (page 112)

5 Brooklyn (page 97)

English Martini

I'll get one of those looks (you know, the kind that seems to imply, "You're a fool, kiddo") from the more staid cocktail makers for even including an "English Martini"—didn't the English propagate the realm of gin, the main ingredient in the Classic Martini (page 24) in the first place? Doesn't the word "gin" come from the English (who distilled the word from the Dutch *genever*, which stands for juniper, from which gin is made)? Isn't the idea of an "English Martini" then the same as saying "shrimp scampi" (as *scampi* means "shrimp" in Italian)? And isn't having a cocktail that features Pimm's No. 1 Cup (a gin-based collage containing quinine plus the mandatory arrangement of secret herbs, unveiled in the 1840s by James Pimm, an oyster-bar owner) and gin sorta silly? The answer to all of the above may be "yes," and if that causes you to shy away from this concoction, so be it. I was offered it by a pal with the above name intact and almost shied away my own self. Lucky for me I didn't, as it's an adult mix that goes down easy during late December evenings surrounded by holiday décor, as well as sprightly spring evenings surrounded by sprouting foliage. **You should be lucky, too.**

Ice cubes

2 ounces **gin** (do I need to say it should be English gin?)

1 ounce **Pimm's No. 1 Cup**

½ ounce **freshly squeezed lemon juice**

Lemon twist for garnish

1. Fill a cocktail shaker halfway full with ice cubes. Add the gin, Pimm's, and lemon juice. Shake well.

2. Strain the mix into a cocktail glass. Garnish with the lemon twist.

Flirtini

Hey there, how you doing? **You're looking fine** in those black boots. You alone? Hard to believe. You come here often? Something in my eye? No, no, I was just winking. Thought it would go nicely with my come-hither smile. Can I buy you a drink? How about a Flirtini? It became popular via that show *Sex and the City* (and was created by King Cocktail, Dale DeGroff). You know, you're pretty royal yourself. Really, let me buy you a drink. And then maybe we can trade numbers? You want to see if you like the drink first? Makes sense to me.

3 **pineapple chunks,**
about 1 inch in size

Ice cubes

½ ounce **vodka**

½ ounce **Cointreau**

½ ounce **fresh
pineapple juice**

3 ounces **chilled
Champagne**

Maraschino cherry
for garnish

1. Add the pineapple pieces to a cocktail shaker or mixing glass. Using a muddler or wooden spoon, muddle well. Fill the shaker or glass half-way full with ice cubes.

2. Add the vodka, Cointreau, and pineapple juice. Shake well (might want to shake those hips too, if being flirtatious).

3. Strain into a large cocktail glass. Top with the chilled Champagne. Garnish with the cherry (and a mysterious smile).

⬆ *A Note: Fresh pineapple is preferred here, but in a pinch you can use canned. Don't blame me if the flirting lacks a little something, though.*

Shaken or Stirred: Does James Bond Really Have the Answer?

Bond's famous "shaken, not stirred" Martini ordering was, I think, an attempt to show just how cool he was, on all levels. Agent 007's Martini had to have that extra iciness because a) he was always in hot situations; b) he was so damn unflappable, no matter the fire; and c) he wasn't like those other men, seated in drawing rooms slowly stirring their pitchers of gin and vermouth. But does it make sense? I think a good shaking helps many drinks, but if you're ponying up for ultra-hip (and expensive) gin or vodka in your Martini, stirring does make sure you get less water in your drink (more ice melts in shaking). I tend to like my Martinis stirred, but that's because I like to make them by the pitcher, so that every guest gets a drink close to the same time. But James Bond is a loner, and I'm a social animal. If making a Martini for someone, it never hurts to ask about a preference.

French Martini

Ooh la la. A lovely Martini variant indeed, attractive in color as well as taste, this one **transports the drinker** straight to an expansive château in the center of France. (Whether the drinker instantly begins speaking French is under study. There have been reports, but nothing has been proved definitively. Myself, I believe that *parler Français vient instantanément, sans aucune communication préalable du buveur.*)

The French connection occurs via the use of Chambord, which is created using the best *framboises noires* (black raspberries) infused in fine Cognac with blackberries, currants, and red raspberries. The end result is a lovely liqueur discovered by Louis XIV in 1685, which has been revered by royals and us peasants ever since.

Ice cubes

1½ ounces **vodka**

1 ounce **Chambord**

¾ ounce **fresh pineapple juice**

½ ounce **freshly squeezed lemon juice**

3 or 4 **frozen raspberries** for garnish

1. Fill a cocktail shaker halfway full with ice cubes. Add the vodka, Chambord, pineapple juice, and lemon juice. Shake well.

2. Add the frozen raspberries to a large cocktail glass. Strain the mix over the raspberries. *À votre santé!*

⤴ ***A Translation (more or less):***
"French speaking comes instantaneously, without any previous communication from the drinker."

Habanero Martini

At one point in our country's cocktail and culinary history, this **fiery persuader** merited a warning, along with a row of flashing red lights: warning, warning, warning. Today, though, most have already heard of the habanero's heat. If you haven't, don't sip this until doing a little research. You don't want to dive in underprepared and get a case of the scorch mouth.

Ice cubes

2½ ounces **silver tequila**

½ ounce **dry vermouth**

1 **habanero chile**

1. Fill a cocktail shaker halfway full with ice cubes. Add the tequila and vermouth. Shake well.

2. Add the habanero to a cocktail glass. Gently, using a muddler or wooden spoon, muddle the pepper. You don't want to pulverize it, just squeeze it a bit.

3. Strain the tequila-vermouth mix into the glass. Serve only to those ready and willing.

Six Obscure Facts to Bring Up at the Bar

Have a desire to get Cliff Clavin-ing (Cliff being the obscure-fact king and confused mailman on the TV show *Cheers*) while sitting with pals at home or at the bar? These facts should get the conversation started (or at least get you the reputation you deserve and desire).

1. Unlike beer and wine, spirits are originally completely clear and colorless; their golden browns and other hues are the result of the aging process or added colors.

2. There are an estimated 49 million bubbles in a bottle of Champagne.

3. Each molecule of alcohol is less than a billionth of a meter long and consists of a few atoms of oxygen, carbon, and hydrogen.

4. The corkscrew was invented in 1860.

5. In ancient Babylon, the bride's father would supply his son-in-law with all the mead (fermented honey beverage) he could drink for a certain period of time after the wedding. Because the ancient Babylonian calendar was lunar-based, this period of free mead was called "honey month," or what we now call the "honeymoon."

6. The longest bar in the world is 684 feet long, or about 208.5 meters, and is located at the New Bulldog in Rock Island, Illinois.

Hazeltini

Though popular reports disagree, the Hazeltini isn't named for the main character in the Shirley Booth sitcom of the 1960s. Instead, the name derives from the use of Frangelico, a hazelnut liqueur produced for more than 300 years in Italy's Piedmont region that traces its name back to a famous monk, Fra Angelico (hence the monk-shaped bottle). Whether you want to **serve these dressed as a maid** (Hazel was a maid on the TV show—perhaps TV's second-most-famous maid, after Florence on *The Jeffersons*) or in a monk's cowl is up to you.

Ice cubes

1½ ounces **vanilla-flavored vodka**

1½ ounces **Frangelico**

½ ounce **sweet vermouth**

Toasted hazelnut for garnish

1. Fill a cocktail shaker halfway full with ice cubes. Add the vodka, Frangelico, and sweet vermouth. Shake as if you were either dusting or swinging a censer.

2. Strain into a cocktail glass. Garnish with a single hazelnut.

A VARIATION: If you're hankering for something a little sweeter, garnish with a piece of hazelnut-flavored chocolate or a chocolate-covered hazelnut.

Italian Martini

Savor this while watching the sun slip over the horizon from the balcony at a seaside hotel in Vernazza or Corniglia or another town in Italy's Cinque Terre, perhaps while appreciating a biscotti or, if partaking before the meal, while nibbling *crostini al funghi*. **The choice is yours** (just know that unless you're looking at me across the gulf between balconies, I'll be jealous).

Ice cubes

2 ounces **gin**

½ ounce **amaretto**

½ ounce **sweet vermouth**

Fresh cherry for garnish

1. Fill a cocktail shaker halfway full with ice cubes. Add the gin, amaretto, and sweet vermouth. Shake well.

2. Strain into a cocktail glass. Garnish with the cherry. *Bella!*

Licorice Martini

Not a flavor that promotes much in the way of middle ground, **licorice is usually loved or hated** (and I'm talking here about the flavor found in black licorice, not the more user-friendly cherry Twizzler flavor). I fall onto the side of loving it, but if you are a hater (even after repeatedly hearing the licorice-related catchphrase, "Don't be a hater"), ignore this recipe altogether and move along. Your moving along only leaves more for those of us who have good taste.

Ice cubes

2 ounces **vodka**

1 ounce **black sambuca** or **other anise-flavored liqueur**

Black licorice whip for garnish

1. Fill a cocktail shaker halfway full with ice cubes. Add the vodka and sambuca. Shake well.

2. Strain into a cocktail glass and garnish with the black licorice whip (you may want to trim it to fit the glass so that it's not flopping all around).

❶ *A Note: Sambuca is a liqueur that is infused with elderberries along with licorice and other ingredients—the bush's scientific name is* Sambucus nigra, *and it grows all over Italy. The liqueur comes in black, white, and red varieties. I like the black here because it goes well with the licorice theme.*

O.K. Martini

Don't be fooled, even for a second, into muddling up this Martini's title into "The Okay Martini," which would distill it down to only so-so, only mediocre, only middling, average, ordinary. The O.K. Martini wears none of the above words on its T-shirt (if a Martini could wear a T-shirt). The names harkens, instead, to Orange Kiss, which was the original title of this cocktail, until some sturdy fellow decided that moniker had too much **fluffy lovey-doveyness** attached to it.

Ice cubes

2 ounces **chocolate-flavored vodka**

1 ounce **orange curaçao**

3 **leaves** and 1 **small sprig orange mint**

1. Fill a cocktail shaker halfway full with ice cubes. Add the vodka and curaçao. Shake well (without kissing the shaker or talking about kissing).

2. Rub the mint leaves around the inside of a cocktail glass, making sure all of the inside gets touched. Discard the leaves.

3. Strain the shaken mix into the glass. Garnish with the mint sprig.

Picasso Martini

When a book is not only interestingly shaped (with the long and short sides switched) but also in a metal case and printed on parchment paper, it's bound to be at least intriguing, and boast a fashionable-buried-treasure air. When the book also—as is the case with *The Martini Diaries* by Leslie Ann Nash, onetime manager of a Paris jazz nightclub in the post–World War II years—features a huge selection of classic and creative Martini variants, it becomes **a treasure in its own right.** Though the recipes and the stories behind them were all "discovered" by Alston Chase, and though the book has the tricky clarification that everything within is a work of fiction, the stories still kick, and the recipes still have kick—enough to start up any jazzy evening. The following is, according to the lore of *The Martini Diaries*, Pablo Picasso's favorite. If there's no Turkish coffee available, substitute regular ol' espresso.

Ice cubes

3 ounces **gin**

½ ounce **brandy**

½ ounce **Turkish coffee,** cooled to room temperature

½ ounce **Simple Syrup** (page 7)

1. Fill a cocktail shaker halfway full with ice cubes. Add the gin, brandy, coffee, and simple syrup. Shake well.

2. Strain into a large cocktail glass. Drink quickly, and then start painting. If you drink enough of these, you may go through all of Picasso's various periods. Don't stop in the Blue Period too long, though—there's no call for the blues.

Pineappletini

As my grandfather used to say, when taking part in late-night spelling bees after a few **tantalizing boozy treats**, "It's always better to be the quizmaster, reciting the words and making the final call of 'correct' or 'incorrect,' than to be the poor soul bumbling over syllable after syllable." Especially when the Pineappletini comes up, throwing those three p's, two n's, two e's, and three i's into the grammatical fray.

Ice cubes

1½ ounces **Van Gogh Pineapple Vodka**

1 ounce **fresh pineapple juice**

½ ounce **green apple-flavored** (or just apple-flavored) **vodka**

3 **fresh pineapple chunks** for garnish

1. Fill a cocktail shaker halfway full with ice cubes. Add the pineapple vodka, pineapple juice, and apple vodka. Shake well (don't get distracted by any "i" before "e" questions).

2. Strain into a cocktail glass. Impale the 3 pineapple chunks on a toothpick or other garnishing device, and drop them into the glass.

➊ *A Note: I enjoy the slight green apple tang here, but if it doesn't align your consonants, go with pineapple vodka solo and use 2 ounces of it.*

Pomtini

Falling both into the health-nut and cocktail-loving categories, this may be **the cocktail that barks up your tree** if you've an eye on healthy living, due to the known and guessed-at benefits that pomegranate juice boasts. That isn't to say that this a) isn't tasty, and b) won't start the party in the way other martinis might. It is, and it will.

If actual pomegranate seeds aren't available for garnishing purposes, a lime slice may be substituted, but a mythical pallor might be cast on the evening. Just ask Persephone (who sacrificed six months of the year to living with Hades in the netherworld just so she could eat six pomegranate seeds—well, that's my take on it), or look it up in the Song of Solomon (which equated the two sides of a pomegranate cut in half to a bride's two cheeks beneath her veil), or other histories that have the pomegranate as a fertility symbol. Whether the legends are based in fact or myth, having the pomegranate present is always better.

Ice cubes	**1.** Fill a cocktail shaker halfway full with ice cubes. Add the vodka, pomegranate juice, and orange juice. Shake well.
1½ ounces **vodka**	
1 ounce **pomegranate juice**	
½ ounce **freshly squeezed orange juice**	**2.** Add the pomegranate seeds to a cocktail glass. Strain the mix over the seeds.
3 or 4 **frozen pomegranate seeds** for garnish	

⊙ **A Note:** *If the pomegranate seeds aren't frozen, that doesn't mean more winter's on the way (as another legend asserts). It only means the drink won't stay chilled as long.*

Raspberritini

I'll admit, the combining of words so they end in "tini" leaves the phrase "gotten out of hand" in the dust, as well as introducing new words to the bar that are almost impossible to pronounce (much less to hear if you happen to be the one making the drinks on a busy, bustling night). But, as I was introduced to this berry delightful mix with the long and awkward name "Raspberritini" as opposed to the more civilized Raspberry Martini, I feel the need to leave it as the former mouthful. Either way, it's a flavorsome medley that doesn't err on the side of seriousness.

Ice cubes

2 ounces **raspberry-flavored vodka**

1 ounce **Chambord**

½ ounce **freshly squeezed orange juice**

Lime wedge for garnish

1. Fill a cocktail shaker halfway full with ice cubes. Add the vodka, Chambord, and orange juice. Shake well.

2. Strain into a cocktail glass. Squeeze the lime wedge over the glass, and then drop it in so it joins the fun.

⬆ **A Note:** *As Chambord dates back to the parties of King Louis XIV of France (the Sun King), don't be embarrassed to break out royal robes, feathered headdresses, and stockings while sipping one of these.*

Red Hot Martini →

Red Hot, Red Hot, Red Hot, get your Red Hot right here, straighten your back right up, bring the flash back into your eyes, wake the demons up and start dancing, get your Red Hot, Red Hot, Red Hot right here, pop the bounce back into your step and the swing back into your style, get your Red Hot, Red Hot, Red Hot. But keep a glass of milk close by. One never knows when the Red Hot is too hot.

Ice cubes

2 ounces **vodka**

1 ounce **Goldschlager cinnamon schnapps**

3 **red hot candies** for garnish

¼ teaspoon **cayenne pepper**

1. Fill a cocktail shaker halfway full with ice cubes. Add the vodka and Goldschlager. Shake well.

2. Add the 3 red hots to a cocktail glass. Strain the mix over the red hots. Sprinkle the cayenne pepper over the surface of the drink so that it floats on the surface. Wash your hands if you managed to get cayenne on them.

⬆ **A Note:** *If the cayenne causes anyone to shy away from this, don't use it. Sometimes it's better to say you're scared if you're scared.*

Rosemary Martini

This drink takes a tidbit of prior planning. If you're not that organized, you can still make it, though. The difference in prep time comes from whether you want to let the vodka really get acquainted with the rosemary, or whether a quick introduction is enough. **The choice is yours.** If going for the long term, add a 750-milliliter bottle of vodka and three decent-sized sprigs of rosemary to a large glass receptacle, one with a lid that attaches securely. Once said lid is secured, let the mix sit for two weeks in a dry, dark place. After the time is up, strain it back into its bottle (leaving the rosemary behind).

If going the quick route and skipping the infusion process, the rosemary should be bruised well, and then added to the shaker in step 1 below. When straining the cocktail, be sure no shaken rosemary bits come along for the ride.

Ice cubes

2¼ ounces **vodka**

½ ounce **sweet vermouth**

¼ ounce **freshly squeezed lemon juice**

Rosemary sprigs (2 if going the quick route mentioned above, 1 if not)

1. Fill a cocktail shaker halfway full with ice cubes. Add the vodka, sweet vermouth, lemon juice, and 1 well-bruised rosemary sprig (unless you've already infused your vodka with rosemary). Shake rapidly.

2. Strain into a cocktail glass. Garnish with a rosemary sprig.

Ruby Martini

When having the gang over to watch *The Wizard of Oz* (or to play the Wizard of Oz board game from 1974, or the newer talking version, or the Monopoly version, or to sing the songs from the movie, or to follow the yellow brick road around the house, or to race flying monkeys, or to philosophize about the relative scariness of lions and tigers and bears, oh my), a tray of cold Ruby Martinis places you in a Dorothy Gale kind of light: able to **ride out tornadoes, take on witches**, and glow throughout the evening. Without the Ruby Martinis, one of your guests may modify an Auntie Em quote and yell across the room, "Now you go serve those hogs Ruby Martinis before they worry themselves into leaving!"

Ice cubes

2½ ounces **citron-flavored vodka**

½ ounce **freshly squeezed ruby red grapefruit juice**

Grapefruit twist for garnish

1. Fill a cocktail shaker halfway full with ice cubes. Add the vodka and grapefruit juice. Shake well, while clicking your heels together 3 times and chanting, "There's no drink like this, there's no drink like this."

2. Strain into a cocktail glass. Garnish with the grapefruit twist and a song.

Ruby Red Martini

The Ruby Red Martini is so utterly different from the Ruby Martini (opposite) that I forbid you or anyone you know to drink it while watching, talking about, or in any way approaching *The Wizard of Oz*. If I even hear an "I'm melting" or "great and powerful Oz" whispered when being served a Ruby Red Martini, **I promptly accompany my drink to the porch.**

Ice cubes

2 ounces **gin**

½ ounce **cherry brandy**

½ ounce **dry vermouth**

Maraschino cherry
for garnish

1. Fill a cocktail shaker halfway full with ice cubes. Add the gin, brandy, and dry vermouth. Shake well (without any heels touching together 3 times).

2. Add the cherry to a cocktail glass. Strain the mix into the glass. Drink heartily, without thinking of Judy Garland (unless it's the Judy from her 1963 TV show).

Saketini

Tracing its lineage back, oh, about 6,000 years, sake has strong champions worldwide. With this in mind, it was only a matter of time before sake and vodka were blended. It's **the law of the bar** that eventually every liquor becomes combined with every other liquor to test the results. Here, the results are positive, and the recipe is mercifully uncomplicated. Also, unlike when sake was made in Japan in 300 A.D., before cultivated yeast was available, there is no need to chew the ingredients (rice, millet, etc.) first and spit them into vats—a bonus by any account.

Ice cubes

2½ ounces **vodka**

½ ounce **sake**

½ ounce **sweet vermouth**

Pickled ginger
for garnish

Cucumber slice
for garnish

1. Fill a cocktail shaker halfway full with ice cubes. Add the vodka, sake, and vermouth. Shake, but not violently.

2. Strain into a cocktail glass. Spear a small piece of pickled ginger to the cucumber slice with a toothpick or very small samurai sword. Garnish the drink with the cucumber-ginger combo.

Smoky Martini

Don't worry those drunken little heads—the numerous smoking bans now in place from Seattle to NYC don't restrict anyone from ordering a Smoky Martini. I won't promise that a single malt-Scotch lover sitting near a chosen bar stool won't give a shake of the head when seeing that someone has the audacity to mix single malt Scotch with other ingredients. Given that, perhaps ordering this from a far-distant corner of the bar (or stirring it up at home) is the safest route. Not that I counsel the safe route in every situation, but if *you* get shaken, the drink might spill. And that's **a tragedy even Shakespeare wouldn't contemplate.**

Ice cubes

2 ounces **gin**

1 ounce **Lagavulin single malt Scotch**

½ ounce **dry vermouth**

Lemon twist for garnish

1. Fill a cocktail shaker or mixing glass halfway full with ice cubes. Add the gin, Scotch, and dry vermouth. Using a stirring rod or long metal spoon, stir well.

2. Strain the mix into a cocktail glass. Garnish with the lemon twist.

⊙ *A Note: Lagavulin is a single malt Scotch distilled in a small bay near the south coast of Islay, where Scotch has been distilled since 1742 (or so the saga says). I like it in this drink because the smokiness builds up in layers, and isn't overwhelming. Other smoky single malts that you might try in this are Talisker and Laphroaig.*

"You can no more keep a Martini in the refrigerator than you can keep a kiss there. The proper union of gin and vermouth is **a great and sudden glory**; it is one of the happiest marriages on earth, and one of the shortest-lived."

BERNARD DEVOTO, *The Hour*, 1951

Strawberry Martini

This is perfect for idyllic late lunches in summer, when a picnic basket overflows with bread, cheese, and fruit, and that favorite fling is corralled for a walk into a shady spot overlooking a field of flowers. **The ingredients here won't weigh down the basket too much,** and think what a star you'll be when unveiling the first Strawberry Martini—the flowering field pales beside anyone who has that kind of foresight.

Ice cubes

2 ounces **vodka**

½ ounce **crème de cassis**

½ ounce **strawberry syrup**

¼ ounce **freshly squeezed lemon juice**

Strawberry slice for garnish

1. Fill a cocktail shaker halfway full with ice cubes. Add the vodka, crème de cassis, strawberry syrup, and lemon juice. Shake well (but not so well that the bucolic nature of the surroundings is disturbed).

2. Strain into a cocktail glass. Garnish with the strawberry slice.

⤴ *A Note: Want to reduce the amount of stuff lugged along to said lovely picnic spot? I think it's okay to premix the vodka, cassis, syrup, and juice in a large glass bottle that has a secure top (increasing the ingredients as needed for multiple martinis).*

3 Drinks to Buy Someone at a Bar when Looking to Impress

There are nights when you want to pick up a pint for a pal, and then nights when you might want to send something special to an unknown lad or lady perched on the barstool opposite yours. These three are sweet choices for that latter situation.

1 O.K. Martini (page 72)

2 Leave It to Me (page 114)

3 Bon Soir (page 248)

Tequilini

My speculation is that the Tequilini has probably 1,000 potential histories (unlike its cousin the Margarita's three possible origins, detailed on page 32), dating to the explosion of "tini" cocktails in the late 1990s and early 2000s. It's **almost a tongue-twister** with the multiple "i" sounds, and since many imbibers find it a thrill to twist their tongues around appealing mixes, as well as to enjoy the boost of tequila, this was a natural to start showing up on cocktail menus. Serve it alongside piquant dishes and when wearing either a wide-brimmed sombrero or tight black pants with silver detailing.

Ice cubes

2½ ounces **silver tequila**

½ ounce **dry vermouth**

½ ounce **freshly squeezed lime juice**

Lime slice for garnish

1. Fill a cocktail shaker halfway full with ice cubes. Add the tequila, dry vermouth, and lime juice. Shake well, singing a mariachi favorite (perhaps "Juan Silveti").

2. Strain into a cocktail glass. Garnish with the lime slice.

⊕ **A Note:** *There are four kinds of tequila:* blanco *(silver),* oro *(gold),* reposado *(rested), and* añejo *(aged). Since this is a mixed drink, I would stick with one of the first two, as the last two are meant for sipping unaccompanied. But within the silver and gold family, feel free to experiment with different tequilas.*

Witch Martini

I'm not swearing in front of a judge under oath that when Donovan wrote his 1966 hit "Season of the Witch" (from the *Sunshine Superman* album), he was **hyped up and giddy** from overindulgence in Witch Martinis. I'm not swearing it, mind you, but I am believing it. Could be that I've had a few too many myself on occasion. Of course, if you haven't, then who's more fortunate?

Ice cubes

2 ounces **citron-flavored vodka**

1 ounce **Strega**

½ ounce **sweet vermouth**

Lemon twist for garnish

1. Fill a cocktail shaker halfway full with ice cubes. Add the vodka, Strega, and sweet vermouth. Shake in a groovy fashion.

2. Strain into a cocktail glass. Garnish with the lemon twist and a bewitching stare.

Strega

Strega has been made by the same family in Benevento, Italy, since 1860, and the legend behind the witch (*strega* means "witch" in Italian) claims that witches from all over the world once gathered in this southern Italian town. My hope is that if witches really did meet there that they consumed a fair amount of this luscious liquid. If you ever have a chance to travel to Benevento and tour the place where Strega is made, you'll see the walnut tree in the building's courtyard, commemorating the legend and the name, as witches supposedly danced wildly around walnut trees. You'll also get to hear (from the amazingly nice folks at the Strega plant) about the 70 herbs and spices that go into this elixir, including saffron and the local wild mint, which grows nowhere else in the world and which has never been cultivated, and hear about three things that set Strega apart: 1) It's a distilled liqueur, and not infused as some others; 2) It uses all local ingredients (following the same recipe handed down from generation to generation of the Alberti family); and 3) It's aged in oak casks before bottling. The end result is a rich golden liqueur, layered with flavors, ideal both before and after dinner. If the witches were looking for a way to entrance drinkers when meeting in Benevento, they found it with Strega. And, as if the liqueur weren't enough of a reason for the trip, the people at Strega also make delicious chocolates (with the chocolate itself made on the premises, and with certain chocolates filled with the liqueur) and the renowned candy *torrone*, a combination of honey, egg whites, roasted almonds, and spices.

Unburied
Treasures

Avast, ye cocktail-loving maties. Strap your strainer to the mizzen-mast. Place your pitchers on the poop deck. Corral your cocktail glasses and stow them under the starboard side. We're shoving off, taking a trip into waters few drink-hounds have sailed for many a long year, circumnavigating the deadly seas of the mundane, sailing past the sirens of the everyday, and heading straight into the islands of lounges long past. That's right, you rabble-rousers seafaring under the skull and crossbones and cocktail-shaker flag, we're on the hunt to find Unburied Treasures.

There's nothing quite as sad as great old drinks lost to the years, left alone by the side of the road like so many rusted bottle openers. It's enough to make one turn into a pirate and start sailing the dusty seas of used and antique bookstores, searching the racks for those gems, those drink recipe collections written years ago and now forgotten by many, solely to turn page after page, keeping both eyes (or one, if a patch is in place) open for that cocktail treasure waiting to be unburied and revealed to friends and family alike at the next walking of the plank, boat christening, or pirate-movie marathon.

The lucky part here for you, dear reader, is that I've swum these seas (at least some of them, as there are always more seas to swim and more caches of gems to find) and have unburied a host of wooden chests bursting with a hoard of treasures. Feast your eyes and mouths on the wonders uncovered—on the Astoria, the Clover Club, and the Brandy Crusta. Get your grubby pirate hands around the Morning Glory, the Eye-Opener, and the blooming White Rose. Satisfy yourself with the riches contained in the Third Rail, the Lorraine, and the Millionaire.

Hold on a minute, matey, before going bonkers over this uncovered bonanza. There's one warning that goes along with the gold. It's not a curse, because nothing this lovely could be cursed, but a warning nonetheless. Unlike some pieces of fortune (that family heirloom gold necklace with the crazy gorilla pendant, for example), these Unburied Treasures aren't meant to be hoarded away and only brought out to be shown to folks from a dedicated distance, behind a glass panel or a group of gigantic bodyguards. These treasures must be shared with all and sundry or the ghosts of Jerry Thomas, Jack Straub, and a white-aproned host of other bartenders of lore will appear out of the heavens and cause lemons to rot, simple syrup to sour, Champagne to unbubble, and parties to crumble. That's a fate of unimaginable sorrow. Don't be shy with serving up these juicy jewels—there's enough to go around, and with them your revelries might become as renowned as the drinks themselves.

14 Juillet

From Paris via the handy 1972 *Quick Guide to Spirits* by Robert Jay Misch, the 14 Juillet uses Armagnac, which is a specific type of brandy made in (you might guess this) the Armagnac region of France. Created from the same type of grapes that give us Cognac, Armagnac isn't double-distilled like Cognac but is aged in the requisite oak casks. It's also not as well known as Cognac, but is, as the French say, très tasty. And there's a board overseeing production to ensure high quality, the *Bureau National Interprofessionnel de l'Armagnac* (or BNIA). The 14 Juillet mixes Armagnac with Cointreau for a posh end result that goes down smoothly after a five-course meal.

Ice cubes

1½ ounces **Armagnac**

1 ounce **Cointreau**

½ ounce **freshly squeezed lemon juice**

1. Fill a cocktail shaker halfway full with ice cubes. Add the Armagnac, Cointreau, and lemon juice. Shake well.

2. Strain into a cocktail glass and serve.

Abbey Cocktail

This monastic special doesn't involve the renting of full-length robes and the shaving of heads. It once was made with Lillet, and has been made with sweet vermouth since Lillet became less well known. But I suggest that when you want to have friends over for a little **communal contemplation of the larger questions**, you omit both of the above and take the Abbey in its pure form of gin, orange juice, and orange bitters.

Ice cubes

2 ounces **gin**

1½ ounces **freshly squeezed orange juice**

2 dashes **orange bitters**

Maraschino cherry for garnish

1. Fill a cocktail shaker halfway full with ice cubes. Add the gin, orange juice, and orange bitters. Shake while chanting (shake more quickly than the chant, though, unless it's a very upbeat chant).

2. Strain into a cocktail glass. Garnish with the cherry and a thoughtful nod.

➕ **A Tip:** *If you don't have orange bitters (shame on you), you might substitute Angostura bitters. But don't say I didn't warn you.*

Drinks for the Links

Golf is a hard sport—even serious golfers have to cool down a bit, usually somewhere along the back nine. The not-as-serious start the cooling down process right at the first tee (especially if there's an on-course bar). Don't have just any old icy concoction, though. Show your dedication by having an appropriate golf-related sipper.

1 Hole-in-One Cocktail (page 112)

2 Golf Links Highball (page 111)

3 Summer Beer (page 403)

4 Clover Club (page 101)

Absinthe Cocktail

First off, forget everything you've been told about absinthe (except the part about it being illegal in every one of the 50 states), if you've been told a bunch of horror stories. If everything you've been told is how at one time absinthe was **an integral part of cocktail culture**, then don't forget it at all. If you've been told it was an anise-flavored spirit, remember that, too. And, if you've been told that it was outlawed due to the wormwood it contains, and that wormwood may very well cause brains to explode, well, remember that, too. But most of all, remember that there are some choice absinthe substitutes available, which allow the making of cocktails that once contained the real thing. The major brands are Absente, Herbsaint, Pernod, and Ricard. I tend toward Pernod, which is more readily available. But don't shy away from experimenting to find which suits your tastes.

Ice cubes

2 ounces **Pernod** or **other absinthe substitute**

1 ounce **Simple Syrup** (page 7)

Lemon twist for garnish

1. Fill a cocktail shaker halfway full with ice cubes. Add the Pernod and simple syrup. Shake exceptionally well, for a good 15 seconds.

2. Strain into a cocktail glass. Squeeze the lemon twist over the glass, and then drop it in.

⊙ A Note: *While illegal in the United States, absinthe is legal in the United Kingdom and in certain other countries. When traveling to these areas, feel utterly free to use absinthe in this Absinthe Cocktail.*

"'Do you mind going to Mauquin's and having an Absinthe cocktail?' **'Absinthe for breakfast . . . Good lord.'**"

JOHN DOS PASSOS, *Manhattan Transfer*

Affinity Cocktail

Back in the day (which is the way to start any story that you want absolutely no one to listen to), I used to pass my nine-to-fives at the now-long-gone Affinity Publishing. When we had the traditional "office holiday party," I unearthed this mighty mix to **make the party more palatable**. I strongly suggest that you try the same.

Ice cubes

1½ ounces **Scotch**

1½ ounces **dry vermouth**

1½ ounces **sweet vermouth**

Maraschino cherry
for garnish

1. Fill a cocktail shaker halfway full with ice cubes. Add the Scotch, dry vermouth, and sweet vermouth.

2. Strain into a large cocktail glass. Top with the cherry. Attempt to keep the drink, and the cherry, away from all co-workers.

Kick Out the Jams at Closing

It's getting late, the closing hour is upon you (either at the bar or at the home bar), and you want to demonstrate this point, gently but forcefully, to the crowd of last-callers in a musical fashion. Basically, you need one of these songs to play to move people out the door. As the saying goes, "You don't have to go home, but you can't stay here." If you're a patron and hear one of these, know that it's time to go.

1. Lynyrd Skynyrd, "Tuesday's Gone" (this really works only on Tuesdays)
2. Rod McKuen, "Seasons in the Sun"
3. Lou Reed, "Street Hassle"
4. MonoStripe, "Green Tea Rockets"
5. Sun Ra, "We Travel the Spaceways"
6. Sammy Kaye, "Why Does It Get So Late So Early?"
7. Nick Curran and the Nitelifes, "Down Boy Down"
8. LL Cool J, "Mama Said Knock You Out"
9. Billie Holiday, "Baby Get Lost"

Americano

This is for those Neapolitan afternoons, when all that can possibly be mustered up vocally is *prego* and *grazie*—the former when asked if you'd possibly be able to drink another Americano and the latter when one is delivered. Luckily, **this afternoon breeze** is so easy to make that no possible fretting can occur.

Ice cubes

2 ounces **Campari**

2 ounces **sweet vermouth**

Chilled club soda

Orange slice for garnish

1. Fill a highball glass almost to the top with ice cubes. Add the Campari and sweet vermouth. Stir, but calmly, like the breeze off the Mediterranean.

2. Fill the glass with club soda. Garnish with the orange slice. Relax.

Antrim Cocktail

I uncovered this in *The Exotic Drink Book*, volume two of Charles H. Baker, Jr.'s, marvelous *Gentleman's Companion*. He says this one was found "in the quaint little overseas club in Zamboanga, on the island of Mindango in the year of grace 1931," invented by one "Monk" Antrim, from Manila. It seems that Mr. Baker generally traveled the world **drinking and eating as much as possible** (he calls it "liquid field work"), which makes me somewhat jealous. After a few Antrim Cocktails, though, I forget about jealousy and am only happy he remembered his pen.

Ice cubes

2 ounces **Cognac**

2 ounces **tawny port**

½ ounce **Simple Syrup** (page 7)

Lemon twist for garnish

1. Fill a cocktail shaker halfway full with ice cubes. Add the Cognac, tawny port, and simple syrup. Shake well.

2. Strain the mix into a cocktail glass. Squeeze the lemon twist over it, and then drop it in the drink.

A Note: Tawny port is a blended wine that has been matured in wooden casks—this maturation process, which is longer than for other ports, is what turns tawny port its namesake color.

"This is a **slow creeper-upper**, so *prends garde*!"

CHARLES H. BAKER, JR., *Gentleman's Companion*

Applejack Cocktail

When you're really good, you deserve an Applejack (as opposed to being called "applejack," which, while it sounds cool enough, doesn't provide nearly the same pleasures). Applejack, or apple brandy, has been used in cocktails since at least 1894, and while an Applejack Cocktail isn't as traditional as an apple for a good teacher, I'm going to go out on a limb and say **the teacher would be happier** with the former.

Ice cubes

2½ ounces **applejack** or **apple brandy**

½ ounce **freshly squeezed lemon juice**

¼ ounce **Simple Syrup** (page 7)

Lemon twist for garnish

1. Fill a cocktail shaker halfway full with ice cubes. Add the applejack, lemon juice, and simple syrup. Shake while thinking of Johnny Appleseed, without whom none of this apple business would be possible.

2. Strain the mix into a cocktail glass. Squeeze the lemon twist over the drink and then drop it in.

Astoria

The Astoria stipulates that someone in the party **wear a cravat**, and that someone in the party carry a cane topped by a dog's head (preferably a dachshund), and that another party member have a floral-topped hat of titanic proportions, and one other boast a small purse that's blinding due to the number of diamonds stuck to it. Once these members are in your party, then start stirring the Astorias.

Ice cubes

2 ounces **gin**

1 ounce **dry vermouth**

2 dashes **orange bitters**

1. Fill a cocktail shaker or mixing glass halfway full with ice cubes. Add the gin, dry vermouth, and orange bitters. Stir well (do not shake—let's be proper here and not bruise the gin).

2. Strain the mix into a cocktail glass. Serve with a back-East accent.

A Note: This cocktail dates to the opening of the Astoria half of the Waldorf-Astoria Hotel in New York, which happened—according to Albert Stevens Crockett's Old Waldorf-Astoria Bar Book *(reprinted by New Day Publishing, 2003)—in 1897 (and he should know).*

Bishop

This tipple predates the twentieth century—by how many years exactly I'm not sure, but the power position that bishops have held for centuries makes me think people have been naming drinks for them, or shaking drinks at them, for a long, long time. Reflecting the splendiferous robes bishops are known to wear, this drink is, at first glance, blinding. Rum and wine? Shouldn't that be enough to get one thrown out of church? But in execution, the Bishop unites like a good sermon. It's strong but goes down smoothly, and the aftereffect is a warm glow. The Bishop is also an ideal mix for those **Saturday sinners/Sunday saints**. If anyone asks what you were doing out late on a Saturday night, or any night, reply, "I was up late in conference with the Bishop," nodding your head reverently.

¾ ounce **Simple Syrup** (page 7)

Lemon wheel

Ice cubes

1 ounce **white rum**

Dry red wine, such as **Cabernet Sauvignon**

Lemon slice for garnish

➕ **A Tip:** I wouldn't break the bank on the wine, as it is being mixed. But neither should it be Mad Dog 20/20. You don't want to anger the Bishop.

1. Add the simple syrup and lemon wheel to a cocktail shaker or mixing glass. Using a muddler or wooden spoon, muddle well.

2. Add about 3 ice cubes and the rum to the shaker. Shake well.

3. Add 3 (instructions go in threes in the more religious drinks) ice cubes to an 8-ounce goblet. Strain the mix from the shaker into the goblet.

4. Top the glass off with red wine. Stir. Garnish with the lemon slice.

A VARIATION: There is also, for those interested, an English Bishop, which involves roasting an orange studded with cloves, then boiling it in port or other wine. (There's no rum in this version.) I wouldn't try this after having a few, though.

"I have come here because my people voted for me, knowing **I was a honest man** and could make as good whiskey and apple brandy at my still as any man."

JACOB GROOM, 1820s Missouri state legislator, apparently honest, if not always grammatically correct

Blinker

Do I dare unearth the admonition, "Don't blink or you'll miss it"? Or does that cliché undermine my credibility? What if I say, "Too many have blinked and missed this aged cocktail, and so it's slipped into the mists of time"? Is that too stuffy and weird old man-ish? What if I say, "Drink this now, quick, before even blinking!"? That seems as right as the Blinker's **tangy-sweet undertones.**

Ice cubes

1½ ounces **bourbon**

¾ ounce **freshly squeezed grapefruit juice**

¾ ounce **grenadine**

1. Fill a cocktail shaker halfway full with ice cubes. Add the bourbon, grapefruit juice, and grenadine. Shake while blinking rapidly.

2. Strain into a cocktail glass. If too much blinking has gone on, garnish with an eyelash brush.

Bobby Burns

Perhaps this Highlands libation wasn't originally assembled in honor of the poet Robert Burns, and was instead named for a cigar salesman known to stand a round for the fellas at the Waldorf-Astoria bar in NYC. Perhaps the original maker of **this potent potable** didn't even know of Robert Burns. Even if this is the case, I still go on record as saying that you and your friends should spend January 25, Robert Burns's birthday (born 1759), celebrating with a few Bobby Burnses in hand. If his poem "Scotch Drink" is read aloud after a second, third, or fourth cocktail, all the better.

Ice cubes

2½ ounces **Scotch**

1 ounce **sweet vermouth**

¼ ounce **Benedictine**

Lemon twist for garnish

1. Fill a cocktail shaker halfway full with ice cubes. Add the Scotch, sweet vermouth, and Benedictine. Shake well.

2. Strain the mix poetically into a cocktail glass. Squeeze the lemon twist over the glass and drop it in.

"O thou, my muse! Guid auld old Scotch drink!
Whether thro' wimplin' worms thou jink,
Or, richly brown, ream owre the brink,
In glorious faem,
Inspire me, till I lisp an' wink,
To sing thy name!"

ROBERT BURNS, "Scotch Drink"

Brandy Crusta

The exotic tone of the name intimates that the Brandy Crusta not only harkens back to a time when people used the word "harkens," but also that it probably involves a bit of ornamentation, both in the making and in the drinking. While not as difficult to make as it might seem when first glancing at the instructions, the Brandy Crusta and the whole crusta family are **a dash fancified**. When consuming them with friends, be sure a smattering of bling (to combine history with modernity) is in evidence, to match attire to occasion.

Sugar

Orange slice

1 **fresh lemon**

Ice cubes

1½ ounces **brandy**

1 ounce **Simple Syrup**
(page 7)

½ ounce **orange curaçao**

¼ ounce **freshly squeezed
lemon juice**

2 dashes **Angostura bitters**

Maraschino cherry
for garnish (optional)

1. Pour a thin layer of sugar onto a saucer or little plate. Wet the outside of the rim of a chilled white wine glass with the orange slice. You don't want it to get sloppy, just a little wet. Holding the glass by the stem, rotate the glass through the sugar, so that the sugar coats only the outside of the rim.

2. Very carefully, peel the rind off half of the lemon, in 1 long spiral strip. You want to get as little of the white pith as possible. Place this spiral in the wine glass.

3. Fill a cocktail shaker halfway full with ice cubes. Add the brandy, simple syrup, curaçao, lemon juice, and Angostura bitters. Shake well.

4. Add about 5 ice cubes to your wine glass. Make sure the lemon rind encircles the ice.

5. Strain the mix from the cocktail shaker into the glass. Garnish with the orange slice (if you feel dirty using the same slice twice, then don't hesitate to use a fresh slice, or 1 slice and a cherry, if it comes to that).

A VARIATION: If you're brandy-deficient, but really want a Crusta, then substitute gin, rum, or even whiskey. While none of the above carries the same sparkling BC flair, all will do in a pinch.

ANOTHER VARIATION: Is the lemon peel too lemony? Is the orange lobby throwing its muscle around? Feel free to use a full orange rind instead of half a lemon rind.

Brandy Scaffa

At one point in history (in the days when men wore long pants year-round and weren't too big on bathing), the scaffa family of drinks was reserved almost 100 percent for males, on account of their **heavy hand with the harder liquors,** and because scaffas are served at room temperature. I suppose it was thought that the more delicate sex wouldn't want a strong, unchilled drink. Whoever decided that obviously didn't have two older sisters. No matter—all of the scaffas now can be recognized and enjoyed by each person in the room, especially during the frosty months.

¾ ounce **green Chartreuse**

¾ ounce **maraschino liqueur**

2 ounces **brandy**

1. Add the Chartreuse to a small wine glass or other similar-sized cordial glass.

2. Add the maraschino liqueur to the glass, pouring it slowly and carefully over the back of a spoon so that it doesn't mix with the Chartreuse.

3. Add the brandy, again pouring slowly over a spoon to make sure it doesn't mingle too much with the maraschino liqueur.

A VARIATION: There are a number of scaffas, with a few constants: They should be served at room temperature, and they should be layered. A first, easy variation, is just to float a dash of Angostura or Peychaud's bitters on top (we'll call this Brandy Scaffa #2). You could also substitute gin, rum, or whiskey for the brandy (changing the name accordingly). If doing this, I would ride with the bitters on top. But that's me.

Brooklyn

It would be a shame for there to be a cocktail rivalry among the NYC boroughs—there's enough intra-city competition as is. That is only reason number one why it's a good thing there's a Brooklyn cocktail to go along with the better-known Bronx (which is on page 22, and which isn't really named after the borough at all) and the even better-known Manhattan (page 31). Another reason is that Brooklyn deserves a drink, one that can be trumpeted and drunk in corners, and in corner bars. A third reason is that this mix has **a well-balanced taste**, and is a cousin to the more established Manhattan with an extra touch of sweetness. Whether that's reflective of the two boroughs isn't for me to decide—but it is a good question to debate over a round of Brooklyns.

Ice cubes

2 ounces **whiskey**
or **bourbon**

1 ounce **dry vermouth**

½ ounce **maraschino liqueur**

2 dashes **Angostura bitters**

1. Fill a cocktail shaker halfway full with ice cubes. Add the whiskey, dry vermouth, maraschino liqueur, and Angostura bitters. Shake well.

2. Strain the mix into a cocktail glass. Garnish with a Brooklyn Dodgers pennant.

Small-Batch Beauties

Though many of the recipes in this book shy away from calling for specific brands of liquors, because in some areas it's still impossible to pick up certain things (and I tend toward inclusionism), if you have a chance to try some smaller-batch items made in any sort of rigorous old-fashioned manner, don't you be shy about trying them. Well-crafted distilled spirits may often be best sipped on their own, but they also can add a very personal touch to a cocktail. There are many distillers now experimenting with more traditional methods, much the way more people are trying traditional preparation methods with food. Going online may be your best bet for research. A company such as Caddell & Williams (www.caddellwilliams.com), which highlights a number of craft distillers (including Germain-Robin, Maison Surrenne, and St. George Spirits, the last of which makes Hangar One vodka), is a great place to start exploring.

Canadian Grenadier

It's good that the second-largest country in the world has a drink honoring its grenadiers. Whether knowing this drink, or ordering this drink, at one of Canada's finest watering holes results in either a round on the house or a **knowing look** from that sexy Canadian on the corner barstool is nothing I would swear to—but that shouldn't stop the proceedings (no matter your country of origin).

Ice cubes

2 ounces **gin**

1 ounce **freshly squeezed lemon juice**

Chilled ginger ale

Lemon slice for garnish

1. Fill a highball glass three-quarters full with ice cubes. Add the gin and lemon juice. Stir twice.

2. Top the glass off with ginger ale. Stir again, this time singing "O Canada." Garnish with the lemon slice.

🔼 *A Note: This drink, as most will note while reading closely, and with a goal of catching this scribe in errors, is a very close cousin to the Horsefeather (page 387). What's really interesting is that the Horsefeather is generally thought of as a Midwestern favorite, and the CG is, of course, from the United States' northern neighbors. Now that's something to bring up at parties.*

Chancellor

This beauty I picked up when swilling my way through David Wondrich's *Esquire Drinks* (Hearst Publishing, 2002), a tome not only a kick in the boozy pants, but also a kick to read, period, with a balance of history, wit, and attitude. Once your hangover from swilling a cauldron of Chancellors dissipates slightly, try a little more "research" under the tutelage of Dr. Wondrich, in hope of attaining a PhD (Pretty Heavy Drunk).

The Chancellor uses Scotch as its base, which isn't seen a ton, due to the strength of character of most Scotches. Scotch doesn't always play nice with mixers. But everyone comes around in the right circumstances. I'd try serving this with your best brogue or, if that's not available, by mimicking Groundskeeper Willie from *The Simpsons*. Sometimes pop culture comes in handy.

Ice cubes

2 ounces **Scotch**

1 ounce **ruby port**

½ ounce **dry vermouth**

2 dashes **orange bitters**

1. Fill a cocktail shaker halfway full with ice cubes. Add the Scotch, port, vermouth, and orange bitters. Shake well.

2. Strain the mix into a cocktail glass. If you must play the bagpipes and wear a kilt while serving, that's your predilection.

"Point of advice: Don't order it [a Chancellor] in an Irish bar. Or any bar, for that matter—better to **err on the side of caution.**"

DAVID WONDRICH, *Esquire Drinks*, 2002

"Come and show me
another city
**with lifted head
singing** so proud
to be alive."

CARL SANDBURG, *Chicago*, 1916

Chicago

When cocktails ruled the earth (or began to rule—let's hope their beautiful reign hasn't ended yet) in the later 1800s and wee hours of the 1900s, there were **cocktails to celebrate everything** from popular plays to starlets to salesmen. It's no surprise, then, that the City of the Big Shoulders had its own blend. What is surprising is the recent forgetting of this Windy City wonder. Try to order it these days at Lincoln Park lounges or Wicker Park watering holes and you'll only get a growl, unless it's not busy in the bar, in which case a big smile might be forthcoming, because you'll have introduced the bartender to a new favorite.

Ice cubes

1½ ounces **Cognac**

½ ounce **orange curaçao**

Dash of **Angostura bitters**

Chilled Champagne

1. Fill a cocktail shaker halfway full with ice cubes. Add the Cognac, curaçao, and Angostura bitters. Shake well, singing, "Chicago is my kind of town."

2. Strain the mix into a Champagne flute. Top off with Champagne. Serve with an ornamented stir stick or an ice pick.

Clover Club

Many of the classics (both well known and in waiting) arrive straight outta the Big Apple, and a majority think of it as being a mecca for cocktails descending from booze's best years. But there were numerous noble drinks built in other cities, too, such as this good-luck treat, which, legend says, comes out of Philadelphia. According to the reliable *Old Waldorf-Astoria Bar Book* (reprinted by New Day Publishing, 2003), the Clover Club once upon a time was a market leader among movers and shakers in the City of Brotherly Love, which translates today to serving it when you're scrutinizing stock portfolios, signing oil-fields contracts, or watching any of the lawyer soaps currently on TV. It'll **provide the backbone** needed for the above activities.

Ice cubes

1½ ounces **gin**

½ ounce **freshly squeezed lemon juice**

½ ounce **grenadine**

1 **egg white,** preferably organic

1. Fill a cocktail shaker three-quarters full with ice cubes. Add the gin, lemon juice, grenadine, and egg white. Shake well.

2. Strain into a cocktail glass. Garnish with a 76ers jersey or a tiny sculpture of Rocky Balboa.

✖ *A Warning: This cocktail does contain raw egg, so don't serve it to elderly guests or guests with compromised immune systems. And don't let the egg be anything but fresh.*

Commando

Its pretty potent punch causes this cocktail to be attractive to special military forces the world over, which may be why it carries **such a strong designation.** Or, it could be the complete opposite. It could be that it's named for those who disdain undergarments—either by choice or by accident—a state of dress colorfully called "going commando." Either way, a few of these help ensure the day goes much more smoothly.

Ice cubes

2 ounces **whiskey**

½ ounce **freshly squeezed lime juice**

¼ ounce **Cointreau**

¼ ounce **Pernod**

1. Fill a cocktail shaker three-quarters full with ice cubes. Add the whiskey, lime juice, Cointreau, and Pernod. Shake well.

2. Strain the mix into a cocktail glass. Be sure you're wearing pants.

Damn the Weather

Isn't it comforting to know that not only is there a drink to request during every disagreeable day—whether due to hot, cold, rain, hail, or tornado—but also that slurpers have been summoning this very amalgamation during awful weather for more than four score and twenty? It's this community of **drinkers across time and space** that makes me feel tingly inside. Or is it the big dollop of gin in this drink? No matter. But do me a favor and, before taking the first sip, toast those who used a Damn the Weather to escape Mother Nature before you.

Ice cubes

2 ounces **gin**

½ ounce **freshly squeezed orange juice**

¼ ounce **sweet vermouth**

¼ ounce **orange curaçao**

1. Fill a cocktail shaker halfway full with ice cubes. Add the gin, orange juice, sweet vermouth, and curaçao. Shake well, raising the shaker skyward in defiance.

2. Strain the mix into a cocktail glass.

⊕ *A Note: If you feel this one needs a garnish, add a maraschino cherry and don't stop to smile about it.*

Delmonico

A kissing cousin to the Manhattan (page 31) both in construction and in locale, this cocktail originates from the famous Manhattan restaurant of the same name. Easy enough, isn't it? But tell friends the tale and instantly you've become **a cocktail hero**–provided the first round has already been administered.

Ice cubes

2 ounces **Cognac**

1 ounce **sweet vermouth**

2 dashes **Angostura bitters**

Maraschino cherry
for garnish

1. Fill a cocktail shaker halfway full with ice cubes. Add the Cognac, sweet vermouth, and Angostura bitters. Shake well.

2. Strain into a cocktail glass. Garnish with the cherry.

➕ **A Tip:** Feel free to experiment with your bitters. Orange bitters might be nice here. You could even change the name to the Orange D if you want to be modernist.

Derby

Not for consuming at the Kentucky Derby (that honor is reserved for the Mint Julep, page 34), this Derby *is* for use at fishing derbies (provided they aren't in city parks that have laws against cocktails), pinewood derbies and soap-box derbies (provided the one piloting those brakeless homemade cars isn't you), and roller derbies (provided that you're tough enough to drink **a slightly elegant and subtle cocktail** at a raucous event like the roller derby).

Ice cubes

2½ ounces **bourbon**

½ ounce **Benedictine**

2 dashes **orange bitters**

1. Fill a cocktail shaker halfway full with ice cubes. Add the bourbon, Benedictine, and orange bitters. Shake well.

2. Strain into a cocktail glass. Serve with a tiny minnow, a wheel bearing, or an arm pad, depending on which derby is being attended.

Dubonnet Cocktail

The very word "Dubonnet" conjures an exotic 1920s French expatriate scene: **flappers, mobsters, musicians** in gold and smoke, authors wearing black in the back room (we gloomy authors), the Moulin Rouge around the next corner, a feather boa stuck in the crook of a chair's back, glasses thick with ice and something slightly strong, a little bitter, a hint of citrus. You may not be able to replicate every bit of that vision, but the drink, luckily, you can remake.

Ice cubes

1½ ounces **gin**

1½ ounces **Dubonnet rouge**

Lemon twist for garnish

⬆ *A Note: Dubonnet is a bitter, fortified wine-based apéritif that comes in two types:* rouge *and* blond *(or red and white). The red is slightly sweeter (but not too sweet) and the white is drier. Both are flavored with herbs and quinine. I think the red works well here, but feel free to test that theory.*

1. Add 5 ice cubes to a mixing glass, cocktail shaker, or other decent-sized glass. Add the gin and Dubonnet.

2. Stir well (you don't want to hurt the Dubonnet's feelings, so stick to stirring and not shaking).

3. Strain into a chilled cocktail glass or large aperitif glass. Squeeze the lemon twist over the glass and then let it join its fellow ingredients.

Earthquake

Hold on to your hats (as well as pictures, unattached CD racks, and lamps) whenever **the floor starts undulating** or whenever an Earthquake starts being shaken. The tectonic plate–moving, pressure-releasing phenomenon doesn't share everything in common with this cocktail, but what they do share is the ability to cause legs to get wobbly, brains to discombobulate, and floors to look unnaturally askew.

Ice cubes

1 ounce **gin**

1 ounce **whiskey**

1 ounce **Pernod**

Maraschino cherry for garnish

1. Fill a cocktail shaker halfway full with ice cubes. Add the gin, whiskey, and Pernod. Shake well while standing in a doorway. Do not shake near a window or under a heavy mirror hanging on the wall.

2. Strain into a cocktail glass. Garnish with the cherry. (When the earthquake strikes, you want to be sure to have food. Who knows when the rescue crews will arrive?)

Ed Dexter

This is from a light volume (a little more than a pamphlet, a chunk less than a book) printed in 1934 called *Irvin S. Cobb's Own Recipe Book*. Mr. Cobb was not only a Southern gentleman but also the author of a novel called *Red Likker*, about the making of whiskey, a process, from what I ascertain, of which Mr. Cobb was amazingly fond—as a Kentuckian, his love of distilling and whiskey was probably instinctual. While including a variety of recipes, the volume is slanted in a certain way, as suggested cocktails and such contain only brands shipped and sold by one Frankfort Distributors. There was time when smallish recipe collections were frequently sponsored in this way, and it made for some entertaining publications—and some entertaining recipes, such as the Ed Dexter.

Ice cubes

2 ounces **bourbon**

½ ounce **orange curaçao**

¼ ounce **Simple Syrup** (page 7)

Lemon twist for garnish

Orange slice for garnish

1. Fill a cocktail shaker halfway full with ice cubes. Add the bourbon, curaçao, and simple syrup. Shake well.

2. Strain Ed into a cocktail glass. Garnish with the twist and the slice.

"Named for a **sincere drinker** and recommended only for such."

IRVIN S. COBB on the Ed Dexter, in *Irvin S. Cobb's Own Recipe Book*, 1934

Eye-Opener

It's a known fact that no one, not even famously energetic early riser Ben Franklin or history's most prolific artist/scientist/bearded robe-wearer Leonardo da Vinci, bounds excitedly from bed every single morning. Some days, the optics can't completely focus no matter how much rubbing or how many carrots. Some days, it's almost too hard to even *see* the end of the bed, much less provide the motor to drive out of it. On these lurching days, I propose ordering out for an Eye-Opener. I'm not guaranteeing you'll **leap up and invent a flying car**, or even that you'll leave the bed. But at least you'll go back to sleep happy.

Ice cubes

1½ ounces **dark rum**

½ ounce **Pernod**

½ ounce **crème de noyaux**

½ ounce **orange curaçao**

1 **egg yolk,** preferably organic

1. Fill a cocktail shaker halfway full with ice cubes. Add the rum, Pernod, crème de noyaux, curaçao, and egg yolk. Shake well (even if eyes are closed), until the shaker gets icy.

2. Strain the mix into a cocktail glass or coffee mug.

⬆ *A Note: If you like your breakfast sweet, add ½ ounce Simple Syrup (page 7), and don't let anyone give you grief.*

❌ *A Warning: As this recipe uses a raw egg, please do not serve it to the elderly or anyone with a compromised immune system.*

⬆ *Another Note: Crème de noyaux is a pink-tinged, sweet, almond-flavored French liqueur made from fruit pits. (Noyaux is French for "fruit pits." It tastes better than it sounds.)*

Frank's Chi Chi

Frank, whoever you are, wherever you are, and however you found the Chi Chi, **I'm donning a grass skirt** in your honor (or, at least, someone at the party will. I'm not saying I don't have the legs for it, but hey, I'm willing to let others do their part). The reason for a grass skirt is the fruity, reclining-under-a-palm-tree-with-feet-dangling-in-the-warm-Pacific nature of the Chi Chi. I suggest you also don the grass skirt. We don't want to dishonor Frank.

Cracked ice

3 ounces **fresh pineapple juice**

2 ounces **vodka**

1 ounce **freshly squeezed lime juice**

1 ounce **freshly squeezed orange juice**

½ ounce **Simple Syrup** (page 7)

Pineapple slice for garnish

1. Fill a large highball glass three-quarters full with cracked ice. Add the pineapple juice, vodka, lime juice, orange juice, and simple syrup. Stir in a chi chi manner (which, to me, means quickly and rhythmically).

2. Garnish with the pineapple slice. (If fresh pineapple is handy, that's a fine idea. If not, canned will suffice.)

3 Great Drinking Songs You Might Not Know, but Might Want to Play in the Bar

There are different appropriate songs for different occasions. You may not know these three, but when sitting in a dusty local tavern wetting your weekend-afternoon whistle, you may want to pick one of them from the jukebox.

1 "There Stands the Glass" by Webb Pierce

2 "Colorado Kool-Aid" by Johnny Paycheck

3 "Chug-A-Lug" by Roger Miller

George's Special

If you ever visit the home of people you've never visited before and they have *The Speakeasies of 1932* (Glenn Young Books, 2003) on their coffee table, give them a hug and know that a pal for life has been greeted. Or, at least, know that you'll probably get a good drink that night. This volume features 36 NYC hot and not-as-hot spots from the Prohibition era, with caricatures of barkeeps and atmosphere for each by the great Al Hirschfeld and descriptions by Mr. Hirschfeld and screenwriter Gordon Kahn. Both gentlemen lived through the dry days and survived with livers damaged and **cocktail-loving souls intact**, and their experience with and exuberance for the bars detailed is dripping from the ink of each pen stroke. Each speakeasy has a recipe for its drink du jour right there on the page, ready for trying.

A fine example from the book is George's Special, served at George's Place, "A businesslike drinking place for purposeful drinkers, who like the jolt of a stiff drink . . . George is the bartender and one of the best in his craft. Expert, but not showy. He keeps his distance."

Ice cubes

2 ounces **gin**

1 ounce **apricot brandy**

1 ounce **freshly squeezed lemon juice**

Maraschino cherry for garnish

1. Fill a cocktail shaker halfway full with ice cubes. Add the gin, brandy, and lemon juice. Shake well.

2. Strain into a cocktail glass. Garnish with the cherry.

The nymph who boasts no borrowed charms,
Whose **sprightly wit my fancy warms**,–
What though she tends this country inn,
And mixes wine, and deals out gin?
With such a kind, obliging lass,
I sigh to take the parting glass.

PHILIP FRENEAU, "The Parting Glass," 1900

Gin and It

What is the "it"? is the first question, certainly. The answer is most definitely not "ice," as this drink is served sans ice. To some, this may seem like going sans pants (which I suppose others might think is a good idea), but it's better than it sounds, and **a great winter thawer.** From what I can ascertain, it's an English drink, which makes a temperate sort of sense, as many drinks in the United States that seem to automatically come with ice come without once across the Atlantic.

2 ounces **gin**

1 ounce **sweet vermouth**

1. Add the gin and sweet vermouth to a mixing glass, cocktail shaker, or other wide-mouth glass. Stir well.

2. Strain the mix into a cocktail glass and serve.

Gin Buck

Also known as the London Buck, and as the grandfather to one of my summer favorites, the Orange Buck (page 177), the Gin Buck starts to appear regularly in post-Prohibition bar and drink guides. Whether this means it was dreamt up by an expat in London or a solid U.S. citizen sick of the bad nature of bootleg gin is up for debate. Who might be up to taking part in this debate after **bucking it through an evening** is about as hard to pin down (but let me say here that it won't be me).

Ice cubes

2 ounces **gin**

½ ounce **freshly squeezed lime juice**

Chilled ginger ale

Lime wedge for garnish

1. Fill an old-fashioned or a similar-sized glass with ice cubes. Add the gin and lime juice (in that order, buck-o).

2. Fill the glass with ginger ale. Stir a couple of well-mannered times with a bar spoon. Squeeze the lime wedge over the glass and then buck it in.

⬆ **A Note:** Sometimes you'll see this one made with lemon juice, and that's okay—but nothing more than okay.

"After two of these, **you'll be able to 'buck'** as well as any bronco."

W.C. WHITFIELD, *Here's How: Mixed Drinks*, 1941

Golf Links Highball

A lucky golfer has a golf cart with a small fridge included, or an insulated golf bag and a caddy strong enough to carry it, and keeps the ingredients for this one **available at any time** on any course. If really lucky, the golfer has both the ingredients to this and to the Hole-in-One Cocktail (page 112). If extremely lucky, he or she has all that and is playing golf somewhere that boasts temperatures warm enough so that those groovy golf shorts are wearable.

Cracked ice

1½ ounces **rye**

¾ ounce **sweet vermouth**

½ ounce **freshly squeezed lemon juice**

½ ounce **fresh pineapple juice**

¼ ounce **dark rum**

Chilled club soda

1. Fill a highball glass three-quarters full with cracked ice. Add the rye, sweet vermouth, lemon juice, pineapple juice, and rum.

2. Top the glass off with club soda. Stir 18 times. Or 9 times, if playing on the smaller course.

Five Easy Party Snacks

Don't let guests go hungry, but don't just put out bags of potato chips and pretzels, either. Bust out these quick creations and still the growling stomachs.

1. Toss together roasted peanuts, cashews, walnuts, and a little spice. I like a hint of cayenne pepper or chili powder to increase thirst. You could also try curry powder or oregano and rosemary. Extra points if you warm them in the microwave before serving.

2. Serve up a platter of sliced carrots, celery, and cherry tomatoes alongside ranch or creamy Caesar dressing and be known as the "healthy" host.

3. Put an 8-ounce square of cream cheese on a serving plate and spread ½ to 1 cup of spicy pepper jelly over it. Serve with sturdy crackers.

4. By hand or in a food processor, mash a 15-ounce can of white beans (drained and rinsed) with about 2 tablespoons of olive oil until smooth. Add salt and pepper, serve alongside French bread rounds, and look sophisticated.

5. Slice some fresh strawberries and drizzle a bit of heavy cream over the top. This is best when just two are partaking, as it's a little flirty.

Havana Cocktail

There are many cocktails that carry the "Havana" handle—on one occasion I opened three aged drink tomes in a row and found three completely different "Havana Cocktail" recipes. All three were pre-Castro books, too, from the age when we weren't restricted from quick Cuba trips to stock up on **fine rum and baseball**. That's one thing that all Havana-named cocktails do have in common: They go well with baseball. They also have rum as the base liquor. Taking both of these provisions into account, shake up a Havana the next time you tote the radio out back to watch the day unfold while listening to your favorite club play through nine. Of the various Havanas to choose from, I like the following, due to its ease of construction and tangy-sweet lemon-pineapple merger.

Ice cubes

2 ounces **Cuban rum** or **other dark rum**

1 ounce **fresh pineapple juice**

¾ ounce **freshly squeezed lemon juice**

Pineapple chunk for garnish

1. Fill a cocktail shaker halfway full with ice cubes. Add the rum, pineapple juice, and lemon juice. Shake well.

2. Strain into a cocktail glass and garnish with the pineapple chunk.

A VARIATION: If drinking out of a cocktail glass seems a bit frou-frou for listening to the ball game, feel free to make this one over ice in an old-fashioned glass. Just add ice cubes, then the rum, then the juices, then stir well. Want to make it even more refreshing? Construct it in a highball glass and top it with chilled club soda. Call it a Havana Cooler and wear a straw hat.

Hole-in-One Cocktail

Tighten up the gold knickers around the knees and **settle on the argyle cotton cap**—no Bermuda shorts or T-shirts emblazoned with "Golfers Do It in the Rough" can be worn if planning on sipping (or gulping) a Hole-in-One once you reach that nineteenth hole. This cocktail's as traditional, and as powerful, as a wooden driver, and won't allow itself to be consumed by a fraternity foursome not giving the links the reverence they deserve.

Ice cubes

2 ounces **Scotch**

¾ ounce **sweet vermouth**

¼ ounce **freshly squeezed lemon juice**

2 dashes **orange bitters**

Maraschino cherry for garnish

1. Fill a cocktail shaker halfway full with ice cubes. Add the Scotch, sweet vermouth, lemon juice, and orange bitters. Shake well, while thinking about the proper place to use a 3-iron.

2. Strain into a cocktail glass. Garnish with the cherry (if you think a cherry doesn't belong on the golf course, then I feel sorry for you).

Jack Rose

It's often unfathomable when a cocktail slips out of the public's mindset. Take the Jack Rose, for example. **Memorably classy and slightly androgynous** name? Check. Admirable blend of sugary, citrusy, and boozy flavors? Check. Appealing origins having to do with the Jacqueminot rose, origins that could potentially be used as a persuasive pickup line? Check. Even considering these points, if ordering the Jack Rose in a bar, one probably ends up talking to a hairy man with a flowery tattoo. The conversation had with said hairy man might end up being interesting in its own right, but the Jack Rose cocktail will surely taste better.

Ice cubes

2½ ounces **applejack**

¾ ounce **freshly squeezed lemon juice**

¼ ounce **grenadine**

Lemon twist for garnish

1. Fill a cocktail shaker halfway full with ice cubes. Add the applejack, lemon juice, and grenadine. Shake until the guests swear they'll work to bring the Jack Rose back into general circulation.

2. Strain into a cocktail glass. Squeeze the lemon twist over the glass and then drop it in.

➕ **A Tip:** *If you want to substitute another apple brandy for the applejack, jump right in.*

A VARIATION: If you don't happen to have grenadine just lying around, substitute Simple Syrup (page 7). You'll be drinking an Applejack Sour.

Landlady

I discovered this beauty at the tail end of one exhaustive weekend hosting distant relatives who forgot the golden rule: Houseguests are like fish, in that after three days they begin to stink. In an attempt to avoid prison, I rifled the handy liquor cabinet, which was dry enough that I'm embarrassed to go into detail. I did have fresh eggs. And I did have a snitch of grenadine. And even **when the cupboard's bare, there's gin**. It turns out that was all I needed—every ingredient in the Landlady close at hand. Remember that tale, friends, when stressed by a houseguest situation. A few of these and even the smelliest fish turns into a rose.

Ice cubes

1½ ounces **gin**

½ ounce **grenadine**

1 **egg white,** preferably organic

Maraschino cherry for garnish

1. Fill a cocktail shaker halfway full with ice cubes. Add the gin, grenadine, and egg white. Shake well.

2. Strain into a cocktail glass or a good-sized cordial glass. Garnish with the cherry.

❌ **A Warning:** *Be sure to use a very fresh egg for the egg white, and do not serve this drink to the elderly or anyone with a compromised immune system.*

Leave-It-to-Me

Does anybody's glass need refilling? Leave it to me. Is some sad lad or lass drooping a bit in the corner? Leave it to me. Is the old dog on the porch making somewhat of an ass of himself? Leave it to me. Want a **scrumptious blend** of apricot, sweetness, and ka-pow? Leave-It-to-Me.

Ice cubes

1½ ounces **gin**

¾ ounce **dry vermouth**

¾ ounce **apricot brandy**

¼ ounce **grenadine**

Lemon twist for garnish

1. Fill a cocktail shaker halfway full with ice cubes. Add the gin, dry vermouth, brandy, and grenadine. Shake well.

2. Strain the mix into a cocktail glass. Squeeze the lemon twist over the glass, and then let it descend.

London Fog →

According to the trustworthy bon vivant Lucius Beebe in his *Stork Club Bar Book* (reprinted by New Day Publishing, 2003), this beverage transports the drinker out of a fog, no matter what its name suggests. It's for the morning after, when feeling—as Norton Pratt, historic editor of the *Boston Telegram*, once wrote—"like a basket of busted bungholes." The London Fog, Mr. Beebe says, was **actor Burgess Meredith's remedy** for this very condition.

Cracked ice

2 ounces **gin**

½ ounce **Pernod**

1. Add about a cup of cracked ice to a mixing glass or cocktail shaker. Add the gin and Pernod.

2. Stir well (so well that it seems you're frappé-ing the mix). Pour everything into an old-fashioned glass. Drink quickly, before the body realizes what's going on.

"Here's **looking up** your old address."

COLONEL HENRY BLAKE, *M*A*S*H*

Lorraine Cocktail

Sorry to disappoint the indie- and underground-music nuts in the audience, but this one isn't named for singer-guitarist Chris Lorraine (of bands the Malinks and the Withholders). And sorry, also, to quiche-heads, because as far as I know this one's not named after the famous brunch favorite, as the Lorraine Cocktail's a genuine nighttime combo, **a little liquid star** to be taken before bedtime, almost guaranteed to generate good dreams. Now, where does that leave this history lesson? Well, at least there's a lot of leeway to come up with a history while consuming Lorraine Cocktails.

Ice cubes

2 ounces **kirsch**

¾ ounce **Benedictine**

½ ounce **freshly squeezed lime juice**

1. Fill a cocktail shaker halfway full with ice cubes. Add the kirsch, Benedictine, and lime juice. Shake well.

2. Strain into a cocktail glass. Garnish with a pillow.

⊙ **A Note:** Sometimes called kirschwasser, kirsch is a young cherry brandy that's dry instead of sweet.

Mahjong Cocktail

The game of mahjong uses groupings of tiles called Chows, Pungs, and Kongs and traces its lineage back to Asia in 800 A.D. The cocktail is **a pretty potent little punch**, merging just three liquors and the water off the shaken ice. Notice the corollaries.

Ice cubes

2 ounces **gin**

½ ounce **white rum**

½ ounce **Cointreau**

Lemon twist for garnish

1. Fill a cocktail shaker halfway full with ice cubes. Add the gin, rum, and Cointreau, but do it strategically. Shake well.

2. Strain into a cocktail glass. Squeeze the lemon twist over the glass. Yell "Mahjong" and release the lemon.

Mamie Taylor

I'd like to think this was kept in a canteen on the hip of Marshal Mamie Taylor, played by little-known 1930s, '40s, and '50s actress Myra Marsh in an episode of the *Hopalong Cassidy* TV show. It's the kind of a drink that a female marshal might swig when out on the prairie or at the saloon, with its considerable plug of Scotch slightly gussied up with old faithful ginger ale. An extra round is on me for anyone nutty enough to know the name of the episode she appeared in—catch me with it the next time we're at a bar together.

Ice cubes

2 ounces **Scotch**

Chilled ginger ale

Lemon slice for garnish

1. Fill a highball glass, or any glass with cowboys on it, three-quarters full with ice cubes. Add the Scotch.

2. Top the glass off with ginger ale, and garnish with the lemon (and a tiny lasso, if available).

Martinez

Named for a California miner in the middle 1800s (probably), the Martinez (hold your breath) has the pleasure of being the father (or grandfather, or great-grandfather) of the Classic Martini (page 24). You get the shaken picture—through the many tosses and turns of the bar, the sweetish Martinez transformed into the drier Martini. Of course, the Martinez is more than likely a descendant itself of the Manhattan (page 31). But all these qualifiers and family trees make me thirsty. Forget them, stop reading, and start shaking.

Ice cubes

1¾ ounces **gin**

¾ ounce **sweet vermouth**

¼ ounce **maraschino liqueur**

2 dashes **Angostura bitters**

Lemon twist for garnish

1. Fill a cocktail shaker halfway full with ice cubes. Add the gin, vermouth, maraschino liqueur, and Angostura bitters. Shake well.

2. Strain into a cocktail glass. Squeeze the lemon twist, then set it free into the glass.

⊙ *A Historical Note: For those keeping track, this drink is featured in Jerry Thomas's 1862 Bar-Tender's Guide, using Boker's bitters, which now, sadly, is unavailable.*

Mary Pickford

Here's an idea: an all-lady cocktail party. Not one where the guests are ladies (though if any ladies need a break from the fellas, that's understandable), but where **the drinks are ladies**. Whip up Mamie Taylors (page 117), Scarlett O'Haras (page 229), and Mary Pickfords. Named for the lovely (what dreamy eyes you had, Mary) star of about 193 silent films, this sipper shares some of her sweetness. And, as Mary was known for philanthropic efforts as well, you should be sure to make enough MPs to share.

Ice cubes

1¾ ounces **white rum**

¾ ounce **fresh pineapple juice**

¼ ounce **maraschino liqueur**

¼ ounce **grenadine**

Maraschino cherry for garnish

1. Fill a cocktail shaker halfway full with ice. Add the rum, pineapple juice, maraschino liqueur, and grenadine. Shake like a little princess (if the princess were a helluva shaker).

2. Strain the mix into a cocktail glass. Garnish with the cherry.

➕ *A Tip:* *Always have a Mary Pickford movie on, at least in the background, when serving this cocktail. It'll bring good luck.*

Top 5 Movie Star Mixes

Ah, the flashing lights of a Hollywood premiere blinking bright over stars as limos block traffic before the blockbuster (or bust) of the week unveils its charms or lack thereof. What to serve (booze-wise) at these galas? One of the following should maintain top billing—just be careful that it doesn't completely steal the spotlight.

1 Rosalind Russell (page 134)

2 Mary Pickford (above)

3 Scarlett O'Hara (page 229)

4 Rhett Butler (page 227)

5 Red Carpet (page 185)

Millionaire

In my dollar-addled mind (as the Snoop Dogg song says, "I've got my mind on my money and my money on my mind"), I can see Mr. Monopoly—or Rich Uncle Pennybags as he's sometimes called—come to life, driving a gold-tinged Rolls, quaffing a freshly poured Millionaire, puffing a Cuban, rolling up to a hotel-packed Broadway to pick up the rents. And it's me that rolled that four and five to land there. I hope he has the courtesy to offer me a drink, because I could use one after paying up.

Ice cubes

1 ounce **white rum**

¾ ounce **sloe gin**

¾ ounce **apricot brandy**

½ ounce **freshly squeezed lime juice**

¼ ounce **grenadine**

1. Fill a cocktail shaker halfway full with ice cubes. Add the rum, sloe gin, apricot brandy, lime juice, and grenadine. Shake well.

2. Strain the mix into a cocktail glass. Garnish with a letter that assures 'em the check is in the mail.

➕ *A Tip:* *If you wanna spin in extra-large style, serve up both the Millionaire and the Million Dollar Cocktail (page 393).*

"There's nought, no doubt, so much the spirit calms as **rum and true religion**."

GEORGE GORDON, LORD BYRON

Mood Indigo

The best way to beat back that blue mood may be to put in an order for this cocktail, which matches up to the mood in hue and strength. But don't wallow alone for too long—in the mood, that is, not the drink. I think that giving up on the whole "alone" trip is **the quickest way out of a blue mood**, when it feels like you've been down for a month of Sundays. Here's a thought: Order or make two Mood Indigos, and offer one to that young man or maid sipping a boring beer. His or her gratefulness will be a sure cure for the blues.

Ice cubes

1 ounce **gin**

¾ ounce **Cognac**

½ ounce **parfait amour**

1 **egg white,** preferably organic

1. Fill a cocktail shaker halfway full with ice cubes. Add the gin, Cognac, parfait amour, egg white, and your troubles. Shake while swaying slightly (to the tune of Duke Ellington's "Mood Indigo," of course).

2. Strain into a cocktail glass and serve.

✖ **A Warning:** *Be sure to use a very fresh egg for the egg white, and do not serve this drink to the elderly or anyone with a compromised immune system.*

Morning Glory

Almost too complicated to be built in the day's early hours, this kitchen-sinker might be better served at noon, once **the cobwebs have been shaken off** and when the eyes are clear enough to pick out each separate part of the liquor cabinet without squinting. It'll be polite to dole it out next to a double-decker Dagwood-ish club sandwich or other foodstuff that matches its abundance of elements.

2 or 3 **ice cubes**

1 ounce **bourbon** or **blended whiskey**

1 ounce **brandy**

¼ ounce **Pernod**

¼ ounce **orange curaçao**

¼ ounce **Simple Syrup** (page 7)

2 dashes **Peychaud's bitters**

Lemon twist for garnish

Chilled club soda

1. Add 2 (or 3 at most) ice cubes to a highball glass. Add the bourbon, brandy, Pernod, orange curaçao, simple syrup, and Peychaud's bitters. Stir well.

2. Squeeze the lemon twist over the glass and drop it in. Top off with club soda. Stir again, but don't strain yourself (especially if it's before noon).

➕ **A Tip:** *If you feel the urge to sing Oasis's "What's the Story, Morning Glory" while constructing this one, please do it at a whisper.*

National

Doesn't the "National" have **a revolutionary ring** to it? I think these should be assembled only when you've overthrown a country (not that I'm advocating anything, of course, that moves you far from the bar). If the energy can't be generated to overthrow a country, then at any rate dress in camouflage and overthrow the weeds that have colonized the backyard. Or, at least, talk down to the weeds from the porch swing. That'll scare 'em.

Ice cubes

2 ounces **rum**

½ ounce **apricot brandy**

½ ounce **fresh pineapple juice**

¼ ounce **freshly squeezed lime juice**

1. Fill a cocktail shaker halfway full with ice cubes. Add everything in a rush. Shake well.

2. Strain into a cocktail glass and serve.

Five Drinks to Have While Reading Comics (Provided You're at Least 21)

It's been a long time since comic books were just for kiddies. There's no reason to hide your love of the brightly colored pages filled sometimes with super-heroic types and sometimes with more everyday folks (like us). And there's no reason not to have the right drink while reading your new monthly comics or a treasured old issue you discovered in the quarter bin at a local shop. Well, there's no reason not to have one of the following while reading—unless you have a tendency to spill.

1. Incredible Hulk (page 168)
2. Captain's Blood (page 206)
3. Scofflaw Cocktail (page 230)
4. Whizz-Bang Cocktail (page 144)
5. Commando (page 102)

Negroni

In my humble opinion, this is one of the world's finest drinks. If the Classic Martini (page 24) is the Superman of drinks, and the Manhattan (page 31) is the Batman, then the Negroni is the Wonder Woman, with its perfect balance of **sweetness, ka-pow, and a hint of bitter** (and never taking itself as seriously as the two fantastic fellows). The Negroni demands balance, though, and must have equality between liquors to reach perfection. This equality does make it a drink that's safe to order at a bar, as long as you keep a friendly eye on the bartender to ensure a steady, uniform pour with the gin, vermouth, and Campari.

Ice cubes

1½ ounces **gin**

1½ ounces **Campari**

1½ ounces **sweet vermouth**

Orange twist for garnish

1. Fill an old-fashioned or a similar-sized glass with ice cubes. Add the gin, Campari, and sweet vermouth. Stir thrice.

2. Garnish with the orange twist.

~~~~~~~~~~~~~~~~~~~~~~~~~~~~~

⬆ *A Note: In the modern world, some make this with vodka. I disagree—which means I keep watch when ordering it at a bar.*

"Dressed in satin tights, fighting for your rights, **she's a wonder, Wonder Woman**."

From the TV theme to *Wonder Woman*

Campari

An Italian aperitif, Campari is known for its vibrant red color and beautifully bitter taste, and it was created by Gaspare Campari. Born in the 1800s in Castelnuovo, Italy, Gaspare became an apprentice *maitre licoriste* (bartender and liqueur mixer) at Turin's Bass Bar at the early age of 14. I'm guessing that the regulations surrounding bartending were different in Italy in the 1800s, or that Gaspare looked much older than his actual years. It was during his time at the Bass Bar that he tested and toiled before finalizing the recipe for his namesake liquor in 1860—a secret recipe that boasts more than 60 all-natural ingredients, including herbs, spices, barks, fruit peels, and cochineal, a crimson dye derived from the cochineal insect.

For the early part of its existence, Campari was sold only throughout Italy. It was Gaspare's son Davide (whom the company is named for today) who took it to an international level. The story is that Davide was working at the Café Campari in Milan when in walked Lina Cavalieri, a very popular opera singer. They hit it off, and all was well, until Lina had to move to Nice after getting a part in an opera there. Davide didn't want to be apart from her, so he decided at that moment to enter Campari into the export market. So, it could be said that Campari has reached its worldwide fame both because of its good taste (alone and as a mixer) and because of love.

Campari is famous for its bitter taste, which some drinkers don't automatically appreciate—though many I've introduced it to have, after an initial wariness, become enamored of it. Campari is drunk by itself as an aperitif, and also mixed, both with juices (such as in the Garibaldi, page 383) and with other liquors (such as in the Negroni, page 123). It's also dreamy mixed with soda water and a lemon twist.

Oriental

According to the (reliable and trustworthy) *Savoy Cocktail Book* (reprinted by Trafalgar Square Publishing, 2000), "In August, 1924, an American engineer nearly died of fever in the Philippines and only the extraordinary devotion of Doctor B. saved his life. As an act of gratitude, the engineer gave Doctor B. the recipe of this cocktail (the Oriental)." That quotation means that **this cocktail is a life saver**, and has a swell story. It may be the only cocktail recipe given in exchange for the saving of a life (no matter how many bar-hounds tell their bartenders that a drink saved their life, it's not the same).

Ice cubes

1½ ounces **rye**

¾ ounce **sweet vermouth**

¾ ounce **orange curaçao**

½ ounce **freshly squeezed lime juice**

1. Fill a cocktail shaker halfway full with ice cubes. Add the rye, sweet vermouth, orange curaçao, and lime juice (leave out the fever). Shake well.

2. Strain the mix into a cocktail glass. Drink a toast to all good stories.

⬆ **A Note:** *If you can't readily find rye, well, I feel for you. Feel okay when substituting bourbon instead.*

Panama Cocktail

I don't believe that Van Halen ever drank any Panama Cocktails—though they did get a bit sweet later down the line—but I still **always sing out "Panama!"** in Halen style when making this treat. The singing gains me an odd look or two, since this is a dessert accompaniment, and people tend to be winding down at this point in the evening. But once I show up at the table, all odd looks turn to smiles. Try it and see what I mean.

Ice cubes

1½ ounces **Cognac**

1 ounce **crème de cacao**

1 ounce **heavy cream**

1. Fill a cocktail shaker halfway full with ice cubes. Add the Cognac, crème de cacao, and heavy cream. Shake well.

2. Strain into a cocktail glass and serve.

⬆ **A Note:** *Yes, this is a close, close cousin to the Alexander (page 18). But, if only so I could insert a reference to Van Halen, it deserves its own mention.*

⬆ **Another Note:** *If you'd like to get fancy, add a chocolate straw as a garnish, or float tiny chocolate hearts on top.*

Perfect

Related closely to several drinks (not the least of which are the Classic Martini, page 24, and the Bronx, page 22), a Perfect cocktail **meshes well into many drinking situations,** for two very reliable reasons. First, it uses gin and sweet and dry vermouths as its only ingredients, and these staples tend to be around most bars and home bars. The second reason is less literal. Often, a host or hostess will ask guests what they want, and the answer will be some variation on, "Just make me the perfect drink." The Perfect cocktail makes deciding what to serve those guests much easier.

Ice cubes

1½ ounces **gin**

¾ ounce **dry vermouth**

¾ ounce **sweet vermouth**

Orange or **lemon slice** for garnish

1. Fill a cocktail shaker halfway full with ice cubes. Add the gin first, and then the dry and sweet vermouths. Shake perfectly.

2. Strain into a cocktail glass. Garnish with either the orange or lemon slice. (I've seen it both ways, and served it both ways depending on mood. Do the same and stay happy.)

Pisco Sour

The Pisco Sour has a lengthy and adventuresome history, he said sonorously. The drink's first notation is probably found in a late 1920s book titled *Lima the City of Kings*, but Europeans made the crucial ingredient, pisco, from the Quebranta grape many years earlier. See, those traveling (some might say conquering) Europeans missed their brandies as well as their poufy beds when "exploring" Peru, and the locally beloved booze, a corn-based liquor called *chichi*, didn't fit their refined palates (though only the "chosen woman" was allowed to make it, a fact you'd think would **enthrall the stuffiest shirt**). Therefore, these fellas distilled a local grape-based anesthetic, and named it after the port that even today sends pisco out into the world.

Ice cubes

2 ounces **pisco**

½ ounce **freshly squeezed lime juice**

½ ounce **Simple Syrup** (page 7)

1 **egg white,** preferably organic

Lime twist for garnish

1. Fill a cocktail shaker halfway full with ice cubes. Add the pisco, lime juice, simple syrup, and egg white. Shake well.

2. Strain the mix into a cocktail glass. Squeeze the lime twist over the mix and then drop it in. Say a word of thanks to ancient Incan emperor Pachacuti, who once had a river rerouted after he was jilted. Said river eventually watered the grape that made the pisco that went in the drink you just made.

❌ *A Warning: Anyone with a compromised immune system probably shouldn't consume raw eggs.*

Port Sangaree

Though the Sangaree sounds tropical, as if it might be **the last beverage served** before entering the Bermuda triangle, it's not fruity in the least. Its heritage is long though, and does have enough side alleys and different turns in its making that it could be seen as a type of alcohol-fueled version of the triangle. The one constant? Nutmeg. Really. With apologies to Jerry Thomas, the original hot bartender, I like my Sangarees tall, so that their breezy nature at least cools me down when I'm wandering lost from deserted island to deserted island.

Ice cubes

½ ounce **Simple Syrup** (page 7)

2 ounces **port** (either ruby or tawny will do)

Chilled club soda

⅛ teaspoon **freshly grated nutmeg**

1. Fill a highball glass almost to the top with ice cubes. Add the simple syrup, then the port.

2. Fill the glass with club soda. Stir gently thrice. Sprinkle the fresh nutmeg over the top.

A VARIATION: There are many possible variations on the Sangaree, using almost any variety of fortification. Burgundy, sherry, and brandy make nice in this recipe. If you'd like to try an ale or a porter Sangaree, that's an enjoyable way to spend an afternoon. Just dispense with the club soda and use enough ale or porter to fill the highball glass.

A WARM VARIATION: Sangarees were also served warm as occasion demanded. For this version, follow the above recipe, without the ice, and use still water instead of bubbly water. To achieve proper temperature, you must shove a red-hot (relatively clean) poker into the drink before the nutmeg is added. Or, you can just add hot water. But where is the fun and adventure in the latter?

Potenta Cocktail

Many bookstores (like some dusty bars) are treasure houses one has to sift through before being rewarded. But **persistence pays off** (like persistence in going into those bars that look a little too dusty from the outside window), as when all of a sudden you uncover a copy of *Applegreen's Bar Book*, originally published in 1899 and written by John Applegreen, formerly of (as the book says) Kinsley's Chicago and the Holland House in New York. *Applegreen's Bar Book* is sized impeccably to fit in the dapper pocket of the turn-of-the-twentieth-century bartender. Though only 90 pages, it's packed with recipes (such as the Snow Ball, found on page 401), wine ideas, and glassware drawings. The bonus in the copy that I found is that one prior owner had written a recipe for the Potenta Cocktail inside the front flap. Not only is this a good cocktail to rediscover, but every time it's consumed by happy masses, the sprit of H.E. Polaud (the name inscribed on the page mirroring the Potenta Cocktail) floats over the gathering, ensuring that a grand time ensues.

Ice cubes

1½ ounces **Dubonnet rouge**

1½ ounces **sloe gin**

½ ounce **Benedictine**

1. Fill a cocktail shaker halfway full with ice cubes. Add the Dubonnet, sloe gin, and Benedictine. Shake heartily, with an eye toward the spirits of past imbibers no longer at the bar.

2. Strain into a cocktail glass and serve.

⬆ *A Note: If you're wondering, "potenta" means powerful or potent. You know what they say about Dubonnet and sloe gin.*

⬆ *Another Note: While H.E. Polaud doesn't suggest it, a lemon twist serves this cocktail well.*

Ramos Fizz

While the Gin Fizz and other fizzes are discussed in this book (on page 384, if you want to get there quickly), the Ramos Fizz deserves its own entry, if not its own chapter. The standard Gin Fizz is a matter of effervescent frolicking; the Ramos Fizz is a perfect testament to the payoffs found only **for those who are supremely dedicated**. With that in mind, don't plan on whipping this one up in seconds when some pals stumble by unexpectedly, or when you want to be directing half your attention to making drinks and half to chatting up a member of the opposite sex. Chaos, and a bad drink, will ensue.

The Ramos Fizz dates back to the late 1880s, and is pure New Orleans: smooth and cool, yet bouncy and dressed to kill. It was invented by Henry C. Ramos, and it's said that he used to have a lengthy line of bartenders successively shake each drink to gain the required consistency. That's what I mean by dedication. This is not one to construct if you don't believe in your shaking ability, or if you're going to arm wrestle later in the evening and need to save your strength.

Cracked ice

2 ounces **gin**

1½ ounces **Simple Syrup** (page 7)

1 ounce **freshly squeezed lemon juice**

1 ounce **freshly squeezed lime juice**

1 ounce **heavy cream**

1 **egg white,** preferably organic

3 drops **orange-flower water**

Splash of **chilled club soda**

1. Fill a cocktail shaker halfway full with cracked ice. Add all of the remaining ingredients except for the club soda. Shake very well for 3 minutes, or 5, or until your hands have to be pried from the shaker.

2. Strain into a Collins glass. The consistency should be very thick. Top with a splash of club soda. The drink should still be thick after the soda is added.

➕ *A Tip: Resist the temptation to substitute orange juice for the orange-flower water. It's not the same. Orange-flower water is an extract made from the distillation of orange blossoms. It's available in gourmet food stores and online.*

✖ *A Warning: Anyone with a compromised immune system probably shouldn't consume raw eggs.*

➕ *Another Tip: This may not be a drink to serve to a large crowd, due to the labor-intensive nature of its construction. But it may be wise to make it with one or two really good friends—friends who wouldn't mind stimulating the cocktail shaker when your arm gets tired.*

Retreat from Moscow

This Cold War chum (that can't be proven, of course, no matter what sort of dazzling incandescents I'm put beneath for questioning) surprisingly enough doesn't contain vodka. Bearing a name such as Retreat from Moscow, and knowing the tender hold on politeness most cocktail creators have, that's **almost impossible to believe**. But look—here's the proof.

Ice cubes

1½ ounces **gin**

1 ounce **kümmel**

½ ounce **freshly squeezed lemon juice**

Lemon slice for garnish

1. Fill a cocktail shaker halfway full with ice cubes. Add the gin, kümmel, and lemon juice, separately, so no one feels that borders have been illegally crossed. Shake well.

2. Strain into a cocktail glass. Garnish with the lemon slice and a well-worn passport.

⬆ *A Note: Kümmel is a liqueur made from caraway seeds, cumin, and other flavorings. See page 133 for more kümmel background.*

Rock and Rye

Doesn't the room go a little hushed when the 6-foot 8-inch, eagle-emblazoned-leather-jacket–wearing, tattoo-boasting, steel-toe-booted, **walking danger of a person** meets the bar and spits out, "Rock and Rye"? If only the bar denizens realized that a true Rock and Rye must have rock candy in it, maybe they'd stop the quivering that's about to spill their drinks.

Ice cubes

2½ ounces **rye whiskey**

½ ounce **freshly squeezed lemon juice**

1 good-sized piece of **rock candy**

1. Fill an old-fashioned or a similar-sized glass with ice cubes. Add the rye and the lemon juice. Stir once.

2. Add the rock candy, propping it somewhat up on the ice (you want the drinker to be allowed to dunk the candy if he or she wants).

⬆ *A Note: When purchasing the rock candy, it's not a bad idea to seek out the kind on a stick. The non-stick kind works, but can get just a little messy.*

⬆ *Another Note: If desired, the Rock and Rye can be shaken, strained, and served in a cocktail glass.*

Roffignac

You must be a bit of a loveable rogue, or a bit of a politician, to quaff a Roffignac. Perhaps you should be both the former and the latter, as is the case with Count Louis Philippe Joseph de Roffignac, who **escaped the revolutionary guillotine** in France and went on to become, in 1820, beloved governor of New Orleans. According to Kerri McCaffety's *Obituary Cocktail: The Great Saloons of New Orleans* (Vissi d'Arte Books, 2001), this drink can be swung together with raspberry syrup or grenadine. I tend toward the raspberry syrup.

Ice cubes

2 ounces **Cognac**

½ ounce **raspberry syrup** or **grenadine**

Chilled club soda

1. Fill a highball glass with ice cubes. Add the Cognac and raspberry syrup. Stir once.

2. Top the glass off with club soda. Stir once again.

⬆ *A Note: This was originally made with a sweetener called Red Hembarig instead of the raspberry syrup, but that, sadly, is no longer available.*

"The harsh, useful things of the world, from pulling teeth to digging potatoes, are best done by men who are as starkly sober as so many convicts in the death-house, but the lovely and useless things, the **charming and exhilarating** things, are best done by men with, as the phrase is, a few sheets in the wind."

H.L. MENCKEN, *Prejudices, Fourth Series*, 1924

Rolls-Royce

Here's another in the lineage of high-stakes cocktails (see the Millionaire, page 119, and the Million Dollar Cocktail, page 393). **I wouldn't try maneuvering an auto** of the same name once a few of these have been consumed. I'm not sure I can suggest even sitting in one in that shape, but hey, if sporting a posh sedan, you have the right to muss it up.

Ice cubes

1½ ounces **gin**

1 ounce **sweet vermouth**

1 ounce **dry vermouth**

½ ounce **Benedictine**

1. Fill a cocktail shaker halfway full with ice cubes. Add the gin, sweet vermouth, dry vermouth, and Benedictine, and put in the clutch. Then shake.

2. Strain the mix into a large cocktail glass. Garnish with a chauffeur and you'll be ready to roll the Rolls.

LIQUEUR SPOTLIGHT

Kümmel

A slightly sweet liqueur, known for its caraway, cumin, and fennel flavor combination, kümmel, Dutch legend says, was first created and distilled by Erven Lucas Bols in 1575 in Holland. Kümmel (sometimes seen in older books as Kimmel) was once very popular in mixed drinks, due to its singular flavor and clear color. Sadly, it's not seen as much today in the United States. It remains very popular in Russia and other parts of Eastern Europe, where the majority of kümmel is both produced and consumed. The liqueur's popularity in Eastern Europe leads all the way back to Peter the Great, who, in 1696, in his quest to build a Russian navy, is said to have traveled to Amsterdam to learn shipbuilding. While in Amsterdam, he paid a side visit to the famous Bols distillery (started by the very same Erven Bols mentioned above). While at the distillery, Peter tasted and fell for kümmel, and brought a few bottles—and the recipe—back to Russia with him. There is also a type of kümmel made in Berlin called Gilka Kümmel. This version lives through a longer distillation before it hits the streets, which leads to a slightly smoother taste, and, some think, a higher quality.

Rosalind Russell

This treat was named after her own self by the actress (star of the films *Auntie Mame*, *The Women*, and the noir classic *Night Must Fall*, among a vast list of others). You don't have to be a celeb or VIP, of course, to name a drink after yourself, but it helps to get it noticed. Having it be **a memorable and heady blend** such as the Rosalind Russell doesn't hurt, either. I suggest before grabbing bottles and pouring for immortality that a few RRs are shaken and at least *Auntie Mame* is watched. It'll instill a number of good ideas, as well as providing inspiration. Just remember Auntie Mame's philosophy: *"Après moi, le déluge."*

Ice cubes

3 ounces **Danish aquavit**

½ ounce **dry vermouth**

Lemon twist for garnish

1. Fill a cocktail shaker halfway full with ice cubes. Add the aquavit and dry vermouth. Shake well.

2. Strain into a cocktail glass. Squeeze the twist over the drink and then drop it in.

↑ *A Note:* As this is a close relation to the Classic Martini (page 24), you shouldn't blush if choosing to add an olive instead of a twist.

↑ *Another Note:* Aquavit is a clear Scandinavian brandy whose name comes from the Latin aqua vitae, or "water of life." If you can't find the Danish variety, which has a caraway flavor, que sera sera.

"My father-in-law, Carl Brisson, **introduced me to this drink** and six months later I married his son."

ROSALIND RUSSELL, quoted in *The Stork Club Bar Book*

Sleeping Giant

In Marion Flexnor's *Cocktail-Supper Cookbook*, published in 1955, she suggests serving the Sleeping Giant before a meal of teriyaki chicken, fried rice, "Korean Pepper Cabbage," French bread, and cucumber-and-onion salad. These around-the-world flavors seem a bit much when jumbled together, but let me set the record straight. After a few of these refreshing mixers, you may skip dinner and get straight to **climbing the beanstalk** (if I can switch giants for a moment). At least take a few nibbles of the cucumber salad, though—you'll be sorry in the morning if you don't eat a bite.

½ cup **ice cubes**

1 ounce **dark rum**

1½ ounces **white rum**

½ ounce **freshly squeezed lemon juice**

½ ounce **freshly squeezed orange juice**

½ ounce **Simple Syrup** (page 7)

4 **pineapple chunks**

1 **maraschino cherry**

1. Add the ice cubes, dark rum, 1 ounce of the white rum, the lemon juice, orange juice, and simple syrup to a blender. Blend well.

2. Pour the mix into a brandy snifter or other fancy glass. Arrange the pineapple chunks on top, and top the pineapple with the cherry. Gently pour the remaining ½ ounce of white rum on top of the fruit. Serve with a small straw.

Wake Up Right with These 5 Friends

Good golly, why does the morning have to come so quickly? Feels like I just hit the hay. And why, while I'm at it, does the sun have to be so nastily bright in the morning? Do you ever find yourself asking these questions? If so, I suggest trying one of the following fab five in the mornings. After one of these, nagging questions slip right out of the window.

1 Eye-Opener (page 107)

2 Golden Dawn Punch (page 300)

3 Corpse Reviver (page 206)

4 We Have to Be at Work by 10 A.M. (page 350)

5 Sun (page 404)

Sunshine Cocktail #1

As much as I enjoy old mister sunshine, which is as much as the next reclining-poolside-in-shorts-and-a-really-good-hat-pour-me-another-one-quick-pass-the-salty-snacks-and-turn-up-the-jams kind of party thrower, I reserve the Sunshine Cocktail #1 and it's slightly fluffier sibling (below) for the drearier days between October 31 and February 28. During those long, dark days, a ray or two isn't needed—it's demanded. **Bring that sunshine back year-round** and watch the room start to glow. Stand up, I tell you, and demand Sunshine Cocktails.

Ice cubes

2 ounces **gin**

¾ ounce **sweet vermouth**

2 dashes **orange bitters**

Orange twist for garnish

1. Fill a cocktail shaker halfway full with ice cubes. Add the gin, sweet vermouth, and orange bitters. (I'd make it Regan's Orange Bitters #6. Who knows how long the winter can be?)

2. Strain the mix into a cocktail glass. Squeeze the orange twist over the glass and then let it relax into the glass.

Sunshine Cocktail #2

A bit more la-di-da at first take than its elder, Sunshine Cocktail #1 (it's the French influence), Sunshine Cocktail #2 nonetheless packs enough punch to **keep the snow and ice at bay**. But don't have so many that you forget all about the snow and ice and pass out in it and lose your toes to frostbite, though that might garner some free drinks—but the toes will be missed in the long run.

Ice cubes

1½ ounces **white rum**

1 ounce **dry vermouth**

½ ounce **crème de cassis**

¼ ounce **freshly squeezed lemon juice**

1. Fill a cocktail shaker halfway full with ice cubes. Add the rum, dry vermouth, crème de cassis, and lemon juice. Shake until you see sunspots.

2. Strain into a cocktail glass. Be sure to don proper sunglasses before drinking, to avoid eyestrain from the bright rays of the sun.

Third Rail Cocktail

This is a dangerous number, to be raised up and knocked down only among familiar friends. But it's not as dangerous as the actual third rail on most subway tracks, which isn't even to be joked about. Nonetheless, this drink **packs a mule's kick.** This isn't meant to scare you away completely: Everyone needs a good kick from a stubborn beast once in a while.

Ice cubes

1½ ounces **white rum**

1 ounce **Calvados**

1 ounce **brandy**

¼ ounce **Pernod**

1. Fill a cocktail shaker halfway full with ice cubes. Add the rum, Calvados, brandy, and Pernod, but carefully (we don't want any trouble). Shake well.

2. Strain into a cocktail glass or small wine glass (I think the wine glass adds a touch of respectability, which could come in handy).

⬆ ***A Note:*** *In Normandy, Calvados is called* le trou normand, *or the "Norman hole," due to its ability to create new space in a full stomach when consumed between the courses during a large meal.*

⬆ ***A Second Note:*** *When the Third Rail was first lit up, it was made using absinthe instead of Pernod. If you're in an absinthe-friendly nation, go that route.*

⬆ ***A Third Note:*** *Calvados is a fairly high-proof apple brandy made in Normandy. If you can't lay your hands on a bottle, another apple brandy would work (but might not seem as dangerous).*

Thistle Cocktail

This tipple is slightly prickly, like the plant whose name it borrows, due to the slightly prickly nature of the main ingredient: Scotch. It also has a soupçon of sweetness on the underside, due to the sweet vermouth, which matches up with the flower's softer thistle down. The flower similarities point out the drink's ability to be swilled favorably by both those revelers looking for **a beverage that bites** and those looking to keep their tongues intact—a nice compromise indeed.

Ice cubes

2 ounces **Scotch**

1 ounce **sweet vermouth**

2 dashes **Angostura bitters**

Maraschino cherry for garnish

1. Fill a cocktail shaker halfway full with ice cubes. Add the Scotch, sweet vermouth, and Angostura bitters. Shake well.

2. Strain into a cocktail glass. Add the cherry.

Valencia

The Valencia sounds vaguely like it was a larger-than-life brick apartment building gone a little seedy, though still the spot to live in, if you're bright-eyed, single, and aspiring toward fashionably scruffy soirées that spin for days. Show up at the Valencia, people say, because there's bound to be a head-splitting after hours. Were you at the Valencia two weeks ago on Friday? I was **lampshading by midnight**. Who's renting that corner place on the second floor of the Valencia, 'cause we gotta keep it in the family. See what I mean? It's only natural, then, to serve the Valencia at the next house- or apartment- or condo-warming. It's celebratory, a bit exclusive, and the ideal start to an inspired evening.

Ice cubes

2 ounces **apricot brandy**

1 ounce **freshly squeezed orange juice**

3 dashes **orange bitters**

Chilled Champagne

Orange twist for garnish (optional)

1. Fill a mixing glass or cocktail shaker halfway full with ice cubes. Add the brandy, orange juice, and orange bitters. Stir well with a long spoon or a new key.

2. Strain the mix into a Champagne flute. Top with Champagne and stir once more.

3. Garnish with the orange twist if desired. If it seems to interrupt the party's flow, forget the twist by the door.

⬆ *A Note: The Valencia makes a nice non-bubbly drink, too. Instead of straining into a flute, just strain into a cocktail glass and leave the Champagne on ice.*

The Bitters Breakdown

One problematic aspect of the modern era is the lack of bitters. There are lots of different kinds, and also lots of bars that don't stock even one variety of bitters, much less two or three. This is a shame, and it would have caused numerous issues back in the day (which in this case equals the days between 1890 and 1940, let's say) if the bitters had been missing. They are too crucial to a host of cocktails to forget them. So, please don't. If you're unsure about what these potions are (it's not your fault, it's the times), bitters are a mixer that contain a liquid combination and distillation of numerous secretive ingredients, including herbs, spices, other plant parts, roots, and more. There are a number of bitters varieties available, but the two seen most often are Angostura and Peychaud's (with the former being more prevalent). There are also other (orange, peach, mint, etc.) bitters obtainable, all of which add a nice touch if you can get them. Especially mentionable in this category is the fairly recent introduction of Gary Regan's Orange Bitters No. 6, which harkens back to the orange bitters of old (orange bitters were a key component in many drinks at one time). Each type of bitters adds its own touch, personality, and essence, as each is different in taste and construction, which is why you see specific bitters called for in specific recipes. If you can't find a particular type of bitters that's called for in a recipe, you can try subbing in another variety—but it will taste different (which might be interesting, but it will be a different drink). Luckily, the bitters mentioned here, as well as the Fee Brothers line of flavored bitters, are all available at your local liquor stores or online. Try a little taste of each if you have a variety, both by themselves and in drinks, and help make the world a slightly better place.

Vieux Carré Cocktail

Named for New Orleans's French Quarter, this intricate delight was invented by Walter Bergeron, who was the head bartender in the Monteleone Hotel in the 1930s. In the '40s, the Monteleone started New Orleans's first revolving bar, which made it easy to convince yourself that the room was actually spinning after a few Vieux Carrés had begun to **take those cares away.**

Ice cubes

1 ounce **rye**

1 ounce **Cognac**

1 ounce **sweet vermouth**

Dash of **Peychaud's bitters**

Dash of **Angostura bitters**

½ ounce **Benedictine**

Lemon twist for garnish

1. Fill an old-fashioned or old-fashioned-wannabe glass halfway full with ice cubes. Add the rye, Cognac, and sweet vermouth, giving each its moment in the sun.

2. Add the Peychaud's and the Angostura bitters. Contrary to popular belief, they do get along, so fear no repercussions.

3. Add the Benedictine, and stir 4 times with a silver spoon (the drink deserves the silver). Squeeze the lemon twist over, and drop it in.

Ward Eight

Politics necessitate a stern drink with a serious history. Politics elicit the worst and best in friends and foes alike. Politics are best debated over a substantial drink to keep the wheels oiled. Politics and alcohol go together like ice cream and very hot hot chocolate (it might burn, but it tastes so fine). Luckily, when the politics get too repetitive, one can pour another Ward Eight. Tracing its lineage to the Locke-Ober restaurant in Boston, the Ward Eight was created way back when to celebrate Mr. Martin Lomasney's election to the state legislature for the Eighth Ward. It still makes **a sturdy companion when the talk gets thick,** and helps to the turn the tide to happier thoughts if the talk gets *too* thick.

Ice cubes

2 ounces **rye**

1 ounce **Simple Syrup** (page 7)

¾ ounce **freshly squeezed lime juice**

½ ounce **grenadine**

Orange slice for garnish

Maraschino cherry for garnish

1. Fill a cocktail shaker halfway full with ice cubes. Add the rye, simple syrup, and lime juice. Shake well, for the people.

2. Add the grenadine and shake twice (once for each side).

3. Strain the mix into a goblet or other stemmed glass. Garnish with the orange slice and the cherry. Sure, the double garnish is excessive, but we live in excessive times.

Whiskey Smash

A relative (I like to think of it as an other-side-of-the-tracks relative) to the Mint Julep (page 34) and the more exotic-sounding Mojito (page 36), the Whiskey Smash, and the other smashes, are included solely because I think the overindulgence of them led to the term "smashed" being a euphemism for "drunk." I can't support my claims with annotations, but send out your next invitation (if having a summer shindig, that is—the Smash is best in summer) with the words "Whiskey Smash" and the time, date, and address and see what creative chaos conspires. **I warned you**.

3 sprigs **fresh mint**

½ ounce **Simple Syrup** (page 7)

¼ cup **cracked ice**

2 ounces **whiskey** or **bourbon**

Lemon slice for garnish

1. Add the mint and simple syrup to a cocktail shaker or mixing glass. Muddle well with a muddler or long wooden spoon.

2. Add the cracked ice and whiskey to the shaker. Stir well, until things are feeling frosty.

3. Pour the mix (do not strain) into a cocktail glass or wine glass. Serve with the lemon slice.

⤴ *A Note: As the whiskey or bourbon is the power player here, don't skimp and pick up a jug of random rotgut. I suggest Maker's Mark or Weller's or, if you can get it, Buffalo Trace.*

A VARIATION: Almost any booze on hand can be made into a smash. I suggest brandy, rum, or rye, but gin and applejack would fit the bill as well. But the mint is essential—don't even whisper "smash" without it.

White Rose

Doesn't this have a dirge-y, haunting sound to it? I see the slow camera shot: a white rose slowly descending onto a blank stone surface while wistful piano music plays softly. Well, forget about that moody action, because the real White Rose is more likely to be served with a bouncy Fats Waller song swinging in the background, and more likely to serve smiles and maybe some back corner cuddling than frowns and moody cinema. Remember to have the floor cleared for dancing, and polish up those shoes.

Ice cubes

1½ ounces **gin**

½ ounce **maraschino liqueur**

½ ounce **freshly squeezed orange juice**

½ ounce **freshly squeezed lime juice**

1 **egg white,** preferably organic

Maraschino cherry for garnish

1. Fill a cocktail shaker halfway full with ice cubes. Add the gin, maraschino liqueur, orange juice, lime juice, and egg white. Shake well while swinging those hips.

2. Strain into a cocktail glass. Add the cherry (don't forget that bouncing cherry).

❌ *A Warning: Do not serve raw eggs to the elderly or anyone with a compromised immune system.*

Whizz-Bang Cocktail

If you haven't heard of *Captain Billy's Whiz Bang*, an at-the-time vaguely vulgar 1920s and '30s men's magazine of yuk-yuks, manly sports poems, bawdy stories, and cartoons (usually centering on flappers or chickens or Prohibition), don't fret, as it wasn't a real history milestone. This lack of knowledge shouldn't keep you from using words like "flapper" and "yuk-yuks" when making Whizz-Bang Cocktails, though—instead, it should encourage it.

Ice cubes
1½ ounces **bourbon**
¾ ounce **dry vermouth**
½ ounce **Pernod**
¼ ounce **grenadine**
2 dashes **orange bitters**

1. Fill a cocktail shaker halfway full with ice cubes. Add the bourbon, dry vermouth, Pernod, grenadine, and orange bitters. Shake well, like an amorous ice-delivery man (which I've been told was a standby in the old-timey joke world).

2. Strain every bit into a cocktail glass. Garnish with nothing.

X.Y.Z. Cocktail

I've never been one for making myself or my guests take moonshine exams (play games, maybe, and toast excessively, yes), but if you can't manage to travel through the alphabet safely and reach those fabulous finishers X, Y, and Z, then you absolutely cannot make this cocktail.

Ice cubes
1½ ounces **rum**
¾ ounce **Cointreau**
¼ ounce **freshly squeezed lemon juice**

1. Fill a cocktail shaker halfway full with ice cubes. Add the rum, Cointreau, and lemon juice. Shake happily, realizing you still know the alphabet song.

2. Strain the mix into a cocktail glass and serve.

Zero Cocktail

This luminous selection shouldn't be discounted because of the diminutive name. Quite the opposite—it should be celebrated because of the **infinite mysteries** and wide-open manner of the zero itself, said numeral being very accepting. Or, at least, that's what I'd reel off when ordering one and being faced with the bartender's wide-eyed stare. When serving the Zero at home, query the people first, to ensure that they appreciate Pernod's strong licorice taste. It's not for everyone (which means there's more for those of us with refined tastes).

Ice cubes

1½ ounces **Pernod**

1¼ ounces **freshly squeezed orange juice**

¼ ounce **grenadine**

Fresh cherry for garnish (or maraschino if fresh is not available)

1. Fill a cocktail shaker halfway full with ice cubes. Add the Pernod, orange juice, and grenadine. Shake well (for at least 0 times 1,000 minutes plus 10 more seconds).

2. Strain the delish combo into a cocktail glass. Garnish with the cherry. (You might not see the cherry, but it's there, and isn't that enough?)

Board Game Beverages

No matter if you're playing real estate mogul in Monopoly or Genghis Khan in Risk or rolling the dice in another old favorite board game, you'll want to have the right cocktail or tall frosty beverage near at hand for luck. But be careful—you don't want to have too many drinks, or you might forget to collect your $200 for passing "Go" or make some other costly strategic error.

1. Monopoly: Boardwalk (page 155) or Millionaire (page 119)
2. Risk: Canadian Grenadier (page 98) or Commando (page 102)
3. Clue: Set Up (page 231) or Corpse Reviver (page 206)
4. Scrabble: X.Y.Z. Cocktail (opposite)
5. Mahjong: Mahjong Cocktail (page 116)

Fresh Faces

It's a delightful world we live within (the majority of the time). The multitudes of reasons are too numerous to list here, so let's focus in on one area that matches up best with the rest of this book: the plain and unmistakable fact that we're lucky enough to be in a cocktail renaissance. This isn't to say, by the way, that there weren't amazing cocktails being created over the past, oh, 70-odd years. There were, and bless those who first made them. It's only to say that in the past couple of decades, the world has seen an explosion in the availability of specialty liquors and liqueurs, combined with an eruption of really creative cocktail inventors, added to an outburst of restaurants, hotels, bars, and even home parties boasting a renewed focus on creative cocktails tailored for the circumstances. As the frenzy of foodies has expanded, so has the frenzy of cocktail enthusiasts and cocktails. This, pals, is a delightful occurrence.

It's delightful enough that it makes having a chapter called Fresh Faces a tad daunting—there is such a multitude of sizzling original drinks that it's problematic to get a handle on half of them. For your sake, I'm up to the challenge. The selection in this chapter by no means wears a shirt saying, "This is it for fresh inventive cocktails" or one that says, "This is a complete overview of every original cocktail created in the past 10 years." Either statement would be a bold lie and get me taken out to the woodshed for a whupping. And there aren't any cocktail shakers in the woodshed.

Fresh Faces doesn't want to get in your face with absolute assertions of any kinds. It's just a small compendium of some of the best creative drinks I've had the pleasure of sampling recently, and a way to introduce these drinks and say, "Here, now, are some hip mixes to introduce at your next swinging social gathering." Some of them use ingredients from far-flung spots (the Candy Corn or the Hernandez, for example), while some put a sparkling spin on old favorites (such as the Bench Press). Some come from hot-spots (like the Mango Batida), some from hot cocktailians (like the Debonair), and some from hot home bartenders (like the Gizmo). There are a few drinks here that have already been around long enough to become legendary (the ubiquitous Cosmopolitan, for one) and a number that should be—and may end up being—legendary (the Dublin 8 seems bound to take off).

While it appears that the thread tying these Fresh Faces together is newness, the actual connection is that they all taste good. Serve them with pride, and with joy, while feeling lucky that you've come of age in this great cocktail century.

43 Blanco
I'm not saying you should order these when actually attending a bullfight (they might be a little light) but, when reclining and pretending to be a bullfighter in your living room or local taverna, this sweet-ish treat hits the bull's-eye, so to speak. It calls for, as the name implies, Licor 43 or Cuarenta y Tres, a Spanish liqueur from the Iberian Peninsula that dates back centuries and boasts the requisite arm-long secret ingredient list. With **a captivating mix** of vanilla, citrus, and herbs, Licor 43 seems designed to go well with cream. But why take my word for it? Serve up a round and poll the room.

Ice cubes

2 ounces **Licor 43**

1 ounce **heavy cream**

1. Fill a cocktail shaker halfway full with ice cubes. Add the Licor 43 and the heavy cream. Shake well.

2. Strain into a cocktail glass. Watch for over-anxious bulls.

A VARIATION: I've left this garnishless, but be open to experimentation. A little freshly grated nutmeg? A lemon twist? A whole vanilla bean? All good ideas.

Albatross

Though the albatross was a good omen in the early parts of Samuel Taylor Coleridge's *Rime of the Ancient Mariner*, the mariner's nutty pegging of it with an arrow has caused the albatross to take on a bad rap. Today it represents something heavy and bad that drags one down. Your mission is to take the albatross back, via this tall swig that should only point to an enjoyable evening, turning this feathered friend back into a good omen. Even if at one point in the evening you mangle his quote to serve your own end a bit ("At length I did serve an Albatross, and Through the booze-fog it came"), an old-school reveler like Coleridge will smile at you for helping to reclaim the fortunes of this big bird.

Ice cubes

1 ounce **gin**

1 ounce **Cointreau**

3 ounces **peach puree** (see Note)

Chilled 7UP or **Sprite**

Peach slice for garnish

1. Fill a cocktail shaker halfway full with ice cubes. Add the gin and Cointreau. Shake well.

2. Fill a highball glass three-quarters full with ice cubes. Strain the gin-Cointreau combo over the ice. Add the peach puree. Stir well while envisioning the ocean.

3. Top the glass off with chilled 7UP. Stir again. Garnish with the peach slice.

A Note: For more on peach puree, see the Bellini (page 373).

Television Tipplers

While you can't equate television characters with the actors portraying them, you can know that if these famous fictional drinkers could actually be at the bar, they'd probably be pretty darn fun. The following are five television tipplers I'd most want to belly up with.

1. **Norm Peterson**, *Cheers*. Everybody at the bar knows his name, which leads to free rounds.

2. **Reginald Van Gleason II**, *The Jackie Gleason Show*. Make the cocktails right and he'll say it: "Ooohh, that's good booze!"

3. **Captain Benjamin Franklin Pierce (Hawkeye)**, *M*A*S*H*. He kept a still in his tent throughout the Korean War. What more do you need?

4. **Fred Sanford**, *Sanford & Son*. Don't be a dummy, step up and share a Mintchipple (a Mint Julep/Ripple combo).

5. **Homer Simpson**, *The Simpsons*. Sure, it would be weird to drink next to an animated character, but it's Homer Simpson. He invented the Flaming Moe.

Almond Joy

While we don't have as many tasty cocktail tributes to screen stars and stage starlets here at the beginning of the twenty-first century as abounded near the start of the past century, we're making up for this lack by concocting more, ahem, adult versions of commercial products (the Flaming Dr Pepper on page 360, for example). The Almond Joy is **the nuttier sibling** of the Mounds candy bar (sometimes you feel like a nut, sometimes you don't), but here it's transformed into a pleasant dessert drink.

Ice cubes

¾ ounce **coconut-flavored rum**

¾ ounce **amaretto**

¾ ounce **crème de cacao**

¾ ounce **heavy cream**

1. Fill a cocktail shaker halfway full with ice cubes. Add the rum, amaretto, crème de cacao, and heavy cream. Shake well.

2. Strain into a cocktail glass. Serve with a smile.

Almost Blue →

A sad song by Elvis Costello, the moment after the sun sets on a day that's boasted blameless blue skies, a celebration at which two out of twenty invitees show up, and this cocktail—I'd say the finale of that list may be the most fun on its own, but I might also say that if you add them all together, the sum of the parts **turns the bluest mood into quite a party**.

Ice cubes

1 ounce **lemon-flavored vodka**

¾ ounce **freshly squeezed lemon juice**

½ ounce **blue curaçao**

½ ounce **Simple Syrup** (page 7)

1. Fill a cocktail shaker halfway full with ice cubes. Add the vodka, lemon juice, curaçao, and simple syrup. Shake those blues away.

2. Strain into a cocktail glass. Drink (repeatedly as needed to turn any frown upside down).

Bamboozler

There's no perhaps about it—the Bamboozler is one of the most fantastic drink names in the multitude of years since the first person unknowingly sipped fermented juice and dug the results. It's only fitting that **this doozy beauty** floats from the fertile brains of Adam Rocke and the artist Shag, who form today's foremost tiki twosome, transporting the colorful Polynesian style into modern life with hip drinks and amazing artwork. The Bamboozler comes from their *Tiki Drinks Deck* (Surrey Books, 2004), which boasts 52 beach beloveds on individual cards done up swanky and sweet. It's ideal for any sunshiny Saturday when you want to bring a little Hawaii home.

Ice cubes

3 ounces **fresh mango juice**

1 ounce **dark rum**

1 ounce **white rum**

1 ounce **vanilla-flavored rum**

½ ounce **maraschino liqueur**

Maraschino cherry for garnish

1. Fill a cocktail shaker halfway full with ice cubes. Add the mango juice, dark and white rums, vanilla-flavored rum, and maraschino liqueur. Shake well, swinging your hips as if it were 1974.

2. Pour the mix into a chilled Collins glass. Garnish with the cherry.

Beach Bum

It isn't a modern phenomenon to enjoy lying back and doing nothing on the beach for long periods of time, to also enjoy a tall cool drink while lying back and doing nothing on said beach, to perhaps enjoy not leaving the beach for days if possible. Not at all. Folks have been beach bums for centuries, when they could afford it or could afford to not care about the cost. This particular refreshing quaff, though, named in honor of **those sun-loving souls** who'd rather not vacate the beach, is more modern. It is, in my sun-addled brain, ideal when you're in that frame of mind that easily ignores sand in the suit in favor of a pleasant lack of responsibilities.

Ice cubes

2 ounces **freshly squeezed orange juice**

1½ ounces **white rum**

½ ounce **freshly squeezed lemon juice**

Chilled 7UP or **Sprite**

Orange slice for garnish

1. Fill a highball glass three-quarters full with ice cubes. Add the orange juice, rum, and lemon juice. Stir lazily.

2. Top the glass off with 7UP. Stir a few more times, but without any dangerous effort. Garnish with the orange slice.

A VIRGIN VARIATION: Sun too bright on your beach? Remove the rum and add an extra ½ ounce of lemon juice, an extra 1 ounce of orange juice, and an extra-dark pair of sunglasses.

Bench Press

While one might have painful memories of the arm-wrenching exercise machine that shares the name Bench Press, don't let that keep you from the long stir spoon and this refreshing quencher. An extension and modification of the Sweet Press (page 404), which is itself a modification of the Presbyterian (page 225), the Bench Press originated on a summer evening when the Mrs. and I had partaken a bit too much at the potato salad bowl. We didn't want to slow the evening's festivities, but our bellies felt as if they'd turned to cement. The combination of bubbles and bitters and lime and gin came straight to the rescue (you *could* call it **a heroic drink**), and kept us cool as part of the bargain. The moral? Anytime you've overindulged at the table but still want a long after-dinner quaff, call out for the Bench Press. If someone looks funny in your direction, just flex your glass.

Ice cubes

1½ ounces **gin**

4 ounces **chilled 7UP** or **Sprite**

4 ounces **chilled club soda**

3 dashes **Peychaud's bitters**

Lime wedge for garnish

1. Fill a Collins or a similar-sized glass with ice cubes. Add the gin.

2. Add the 7UP and club soda at the same time. Add the Peychaud's bitters.

3. Squeeze the lime wedge over the glass and drop it in. Stir well with a bar spoon or tiny barbell.

⬆ **A Note:** *You can go higher on the gin here if the night demands it. Just be sure to keep the balance of 7UP and club soda at half and half.*

⬆ **Another Note:** *I like Peychaud's bitters here, for its curative nature. But if you only have Angostura or orange bitters handy, they work in a pinch.*

Licor 43

A fresh favorite from the Iberian Peninsula in Spain, Licor 43, also known as Cuarenta y Tres, has recently lit bar menus on fire, with its ability to be used in a wide variety of cocktails and long tall sippers, and its mutable nature that allows it to be a tasty participant in sweet treats and stiffer mixes. It has a sweet, citrus-vanilla flavor. However, one mustn't be fooled by the more recent surge in Licor 43 popularity. This liqueur (or at least a similar great-great-grandmother) has been served in Spain since Hasdrubal in 237 B.C. Or thereabouts. You see, when General Hasdrubal founded Carthago Nova, a number of liqueurs were developed for the general's Carthaginian warriors, in order both to encourage them in battle and to add a little more fun to the many victory festivals after battle. The liqueurs were almost lost in 206 B.C., when the Roman army, headed up by Publio Cornelious Escipion, attacked and conquered Carthago Nova. After the conquest, the Romans tried to destroy all of the liqueurs, but the Carthaginians hid the recipes and a number of small presses and stills to keep the liqueur tradition alive. Eventually, peace came around and the Romans become fans of the Carthaginian liqueur, and it eventually started being exported around the world. Today, that Carthaginian liqueur is called Licor 43.

Boardwalk

You might be under the boardwalk, down by the sea, on a blanket with your baby, wanting to **pour the perfect blend** for the occasion (in which case you'd better plan ahead, as you'll need to bring ice). Or, you might desire to sip an appropriate cocktail to celebrate buying Boardwalk during the early stages of a marathon Monopoly game. Or, it might be that you recently inherited or purchased a bottle of imported maraschino liqueur and are searching for an appetizing way to use it. Whichever scenario describes your afternoon agenda, the Boardwalk makes a great companion.

Ice cubes

2 ounces **vodka**

½ ounce **dry vermouth**

½ ounce **maraschino liqueur**

½ ounce **freshly squeezed lemon juice**

1. Fill a cocktail shaker halfway full with ice cubes. Add the vodka, dry vermouth, maraschino liqueur, and lemon juice. Shake well (much like you'd shake the dice when really needing doubles).

2. Strain into a cocktail glass and serve.

C&A

Oftentimes I find that a friend sets me up with a drink and I have to knock my noggin against the wall—why didn't I think of that years ago? It's that way with the C&A, which simply pairs two of my favorites, Campari and San Pellegrino Aranciata, into **an unflappable mix** that keeps guests sparkling and keeps a host from having to sweat over any nutty preparations. That simplicity makes this ideal for larger gatherings where you're tripling up as drink maker, badminton referee, and matchmaker. There'll even be extra time to ensure *your* glass always stays full, which is a crucial component to any good party.

Ice cubes

2 ounces **Campari**

Chilled San Pellegrino Aranciata

Lemon, lime, or **orange slice** for garnish

1. Fill a highball glass with ice cubes. Add the Campari, and then the San Pellegrino Aranciata. Stir well.

2. Garnish with a slice of lemon, lime, or orange. It seems like orange would be the obvious choice, but all three add a little something different, so experiment.

↥ *A Note: San Pellegrino Aranciata is an Italian orange soda with a light touch of bitterness. It's readily available in grocery stores, which is good, because no other orange soda works as a good substitute here.*

Candy Corn

It's extraordinary that a drink using Licor 43, a Spanish liqueur, and Amarula Cream, an African liqueur, is named after an American candy that was initially eaten in the 1880s and first produced commercially by the Wunderle Candy Company of Philadelphia. It just goes to show that today's imaginative cocktail creators have a) a wealth of resources at their disposal, b) a craving for drinks that match childhood favorites, and c) a lot of time on their hands. As you might guess, the Candy Corn is **a sweet suitor**, best suited for after dinner (or mid-afternoon, if you get those kinds of cravings).

Ice cubes

1 ounce **Licor 43**

1 ounce **Amarula Cream**

1 ounce **orange curaçao**

1 **candy corn** for garnish (optional)

1. Fill a cocktail shaker halfway full with ice cubes. Add the Licor 43, Amarula Cream, and curaçao. Shake well.

2. Strain into a cocktail glass. If you must, garnish with the candy corn (of the actual candy variety).

⬆ *A Note:* Amarula Cream is made from the fruit of the marula tree, a wild African tree that has never been cultivated. Its flavor boasts hints of caramel, chocolate, vanilla, and butterscotch.

Four Movie Bars

There are some movies that feature stars having drinks, and some movies where the bar or lounge itself becomes a character. Anytime you want to feel close to a famous cinematic watering hole, check out one of these classics.

1. **Rick's Café Américain**, from *Casablanca*

2. **St. Elmo's Fire**, from the eponymous movie

3. **House of Games**, from the eponymous movie

4. **Double Deuce**, from *Road House*

Century Sour

If a young lad or lady desires to start up a career behind the stick (as bartending was and is called by those in the know), he or she would be well served to start by reading Mardee Haidin Regan's *The Bartender's Best Friend* (John Wiley & Sons, 2003). Not only does it contain the basic, intermediate, and advanced hints, tips, rules, and instructions for barkeeps of all types, it also presents an array of terrific recipes, including the Century Sour, which was itself adapted from a recipe from King Cocktail, Dale DeGroff, and which uses Alizé passionfruit liqueur. Add in the fact that *The Bartender's Best Friend* has an easily wiped down cover (which means it's a book that's actually usable behind the professional bar) and you can understand why **it's a favorite**.

Ice cubes

1 ounce **Alizé passionfruit liqueur**

1 ounce **apricot liqueur**

¾ ounce **freshly squeezed lemon juice**

Lemon twist for garnish

1. Fill a cocktail shaker halfway full with ice cubes. Add the Alizé, apricot liqueur, and lemon juice. Shake well.

2. Strain into a cocktail glass. Garnish with the lemon twist.

Cherry Bomb

People often say, "Life was simpler when I was young." Sometimes I think these folks forget how chaotic youth is, but in the case of the Cherry Bomb I'm inclined to agree. When I was 10 years old, "cherry bomb" meant a small explosive used around the Fourth of July to drive my parents, sisters, and neighbors nutty. Now, there are probably 133 different recipes for a Cherry Bomb cocktail (as well as a Cherry Bomb tattoo parlor in Chicago, a Cherry Bomb sex toy site, and Cherry Bomb, the grooviest band in Kansas City). I'd say it would be too baffling if I didn't already have a favorite, clear-cut, exquisite recipe that always **cuts through the confusion**. The fact that this recipe is a bit of a knockout only makes it that much easier to forget the others.

Ice cubes

2 ounces **vodka** (if you can get cherry-infused vodka, use it here)

¾ ounce **white crème de cacao**

¼ ounce **grenadine**

Maraschino cherry for garnish

1. Fill a cocktail shaker halfway full with ice cubes. Add the vodka, crème de cacao, and grenadine. Shake well.

2. Strain into a cocktail glass. Garnish with the cherry.

Cinnamon Snap

While snapping loudly in someone's face (whether to underline a point or put a quick stop to an unwanted interruption) constitutes an insult from Bombay to Boise, placing a Cinnamon Snap in front of the same face is the opposite of insult—instead, it's a compliment, and may just garner, instead of a punch in the nose, **a kiss on the cheek**.

1 ounce **amaretto**

¾ ounce **freshly squeezed orange juice**

½ ounce **cinnamon schnapps**

½ ounce **heavy cream**

Orange slice for garnish

1. Fill a cocktail shaker halfway full with ice cubes. Add the amaretto, orange juice, cinnamon schnapps, and heavy cream. Shake well, with short, snap-like shakes.

2. Strain into a cocktail glass. Garnish with the orange slice.

⬆ *A Note: While the intro alludes to a kiss, no promises of actual kisses have been given. So don't call my lawyers if you don't get to smooching once you've served the Cinnamon Snap.*

Coquelicot

While not as mind-expanding as certain forms of its English translation ("the poppy"), the Coquelicot does introduce an assortment of tropical flavors that flit about on the tongue in a way that promises those taste-focused parts of the brain **an awfully happy experience**. The brain particularly enjoys this revitalizing beverage if both it and body are draped on warm sand or warm deck chair on a particularly luminous beach. At least that's the suggestion of Maile and Matt Bohlmann, cocktail connoisseurs who introduced me to this and who have a little Hawaii and a little Arizona desert in their background—so they understand on a deep level about refreshing drinks.

1 cup **crushed ice**

1 small, ripe **banana**

1½ ounces **white rum**

1½ ounces **cream of coconut**

1 ounce **freshly squeezed lime juice**

Whipped cream for garnish

Freshly grated lime zest for garnish

1. Add the ice, banana, rum, cream of coconut, and lime juice to a blender. Blend well, until you can almost smell the ocean.

2. Pour into a tall glass or large goblet. Top with the whipped cream and a little freshly grated lime zest. Serve with a straw and a hula skirt. If you have a ukulele, serve with that, too.

Cosmopolitan

Popular enough in today's alcohol arena as to almost need no introduction (famous through TV appearances combined with impeccable timing and the necessary good taste), the Cosmopolitan is so popular as to be completely comfortable with a shortening of the name to "Cosmo." Isn't that the height of heights? Indeed, some might argue that it is no longer a fresh face, though on the cocktail timeline, it is. For years this fav was surrounded by a bit of mystery, with arguments over who created it and where and how. Cocktail detective Gary Regan broke the final word that it was created originally by Toby Cecchini, a New York City bartender who for years wouldn't admit to the invention, saying, "Nobody believed me when I lay claim to it, so I took to denying it instead." Turns out he was introduced to a rough variation of the drink by a fellow bartender (name of Mesa) and, liking the color, polished the formula until it became the mix now slurped all over the world.

Ice cubes

2 ounces **Absolut Citron vodka**

1 ounce **Cointreau** or **triple sec**

1 ounce **cranberry juice cocktail**

½ ounce **freshly squeezed lime juice**

Lime slice for garnish

1. Fill a cocktail shaker halfway full with ice cubes. Add the vodka, Cointreau, cranberry juice, and lime juice. Shake well.

2. Strain into a large cocktail glass (large enough to hold the ego of a drink so popular). Garnish with the lime slice.

Debonair

From one of Gary and Mardee Haidin Regan's many excellent cocktail and liquor books (the one in this case being the lovely *New Classic Cocktails* [John Wiley & Sons, 1997]), the Debonair was created by the Regans in 1993. It's created after the example of the Whiskey Mac, a 1960s British drink made with blended Scotch and ginger wine, but here updated using a newer creation, Original Canton Delicate Ginger Liqueur, which was introduced into the United States in the 1990s. The result is **a complex but subtle blending** of flavors.

Ice cubes

1 ounce **Original Canton Delicate Ginger Liqueur**

2½ ounces **single malt Scotch** (Gary and Mardee suggest Springbank or Oban, and I would trust their taste if I were you)

Lemon twist for garnish

1. Fill a mixing glass halfway full with ice cubes. Add the ginger liqueur and Scotch. Stir well with a long, thin, elegant, metal spoon (you must match the stirrer to the drink).

2. Strain into a chilled cocktail glass. Garnish with the lemon twist.

LIQUEUR SPOTLIGHT
Cointreau

Sometimes referred to as a high-end type of triple sec (some would say the original type) and sometimes referred to as its own animal in the liqueur world, Cointreau is made in Saint-Barthélemy-d'Anjou, which lies outside of Angers, in France. But the sweet and bitter oranges whose peels bring Cointreau its distinctive flavor now come from different parts of the world, including Haiti and Spain. The secret recipe was originally written, tested, and tasted by confectioner Adolphe Cointreau and his brother Edouard-Jean, who, as the tale is told today, once said about their namesake liqueur, "I wanted to combine crystal clear purity with the subtlety of tastes obtained from the perfect harmony of sweet and bitter orange peels." The brothers set up the first Cointreau distillery in 1849, though the first bottles weren't sold to the public until 1875. Now, Cointreau is sold in more than 200 countries, and is enjoyed both before and after dinner and both by itself and mixed in a variety of drinks. A simple, elegant pairing is Cointreau and tonic water, garnished with a lime wedge.

Dish It Up Cocktail

This was created by me in the 2005 holiday season for the fine folks at Dish It Up, a kitchen store in the Magnolia neighborhood of Seattle. (Visit them at www.dish-it-up.com. They have everything a home or pro cook needs, as well as an absolutely lovely test kitchen in the back, where they host classes of all kinds.) This cocktail uses satsuma tangerine juice (the satsuma's a Northwest fall staple), orange bitters, Cointreau, and parfait amour, as well as an agreeable helping of chocolate-flavored vodka. The result is **an adult cocktail** layered with different orange tones.

Ice cubes

1 ounce **chocolate-flavored vodka**

1 ounce **Cointreau**

¾ ounce **freshly squeezed satsuma tangerine juice**

¼ ounce **parfait amour**

2 dashes **orange bitters**

Satsuma section, peeled, for garnish

1. Fill a cocktail shaker halfway full with ice cubes. Add the vodka, Cointreau, satsuma juice, parfait amour, and bitters. Shake well.

2. Strain into a cocktail glass. Garnish with the satsuma section skewered on a toothpick.

⬆ *A Note: If you can't get fresh satsuma juice, try adding just a splash of lemon juice to regular orange juice. Satsumas boast a signature slight tang that's necessary to the flavors here.*

Dublin 8

This Irish special (by way of the Midwestern United States) owes its birth to love and Jeremy Sidener, a bartender extraordinaire and manager of Louise's Bar and the Eighth Street Tap Room in Lawrence, Kansas. Mr. Sidener was chatting up a charming Irish lady and thought the conversation would take a fortuitous turn if he constructed a new drink for her right there and then. This move wasn't coming out of left field, as bartenders enjoy both drink experimentation and flirtation. Thus the Dublin 8 was born. While tasty year-round, it's especially **a hit on St. Patrick's Day** (letting you put those nasty green beers aside). Oh, and as far as the drink's ability as a romance aid? Let me just say that the two mentioned in the story above are now married.

Ice cubes

2 ounces **Irish whiskey** (Bushmills makes the trip safe)

3 ounces **freshly squeezed orange juice**

3 ounces **chilled ginger ale**

Lime quarter for garnish

Lime slice for garnish

1. Fill a 10-ounce highball or a similar-sized glass three-quarters full with ice cubes. Add the whiskey.

2. Add the orange juice and ginger ale at the same time, so that we don't have any arguments over who's more important to the effort.

3. Squeeze the lime quarter over the glass, and then drop it in. Stir gently. Garnish with the slice of lime.

Emerald Drop →

I'm not one for hypothesizing, but I believe it's the tang of the barbecue sauce from the grill connecting with the citrus of the orange juice, basted within the propensity of melons in summer, sauced by the reflection of the sun into the colorful nature of this cocktail, that makes the Emerald Drop **one of my favorite summer shakers.** Serve this up during a picnic with a stack of slow-cooked and spicily sauced favorites and the smiles will be as wide as the shorts are short.

Ice cubes

1½ ounces **mandarin-** or **orange-flavored vodka**

1 ounce **freshly squeezed orange juice**

½ ounce **Midori melon liqueur**

Maraschino cherry for garnish

1. Fill a cocktail shaker halfway full with ice cubes. Add the vodka, orange juice, and melon liqueur. Shake, but in a manner that doesn't resemble exercise.

2. Strain into a cocktail glass. Garnish with the cherry. (No matter how hot, don't forget the cherry. You may get a riot.)

Esteem

This graceful glass-filler should be brought out when entertaining an influential college professor, a boss who builds—instead of shakes—your confidence, a writer whose work brings you to the "I laughed, I cried" stage, or any **friend who always has your back,** no matter the situation. Esteem is what you have for these folks—why not serve it, too?

Ice cubes

1½ ounces **gin**

½ ounce **anisette**

½ ounce **freshly squeezed lime juice**

Chilled Champagne

1. Fill a cocktail shaker halfway full with ice cubes. Add the gin, anisette, and lime juice. Shake well.

2. Strain the esteemed mix into a Champagne flute or white wine glass. Top it off with chilled Champagne.

🔼 **A Note:** *Anisette is a slightly sweet anise-flavored liquor. With this in mind, perhaps the Esteem isn't the drink to serve if one of your guests has an aversion to black licorice. Unless the esteem you hold them in is low.*

"Just fancy, they gave me drink, fed me!
Such bread, **it was exquisite!** *Délicieux!*
And the vodka, I never tasted any better.
And they would not take a penny for anything."

VASENKA VESLOVKSY, in *Anna Karenina*, by Leo Tolstoy

Farmer

A mix made for all the Midwesterners in the house, the Farmer echoes that wide-open combination of **stark loveliness and sparseness** found in the Great Plains region. With that backbone, it's a simple mix, but one that serves up strong when rocking slow on the rear porch, watching the sun go down over the back forty.

Ice cubes

2 ounces **bourbon**

½ ounce **Grand Marnier**

½ ounce **freshly squeezed orange juice**

1. Fill a rocks or a similar-sized glass three-quarters full with ice cubes. Add the bourbon. Lovely, isn't it?

2. Add the Grand Marnier and orange juice. Stir, but just barely.

Gizmo

From the muddled (which when speaking of cocktails is a top-notch compliment) mind of bartender, chef, bar-stool sitter, and current chief Husky Boy (the *Husky Boy* being a 'zine devoted to food and drink) Jeremy Holt, the Gizmo is, according to Jeremy, a gin-based pseudo-Cosmopolitan. It was developed one year on the day after Thanksgiving while cleaning out the fridge and, one would guess, needing a little something to help make the post-Thanksgiving party rearranging less of a chore.

Ice cubes

2½ ounces **gin**

1 ounce **homemade cranberry sauce**

½ ounce **Simple Syrup** (page 7; optional)

1. Fill a cocktail shaker halfway full with ice cubes. Add the gin, cranberry sauce, and simple syrup if using (if you're not into the sweets, omit the syrup). Shake exceptionally well.

2. Strain into a cocktail glass. Garnish with a side of turkey leg or, for vegetarians, a hunk of stuffing on a toothpick.

⬆ *A Note: Not sure about making homemade cranberry sauce? Try this: Add one 12-ounce bag fresh cranberries, the juice and zest of 1 orange, and 1 cup sugar to a saucepan. Cover and simmer over medium heat until desired sauce texture is reached.*

Three Men, a Woman, and a Menagerie Walk into a Bar

A man walks into a bar with a slab of asphalt under his arm and says, "A drink, please, and one for the road."

A man walks into a bar, holding a set of jumper cables. The bartender says, "You can come in, but don't start anything!"

A man walks into a bar, sits down, and orders a beer. The bartender brings it and some peanuts over. A few seconds later, the man hears a small voice say, "You look nice today." A few minutes later, he again hears a small voice, saying, "That's a nice tie." The guy asks the bartender, "Who is that talking?" The bartender replies, "Those are the peanuts. They're complimentary."

A woman goes into a bar and asks for a "double entendre." So the bartender gives it to her.

A neutron walks into a bar and orders a beer. The bartender sets the beer down and says, "For you, no charge!"

A kangaroo walks into a bar. He orders a beer. The bartender says, "That'll be $10. You know, we don't get many kangaroos coming in here." The kangaroo says, "At $10 a beer, it's not hard to understand why."

A grasshopper walks into a bar. The bartender says, "Hey, hey, it's you, we have a drink named after you. You're a celebrity." The grasshopper replies, "You've got a drink named Steve?"

A baloney and cheese sandwich walks into a bar and orders a beer. The bartender says, "I'm sorry, we don't serve food."

A priest, a rabbi, a nun, a blonde, a polar bear, a giraffe, and a penguin walk into a bar. The bartender says, "Hey, what is this, some kind of a joke?"

HAG Cocktail

While having acronymic drink names seems maybe too insider, in the case of the HAG I had to insist, or suffer having a drink called the Home and Garden Cocktail, which makes me shudder. **The story is an old one**—sign up to work for a giant company in their home and garden division to find out when the sales are happening on cocktail shakers and then get drafted to create a signature cocktail for a company function. You've heard it many times before, I'm sure.

What you may not have heard about is this dandy drink, which uses vodka, apple juice, loganberry liqueur, and a cherry. The ingredients (except the vodka, which was brought aboard to add that warming fortitude one needs to survive a company function) relate in their relationships to Washington state, which is known for apples, cherries, and loganberries.

Ice cubes

2 ounces **apple juice**

1 ounce **vodka**

½ ounce **loganberry liqueur**

Fresh cherry for garnish (or maraschino, if fresh is not available)

1. Fill a cocktail shaker halfway full with ice cubes. Add the apple juice, vodka, and loganberry liqueur. Shake well.

2. Drop the cherry into the bottom of a cocktail glass. Strain the mix into the glass. Drink in thanks to all that Washington state offers the world.

⬆ **A Note:** For loganberry liqueur, try the Clear Creek Distillery (www.clearcreekdistillery. com). If you can't get a loganberry liqueur, sub in a raspberry liqueur, such as Chambord.

Hernandez

This lovely fall and winter favorite was fashioned at a celebration for friends and fellow cocktail enthusiasts Ean and Reba Hernandez. As Ean is of Spanish descent and very interested in all things Spanish, it's only right that this employ the lovely Spanish liqueur Licor 43 or, simply, Cuarenta y Tres, which is a smooth golden liqueur from the Iberian Peninsula that has been made for hundreds of years. The result is a hearty, nutty cocktail that's **ideal either before or after dinner**, and that warms your guests up on a cold evening.

Ice cubes

1½ ounces **Licor 43**

1 ounce **sweet vermouth**

2 dashes **Peychaud's bitters**

Fresh cherry for garnish (or maraschino, if fresh is not available)

1. Fill your favorite cocktail shaker halfway full with ice cubes. Then add the Licor 43, humming the Spanish national anthem.

2. Add the vermouth and the bitters. Shake in matador style (which I would suggest equals hearty shaking).

3. Place the cherry in the bottom of a cocktail glass. Strain the mix into the glass and serve with a flourish.

A Note: When serving this without a cherry, it's called the Dirty Hernandez. I don't suggest it, but sometimes you have to do what you have to do.

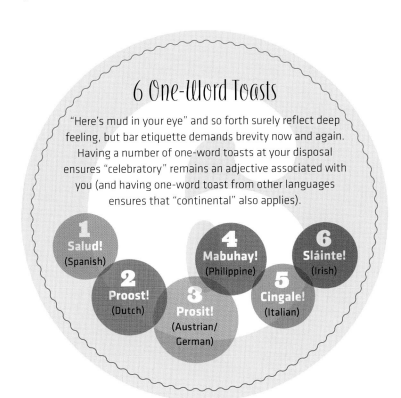

6 One-Word Toasts

"Here's mud in your eye" and so forth surely reflect deep feeling, but bar etiquette demands brevity now and again. Having a number of one-word toasts at your disposal ensures "celebratory" remains an adjective associated with you (and having one-word toast from other languages ensures that "continental" also applies).

1 Salud! (Spanish)

2 Proost! (Dutch)

3 Prosit! (Austrian/German)

4 Mabuhay! (Philippine)

5 Cingale! (Italian)

6 Sláinte! (Irish)

Incredible Hulk

When I was very young, I spent many Saturday mornings heading to downtown McPherson, Kansas, with my pa, to make two stops. The first was at Daylight Doughnuts, where I developed a dangerous love of bearclaws, and the second was the unnamed newsstand/ comic book store next door. At the time, comics were fairly inexpensive (I'm not saying exactly how inexpensive, to diffuse any awkward age questions), and I bought bundles, with the majority of my dollars going toward the *Incredible Hulk* and crossovers featuring Mr. Hulk. That's a lot of back story, I realize. How else, though, could I convince you that my obsession with creating an Incredible Hulk cocktail isn't just faked? It took a while to construct the right balance (if you know Hulk lore, you'll realize his trademark green color has changed a lot—this also made cocktail construction difficult) of **bluster and muscle and slight childishness**. It also took the introduction of Hpnotiq to the U.S. market. With a trademark blue hue and fragrant mix, along with a vaguely supervillain-esque name, Hpnotiq brings the Hulk off the page and into the glass.

Ice cubes

1 ounce **brandy**

1 ounce **Hpnotiq**

1 ounce **freshly squeezed orange juice**

Lime twist for garnish

1. Fill a cocktail shaker halfway full with ice cubes. Add the brandy, Hpnotiq, and orange juice. Shake well (as if you had biceps the size of bulldogs).

2. Strain into a cocktail glass. Garnish with the lime twist (and a remnant of a shirt that has been reduced to tatters).

⬆ *A Note: When sipping Incredible Hulks with pals, it's just fine to say, "Don't make me angry . . . you wouldn't like me when I'm angry," to any guest who reaches for your cocktail.*

Jasmine

With such a lovely name, there are bound to be multiple versions of a Jasmine, as well as multiple folks claiming ownership of the first Jasmine cocktail—and there are. You might also—and this is my path— **avoid all conflicts or arguments** about who made what when, by simply shaking, and then, without hesitation, drinking.

Ice cubes

1 ounce **gin**

½ ounce **Campari**

½ ounce **Cointreau**

½ ounce **freshly squeezed lemon juice**

¼ ounce **Simple Syrup** (page 7)

Lemon twist for garnish

Jasmine flower for garnish (optional)

1. Fill a cocktail shaker halfway full with ice cubes. Add the gin, Campari, Cointreau, lemon juice, and simple syrup. Shake considerably.

2. Strain into a cocktail glass. Garnish with the lemon twist and the jasmine flower, if desired.

A VARIATION: Is the simple syrup taking this into too sugary territory for you? Omit it with my blessing.

Seven More Obscure Facts to Bring Up at the Bar

Looking to expand the bar dialogue even more?
See pages 70 and 450.

1. In the three months before his liberation, one famous prisoner in France's infamous Bastille prison consumed 12 bottles of brandy, 121 bottles of beer, and 167 bottles of wine.

2. Samshu is a Chinese liquor distilled from rice that has been boiled under pressure. The word *samshu* comes from the Chinese *shao chiu*, which means "burn wine."

3. According to Herodotus, ancient Persians would only discuss important political affairs when under the influence of wine.

4. A "brimmer" is a glass whose contents go up to touch the rim, and a "bumper" is a glass so full that the contents peak in the middle of the top of the glass. Usually used in reference to wine, these terms can be used at other times as well.

5. Prehistoric nomads made beer from grain and water before learning to make bread.

6. The word "vodka" is a diminutive of the word *voda*, which is Russian and means "water." The first documented production of vodka in Russia happened at the end of the ninth century, but the first known commercial distillery was at Khylnovsk about 200 years later.

7. At one point, the recorded contents of Thomas Jefferson's wine cellar included 15 bottles of Madeira, four of "Lisbon wine for common use," 54 bottles of cider, and 83 bottles of rum.

Listen to Your Elders

Not only one of the sweetest folks in all the land, an accomplished baker, a keen conversationalist, and a snappy dresser, Rebecca Staffel was also at one time both my literary agent and the senior editor of the cookbooks section at Amazon.com. She understands her food and her alcohol, and is to be trusted on most matters of taste. Rebecca introduced me to the following breezy arrangement in the summer of 2005, and I was, and am, **dazzled by its delicacy**. I suggest serving it at lawn parties both of the daytime and nighttime variety, when you want to be classy, but also want to, as the kids say, get jiggy with it.

Ice cubes

1½ ounce **Hendrick's gin**

½ ounce **elderflower syrup**

Chilled Champagne

1. Fill a cocktail shaker halfway full with ice cubes. Add the gin and elderflower syrup. Shake well.

2. Strain the mix into a cocktail glass. Top with the Champagne.

⬆ *A Note: Elderflower syrup is made from the elderberry flower and is available at most specialty food shops. It's high in vitamin C, which means this drink is a healthy one. But don't let that keep you away from it.*

⬆ *Another Note: While you could substitute another gin for Hendrick's (which is a small-batch Scottish gin), don't ever serve a Listen to Your Elders with a different gin to Miss Staffel, unless you're looking for trouble.*

A SLIGHT VARIATION: If you can lay your hands on edible flowers (and I don't mean just grabbing whatever's pretty in the backyard—which leads to stomachaches) at a local gourmet shop, they make an ideal garnish for this one.

Lollipop

Lollipop lollipop, oh lolli lolli lolli . . . Charming song, and this is **a charming swallow**. The resemblances end there, though, as do most resemblances between the candy and the cocktail. I never had a lollipop quite like this at any tender age, I can tell you, which my liver is probably the better for. And don't let any fellow revelers catch you licking the drink—that'll lead to strange looks and probably end with you being cut off.

Ice cubes

1 ounce **Cointreau**

¾ ounce **green Chartreuse**

¾ ounce **kirsch**

¼ ounce **maraschino liqueur**

1. Fill a cocktail shaker with ice cubes. Add the Cointreau, Chartreuse, kirsch, and maraschino liqueur. Shake childishly.

2. Strain into a cocktail glass. Serve with a white stir stick (to complete the lolli illusion).

Mango Batida

Cuddled into a cozy-but-cultured space on NW 45th Street in Seattle, tucked in around cute houses, one discovers the Sambar, which features creative cocktails alongside scrumptious small bites (including the best *frites* I've ever snacked on). While the food should always be sampled, **it's the cocktails that count**, as gourmet in their way as the French menus in Le Gourmand (the fabulous restaurant that shares the Sambar's building). All the liquor options at the Sambar are worth trying (maybe over a few visits), but if you head over in summer, go with the Mango Batida first—you won't be shy about talking it up afterward.

2 ounces **cachaça**

½ ounce **freshly squeezed lime juice**

½ ounce **mango puree** (see Note)

1. Fill a cocktail shaker halfway full with ice cubes. Add the cachaça, lime juice, and mango puree. Shake well.

2. Strain the mix into a cocktail glass.

⊕ *A Note: To make the mango puree, just add peeled pieces of mango to a food processor, adding a little water if needed. You want the end result to be smooth in consistency. Or you can order mango puree from Perfect Purée of Napa, California (www.perfectpuree.com).*

Melon Ball

It's curious how certain drinks become almost inexplicably popular. Case in point: the Melon Ball, garnering order after order at college haunts and young professional hangouts. It's not that it's a bad drink—not at all. But it's not, in my mind, an automatic knockout, or a life-rearranger, or worthy of any drink-fueled iambic epic, though you'll see more folks ordering it than other cocktails that are in those categories. The Melon Ball is fruity, and clever in color, and **neither too sweet nor too sour** nor too strong. Maybe it's this middle-of-the-road-ness that did it, or maybe Midori had a really keen ad campaign. Whichever, don't let its popularity push you from serving these up, especially on a late summer evening when the temperature is just starting to cool. If you happen to own a melon baller, use it to make little melon rounds to garnish your drink.

Ice cubes

1½ ounces **Midori melon liqueur**

1 ounce **vodka**

4 ounces **freshly squeezed orange juice**

Honeydew chunk or **lime slice** for garnish

1. Fill a highball glass three-quarters full with ice cubes. Add the Midori and vodka. Stir twice (once for each).

2. Top the glass off with orange juice. Stir 3 more times. Garnish with a piece of honeydew or a lime slice, or both.

A VARIATION: Want a bubbly Ball? Cut back to 2 ounces orange juice and add 2 ounces 7UP or Sprite.

A SECOND VARIATION: I've seen this made with pineapple juice instead of orange juice, and while I wouldn't follow that route, it could add a tropical angle.

Metropolitan

With its classy name that fetches to mind **twinkling chandeliers, black ties, and shimmery gowns**, and its classic ingredients list, it wouldn't surprise me much if the Metropolitan dated circa 1929. However, it is, to my loose detecting, a more modern mix. Having said that, naturally, I've now doomed myself to an eternity of letters, e-mails, and angry calls railing against me for missing the many Metropolitan mentions in bar books from Jerry Thomas on up. People, get a grip. Before hassling me, pour yourself a Metropolitan and realize that time spent griping at a simple scribe such as myself is time spent not drinking cocktails.

Ice cubes

1½ ounces **brandy**

1 ounce **sweet vermouth**

¼ ounce **Simple Syrup** (page 7)

2 dashes **Angostura bitters**

1. Fill a cocktail shaker halfway full with ice cubes. Add the brandy, sweet vermouth, simple syrup, and bitters. Shake well, and stylishly.

2. Strain into a cocktail glass.

⌁ **A Note:** *"Metropolitan" is such a hip name that I've seen multiple drinks attached to it. With that fact firmly entrenched in your front matter, check with the bartender when ordering this one at the local watering hole, to make sure you and she or he agree on the ingredients. You never want to be disappointed at the bar.*

Millennium Cocktail

On those dreary days when things are going rotten, the car has a flat, the job stinks, a pigeon let loose on your new loafers, etc., etc., and you think that being alive at any other time in history would be better, remember, first off, that you haven't had to live through Prohibition, and second, that you live in the age of Regan (Gary and Mardee Haidin Regan, that is), an age in which they were kind enough to create the Millennium Cocktail to **start this new century**.

Ice cubes

2½ ounces **bourbon**

½ ounce **peach schnapps**

3 dashes **Angostura bitters**

Lemon twist for garnish

1. Fill a mixing glass or cocktail shaker halfway full with ice cubes. Add the bourbon, schnapps, and bitters. Stir well.

2. Strain into a cocktail glass. Garnish with the lemon twist. Enjoy the moment.

Mind Eraser

Oh no, not the Mind Eraser, which sounds hauntingly like a futuristic tool to wipe out the free thoughts of all liberty-loving citizens, turning us into drones buzzing around cubes in some corporate hive, waiting for that clock to tick to 5 P.M. . . . oh, wait, the Mind Eraser *here* is designed to produce forgetfulness of that corporate world, which is why it's an excellent way to **expunge a long week** once Friday afternoon rolls around. You have my permission, by the way, to gather up all close-at-hand co-workers and secure the nearest watering hole at 4 P.M. this Friday, instead of 5. Tell your boss I said it was okay.

Ice cubes

2 ounces **vodka**

2 ounces **Kahlúa**

1½ ounces **chilled club soda**

1. Fill an old-fashioned glass three-quarters full with ice cubes. Add the vodka and Kahlúa. Stir well.

2. Add the club soda. Stir 10 more times. Drink promptly.

A VARIATION: The Mind Eraser gets uncommon when using chocolate-flavored vodka—it becomes almost like a chocolate-coffee soda. Maybe a cherry is needed in this situation.

Mountain

I can't readily recall if I first consumed one of these on a mountain—a fact pointing to the fairly strong nature of this cocktail. Don't serve or order one when actually climbing a mountain, skiing down a mountain, or skydiving over a mountain. Keep it to those fireside talks when the mountain adventures are in the past. It'll **keep your whistle wet** as you tell the tale of the mountain to a throng of entranced listeners who have no idea that you never even left the lodge.

Ice cubes

1 ounce **white rum**

1 ounce **freshly squeezed orange juice**

½ ounce **vodka**

½ ounce **Tia Maria**

Lemon twist for garnish

1. Fill a cocktail shaker halfway full with ice cubes. Add the rum, orange juice, vodka, and Tia Maria. Shake well.

2. Strain the mix into a cocktail glass. Squeeze the lemon twist over and then let it float into the drink.

Nutty C

Gimme a C, a nutty C, that tastes so sweet and tropically that it **makes you want to sing and dance**, and possibly take off your pants (in the vaudevillian way, not the stripper way). Gimme that C, that Nutty C, that takes you back to old Ha-wai-i, that goes up dandy, on a beach that's sandy, and goes down easy, on a beach that's breezy.

Ice cubes

4 ounces **fresh pineapple juice**

2 ounces **dark rum**

2 ounces **amaretto**

Pineapple chunks for garnish (optional)

1. Fill a highball glass with ice cubes. Add the pineapple juice, rum, and amaretto. Stir with a song in your heart and a stir stick in your hand.

2. Garnish, if you'd like, with the pineapple chunks on a toothpick.

A VARIATION: Serve this in a hollowed-out pineapple shell, if you like.

Orange Buck

A favorite among the posse I rode with at Kansas State U, the OB came to mention one leisurely summer Manhattan (Kansas) afternoon when I and a few co-workers at the revered Hibachi Hut restaurant began adding up how many days old we were (ah, bar games). After adding and subtracting for leap years and muddled brains, it became apparent that I was only weeks away from turning 10,000 days old. In some primeval valley there's a yet-to-be-discovered culture that celebrates the 10,000th day with **much whooping and hollering**. With anthropology foremost in mind, I decided to have my own 10,000th day party, and picked the Orange Buck to be the signature drink.

The Orange Buck has since been one of my preferred summer refreshers. Not too robust (but robust enough to matter), slightly citrusy, slightly gingery, and very cooling, it pays the warm weather bill. A younger relative of the Gin Buck (page 110), the Orange Buck adds orange juice and sticks with lime (often the Gin Buck is made with lemon juice). The result is worthy of any July festivity.

Ice cubes

3 ounces **gin**

2 ounces **freshly squeezed orange juice**

2 ounces **chilled ginger ale**

Lime wedge for garnish

Lime slice for garnish

1. Fill a highball or comparably sized glass three-quarters full with ice cubes. Add the gin.

2. Add the orange juice and ginger ale, concurrently. We don't want any hurt feelings between the mixers. Stir, but don't get wacky about it.

3. Squeeze the lime wedge over the glass and drop it in. Garnish with a lime slice.

A VARIATION: The Orange Buck recipe plays well with other liquors. For example, adding rum instead of gin equals a New Orleans Buck.

⬆ *A Note: The Orange Buck can be poured in bigger and smaller glasses than the 8-ounce highball alluded to above. Just be sure that for every 1½ parts gin, you use 1 part ginger ale and 1 part orange juice.*

✕ *A Warning: I've said it before: Folks consuming a number of Bucks may waver into childish sayings, such as "Buck you" and "That's Bucked up." And I think it's just fine that they do.*

Oreo Cookie

O-O-O-ice cold booze makes this Oreo Cookie a dangerous combination, when a dark, delicious cookie turns into an icy drink sensation. Leave the milk for the kids, though.

Ice cubes

¾ ounce **vodka**

¾ ounce **Kahlúa**

¾ ounce **crème de cacao**

¾ ounce **Bailey's Irish Cream**

Oreo cookie
for garnish (optional)

1. Fill a cocktail shaker halfway full with ice cubes. Add the vodka, Kahlúa, crème de cacao, and Bailey's. Shake it, cookie, shake it.

2. Strain into a cocktail glass. If cutesy is the plan, garnish with a real Oreo cookie.

Peachy Keen

While the name echoes a dessert listed on a 1950s diner menu, don't think this peach pleasure should appear solely when the girls are sporting poodle skirts and Peter Pan collars and the boys are strutting around in letter sweaters. Since the Peachy Keen uses peach liqueur, specifically Liqueur de Pêche de Vigne de Bourgogne (which is becoming more widely available, and which uses wild peaches from Burgundy), it should be served whenever peaches are in season. If the peaches aren't fresh, the drink goes from "keen" to "square" in less time than it takes to shake it.

1 **peach half,** skinned and cubed

½ ounce **freshly squeezed lemon juice**

Ice cubes

1½ ounces **vodka**

1 ounce **Liqueur de Pêche de Vigne de Bourgogne** or **other good-quality peach liqueur**

Peach slice for garnish

1. Add the peach cubes and lemon juice to a cocktail shaker. Using a muddler or wooden spoon, muddle well.

2. Fill the cocktail shaker halfway full with ice cubes. Add the vodka and Liqueur de Pêche de Vigne de Bourgogne. Shake well.

3. Strain into a cocktail glass. Garnish with the peach slice.

Peter Sellers

There are many personalities who deserve a named drink in their honor but who have failed to garner this highest praise. For some time, legendary madcap actor Peter Sellers resided in this distressing category. Recently, however, four pharmacists named Brad, Brett, Bob, and Jeremy took a three-week voyage across the nation in a rented RV. Naturally, they needed **a deliberate drink for the adventure** (before you *tsk tsk tsk*, let me assure you that the drinks were only poured for those not driving). The following combination is what they created and then named in honor of the darkly comic, slightly manic, and always versatile Sellers. It's an honorable tribute, I believe, and one which should be consumed recklessly during your next Inspector Clouseau film festival.

Ice cubes

2 ounces **fresh ruby red grapefruit juice**

1½ ounces **gin**

Dash of **Peychaud's bitters**

Chilled Squirt or **other grapefruit soda**

1. Fill a Collins or a similar-sized glass three-quarters full with ice cubes. Add the red grapefruit juice, gin, and a good dash of Peychaud's. Stir 4 times.

2. Top off the glass with the chilled Squirt. Stir 4 more times.

Five Writers to Read and Drink with (if They Were Still Alive, That Is)

The story of the hard-drinking writer almost feels clichéd—have there really been so many? It's almost the case that everyone drinking thinks they can write a good book. Who knows, maybe they could, if the bar just had an extra pen. These five famous authors did.

1. **Mark Twain:** "Sometimes too much to drink is barely enough."
2. **William Butler Yeats:** "The problem with some people is that when they aren't drunk, they're sober."
3. **Dorothy Parker:** "I like to have a Martini, two at the very most, at three I'm under the table, at four, I'm under the host."
4. **Dylan Thomas:** "I've just had 18 straight whiskies. I think that's the record."
5. **Ernest Hemingway:** "Always do sober what you said you'd do drunk. That will teach you to keep your mouth shut."

Petit Zinc

While small in name, and not too huge in actual ounces, the Petit Zinc makes its move in taste, with **a multifaceted mixing** of orange flavors coming from Cointreau and orange juice, underlined by the faintly bitter appeal of sweet vermouth. It is ideal both for fireside chats in the family room following dinner and predinner parlay in the parlor room, but the only real problem with the Petit Zinc is the garnish, as I've seen it both with an orange slice and a cherry. I say go with the slice if serving to more than two people.

Ice cubes

1 ounce **vodka**

½ ounce **Cointreau**

½ ounce **sweet vermouth**

½ ounce **freshly squeezed orange juice**

Orange slice or **maraschino cherry** for garnish

1. Fill a cocktail shaker halfway full with ice cubes. Add the vodka, Cointreau, sweet vermouth, and orange juice. Shake well, but with small motions.

2. Strain into a cocktail glass. Garnish with the orange slice or cherry.

A VARIATION: On the always helpful (and enjoyable) Drink Boy (www.drinkboy.com) Web site, it's noted that this should be made with fresh Seville oranges, and if they're not available, ¼ ounce lemon juice should be added to match the taste. My advice? Always have faith in the Drink Boy.

Phantasm Fizz →

Like the ghost of a bubbly dessert drink—seeking Joseph Stalin (perhaps when he was tired of drinking the vodka and red wine he usually quaffed) without **the desire for conquest**, the Phantasm Fizz appears ("to appear" is the meaning of the Greek *phantasma*), almost floating across the counter, almost a haze in the distance, but closer, closer, closer—until it reaches your waiting hand. Drink it! You must! It's preordained.

Ice cubes

1½ ounces **vodka**

1 ounce **heavy cream**

½ ounce **Galliano**

Chilled club soda

1. Fill a cocktail shaker halfway full with ice cubes. Add the vodka, heavy cream, and Galliano. Shake well, or relegate yourself to flailing away centuries wandering the mists of time.

2. Fill a highball glass with ice cubes. Strain the mix over the ice. Top with club soda. Garnish with a warning: Leave this drink unfinished at your own risk.

⬆ *A Note: Some researchers into the paranormal believe that the Phantasm Fizz is even more unnatural when topped with a touch of whipped cream.*

Presidential

Keep this one near to you and yours during those cold Januarys and Februarys, so that you're always **ready for appropriate toasts** (George Washington's, Abraham Lincoln's, and my birthdays—as well as the combined President's Day) and ready to keep the belly warm if the heat goes off due to a snowstorm. A strapping mix, the Presidential doubles as a mediator if you and a comrade can't agree on the historical merits of a past or current president.

1 ounce **Simple Syrup** (page 7)

2½ ounces **bourbon**

¾ ounce **freshly squeezed lime juice**

Ice cubes

Lime slice for garnish

1. Add the simple syrup to a double old-fashioned glass or another 10- to 12-ounce tumbler that has the requisite wide mouth.

2. Add the bourbon and lime juice to the glass, calmly and coolly.

3. Add ice cubes to the glass and mix with a stirrer. Garnish with the slice of lime. Sip slowly, taking in all the scents and savoring the drink like fine conversation.

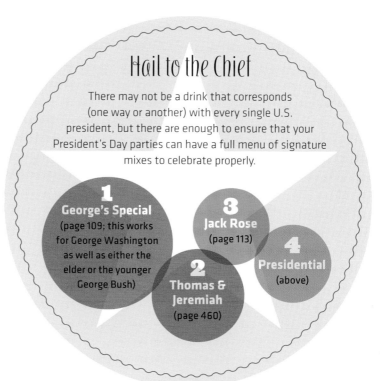

Hail to the Chief

There may not be a drink that corresponds (one way or another) with every single U.S. president, but there are enough to ensure that your President's Day parties can have a full menu of signature mixes to celebrate properly.

1
George's Special
(page 109; this works for George Washington as well as either the elder or the younger George Bush)

2
Thomas & Jeremiah
(page 460)

3
Jack Rose
(page 113)

4
Presidential
(above)

Pumpkin

Often, you come across innovative drinks unexpectedly. Example A: Rome, Italy, where my wife and I had an enlightening, entertaining, and historical no-line-waiting tour of the Vatican museums given by Tony Polzer (who heads up 3 Millennia Tours, www.threemillennia.com). After the tour, Tony set us up with perhaps the preeminent pizza in Rome, including a *quattro formaggi* slice grand enough to move to Italy for, and we copped a squat and ate and chatted. During the chat, Tony revealed that he provides tours not only of ancient Rome and the Vatican but also of Rome nightlife, including a tour highlighted by a couple of hot drinks he created. All were interesting mixes, but the top, and most engaging? The Pumpkin, which **goes pyrotechnic and gets a little fancy** via a swoosh of fresh cinnamon.

2 ounces **Kahlúa**

¾ ounce **Bailey's Irish Cream**

½ ounce **Goldschlager**

Ground cinnamon

1. Add the Kahlúa and Bailey's to an old-fashioned glass. Stir briefly.

2. Float the Goldschlager on top of the mix, pouring it over the back of a spoon if necessary. Carefully light it on fire, using a long-handled match just touched to the liquid's edge. Keep a moist kitchen towel nearby for safety's sake.

3. Sprinkle the cinnamon over the flames. Blow out. Drink, but be careful not to burn your mouth.

Rebecca

Creating a cocktail for a special occasion or a friend, or a combination of both, might be a daunting affair—so much could go wrong, and then **it's all on your shoulders**. But by keeping the recipe fairly simple, and by knowing your audience, you may end up with a sipper as scrumptious as the Rebecca.

I first made the Rebecca to celebrate Seattle-area bon vivant Rebecca Staffel's departure from Amazon.com, where she was the long-time cookbooks editor. Rebecca loves her bubbly, so I knew I wanted to use a little Champagne and, at the time, I had just moved into a house boasting a large raspberry patch in the backyard, so I knew I wanted to add a few of those to the mix. After that, the other ingredients practically flew off the shelves, begging to be a part of it.

Ice cubes

2 ounces **vodka** (if you have raspberry-infused vodka, don't shy away from using it)

1 ounce **Chambord** or **other raspberry-flavored liqueur**

4 or 5 **frozen raspberries**

Chilled Champagne

1. Fill a cocktail shaker halfway full with ice cubes. Add the vodka, and then the Chambord. Shake for at least 10 seconds.

2. Add the frozen raspberries to a cocktail glass. Strain the vodka-Chambord arrangement into the glass over the raspberries.

3. Top off the glass with Champagne (don't feel the need to overflow, though—you want to be able to serve this without fear of spillage).

⬆ *A Note: If possible, use raspberries that have been freshly picked, gently washed, carefully dried, and quickly frozen. The frozen raspberries not only provide a sweet and tangy treat once they meet the mouth at the end of the drink, but they also help to keep the ingredients chilled.*

"There comes a time in every woman's life when **the only thing that helps** is a glass of Champagne."

KIT MARLOWE (Bette Davis), in *Old Acquaintance*, 1943

Red Carpet

Created one spring by me and my boss at the time (see, the workers and the bosses can get along, as long as there are bosses like Ara Jane Olufson), the Red Carpet was specifically invented for use as a fresh signature cocktail at an Academy Award–watching party. To match the occasion, **something a bit bubbly, a bit classy sounding**, and still a bit silly was demanded. The Red Carpet fits that Hollywood bill perfectly.

It uses sour cherry syrup, which will be available at the gourmet food store that I hope is right up the block. (Doesn't everyone have a gourmet food store up the block? If not, whom can we blame?) If you can't hunt down the sour cherry syrup, try 3 parts grenadine to 1 part fresh lemon juice. While talking substitutions, if orange-flavored soda water is scarce in your neighborhood, use regular club soda with a splash of freshly squeezed orange juice added to the shaker.

Ice cubes

1½ ounces **gin**

¾ ounce **sour cherry syrup**

Chilled orange-flavored club soda

Orange slice for garnish

Fresh cherry for garnish (or maraschino, if fresh is not available)

1. Fill a cocktail shaker halfway full with ice cubes. Add the gin and sour cherry syrup. Shake well, knowing that the paparazzi are watching your every move.

2. Fill a highball glass halfway full with ice cubes. Strain the mix into the glass.

3. Top off the glass with club soda. Garnish with the orange slice and the cherry (2 cherries if you pick all the winners on that particular Oscar night).

Sabra

Intriguing, isn't it? While the name means, in Hebrew, "cactus flower," this drink as I've read about it and made it doesn't contain cactus or cactus juice and sadly isn't even garnished with a cactus flower (though if a cactus flower is readily available and edible, you should give it a whirl). The Sabra is **an austere and balanced duo,** with vodka and Godiva chocolate liqueur, and fits those evenings when you want to wind down with a dessert-style drink, but don't want to go overboard on the sweetness. I've seen it served as a shot, but I like it cocktail style, sipped and with a garnish.

Ice cubes

1½ ounces **orange-** or **mandarin-flavored vodka**

1½ ounces **Godiva chocolate liqueur** or **other chocolate liqueur**

Orange slice for garnish

1. Fill a cocktail shaker halfway full with ice cubes. Add the vodka and chocolate liqueur. Shake well.

2. Strain into a cocktail glass. Garnish with the orange slice.

⊙ *A Note: This is a somewhat delicate drink, and therefore it looks best with a light garnish. With this in mind, try using a satsuma tangerine or mandarin orange slice rather than a regular orange slice.*

Six Historic Bars

They may have changed in atmosphere and ownership since they first became highlights on the tour of historic bar spots. They may get a little crowded, or they may be more off the beaten path. However, these six bars are worthy pilgrimages for any cocktail lover, because they've birthed some incredible combinations.

1. Harry's Bar, Venice, Italy: birthplace of the Bellini (page 373)
2. The Waldorf-Astoria, New York, New York: birthplace of the Bronx cocktail (page 22)
3. Harry's New York Bar, Paris, France: birthplace of the Bloody Mary (page 21)
4. Locke-Ober, Boston, Massachusetts: birthplace of the Ward Eight (page 140)
5. Long Bar, Singapore: birthplace of the Singapore Sling (page 399)
6. The Carousel Bar, New Orleans, Louisiana: birthplace of the Vieux Carré (page 140)

Silver Streak

It's reassuring to know that the modern cocktail revolution stretches worldwide (much like the cocktail heydays of the past), and that there are powerful practitioners of the art everywhere you can land a plane (and many places you can't). Speaking of fine shakers outside of the United States, one of the best bar scribes in Britain is Ben Reed, who has a number of books brilliant in drinks and looks. The following recipe is taken from his book, *The Art of the Cocktail* (Ryland Peters & Small, 2004), and harkens back to past last calls in its **lovely simplicity** and use of kümmel (a liqueur made at least partially from caraway seeds that doubles as a digestif).

Ice cubes

1 ounce **vodka**

1 ounce **kümmel**

⬆ *A Note: If your vodka is already chilled, feel free to skip step 1 and just pour the vodka over the ice.*

1. Fill a cocktail shaker halfway full with ice cubes. Add the vodka. Shake well.

2. Fill a rocks or other short, squat glass with ice cubes. Strain the vodka over the ice.

3. Add the kümmel. Stir with aggression.

Social

For many, it's Mondays. For me, it's Tuesdays. For some, even Wednesdays are that deadliest day of the week, the day lips don't even form "hello" when walking past friends in the halls or city streets, where the number of words one feels like speaking could barely fill a thimble (if words had weight and took up space, that is). Circumvent *your* normally silent day by prescribing yourself a few Socials before any social situations. They **loosen the tongue and lighten the spirit.**

2 **orange slices**

Ice cubes

1½ ounces **vodka**

¾ ounce **Citrónge liqueur**

2 dashes **orange bitters**

⬆ *A Note: Citrónge liqueur is created by combining a grain alcohol, bittersweet Jamaican and Haitian oranges, cane sugar, and magic. See page 63 for more Citrónge background.*

1. Add 1 orange slice to a cocktail shaker or mixing glass. Using a muddler or long wooden spoon, muddle the slice well (this is a good way to relieve aggression, too).

2. Fill the cocktail shaker halfway full with ice cubes. Add the vodka, Citrónge, and orange bitters. Shake 3 times.

3. Strain the mix into a cocktail glass. Garnish with the second orange slice. Speak freely.

Sookie Cocktail

Not only does it claim a fascinating name (which rhymes so well in so many situations), the Sookie Cocktail also claims an engaging mix of flavors that crisscross the globe, using Kahana Royale Macadamia Nut Liqueur and Maker's Mark Kentucky bourbon (or, if you have to, a comparable bourbon). It's all accented by just a splash of freshly squeezed orange juice. **Sounds nutty?** You bet, but that's what makes it an excellent choice for a night of madcap gaming (I suggest the word-making game Quiddler) or a night of watching Marx Brothers movies, starting with *Duck Soup*.

Ice cubes

1½ ounces **Maker's Mark Kentucky bourbon**

1 ounce **Kahana Royale Macadamia Nut Liqueur**

½ ounce **freshly squeezed orange juice**

1. Fill a cocktail shaker halfway full with ice cubes. Add the bourbon, macadamia liqueur, and orange juice. Shake well, as if being chased by a rottweiler who might just take a nip from your backside if you don't shake ferociously enough.

2. Strain into a cocktail glass and serve.

⬆ *A Note: Kahana Royale Macadamia Nut Liqueur is made from roasted macadamias blended with the always mysterious "exotic natural flavorings." A little sweet, it works well in cocktails, solo over ice, or paired with vanilla ice cream for a delish dessert.*

"Bourbon's the only drink. You can take **all that Champagne stuff** and pour it down the English Channel."

MRS. STEVENS (Jessie Royce Landis), in *To Catch a Thief*, 1955

Sunsplash

With the ease of travel in this modern world, is it any surprise at all that folks head toward the beaches in huge numbers? Luckily, there are innovative drinks continually being created to keep those beaches full of happy vacationers. Luckily, also, many of these new mixes, such as the Sunsplash, feature **a virtuous amount of fresh citrus** and other juices, to make sure that the beach-goers stay somewhat healthy and hydrated.

Ice cubes

1½ ounces **orange-flavored vodka**

1 ounce **freshly squeezed orange juice**

½ ounce **Cointreau**

½ ounce **freshly squeezed lime juice**

½ ounce **cranberry juice cocktail**

Lime slice for garnish

1. Fill a cocktail shaker halfway full with ice cubes. Add the vodka, orange juice, Cointreau, lime juice, and cranberry juice cocktail. Shake well.

2. Strain into a large cocktail glass. Garnish with the lime slice, a pair of flip-flops, and a swimsuit. How revealing a suit is up to you.

A VARIATION: Want to up the refreshing ante of your Sunsplash? Try straining the mixture into a highball glass half full of ice cubes, and then topping it with chilled 7UP or Sprite. Call it a Bubblesplash.

Let's Get This Party Started

Most folks have their own opinion of what to slip into the CD player to turn a dull bar into a rollicking good time or to liven up a party that's missing a step. But if you for some odd reason all of a sudden find yourself unsure of whom to turn to in these situations, then I suggest one of these songs (which cover a wide spectrum of tastes):

1. Rolling Stones, "Street Fighting Man"
2. Devo, "Gut Feeling"
3. James Brown, "Get Up (I Feel Like Being a) Sex Machine, Pt. 1"
4. Stooges, "Search and Destroy"
5. Public Enemy, "My Uzi Weighs a Ton"
6. Willie Nelson, "Whiskey River"
7. Minutemen, "I Felt Like a Gringo"

Chartreuse

In 1605, the monks at a Chartreuse monastery in Vauvert, outside Paris, were given a gift from the marshal of King Henri IV, François Hannibal d'Estrees (at this time, the Chartreuse Order of cloistered monks, or Carthusians, was already 500 years old). He presented them with a manuscript titled "An Elixir of Long Life." An antique, the manuscript wasn't even completely understood at first, but slowly it was transcribed. The manuscript described, and had a recipe for, a healing elixir. The deciphering of the manuscript took so long that the elixir didn't begin being used by the monks until 1737, at which time it was renamed Chartreuse Elixir, and sold in limited quantities to the public. Though its history has taken many turns since then (including one that had the liqueur made in Spain, when the monks were exiled in 1903), that same recipe is still made today, and only in France.

There are now four variations of Chartreuse: Elixir Végétal de la Grande-Chartreuse, extra aged V.E.P. Chartreuse, and the better known Green Chartreuse and Yellow Chartreuse. The recipes (ingredients and preparation techniques) for these liqueurs are known only by two monks at any given time, but it is known that 130 herbs, roots, leaves, spices, and other natural products are contained within Chartreuse, and that the liqueur is placed into oak casks to mature before being bottled and delivered worldwide. Green Chartreuse has a strong, herbal taste, which warms as it travels through the body, and while Yellow Chartreuse echoes the Green's herbal nature, it is sweeter and milder. Both are best served cold, either solo on the rocks or mixed into a shaken cocktail.

Supersonic

I'm not going to get all rah-rah here, or jump out of the stands and **tear down the hoop**, but you aren't a real fan if you haven't devoured a drink named after your favorite sports team. And if your top team doesn't have a drink, try this one, tagged after *my* b-ball heroes, the Seattle Supersonics. If you like it, maybe you should switch loyalties?

Ice cubes

1½ ounces **gin**

1 ounce **green Chartreuse**

½ ounce **freshly squeezed lime juice**

Splash of **Simple Syrup** (page 7)

Lime twist for garnish

1. Fill a cocktail shaker halfway full with ice cubes. Add the gin, Chartreuse, lime juice, and simple syrup. Shake in a dunking motion.

2. Strain into a cocktail glass. Squeeze the lime twist over the drink, and then shoot it into the glass (from 3-point range if you have the skills).

Sweet Cherry

Tall and harmonious, Sweet Cherries are perfect when having a patio or porch soirée that rests between "mellow" and "complete relaxation." A little soft and sweet music on the stereo (some early '60s pop works well in this situation), lightweight shoes and no socks on the feet, a series of simple snacks (perhaps basic bruschetta with basil, tomatoes, and olive oil paired up with pear and Pecorino slices), and a Sweet Cherry for each attendee **makes the afternoon a better place**.

Lemon slice

5 to 8 leaves **fresh mint**

Ice cubes

1 ounce **Stolichnaya Vanil vodka**

1 ounce **Effen black cherry vodka**

½ ounce **maraschino liqueur**

½ ounce **freshly squeezed lemon juice**

Chilled club soda

Cherry (a Bing cherry, if possible) for garnish

1. Add the lemon slice and mint leaves to a Collins glass. Using a muddler or wooden spoon, muddle well.

2. Fill the glass three-quarters full with ice cubes. Add the vanilla and black cherry vodkas, maraschino liqueur, and lemon juice. Stir breezily.

3. Top off the glass with club soda. Stir again, and again, and once again. Garnish with the Bing cherry.

This Year's Model

The jury remains out on whether **this preferred pet** got its title from the Elvis Costello album, from the creator's admiration of the latest Corvette featured on the lot, or from a particularly catty male or female walking the runways to display contemporary fall fashions. The jury is in on using freshly squeezed orange juice here, though, and the verdict is a resounding "yes." The jury still debates on whether to garnish this cocktail with a single pineapple chunk set in the glass's bottom or speared on a toothpick, or to garnish with a half-wheel of pineapple draped onto the glass's rim. Guess what? You are the jury.

Ice cubes

1½ ounces **white rum**

½ ounce **apricot brandy**

½ ounce **freshly squeezed orange juice**

½ ounce **fresh pineapple juice**

Pineapple chunk for garnish (or a pineapple half-wheel if courageous and hungry)

1. Fill a cocktail shaker halfway full with ice cubes. Add the rum, brandy, orange juice, and pineapple juice. Shake well.

2. Strain into a cocktail glass. Garnish with one of the pineapple options mentioned above.

Thug Passion

Okay, it may seem peculiar to feature a drink lifted from a song, but "Thug Passion" is a song by Tupac Shakur, off one of the top five rap albums of all time, *All Eyez on Me*. This would be a moot point if the drink weren't **a superior synthesis**, one that balances out the sweetness of Alizé with a drier, and more animated, Champagne. In the song, it's said that the bubbly in question needs to be Cristal, but if you substitute a lesser known, and lesser priced, dry Champagne, I don't think you'll need to hang your head in shame.

2 ounces **Alizé**

4 ounces **chilled Champagne**

Small **lemon slice** for garnish (optional)

1. Add the Alizé to a flute glass. Top off the glass with the Champagne.

2. Stir briefly. If it needs a garnish, go with a small lemon slice.

↻ A Note: *If the Champagne isn't chilled completely and utterly, add an ice cube when adding the Alizé to the glass.*

↻ Another Note: *There are now available multiple varieties of Alizé, but for this stick with the original (called, ahem, Gold Passion), a liqueur made with passionfruit juice and Cognac.*

Tidal Wave

No one doubts the damage that a genuine tidal wave is capable of inflicting. However, the shared name shouldn't frighten you away from this bracing and fruity brew. It does feature two liquors, though, so don't overconsume. Instead, think of this solely as a miniature tidal wave, one that has only **enough oomph for refreshing** you or any others who are partaking, and not as a phenomenon that could pull up trees by the roots.

Ice cubes

1½ ounces **cranberry juice cocktail**

1 ounce **white rum**

1 ounce **orange-flavored vodka**

½ ounce **freshly squeezed lime juice**

Lime slice for garnish

1. Fill a cocktail shaker halfway full with ice cubes. Add the cranberry juice, rum, vodka, and lime juice. Shake well, to the beat, of course.

2. Strain into a cocktail glass. Garnish with the slice of lime, some seriously high boots, and a sparkly shirt.

A VARIATION: Make this even more refreshing by straining the shaken mixture into a highball glass half full of ice cubes. Then top it off with club soda. Stir well, garnish with the lime, and start shaking that rump.

Tuscan Mule

When you make a first trip (or second, third, or fourth trip) to the central interior of Italy, be it central Tuscany or Umbria, and you're relaxing on a hilltop (perhaps the most beautiful hilltop you've ever been on) outside of your beautiful rented villa (try www.amicivillas.com if you haven't yet picked a favorite villa hook-up), and the sun is sinking, but still high enough in the sky that you need to be cooled down a bit for maximum enjoyment and need a liquid sidekick to the Pecorino, olive oil, and bread, whip together a Tuscan Mule. After one, **you may be inspired to paint** or sculpt a bit; after two you may want to stay in Italy indefinitely; after three you may start singing Verdi's *Nabucco*; and after four you may start braying like a mule. So, stick to three—there's no call for an international incident.

Ice cubes

1½ ounces **Tuaca**

Chilled ginger ale

Lime wedge for garnish

1. Fill a highball glass with ice cubes. Add the Tuaca.

2. Top off the glass with ginger ale (leave about ¼ inch at the top to avoid spilling and killing the grass).

3. Squeeze the lime wedge over the glass, and then drop it in. Stir well. *Salute!*

Urban Bourbon

Sophisticates should enjoy this chic sipper, which combines the musculature of bourbon with the vanilla tang of Tuaca. Whether drinking this with gentlemen or ladies, I think it should be understood that all outfits must be refined and cool—**no suit coats sporting patches on the arms** allowed. The apparel attitude apparent at any gathering featuring the Urban Bourbon underlines this drink's ability to shine as the feature cocktail at a dress-up holiday party, especially those occurring during winter (the bourbon provides a warming that's welcome in winter).

Ice cubes

2 ounces **bourbon**

¾ ounce **Tuaca**

Lemon twist for garnish

1. Fill a cocktail shaker halfway full with ice cubes. Add the bourbon and Tuaca. Shake well.

2. Strain into a cocktail glass. Garnish with the lemon twist.

Vodka Slippery Knob

I first wandered into this captivatingly named drink while perusing a laminated one-page listing of alcoholic favorites. It was laminated, I'm guessing, to make it easy to wipe off when a little unexpected spillage occurs. Keep that in mind and watch the pouring when making this Martini cousin for a sophisticated gathering—the classics book club, for example, or the monthly philosophical society meeting. There's no call to serve a cocktail with this kind of a name in an uneducated setting.

Ice cubes

2½ ounces **vodka**

½ ounce **Grand Marnier**

Lemon twist for garnish

1. Fill a cocktail shaker or mixing glass halfway full with ice cubes. Add the vodka and Grand Marnier. Stir well, being careful not to let anything spill over the edges.

2. Strain into a cocktail glass. Garnish with the lemon twist.

⊕ **A Note:** An orange slice can sub for the lemon twist here.

"Wine is **bottled poetry**."

ROBERT LOUIS STEVENSON

Whistling Orange

The contest is thus: After two or three Whistling Oranges, see which brunch reveler (I say brunch because the Whistling Orange was **born for weekend brunches**) has the whistling chops to indulge everyone within hearing distance with a whistled version of at least the first verse and chorus of the Rolling Stones's classic, "Satisfaction." I choose that song because of its recognizable licks, and also because this mirrors the song in its purity, simplicity of construction, and citrusy essence.

2 ounces **chilled freshly squeezed orange juice**

2 dashes **orange bitters**

6 ounces **chilled white wine** (see Note)

1. Add the orange juice and orange bitters to a white wine glass. Stir once with a graceful spoon.

2. Add the chilled white wine. Stir once more (with the graceful spoon).

⊕ *A Note: When choosing a white wine for the Whistling Orange, pick one that's dry, light, and not too sweet, such as a good Sauvignon Blanc.*

⊕ *Another Note: It may be necessary to add a single ice cube to the drink if the orange juice isn't chilled. Serving it even slightly warm won't have anyone whistling.*

Yellow Cake

Is this drink as good as the yellow cake your grand-mother, or aunt, or mother made when you were a wee lad or lass? Doubtful. Would it translate into **an agreeable accompaniment** to a huge slice of that yellow cake right now, today, this instant? Definitely.

Ice cubes

1 ounce **vanilla-flavored vodka**

1 ounce **Cointreau**

1 ounce **fresh pineapple juice**

Lemon twist for garnish (optional)

1. Fill a cocktail shaker halfway full with ice cubes. Add the vodka, Cointreau, and pineapple juice. Shake well.

2. Strain into a cocktail glass. Garnish with the lemon twist, if you'd like. (I like my Yellow Cake to have just a hint of lemon in it. If you don't, leave the twist out.)

An Obscure Reliquary

The night is dark and cloudy, with no moon in sight, the hour is midnight, there's a raven circling above, in the distance an animal howls, and an icy wind rages across the hills and catches you right under the chin.

Wait, is that a dragging footstep in the distance? A peg-legged man? Is that slight squawking you hear a bicycle creeping up, or a skeleton's bones or the whispered tones of a cowled character speaking in a foreign dialect? It's getting closer, and closer, and closer. Should you run? Hide? Scream?

Instead of letting the neck hairs stand on end, introduce yourself without fear to the cast of unnatural-sounding liquid delights, lesser-known bar characters, and calamitously titled cocktails that make up An Obscure Reliquary. Blow the dust off of this chapter's contents and become surrounded by a few of the most dangerous drinks, designed to ward off serious storms by inviting the monsters into the room. Of course, the only thing you really have to fear is a hangover (in certain situations), or that you'll be guilty by association when the crimes in the chapter are released to the light of day.

You doubt me? You have no dread of walking with the Black Dog over the Blood and Sand? Going face to face with Green Dragon, the Jabberwock, or the Rattlesnake? Becoming acquainted with the arcane knowledge of the Corpse Reviver, Satan's Whiskers, or Widow's Kiss doesn't cause your stomach to flutter and your hands to quiver? You, bold one, courageous one, heroic one, are made of stern and strong stuff—but be sure to carry a golden shaker and a strainer made of pure silver.

Or, maybe, you actually like to walk on that dark side a bit, even enjoy facing up to the more far-out fancies, and think that dancing with Zombies or Black Friars under the full moon is a kick in the pants. Or maybe you yearn for new experiences in all forms, whether it's consuming Monkey Brains and Nude Eels or sidling up to Godfathers and Presbyterians. These, then, are the drinks for you and your partners in crime—the amalgamations served up not to ward off the strange and scary, but to welcome them. Drink deep and welcome the weirdness that transpires, but don't say when waking up tomorrow that I didn't warn you.

Asylum

After a few of these, **you may never want to check out**. In David Wondrich's *Esquire Drinks* (Hearst Publishing, 2002), a bedlam you'd be smart to check in to, if you've the liver and courage, this potion is attributed to William Seabrook, who wrote a tome about his time in Haiti and blood voodoo baptisms as well as a second volume about his time in the white jacket in the white rooms trying to break his booze habit. Said second volume is titled *Asylum*. Call the shrinks.

Ice cubes

1½ ounces **Pernod**

1½ ounces **gin**

½ ounce **grenadine**

1. Add 3 to 5 ice cubes to an old-fashioned glass. Add the Pernod, gin, and grenadine, under lock and key.

2. Stir well with a bar spoon, stirring rod, or set of keys.

Five Darn Good Dive Bars

On one particular episode of *The Simpsons*, an unsuspecting sweatered gentleman wanders into Moe's Tavern from a newly created Springfield walking mall (after going through a long tunnel). Once there, he declares, "This isn't a faux dive, this is a dive." Walk into any of the following bars thinking that they'll be "faux" and you'll be sorry. Walk in looking for a fine American dive, and you'll be ecstatic.

1. Pete's Pub, Boston, Massachusetts
2. O'Connor's, Brooklyn, New York
3. Inner Town Pub, Chicago, Illinois
4. Dirty Frank's Bar, Philadelphia, Pennsylvania
5. Dive Bar, Cleveland, Ohio

Black Dog

If you're out walking 'round midnight during a regular rip-snorter, with lightning, rain, thunder, etc., and it suddenly goes dead calm, and you see a black dog ahead, with eyes like pulsing hearts, teeth like knives, and a cavernous growl that seems to emanate from the earth itself, please don't feel the need to stop by and tell me about it. If you believe old wives' tales, you should spend your last two hours in this mortal coil in a more fitting manner. If your Black Dog sighting is of the liquid variety, it's another story entirely. Not that I'm promising you will be bound for a run of blameless luck, or will avoid the next life-stopping afternoon with the in-laws, or should bet the Porsche on the next hand without even flipping your hole cards. However, the chances of ending up with teeth marks in your posterior are much, much reduced.

Ice cubes

2 ounces **dark rum**

1 ounce **dry vermouth**

Lemon twist for garnish

1. Fill a cocktail shaker halfway full with ice cubes. Add the dark rum and vermouth. Shake as if being chased by Black Pete himself.

2. Strain the mix into a cocktail glass. Squeeze the lemon twist over the darkness, and then let it descend. Doesn't it look somewhat like a deadly canine eye watching you?

A VARIATION: Some appreciate this with a black olive instead of a lemon twist. I am not counted among those worthies.

Black Friar

The Black Friar cocktail is less potent than the Inquisition, though it is a long-cowled stride rougher than badger Friar Tuck in the animated 1973 *Robin Hood*. Featuring both vodka and whiskey brought under the service of coffee liqueur, the Black Friar speaks a serious sermon indeed. If your sentiment is sitting firmly in "moody artist" realm (too much existential literature or too much time staring at Francis Bacon paintings?), my proposition is to throw a party that features dueling Black Dogs and Black Friars. Make everyone wear bright orange, yellow, and red T-shirts and shorts under the black turtlenecks and jeans, though, because after a few rounds folks'll be more looped than pooped.

Ice cubes

2 ounces **coffee liqueur** (Kahlúa works fine)

1 ounce **vodka**

1 ounce **whiskey** (I suggest a neutral blended variety)

1. Fill a cocktail shaker halfway full with ice cubes. Add the coffee liqueur, vodka, and whiskey. Shake well.

2. Strain into a cocktail glass. And cheer up.

⊕ *A Tip: If this feels a little naked (and we all know how bad that is), garnish each drink by floating 3 coffee beans on top.*

"Let us **open a bottle** and do our best to save each other's souls."

FRIAR TUCK (Michael McShane), in *Robin Hood: Prince of Thieves*, 1991

Blood and Sand

While sounding south of uncomfortable in both name and ingredient list, the Blood and Sand is actually a pleasing companion in no way related to a shark attack. It even has an undercurrent of sweetness, much like a repentant villain at the end of a splattery movie. I've been told by a reliable source that this one makes the ideal accomplice to the monthly horror movie gathering—refuse this advice at your own risk.

Ice cubes

¾ ounce **Scotch**

¾ ounce **cherry brandy**

¾ ounce **sweet vermouth**

¾ ounce **freshly squeezed orange juice**

Orange slice for garnish

1. Fill a cocktail shaker halfway full with ice cubes. Add the Scotch, cherry brandy, sweet vermouth, and orange juice. Shake well.

2. Strain into a cocktail glass. Garnish with the orange slice (unless it's been kidnapped).

Brain Hemorrhage

Many may feel that this distressingly named drink better belongs in the Collegiate Classics chapter (if anyone in the room over the age of 30 has ordered this, it's okay to shake your head in despair). However, my take is that this nasty trick is best served during the weekly viewing of a hospital soap (daytime or evening), as those shows seem to revel a bit in the gross-out factor, while maintaining, at least in the evening, a sheen of respectability.

Ice cubes

1½ ounces **peach schnapps**

1 ounce **Bailey's Irish Cream** or **other cream liqueur**

½ ounce **grenadine**

1. Fill a small wine glass with ice cubes. Add the peach schnapps.

2. Float the Bailey's on top of the schnapps (pouring it slowly over the back of a spoon if necessary, to avoid mixing it with the schnapps).

3. Drizzle the grenadine over the Bailey's. Do not stir. Ooky, isn't it?

⬆ *A Note: Many serve this as a shot, but I find the swirling brainy-ness better in a glass. If shooting, cut back to ¾ ounce schnapps and ½ ounce Bailey's.*

Caipirinha

No longer on the same continent as the "obscure" or "bloody-and-odd" or "wacky" others in this chapter, the Caipirinha (pronounced ki-pea-REE-nya) has become a **belle of the bar** recently. The national drink of Brazil, the Caipirinha uses cachaça, a liquor distilled from sugar cane that's becoming more and more available at stateside liquor stores. This means that the samba can start up for your at-home Carnival on any of the 365 days of the year. If you invite me, don't expect me to wear that tiny bikini with all the sparklies and tassels. It's plumb tattered from overusage.

½ **lime,** cut into quarters

1 tablespoon **light** or **dark brown sugar**

Cracked ice

2 ounces **cachaça**

1. Add 3 of the lime quarters and the brown sugar to a mixing glass or cocktail shaker. Muddle well (pretend that you're in a conga line and that the person whose hips you're holding is a very good dancer).

2. Fill an old-fashioned glass three-quarters full with cracked ice. Add the cachaça.

3. Pour the lime-sugar muddle into the glass with the cachaça. Stir well, making sure the sugar dissolves completely.

4. Garnish the glass with the remaining lime wedge.

A VARIATION: No cachaça? Vodka works well in its place (if not traditionally accurate), as long as the name changes to Caipiroska.

Captain's Blood

Argh, shiver me timbers, and yo-ho-ho. If the Captain's Blood is flowing across the mizzenmast, it may be time to **give up the ship**. Or invite the marauders over, where you can splice the mainbrace in proper fashion—eye patches, peg-legs, cutlasses, and black hats required.

Ice cubes

2½ ounces **dark rum**

½ ounce **freshly squeezed lime juice**

2 dashes **orange bitters**

Lime slice for garnish

1. Fill a cocktail shaker halfway full with ice cubes. Add the dark rum, lime juice, and orange bitters. Shake, matey, shake.

2. Strain into a cocktail glass and garnish with the lime slice.

Corpse Reviver

After a night of Zombies (page 242), Brain Hemorrhages (page 204), Scorpions (page 316), and Your Favorite Aunts (page 240), even the most constitutionally sound are bound to feel a bit under-the-ground the next A.M. In those, ahem, dead situations, the Corpse Reviver is **assured to bring one back to life**. Or at least it will get you to sit up straight and take notice of the morning's brightness.

Ice cubes

1½ ounces **brandy**

1½ ounces **applejack** (or apple brandy)

¾ ounce **sweet vermouth**

1. Fill a cocktail shaker halfway full with ice cubes. Add the brandy, applejack, and sweet vermouth. Shake well.

2. Strain the mix into a cocktail glass. Garnish with a tombstone, if a small one is available.

"It's **alive**, alive!"

DR. HENRY FRANKENSTEIN (Colin Clive), in *Frankenstein*, 1931

Dark and Stormy

It was a dark and stormy kind of night. A shot rang out. No, wait, a highball rang out. It was **tall, and bubbly, and unflappable,** but with a kick that could knock you out of bed in the morning and get you to make breakfast, or at least make the bed, after a night solving mysteries (even if it's solely the game of Clue) and drinking Dark and Stormys with a whole force of friends. Who got to wear the fedora and who the trench coat? That's the true mystery.

Ice cubes

2 ounces **dark rum**

Chilled ginger beer

Lime wedge for garnish

⬆ **A Note:** *From the real detectives polled, it was determined that the Dark and Stormy should always be made with Bermudan dark rum.*

1. Fill a highball glass three-quarters full with ice cubes. Add the dark rum.

2. Top it off very carefully with ginger beer. Not too fast, or you'll be spotted by the dame or dude you've been tailing. And you'll spill ginger beer all over the countertop.

3. Squeeze the lime over the top, and then let it drop in like a shoe (a gumshoe, that is).

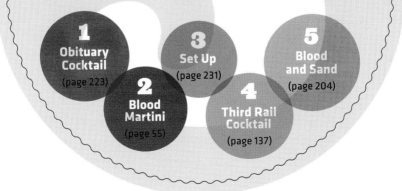

5 Cocktails to Kill While Reading Agatha Christie

Dame Agatha has millions of copies of her mysteries in print and legions of fans (still), and yet no one has suggested the right alcohol accompaniment for paging through any of her great Hercule Poirot or Miss Marple whodunits. Until now, that is. If Agatha Christie isn't your mystery writer of choice, I think these go down easy (easier than arsenic) with other writers, too (even the more hardboiled like Raymond Chandler and modern masters like Walter Mosley), as long as murder is served alongside.

1 Obituary Cocktail (page 223)

2 Blood Martini (page 55)

3 Set Up (page 231)

4 Third Rail Cocktail (page 137)

5 Blood and Sand (page 204)

Devil Cocktail

This little charmer matches up well with the many fables of Mr. Scratch, in that it **has a sweet tongue but a fiery aftertaste**. In this case, it's not the brimstone heating things up, but a pinch of cayenne. Because of the heat, no matter your religious preferences or lack thereof, follow the golden "do unto others" rule and be gentle when preparing this drink.

Ice cubes

2 ounces **brandy**

½ ounce **white crème de menthe** (green works, too, but looks yucky)

Pinch of **cayenne pepper**

1. Fill a cocktail shaker halfway full with ice cubes. Add the brandy, crème de menthe, and cayenne pepper (wash your hands after adding the cayenne or you'll be sorry later in the evening). Shake well.

2. Strain into a cocktail glass. Garnish with a glass of water, or some good bread and cheese to soothe the burning sensation.

LIQUEUR SPOTLIGHT
Dubonnet

A relative of the vermouth family, Dubonnet is a French fortified wine that has been flavored with herbs, spices, and quinine. Dubonnet traces back to French wine agent Joseph Dubonnet, who in 1846 decided that he wanted to make his own flavored fortified wine (many varieties had become popular by that time). As bitters, mostly in "medicinal" mixes, were very popular, he decided to flavor his wine with quinine as well as herbs. To balance out the quinine, he used a sweeter Greek wine. Originally he served his concoction only to friends and family, but his combination soon became so popular that he began selling it to the general public. Today, there are two versions of Dubonnet: Rouge, or red, is made from red wine that's been flavored with a bit of quinine and assorted spices, with a slightly sweeter result; Dubonnet blanc, also called white or blond, is made from white wine, with herbs and quinine added. The result is dryer than the rouge version. Both are drunk as apéritifs, and also mixed in many different cocktails.

Dog's Nose

An oldie from within what David A. Embury calls the "Arf and Arf" theme, this tail-wagger might cause consternation to those not taking the time to take it out for a walk, due to the awkward pairing of gin and porter. But give it a try on a rainy late fall afternoon and see how surprisingly ideal it is. Thank Mr. Charles Dickens, who mentions it first in *The Pickwick Papers* and also in the lesser-known, but amazing, *Our Mutual Friend*. If it was **good enough for Dickens**, then it should still hold up for today's dogs.

12 ounces **porter**

1½ ounces **gin**

½ ounce **Simple Syrup** (page 7)

Freshly grated nutmeg

1. Add the porter to a heavy saucepan. Slowly heat it up over medium heat (if you're in a hurry, use the microwave), but don't let it boil.

2. Once the porter is good and warm, pour it into a large, heatproof glass. Add the gin and simple syrup. Stir well.

3. Sprinkle nutmeg over the top of the drink. Don't add too much (there's no need for a full layer of nutmeg), but be sure to use enough so that the aroma makes the rain recede.

⊕ *A Note:* *If you feel the plain simple syrup is too light, try this one with simple syrup made from brown sugar.*

"For the rest, both the tap and parlour of the Six Jolly Fellowship Porters gave upon the river, and had red curtains matching the noses of the regular customers, and were provided with comfortable fireside tin utensils, **like models of sugar-loaf hats**, made in that shape that they might, with their pointed ends, seek out for themselves glowing nooks in the depths of the red coals, when they mulled your ale, or heated for you those delectable drinks, Purl, Flip, and Dog's Nose."

CHARLES DICKENS, *Our Mutual Friend*, 1865

East India Cocktail

This mix points to two things. First, the East India Company must have had **tremendous power in the biz world** of yesteryear (there aren't many cocktails named after sixteenth-century trading powers). And, second, even giant implacable companies often go adrift, leaving only sugary cocktails in their wake (which points out another fact—be gentle with the syrup here, or this one might be trouble on the teeth).

Ice cubes

1½ ounces **brandy**

1 ounce **orange curaçao**

¼ ounce **maraschino liqueur**

¼ ounce **raspberry syrup**

2 dashes **Angostura bitters**

Lime wedge for garnish

1. Fill a cocktail shaker halfway full with ice cubes. Add the brandy, curaçao, maraschino liqueur, raspberry syrup, and Angostura bitters. Shake well.

2. Strain into a cocktail glass. Squeeze the lime wedge over the glass, and then let it leave your fingers and sail into the glass as if it were a ship leaving port.

El Presidente

Don't get stuck in front of the firing line at the next insurrection. (I'm postulating that most take part in at least two revolutions. If this isn't the case, tell me why the neighbors keep screaming in my direction? Could their repeated chants of "quit that racket" not equal a call to arms in the name of liberty?) Have an El Presidente **ready to strain at a moment's notice,** to placate whomever wins that final battle.

Ice cubes

1½ ounces **white rum**

½ ounce **dry vermouth**

½ ounce **freshly squeezed lime juice**

½ ounce **grenadine**

Lime twist for garnish

1. Fill a cocktail shaker halfway full with ice cubes. Add the rum, dry vermouth, lime juice, and grenadine. Shake in a marching fashion.

2. Strain into a cocktail glass. Garnish with the lime twist and a reactionary viewpoint. If you must, a small toy machine gun may also be used as a garnish.

Fog Cutter

Behold the relentlessness of the sea, hammering the beaches in sun, rain, and fog—the last being the most dangerous, with air like proverbial pea soup and the haunting ship's horns **bellowing like a dangerous sea beast** while good sailors hold the mizzenmast (or any old mast) and pray that the lighthouse opens this particular dark night and calls them in to safety. One would think that as the lighthouse cuts the fog with clearer sailing and safe harboring in mind, a sweeping drink called the Fog Cutter would operate the same function for those in a sea of bars. Well, one might *think* that, but one would be wrong, as the Fog Cutter tends toward making those sailing in it foggier, and not less so. There are three boozy beasts that form this fog machine (rum, brandy, and gin). The classic sherry float on top adds another layer of haze, too. This is not to be taken when actually piloting a ship, no matter what the cargo.

Ice cubes

2 ounces **freshly squeezed orange juice**

1½ ounces **white rum**

1 ounce **brandy**

1 ounce **freshly squeezed lemon juice**

½ ounce **gin**

½ ounce **orgeat syrup**

¼ ounce **sherry**

Orange slice for garnish

1. Fill a cocktail shaker halfway full with ice cubes. Add the orange juice, rum, brandy, lemon juice, gin, and orgeat syrup. Shake well.

2. Fill a highball glass three-quarters full with ice cubes. Strain the shaken fog into the glass. Top with the sherry. Garnish with the orange slice and a lifejacket.

A Note: Orgeat is an almond-flavored syrup, best known for its key role in the Mai Tai (page 29). It's available in gourmet and specialty food stores and sometimes in coffee shops.

Godfather

Someday, and that day may never come, I'll call upon you to do a service for me. It will be a service involving bourbon and amaretto (but not too much amaretto) over ice. I'll say, stir it, but not too much. And **if I'm feeling generous**, I'll let you serve it with a Sicily-shaped stir stick.

Ice cubes

2½ ounces **bourbon**

1 ounce **amaretto**

1. Fill an old-fashioned or similar-sized glass with ice. Add the bourbon, by itself (it deserves the respect).

2. Add the amaretto. Stir 3 times (and then forget about the third movie).

Goldfish Cocktail

Shame on any reader who saw the title of this refined association and thought it would entail gulping a live goldfish. While named after one of our aquatic acquaintances, it isn't a sideshow. Instead, it is a lovely drink that may recall the sea, but may also be a first-rate accompaniment to an early evening Go Fish tournament or other card-playing soirée. Deal them quick, toss a few back, and **watch the hours swim by**.

Ice cubes

1½ ounces **gin**

¾ ounce **Goldwasser**

½ ounce **Cointreau**

¼ ounce **freshly squeezed lemon juice**

Lemon twist for garnish

1. Fill a cocktail shaker halfway full with ice cubes. Add the gin, Goldwasser, Cointreau, and lemon juice. Shake well.

2. Strain the mix into a cocktail glass. Squeeze the lemon twist over it and then drop it in.

A Note: *Goldwasser is a slightly spicy, slightly orange-flavored liqueur that contains actual gold flakes (which look like little goldfish in the above recipe, I suppose). The theory goes that the flakes were first inserted due to gold's curative powers.*

Green Dragon Cocktail

If you happen to be hiking through a remote mountainous region late on a thundering eve, and stray into a murky cave, and all of a sudden are surrounded by piles and piles of doubloons, diamonds, emeralds, etc., and you can't summon the strength to split instantly, then my suggestion is to offer the scaly owner of said hoard (I'm thinking dragon here, folks) one of these minty knockouts. And then, **when you wake up, pour one for yourself.** Or if you're just hosting a Dungeons & Dragons night for nostalgia's sake—who am I to judge?—go out of your way to acquire the ingredients for this fantasy fave. That way you can slay a number of dragons before the dragons slay you.

Lemon wedge

3 sprigs **fresh mint** or a handful of **leaves**

Ice cubes

2 ounces **gin**

¾ ounce **kümmel**

3 dashes **orange bitters**

Lemon slice for garnish

1. Add the lemon wedge and mint sprigs (or a good group of fresh mint leaves) to a mixing glass or cocktail shaker. Muddle well with a muddler, wooden spoon, or battle axe.

2. Fill the mixing glass or cocktail shaker halfway full with ice cubes. Add the gin, kümmel, and orange bitters. Shake well.

3. Pour everything, ice and all, into a small wine glass. Garnish with the lemon slice.

⬆ *A Note: Kümmel is a cumin- and caraway-flavored liqueur.*

⬆ ***Another Note:*** *In* The Savoy Cocktail Book *version of this recipe (which is the first I saw), it's made with peach bitters. I enjoy the orange, but if you can pick up the peach, give it a whirl for historical accuracy.*

A VARIATION: For some, the bruised-up mint and lemon amounts to too much dragon droppings. If this sounds like you, then strain everything into a cocktail glass in step 3 above. It won't be quite as much fun, but neither will you get mint in your mustache.

Harvey Wallbanger

Not as obscure or hazardous as others in this chapter, the Harvey Wallbanger still hovers on the outskirts of modern society. (What is a "wallbanger," many ask, with a barely discernable quiver in their voices. Is it violent? Is it underground? A 1970s sexual trend? A California surfer who liked Galliano with his screwdriver?) This wasn't always the case. In the jolly 1970s, the HW gained expansive popularity, showing up on T-shirts, buttons, and undergarments. Today, it seems almost an afterthought, or a component of the Sloe Comfortable Screw Up Against a Wall (page 348). That's a shame, honestly, because the Harvey Wallbanger is cozy both on a summer's day and as **an accompaniment to a bubble bath**. I prefer the latter (with a good book in the other hand), but try both and report back.

Ice cubes

2 ounces **vodka**

5 ounces **freshly squeezed orange juice**

½ ounce **Galliano**

1. Fill a highball glass three-quarters full with ice cubes. Add the vodka, and then the orange juice. Stir briefly.

2. Float the Galliano on top of the juice and vodka. Put your feet up. Ahhhh.

Headshrinker

If ever you've had enough of a) work; b) family; c) class (for those over-21 students); or d) work, and need a good excuse to cut out, take a breather, and have a sit-down and a refreshing beverage, I've signed off on you, saying, "Oh, I need to visit my Headshrinker," with one of those **hazy bursts of laughter** that guarantees no one follows up the statement with any further questions.

Ice cubes

1½ ounces **vodka**

1 ounce **blackberry brandy**

½ ounce **freshly squeezed lemon juice**

Lemon twist for garnish

1. Fill a cocktail shaker halfway full with ice cubes. Add the vodka, brandy, and lemon juice. Shake while shaking your head. Hey, shake your whole body. You deserve it.

2. Strain into a cocktail glass. Squeeze the lemon twist over the glass and drop it in.

Jabberwock Cocktail

Without jaws that bite or claws that catch, it may be that you don't need to beware this cocktail. However, **visions of enlarged unspeakable creatures** can occur if enough Jabberwocks are downed. Whatever you do, though, remember to shun the frumious Bandersnatch.

Ice cubes

1½ ounces **gin**

1 ounce **dry sherry**

1 ounce **Dubonnet blanc**

1 dash **orange bitters**

Lemon twist for garnish

1. Fill a large mixing glass halfway full with ice cubes. Add the gin, sherry, Dubonnet, and orange bitters.

2. Stir well. (I think stirring helps reduce the chance of the sherry getting knocked about by the gin and Dubonnet. Sherry is a little in need of protection.)

3. Strain into a cocktail glass. Squeeze the lemon twist over the top of the drink and drop it down.

A Note: Originally the Jabberwock was made with Caperitif, a South African herbal liqueur, instead of Dubonnet. Caperitif is no longer available without time travel (or at least I haven't uncovered any), hence the change in the above recipe.

Another Note: Dubonnet is a French fortified wine that has had quinine, herbs, and spices added to it. There are two versions, blanc and rouge. For more on Dubonnet, see page 207.

Jamaican Ten Speed

On the Amazon.com Web site (said company once employed this author), estimable cocktailians, authors, and all-around charmers Gary and Mardee Haidin Regan once wrote up a Cocktail of the Month column packed with history, wit, and, of course, hot cocktail recipes. As the lucky person who coordinated getting the columns posted at the right times, I always had first view and lorded that fact over my boozehound pals. **One of the most interesting mixes** I learned about through the Regans' column is the Jamaican Ten Speed. Created by Roger Gobler, who worked the bar at the Café Terra Cotta in Scottsdale, Arizona, the Jamaican Ten Speed, or J.T.S., was discovered by the Regans when they were judging a cocktail contest in Phoenix. It boasts a fairly lengthy (and sort of strange, at first glance) list of ingredients that ride together perfectly.

Ice cubes

1 ounce **vodka**

¾ ounce **Midori melon liqueur**

½ ounce **half-and-half**

¼ ounce **crème de banane**

¼ ounce **Malibu rum**

1. Fill a cocktail shaker halfway full with ice cubes. Add every other ingredient, but delicately.

2. Strain all 10 speeds into a cocktail glass. Kick down the kickstand and relax.

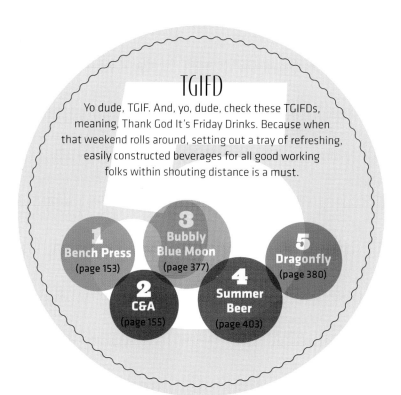

TGIFD

Yo dude, TGIF. And, yo, dude, check these TGIFDs, meaning, Thank God It's Friday Drinks. Because when that weekend rolls around, setting out a tray of refreshing, easily constructed beverages for all good working folks within shouting distance is a must.

1 Bench Press (page 153)

2 C&A (page 155)

3 Bubbly Blue Moon (page 377)

4 Summer Beer (page 403)

5 Dragonfly (page 380)

Jellyfish Cocktail →

Almost peaceful in appearance (or ghost-like, depending on your ability to see the supernatural in all things), the jellyfish lulls many into forgetting the sting those tendrils pack. This cocktail, while it won't float calmly in the ocean, does share **a potentially forgotten sting** with its namesake. Wear a wetsuit when submerging in the cocktail, as you would when swimming near the marine medusa, to avoid any unnecessary messes or stings.

Ice cubes

1½ ounces **vodka**

1½ ounces **blue curaçao**

1½ ounces **white sambuca**

½ ounce **cream**

1. Fill a highball glass with ice. Add the vodka.

2. Carefully, slowly (watch out!) drizzle in the curaçao, avoiding mixing it too much with the vodka.

3. Add the sambuca in the same manner as the curaçao.

4. Float the cream on top of the mix, pouring it slowly over the back of a spoon if necessary. Stir delicately, so that the Jellyfish doesn't completely combine, but swirls instead.

Jersey Lily

A lovely, if slightly ominous-looking Pousse Café (page 268) -style sipper, the Jersey Lily is probably named after British actress Lily Langtry. Or it could be named after the Arizona ghost town Jersey Lily, which never boasted much more than a post office, and never released more than $7,000 of **the fortune in gold** supposedly buried in them thar hills (truth be told, the town was named after the actress, too, so either way, this drink traces its way to her).

2 ounces **green Chartreuse**

1 ounce **Cognac**

5 dashes **Angostura bitters**

1. Pour the Chartreuse slowly into a liqueur or cordial glass. Pouring over a spoon or just very carefully, float the Cognac on top of the Chartreuse.

2. Instead of the normal dashing, softly float the 5 drops of Angostura bitters on top of the Lily. Drink while dreaming of gold (of either the mineral or celluloid kind).

A VARIATION: If you leave the bitters by the side of the road, and go halvsies with the Cognac and Chartreuse, you've moved all the way over the bridge to drinking just the Jersey.

Kitchen Sink

Can you envision a drink that uses so many alcohol varietals that you say "No way, not even on a dare, I'm not that foolish, I respect my liver too much, not even if I was paid or hypnotized"? You might expect that an amalgamation called the "Kitchen Sink" would be that very drink, lending itself to hyperbolic refusals like the above. Ha! You've been fooled, friends. While powerful and, yes, containing three big booze boys, this cocktail isn't nasty in the least. I suggest not telling your pals this when serving–**make it sound awful**, and then goad them into taking that first slug. Afterward, the laughs should be rolling from the room's corners.

Cracked ice

¾ ounce **rye**

¾ ounce **gin**

¾ ounce **apple brandy**

½ ounce **Simple Syrup** (page 7)

¼ ounce **freshly squeezed lemon juice**

¼ ounce **freshly squeezed orange juice**

1 **large egg,** preferably organic

1. Fill a cocktail shaker halfway full with cracked ice (you want this good and frothy, and the cracked ice helps). Add all of the remaining ingredients. Shake well.

2. Strain into a large cocktail glass. Garnish with anything you can think of quickly, before the froth disappears.

✖ *A Warning: This does contain raw egg, so be sure your egg is fresh. This shouldn't be served to guests who are elderly or who have compromised immune systems. Though it is an important ingredient, this also can be constructed without an egg. Just call it "The Sink."*

Seven Cocktails You Might Not Serve Your Parents

It may be the name, or it might be the nasty ingredient mix (well, usually it's just the name), but none of these are going to be big hits around the Sunday night dinner table.

1. Brain Hemorrhage (page 204)
2. Corpse Reviver (page 206)
3. Duck Fart (page 333)
4. Purple Panties (page 343)
5. Screaming Orgasm (page 347)
6. Nude Eel Cocktail (page 222)
7. Sloe Comfortable Screw (page 348)

Monkey Brain

For those feasts when you're a guest along with Indiana Jones at the Temple of Doom, and the scuttling course (bugs) and the squirmy course (snakes) have crept along into the *coup de grâce*—or Monkey Brain—course, I **always have a shaker of these at the ready**. That way, instead of insulting the hosts, you can say, coolly, "I only *drink* my Monkey Brains."

Ice cubes

2 ounces **Apfelkorn**

1 ounce **Bailey's Irish Cream**

¼ ounce **grenadine**

A Note: *Apfelkorn is a sweetish German liqueur created by blending a wheat-based spirit with apples.*

1. Fill a cocktail shaker halfway full with ice cubes. Add the Apfelkorn and Bailey's. Shake well (like a whip, I would say).

2. Strain the brainy mix into a cocktail glass. Add the grenadine. Stir once, to increase the gristly-looking nature of the drink.

Monkey Gland

Seemingly the final ingredient used by a witch doctor when making a potion to finally turn Tarzan into a full-fledged gorilla, or a black market commodity renowned for its ability to **turn a lunkhead into a Lothario**, or the latest reduction aid for the haute-est of haute-cuisine sauces, the Monkey Gland is, instead, a first-rate thirst-quencher.

Ice cubes

1½ ounces **gin**

1 ounce **freshly squeezed orange juice**

½ ounce **Pernod**

¼ ounce **grenadine**

1. Fill a cocktail shaker halfway full with ice cubes. Add the gin, orange juice, Pernod, and grenadine. Shake well.

2. Strain into a cocktail glass. When drinking, remember that zero monkeys were harmed during the making of this drink.

Moscow Mule

Though we take vodka (or *gorzalka*, as it used to be called in eleventh-century Poland) for granted as a base spirit in cocktails, it wasn't always at such a high level of popularity. Its big boost came in the 1950s (the buttoned-down decade that needed more clear, unfragrant liquor), and came out of a Los Angeles hot spot called the Cock and Bull, where the owner of said spot hung with the distributor for a newly imported vodka called Smirnoff. These two bright boozehounds figured, rightly, that the way to the average drinker's consciousness was through an ad campaign featuring a tasty new mixture. Through this marketing scheme the Moscow Mule was born, **vodka ran through the streets** like high-proof water, and the copper tankard business boomed (for a while, at least).

Ice cubes

2 ounces **vodka**

1 ounce **freshly squeezed lime juice**

Chilled ginger beer

Lime wedge for garnish

⊕ *A Note: As alluded to above, this was originally served in a copper tankard. If you have a copper tankard lying around, use it wisely. And often.*

1. Fill a highball glass three-quarters full with ice cubes. Add the vodka, lime juice, and ginger beer.

2. Squeeze the lime wedge over the drink and then submerge it. Stir well.

A VARIATION: If you want to go the regional, as opposed to the international, route, switch the vodka with Southern Comfort and the lime juice with lemon juice. You'll be riding a Missouri Mule.

Nude Eel Cocktail

There should be a very loud band called the Nude Eels. They could play a show with the Monkey Brains (page 221). It could be a tribute concert where they only play Zombies (page 242) covers. **Hit the bar heavily** before the show, because said bar is having specials on all drinks sharing the names of the bands in question. Once you pick your poison, stick with it, though—none of these three drinks plays as well with each other as the fictitious bands in this dive.

Ice cubes

1 ounce **gin**

1 ounce **Cognac**

1 ounce **Dubonnet rouge**

1 ounce **yellow Chartreuse**

1. Fill a cocktail shaker halfway full with ice cubes. Add each member of this combo to the shaker. Shake well while screaming loudly (you have to scream to make yourself heard due to the excessive volume emanating from the Marshall stacks).

2. Strain into a large cocktail glass. Garnish with a bloody guitar pick.

Obituary Cocktail

Taken from Kerri McCaffety's beautiful book of the same name, which celebrates classic New Orleans saloons, the Obituary Cocktail is a **Martini variation with a deadly twist**, at least by today's modern standards—absinthe. The cocktail was created at the beginning of the twentieth century at Lafitte's Blacksmith Shop, whose aged bricks and cypress beams have stood since 1772 and where a saloon has stood since the early 1800s.

Ice cubes

4 ounces **gin**

1 ounce **dry vermouth**

1 ounce **Pernod** (a friendly absinthe substitute)

1. Fill a cocktail shaker halfway full with ice cubes. Add the gin, dry vermouth, and Pernod. Shake until you see the ghost of Jean Lafitte (or until the drink is well chilled).

2. Strain into a large cocktail glass.

⬆ ***A Note:*** *Absinthe is an anise-flavored spirit that was once very popular in cocktails, until it was made illegal in many parts of the world due to the fact that it includes wormwood, which supposedly can cause many unhealthy side effects. In recent years it has enjoyed a revival in Europe.*

"L'amore fa passare ill tempo; ill tempo fa passare l'amore."
(Love makes time fly; **time makes love fly**.)

Inscription scrawled on the wall by Italian sailors at Lafitte's Blacksmith Shop

Pink Squirrel

Be warned, the Pink Squirrel is lurking around the corner, waiting with bated breath to strike any who don't join its legion of branch-squatters. The legend of the Pink Squirrel is only to be whispered in the full light of the sun, as it's evil, gruesome, and full of cotton candy. Don't ever say "pink squirrel" five times while looking at a plate of walnuts, or the beast itself will arise from the tree trunk to gnaw you with its tiny pink teeth. . . . No matter how hard you try, it's awkward to make a frilly squirrel sound menacing in the manner of a devil dog, axe murderer, or bloodthirsty giant mutated rabbit. The drink is as sugary as the idea, which is why I like to serve it with dessert—a little bubblegum ice cream or chocolate cream pie. I figure, once you're going sweet, never go halfway.

Ice cubes

1 ounce **crème de noyaux**

1 ounce **white crème de cacao**

1 ounce **heavy cream**

1. Fill a cocktail shaker halfway full with ice cubes. Add the crème de noyaux, crème de cacao, and heavy cream. Shake well.

2. Strain into a cocktail glass.

A VARIATION: If you can't easily get the pink, almond-flavored crème de noyaux, then bounce the crème de cacao up to 1¾ ounces and add ½ ounce of grenadine. Call it a Sickly Pink Squirrel.

⬆ *A Note: If this squirrel seems a little naked, try garnishing it with a peppermint stick.*

Presbyterian

Ideal for sitting and sipping as the sun goes down, the Presbyterian is completely tolerant, and it tastes dandy no matter what the drinker's religious preference is. As long, that is, as said drinker **holds a sure hand** on the club soda siphon and ginger ale bottle, ensuring equality between mixers.

Ice cubes

1½ ounces **bourbon**

Chilled club soda

Chilled ginger ale (or 7UP, if the mood takes you)

Lemon twist for garnish

1. Fill a highball glass three-quarters full with ice cubes. Add the bourbon.

2. Very carefully, fill the glass with equal parts club soda and ginger ale. Stir 3 times clockwise for the club soda and 3 times counter-clockwise for the ginger ale.

3. Garnish with the lemon twist.

↑ *A Note: I've seen the Pres (as it's called by late Sunday afternooners) made with both ginger ale and 7UP. I believe the former is more historic, but the latter is in no way offensive.*

LIQUEUR SPOTLIGHT

Crème de Noyaux

This liqueur is the pits—literally. Crème de noyaux is created from fruit pits, or "stones" (most often apricot or peach). The word *noyaux* is actually French for "pits" or "cores." However, it doesn't taste like the pits, instead boasting a delightful almond flavor. And, it doesn't look like the pits, instead being a light red or pink (which some might call a light red). It's lovely both for flavoring a drink and for adding a glowing color that helps set the mood, match a dinner party's theme, or simply look sweet. Try it not only when called for, but also as a nutty substitute for triple sec (in a Margarita, for example).

Crème de noyaux isn't as popular (or, sadly, as readily available) as it once was, though it's still used by discerning drink makers who want a hint of sweet almond in a drink. Its popularity may have peaked in the 1970s, as it was a key ingredient in the Pink Squirrel (opposite), which was all the rage at the time.

Rattlesnake Cocktail

Sshhhh. Can you hear it? Right beyond the sagebrush and under the sandstone? It's that faint rattling noise that in every movie Western means some poor cowboy's ankle is about to be impaled by long, curving, poisonous teeth. Rattlesnakes, I thought at one point in my impressionable youth, are everywhere. That is why I still think it's always good to have a party of six people around when drinking Rattlesnake Cocktails. You need **someone to share the pain.** Serves 6

Ice cubes

9 ounces **rye** (if you really can't find rye, use a mean bourbon)

3 ounces **Pernod**

3 ounces **freshly squeezed lemon juice**

4 dashes **Peychaud's bitters**

1. Fill a large cocktail shaker halfway full with ice. Add the rye, Pernod, lemon juice, and bitters. Shake very well.

2. Strain the mix equally into 6 cocktail glasses or cordials made from snakeskin. Drink warily.

⚓ *A Note: This is a large snake. If your cocktail shaker isn't of the large snake-holding variety, build this in a pitcher, and stir until your arms get numb.*

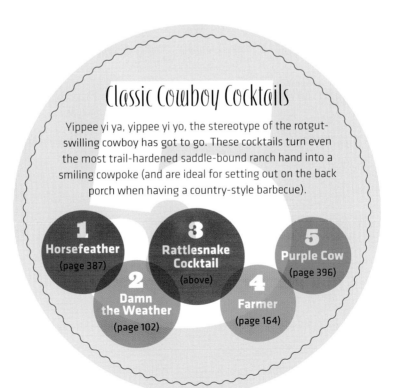

Classic Cowboy Cocktails

Yippee yi ya, yippee yi yo, the stereotype of the rotgut-swilling cowboy has got to go. These cocktails turn even the most trail-hardened saddle-bound ranch hand into a smiling cowpoke (and are ideal for setting out on the back porch when having a country-style barbecue).

1 Horsefeather (page 387)

2 Damn the Weather (page 102)

3 Rattlesnake Cocktail (above)

4 Farmer (page 164)

5 Purple Cow (page 396)

Rhett Butler

When released in 1939, *Gone with the Wind* was a Technicolor phenomenon—perhaps the most popular movie of all time (at least in percentage of the population who saw it when it was in theaters), and beloved by audiences to a level not yet matched. Beyond all that **fine-and-dandy-ness**, beyond the Academy Awards, beyond the six-hour TV mini-series based on the follow-up novel, *Scarlett, Gone with the Wind* also spawned two fine cocktails named after its most recognizable characters, the tangier Rhett Butler here and the Scarlett O'Hara (page 229). When serving both at a Southern-style hootenanny, I suggest making them at opposite sides of the room to avoid any scandalous incidents.

Cracked ice

2 ounces **Southern Comfort**

½ ounce **orange curaçao**

½ ounce **freshly squeezed lime juice**

½ ounce **freshly squeezed lemon juice**

Lemon twist for garnish (optional)

1. Fill a cocktail shaker halfway full with cracked ice. Add the Southern Comfort, curaçao, lime juice, and lemon juice. Shake well.

2. Strain the mix into a cocktail glass. Squeeze the lemon twist over the drink, if using, and then curl it around the edge of the glass so it looks like a flame.

Rusty Nail

I once stepped on a rusty nail and almost had to have my foot removed. It was far, far less pleasant than this Scotch-Drambuie symphony, said drink having little chance of infecting your body with tetanus. Instead, it can instill one with **a penchant for bringing out the bagpipes** and jigging around the yard. If it's the front yard, be sure to wear a little something under the kilt. As Scotch is the main ingredient, with the Drambuie providing the significant shading, the Rusty Nail reflects heavily the type of Scotch used. I suggest a hearty blended Scotch such as Chivas or J&B, but experiment and find your favorite. Single malt scotches can also be tried, with fine, fine results.

Ice cubes

2 ounces **Scotch**

1 ounce **Drambuie**

Lemon twist for garnish (optional)

1. Fill an old-fashioned glass with ice cubes. Add the Scotch and Drambuie, allowing them to greet each other like the old pals they are.

2. Stir, but not excessively. If you're feeling frisky, squeeze the lemon twist over the top and then plop it into the drink.

⬆ *A Note: Drambuie is a lively but smooth combination of aged Scotch, honey, and secret ingredients passed down from silent generation to silent generation. In Gaelic, it means "the drink that satisfies." Keep that bit of trivia in mind for making pocket change on bar bets.*

"My God, **so much I like to drink Scotch** that sometimes I think my name is Igor Stra-whiskey."

IGOR STRAVINSKY

Satan's Whiskers

Only partake in this demonic blend if wearing a red cape and those Styrofoam-esque red devil horns that attach to the head (and perhaps drawers that say "little devil" on them in fiery letters). If daring to drink the Satan's Whiskers without proper attire, no one but you is responsible for the consequences. (I'd say the only consequences are looking less silly, but they may equal having less fun, too.)

Ice cubes

1 ounce **gin**

1 ounce **dry vermouth**

1 ounce **sweet vermouth**

1 ounce **freshly squeezed orange juice**

½ ounce **Grand Marnier**

2 dashes **orange bitters**

1. Fill a cocktail shaker halfway full with ice cubes. Add the gin, the dry and sweet vermouths, orange juice, Grand Marnier, and orange bitters. Shake well.

2. Strain into a large cocktail glass.

A VARIATION: If you substitute orange curaçao for the Grand Marnier, you're slurping a Curled Satan's Whiskers. Wouldn't that serve the old devil right?

Scarlett O'Hara

It's only fitting that the Scarlett O'Hara, like the Rhett Butler (page 227), uses Southern Comfort as its main building block—both were created in homage to the quintessential Southern movie. As *Gone with the Wind* won a number of Academy Awards (including one for Vivien Leigh as Scarlett), you might want to roll this, the Rhett B., and the Red Carpet (page 185) out at your next Academy Awards gala. Then the accolades will all end up in your lap.

Ice cubes

2 ounces **Southern Comfort**

1 ounce **cranberry juice cocktail**

½ ounce **freshly squeezed lime juice**

1. Fill a cocktail shaker halfway full with ice cubes. Add the Southern Comfort, cranberry juice cocktail, and lime juice. Shake well (as if tomorrow really weren't another day).

2. Strain into a cocktail glass.

A VARIATION: If you're in the midst of a hot Southern summer, try blending this up instead of shaking it. Just add the liquid ingredients, plus 1 cup of ice, to a blender, blend well, and cool down.

Scofflaw Cocktail

This is for all the criminals in the house. (Here's hoping they're criminals solely while playing video games or during daydreams after reading Dashiell Hammett.) Is it reassuring or depressing that folks have always dug aping the criminal? I'll let everyone drinking a Scofflaw right this moment pick the locks on their own minds. Myself, I think I'll discharge another **one of these brightly balanced cocktails** and watch Kubrick's *The Killing*, as a Scofflaw partners particularly well with black-and-white crime films.

Ice cubes

2 ounces **rye**

1½ ounces **dry vermouth**

½ ounce **freshly squeezed lemon juice**

½ ounce **grenadine**

2 dashes **orange bitters**

Lemon slice for garnish

1. Fill a cocktail shaker halfway full with ice cubes. Add the rye, dry vermouth, lemon juice, grenadine, and orange bitters. Shake well, you dirty rat.

2. Strain into a large cocktail glass. Garnish with the lemon slice, if only to keep folks' hands busy and away from their Tommy guns.

A VARIATION: If you can't buy, beg, borrow, or steal some rye, you could use bourbon. It will diminish your tough-guyness, though.

Serpent's Tooth

Okay, you've been known to read Harry Potter and other fantasy books marketed mainly to the under-18 crowd. Okay, you've been known to secretly or openly enjoy the odd Renaissance faire, once even donning a pointed wizard's touk. Okay, you once wore chain mail for Halloween (or wished you had). None of that means you shouldn't also **enjoy a more modern cocktail.** Enter the Serpent's Tooth.

Ice cubes

1½ ounces **Irish whiskey**

1 ounce **sweet vermouth**

½ ounce **kümmel**

½ ounce **freshly squeezed lemon juice**

3 dashes **Angostura bitters**

1. Fill a mixing glass or cocktail shaker halfway full with ice cubes. Add the whiskey, sweet vermouth, kümmel, lemon juice, and Angostura bitters. Using your staff, sword, or a long thin spoon, stir well.

2. Strain into a large jewel-encrusted goblet or cocktail glass. Garnish with a fang, or nothing at all.

Set Up

If you haven't seen the 1949 Robert Ryan boxing pic that shares a name with this cocktail, then I suggest renting it. It's just over 71 minutes, all in real time, and by the moment the last scene fades to black you'll want to sit with the lights off and **consume a steady stream** of these. Not because the movie's bad (it's darn good), but because it's more than a little depressing, with its rough fight sequence and no-feel-good ending. Here's a thought—the first time you serve these, watch the film. The next time, invite your pals over and have a Rock 'Em Sock 'Em Robots tourney. That way you'll have balanced out the sad movie with a fun fight night.

Ice cubes

2 ounces **bourbon**

1½ ounces **freshly squeezed orange juice**

½ ounce **Pernod**

1. Fill an old-fashioned or other short, squat glass with ice cubes. Add the whiskey, orange juice, and Pernod.

2. Stir well.

Shark

Da dum, da dum, da dum. Da dum, da dum, da DUM. Then, your legs are chewed off about mid-thigh and that teeny thong bikini or groovy board short is for naught. Who'll see it when you've been used as belly liner for the great white 1970s movie star? To ensure your beach skimpies are seen, stay away from the water altogether. Instead, mix up a Shark and **become the consumer** rather than the consumed.

Ice cubes

1½ ounces **vodka**

1 ounce **blue curaçao**

½ ounce **freshly squeezed grapefruit juice**

Chilled ginger ale

1. Fill a highball glass three-quarters full with ice cubes. Add the vodka, curaçao, and grapefruit juice. Stir once (watching for fins).

2. Fill the glass up with ginger ale. Stir well with a shark-shaped stirrer.

"Here's to **swimmin'** with bow-legged women."

QUINT (Robert Shaw), in *Jaws*, 1975

Sleepy Hollow

It's a smidgen odd (though I haven't lost my head over it) that a fresh mix such as this drink, with its hint of apricot and lemon and sweet undertone, is matched up forever in our cocktail lore with the legend of a headless fella riding a black mare (probably accompanied by a Black Dog, page 201) and causing general chaos. Perhaps it's the heavy helping of gin, put in, no doubt, **to get one through the sleepless night** after reading said Irving story. Whatever the reason, when serving up the Sleepy Hollow, I suggest placing a headless mannequin in the shower with the curtain slightly closed and only candles for light to freak out the guests. They'd expect nothing less (or maybe they'd expect a bit more—on the mannequin's body, that is).

½ cup **fresh mint leaves,** plus a sprig for garnish

¾ ounce **freshly squeezed lemon juice**

½ ounce **Simple Syrup** (page 7)

Ice cubes

2½ ounces **gin**

½ ounce **apricot liqueur**

1. Add the mint, lemon juice, and simple syrup to a mixing glass or cocktail shaker. Using a muddler or hefty wooden spoon, muddle well.

2. Fill the cocktail shaker or glass halfway full with ice cubes. Add the gin and apricot liqueur. Shake as if you heard the horseman's hoofbeats coming.

3. Strain into a large cocktail glass. Garnish with a sprig of mint and a swizzle stick topped by a plastic head.

🔁 **A Note:** *Some apricot liqueurs are brandy based, and some are not. You want the variety that is not brandy based in this drink. If you can't find apricot liqueur, you could use apricot syrup (use a little less).*

A VIRGIN VARIATION: Want to go to Sleepy Hollow but not fall asleep? Remove the gin and use 1½ ounces lemon juice instead, and substitute 1 ounce apricot syrup for the apricot liqueur. It's going to be tangy, but still tasty.

Stomach Reviver Cocktail

There's an archaic Etruscan myth that says if you throw a wild wingding and serve both Corpse Revivers (page 206) and Stomach Revivers, the dead rise up and walk the earth. The kicker? **They're always hungry.** I think this myth is the basis of all the great George Romero movies (as well as the brilliant *Shaun of the Dead*—any movie that has its hero/heroine go to the pub to escape the zombie horde is okay by me).

Ice cubes

1½ ounces **brandy**

1 ounce **kümmel**

½ ounce **Fernet Branca**

2 dashes **Peychaud's bitters**

1. Fill a cocktail shaker halfway full with ice cubes. Add the brandy, kümmel, Fernet Branca, and bitters. Shake like the undead. No, wait, that's too slow. Shake much more quickly than the undead.

2. Strain the mix into a cocktail glass.

↥ *A Long Note: It's interesting that this drink contains both Fernet Branca and bitters (as Branca is extra bitter in its own right). Since both are considered excellent at alleviating the pain of eating a bit too much, I suppose the originator of the Stomach Reviver wanted to ensure that it would revive any stomach, no matter how overstuffed. Fernet Branca is not automatically to everyone's taste, so you may need to alter this recipe a bit to down the dosage.*

Dating back to 1845, Fernet Branca has a secret recipe that is still, today, hoarded by the family as if it were gold (which in a way it is, as it is very popular in Italy and worldwide). It is known that the recipe contains 27 herbs picked off of 4 continents, including aloes, gentian root, rhubarb, gum myrrh, red Cinchona bark, and the spices colombus, galangal, and my special favorite, zedoary. Really, having a drink containing Fernet Branca is like traveling the world in one sip. So get off your bitters fear and dive in—your stomach will thank you.

Tiger Milk

Forget that nutrition bar with its orange wrapper and triathlete benefits. Forget for a second that you ever heard the word "athlete." If you want to feel tip-top, all that exercising *might* work (I mean, studies show and all, but who reads those studies?), but the old remedy of a platter packed with Tiger Milk cocktails is **a sure thing** in the world of healing and feeling fine. I suggest serving this to a whole feline pack of friends, preferably in the early evening hours. That's when tigers like to hunt.

Cracked ice

2 ounces **brandy**

½ ounce **heavy cream**

½ ounce **milk**

Freshly grated nutmeg for garnish

1. Fill a cocktail shaker halfway full with cracked ice. Add the brandy, cream, and milk. Shake for about 1 minute, but stealthily, like you were stalking prey.

2. Strain into a cocktail glass. Sprinkle the nutmeg over the top (you don't want to completely cover the top, but you do want a decent amount).

A Note: *You'll want to use cracked ice here, for proper frothing.*

Velvet Hammer

Want **a knockout with a gentle touch**? Need to have dessert, but desire it to be served at a high proof? The Velvet Hammer is the right answer to these emotional questions.

Ice cubes

2 ounces **vodka**

¾ ounce **white crème de cacao**

½ ounce **heavy cream**

Ground cinnamon for garnish

1. Fill a cocktail shaker halfway full with ice cubes. Add the vodka, white crème de cacao, and heavy cream. Shake well.

2. Strain into a cocktail glass. Sprinkle a light layer of cinnamon over the top.

A VARIATION: If cinnamon doesn't get your hammer hammering, try a little freshly grated nutmeg.

Volga

It's as if I never left: in a canoe. On the longest river in Europe, the Volga. Ice in every direction. Bears and bear-like animals along the banks. A storm railing against the canoe for every one of the 2,300 miles. Crazy birds circling, waiting for the canoe crash to pick the remains clean from splinters. Water splashing over the sides like a curse. And then the sturgeon, with their beady eyes, tracing my progress from the deep pockets. The banks birthed jagged rock after jagged rock, taunting me with possible capsize after capsize. But did I worry? No, sir, and no, ma'am. I poured a Volga and sat back and smiled. **If you're ever stuck on a long river**, I suggest doing the same.

Ice cubes

2 ounces **vodka**

¾ ounce **crème de cassis**

½ ounce **heavy cream**

2 **raspberries** for garnish

1. Fill a cocktail shaker halfway full with ice cubes. Add the vodka, crème de cassis, and heavy cream. Shake well.

2. Add the raspberries to a cocktail glass. Strain the mixture into the glass. *Na vashe zdorov'ye!*

⬆ *A Translation:* "To your health!"

White Lion

Roarrrrr. This lion lets loose the roar with a full grin of teeth, but **the bite isn't quite so sharp** as to cut anyone on a first nip. After the second bite (or, in this case, drink), sure, it's a little more ferocious, but not dangerous. After that, you might feel the scars the next morning.

Ice cubes

1½ ounces **white rum**

1 ounce **orange curaçao**

½ ounce **freshly squeezed lemon juice**

½ ounce **raspberry syrup**

½ ounce **Simple Syrup** (page 7)

Lemon twist for garnish

1. Fill a cocktail shaker halfway full with ice cubes. Add the rum, curaçao, lemon juice, raspberry syrup, and simple syrup. Shake well, while roaring.

2. Strain into a large cocktail glass. Garnish with the lemon twist.

White Spider

Long ago, in the dawn of recorded history, when magnificent snowy mountains rose outside the swinging oaken door of every town tavern and the howling wind seemed lifelike on those sinister snowy eves, parents would send children scared into their beds by telling the story of the White Spider, living just outside the village boundaries, waiting to take bad girls and boys to its webby lair and drain their blood. Scary, isn't it? The part the kids didn't hear, and which I am only telling you now because you've come of age (that's past 21), is that after the children's beds were filled, the parents would order up a round of these White Spiders and **party down, heedless** of any gloomy weather.

Ice cubes

1½ ounces **gin**

1 ounce **Cointreau**

½ ounce **freshly squeezed lemon juice**

½ ounce **Simple Syrup** (page 7)

Lemon twist for garnish

~~~~~~~~~~~~~~~~~~~~

⬆ *A Numerical Note: For those keeping track, we've now used 162 lemon twists in this book.*

1. Fill a cocktail shaker halfway full with ice cubes. Add the gin, Cointreau, lemon juice, and simple syrup. Shake for at least 16 seconds (2 seconds for each leg).

2. Strain into a cocktail glass. Squeeze the lemon twist over the glass and then drop it in.

A VARIATION: If, later in the evening, you're out of simple syrup and aren't up to making more, and are also out of twists and not comfortable at this late hour using the garnishing knife, it's just dandy to make this drink without either the syrup or the twist. You'll just be serving a White Lady.

ANOTHER VARIATION: You might also see a White Spider cocktail that's solely vodka and white crème de menthe—a Vodka Stinger, by another name. If you order up a White Spider in a bar and get this latter choice, don't complain. It's darn tasty, too.

Widow's Kiss

If you think of this merger in a friendly but somber way (the poignant kiss on the cheek from a widow at a funeral, perhaps), it's **not so terrifying**. If you think of it in the arachnid sense (meaning the black widow's kiss, which translates into pain, agony, and death if you're the husband), it's a yell-inducer. If you're going for the latter at a creepy Halloween soirée, then I suggest serving your Widow's Kisses along with White Spiders (page 237) and reveling in the eight-legged frightening fun.

Ice cubes

1½ ounces **Calvados**

¾ ounce **yellow Chartreuse**

¾ ounce **Benedictine**

1 dash **Angostura bitters**

1. Fill a cocktail shaker halfway full with ice cubes. Add the Calvados, Chartreuse, Benedictine, and bitters. Shake well.

2. Strain into a cocktail glass. Serve with a kiss (if you're exceptionally brave).

⬆ *A Note: If you can lay your hands on honest-to-goodness Calvados from Normandy, France, then definitely use it. If not, then any good apple brandy can sub in.*

Six Halloween Horrors (of the Alcohol-Based Variety)

Many legends about Halloween populate folklore (including the legend of Jack O'Lantern, which involved an Irish fella fond of his cups who tried to get the devil to pay for the last round on a Saturday eve and ended up wandering in a bar-less limbo forever). One says that if you have a Halloween party without the properly chilled cocktails, your name forevermore becomes a curse in the mouths of attendees of said party. Don't jump back in fear—brew (and shake) up one of these and have your ghoulish party live in infamy.

1. Sleepy Hollow (page 233)
2. Tonga Punch (page 319)
3. Phantasm Fizz (page 180)
4. Satan's Whiskers (page 229)
5. Bloody Mary (page 21)
6. Witch's Brew (page 239)

Williwaw

Oh, the Williwaw. Is it a sort of droopy poncho-esque attire, a pudgy mythological beast, or an island off the coast of Bora Bora? The answer to this question should be found in *VIPs All New Bar Guide* (Gold Medal Books, 1960), as that's where I found the Williwaw. But no, *VIPs* has no Williwaw history or definition, though it does have a host of cartoons, a section of bar challenges called "Drinking Is Fun," and an assortment of early-'60s jokes, such as: "A barfly was having a quiet drink in his favorite saloon when he noticed that the stranger standing next to him was alternately drinking Scotch and bourbon. This was too much for the barfly, who asked, 'How can you drink like that?' 'Simple,' the stranger replied. 'I just got paid.'" Ba-dump-bump.

Ice cubes

1½ ounces **brandy**

1 ounce **cherry brandy**

½ ounce **Simple Syrup** (page 7)

2 dashes **Angostura bitters**

1. Fill a cocktail shaker halfway full with ice cubes. Add the brandy, cherry brandy, simple syrup, and Angostura bitters. Shake Williwaw well.

2. Strain into a cocktail glass. Serve with a laff.

Witch's Brew

According to the *Comprehensive Pictorial Encyclopedia* of 1943, a witch is "a woman who, according to pop superstition, is believed to possess dangerous powers of magic or witchcraft." This may be true (though it also says a python is a large tropical snake, and we know it's a purple drink on page 345). If so, then a Witch's Brew should be a dangerous drink. The range of ingredients may also point to this supposed dangerousness. The question you should ask isn't whether the drink is dangerous, though—it's whether you're going to let a little perceived danger worry you away.

Ice cubes

1½ ounces **Strega**

½ ounce **white crème de menthe**

½ ounce **freshly squeezed lemon juice**

½ ounce **freshly squeezed orange juice**

¼ ounce **Pernod**

Lemon slice for garnish

Fresh mint sprig for garnish

1. Fill a cocktail shaker halfway full with ice cubes. Add the Strega, crème de menthe, lemon juice, and orange juice. Shake well.

2. Strain into a cocktail glass. Float the Pernod on top, pouring it carefully over the back of a spoon if necessary. Garnish with the lemon slice and mint sprig. Drink with a cackle and while wearing a tall black hat.

Your Favorite Aunt

This one is good to know if you're interested in raking in the gifts around the holiday season, or the accolades around any family gathering. My perception is that not only aunts, but also uncles, grandparents, and second or third cousins **start singing your praises** once you've sent out the third round of Your Favorite Aunts, whatever the occasion. And after the next round they may start changing their wills.

Ice cubes

1 ounce **gin**

1 ounce **brandy**

1 ounce **sweet vermouth**

½ ounce **freshly squeezed lemon juice**

½ ounce **Simple Syrup** (page 7)

Fresh cherry for garnish (or maraschino if fresh is not available)

1. Fill a cocktail shaker halfway full with ice cubes. Add the gin, brandy, sweet vermouth, lemon juice, and simple syrup. Shake well, thinking fondly of every relative in the room (if the room is full of just friends, consider them non-blood relatives).

2. Strain into a large cocktail glass. Garnish with the cherry.

Zombie

Ah, the undead. Gotta love 'em. Unless they're eating your brain, of course. The way they stumble and mumble around, the way they keep at their goals, whatever the obstacles, their shuffling dance style, how well they both scare and amuse. It's completely fitting that they have a classic drink named after them. The report is that the first Zombie was created in 1939 by Don the Beachcomber at the Hurricane Bar during the World's Fair for a particularly hung-over customer (although society drunk, classy writer, world traveler, and raconteur Charles Baker, Jr., says he created it two years earlier). Like a horde of zombies, this brain fuzzer spread from tiki bar to tropical lounge to beach saloon. Before long, every booze slinger said his version was not only the finest, but also the original. The fact, from what I've been able to ascertain, is that Don never published his recipe, and so unless he rose from the dead (in a good mood, and not just looking for brains), everything is conjecture. I think the below recipe uses the requisite multiple rums, **gets one through the night in a delightful fashion**, and numbs the brain in a style conducive to the zombie shuffle, as well as the stumbling and mumbling.

Ice cubes

1 ounce **white rum**

1 ounce **amber rum**

1 ounce **dark rum**

¾ ounce **freshly squeezed lime juice**

¾ ounce **fresh pineapple juice** (if you can only get presweetened pineapple juice, omit the simple syrup and double the pineapple juice)

½ ounce **apricot liqueur** or **apricot brandy**

½ ounce **papaya juice**

½ ounce **Simple Syrup** (page 7)

½ ounce **151-proof rum**

Lime and **lemon wheels** for garnish

Fresh cherry for garnish (or maraschino if fresh is not available)

Fresh mint sprigs for garnish

Confectioners' sugar for garnish

1. Fill a cocktail shaker halfway full with ice cubes. Add the white, amber, and dark rums, the lime juice, pineapple juice, apricot liqueur, papaya juice, and simple syrup. Shake much more quickly than you can imagine the undead could shake.

2. Pour the mix (ice and all) into a Zombie glass, large Collins glass, or other glass in the 14-ounce range.

3. Float the 151-proof rum on top of the drink, pouring it over the back of a spoon if necessary. Garnish with a lime wheel, a lemon wheel, a cherry, and 2 mint sprigs.

4. Lightly sprinkle confectioners' sugar over the drink, garnishes and all. Serve with a straw, and, if serving the second round, a bed.

VARIATIONS: Obviously, there are as many variations to this drink as there are zombie movies. You may also garnish this drink with fresh pineapple spears, orange slices, and even slices of star fruit. Some suggest using orgeat syrup and omitting the apricot liqueur. Others insist that the 151 rum be Demerara. Another variation uses freshly squeezed orange juice. I wouldn't feel the need to try them all—just be aware of this when you order one in a bar. The underlying chorus, which is "enough rum to knock you into and back out of the afterlife," always sings the same. That song means that one Zombie is goofy fun, two is probably a bit mind-anesthetizing, and more than two may leave you feeling as if you were hit by a rum truck.

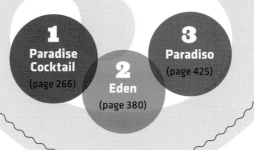

3 Drinks for the Afterlife

I'm no theologian, but if there is a big bar in whichever version of the happy part of the afterlife you believe in, my guess is that one of these three mixes is on special. And I'll bet it's made divinely.

1
Paradise Cocktail
(page 266)

2
Eden
(page 380)

3
Paradiso
(page 425)

Dinner for Two

The lights are dimmed; the music is leisurely and low; candles are lit and placed strategically; there's a simple but elegant meal ready to be served; clothes are chosen to show that sexy side while still maintaining a nonchalant edge (don't give it away); a few flowers twist in a vase on the table; your current flame is mere minutes away from ringing the bell; and then it hits you . . . what cocktails could possibly be perfect accompaniments for an evening as starry-eyed as this?

When the romance signal lights start blinking, don't muss that coiffed hair going wild with stress. Untie the pages of Dinner for Two and fan those flames. The velvety-talking drinks in this chapter—which are all built to serve two, naturally—know when to take the mood from fair to fantastic, whispering softly when the occasion needs it (via the scrumptious Magnolia Blossom Cocktail or the Silk Stocking) or notching up the heat a tad for those more intense after-midnight rendez-vous (perhaps with the Cupid Cocktail or the Kiss in the Dark).

Whatever the mood you and yours are making, Dinner for Two has a mix to match, whether it's a sophisticated evening with subtle flirtations (this book's lovelorn columnist suggests the Bon Soir), a meal that's slipped into dullsville and demands re-invigoration in the form of a liquid kick-in-the-amorous-pants (here you want to unveil the Bustier), or a late-night, past last call, sorta romantic occasion (you'll want to serve a Night Cap or two).

This chapter's line-up of sultry sippers is as bountiful as a booty-shaking bass line when it comes to livening up a night full of lovers, so do be careful. Start serving these mightily moving mixes to any old house or dinner guest and the potential for an affair is bound to run high, which means you must be judicious with whom you pour the Dinner for Two selections. There's no need to ruin any friendships.

Angel's Tit

The AT (see how modest I am?) wasn't always such a blue drink—I mean blue in the movie way and not the color way. It used to be just an Angel's Tip, as if the drink itself were **an extension of the celestial**. In the middle of the past century, when folks were hungry for more human pleasures, this one changed its tune from heavenly choir to sultry saxophones. While the name got sexed up, the ingredients stayed that same. Funny how that works. **Serves 2**

4 ounces **crème de cacao**

2 ounces **heavy cream**

Whipped cream for garnish

Maraschino cherries for garnish

1. Pour the crème de cacao equally into 2 large cordial glasses. Using the utmost care, as well as a bar or other spoon, float the heavy cream on top of the crème de cacao.

2. Top each drink with a small swirl of whipped cream, being careful not to inadvertently mix the heavy cream and crème de cacao. Top each with a cherry. And a leer, of course.

A VARIATION: I first heard about this variation in Seattle's Athenian Inn, a restaurant in the Pike Place Market that was one of the first places in Seattle to have a liquor license (in 1933). If you remove the cherry and the whipped cream, this is called a King Alphonse.

Black Pearl →

This classy combo oozes Monte Carlo smoothness. If serving this to a prospective paramour, I'd expect you to be wearing at least one silky item, and one other item that **sparkles when the moon finds its way** through the half-drawn curtains. Where the silk and sparkle appear in your ensemble might depend on how many Black Pearls you've served, or been served. **Serves 2**

Ice cubes

2 ounces **Cognac**

2 ounces **Tia Maria**

Chilled Champagne

Maraschino cherries for garnish

1. Fill a cocktail shaker halfway full with ice cubes. Add the Cognac and Tia Maria. Shake well.

2. Strain the mix into 2 flutes or wine glasses (though the latter won't get you any smooth-move points). Top with Champagne. Garnish each with a cherry, either dropped in or speared and floated on top.

⬆ *A Note: Tia Maria is a dark and rich coffee liqueur made from a cane-based spirit, Jamaican coffee, vanilla, and sugar, and it is becoming increasingly popular.*

Bon Soir

Everyone knows that if you drop a little French into your romantic nighttime, sparks soon fly. Or is that just in the movies? I'm not prepared to provide a final answer (leave that to any old advice columnist dishing on how to fire up a dull love life), but I am prepared to say that this refreshing combo is ideal for consuming before a meal. Really, serve it as you open the door for a date (or even for just a friendly evening) and **everyone ends up happy. Serves 2**

Ice cubes

2 ounces **parfait amour**

2 ounces **Benedictine**

Chilled ginger ale

1. Fill 2 highball glasses with ice cubes. Add 1 ounce of parfait a'mour and Benedictine to each glass.

2. Top each glass with the ginger ale. Stir well. I've read that this should be served with a straw, but I am on the fence about that. Sure, a straw is a good time, but does it set the right mood? Maybe if you're feeling exceptionally playful.

Brandy Champerelle

A dance in which long poufy skirts are both annoying and **maddeningly attractive**? A mushroom planted in boozy soil from which aphrodisiac tea can be brewed? A horse that once won at 100 to 1? A lesser-known and exceedingly limber way of kissing behind the ear? A member of the pousse café family of layered drinks? I'll take question five and call it a night. **Serves 2**

2 ounces **orange curaçao**

2 ounces **yellow Chartreuse**

2 ounces **brandy** (or Cognac, to be high end)

1. Add 1 ounce curaçao to each of 2 cordial or similar glasses. Without shaking a bit (you picked the right question above, so relax), float 1 ounce Chartreuse on top of the curaçao in each glass, pouring it slowly over a spoon if necessary.

2. Float 1 ounce brandy on top of the Chartreuse in each glass, again using a spoon if necessary.

Benedictine

Benedictine has a dramatic history—we're lucky it's even around today. For many years, the secret recipe for this liqueur was lost. Alexandre Le Grand gets the credit for unearthing the recipe. In 1863 he found a book of spells, within which was the secret recipe. After some deciphering, our liqueur hero recreated the recipe, updated it a bit, and called it Benedictine.

But how did such a fabulous recipe become lost in the first place? The recipe sprung out of the Renaissance, during which a French monk named Dom Bernardo Vincelli (originally named Dom Bernar), residing at the Abbey of Fécamp, mixed a healing elixir using 27 plants and spices gathered from across the world. This original Benedictine recipe became very popular, but during the French Revolution a noble bought it, put it in his library, and then lost it (and perhaps his head) in the confusion. Lucky for us, Alexandre Le Grand knew a good spell when he saw it.

Benedictine's unique flavor is a result of its secretive list of 27 ingredients—a list that includes angelica, hyssop, juniper, myrrh, saffron, aloe, arnica, and cinnamon. The combination's herbal tones are backed by an underlying potency, which makes even a small amount of this liqueur a key component in a variety of cocktails, including the Bobby Burns (page 94) and the Lorraine Cocktail (page 116). It's also drunk by itself, sometimes over ice, before a meal. Also, Benedictine is popular in its B&B form, where it's premixed with brandy.

Bridal Path

Don't assume that this drink alone equates to a couple taking that walk (some say it's a short walk, some a long walk) into matrimony. I hear **a ring is also needed**, and think that an agreeable dinner at least might be in order, for starters. But trying to walk that path without having this Bridal Path as part of the process? I see clouds on the marital horizon—dark, dark clouds. **Serves 2**

Ice cubes

4 ounces **vodka**

1 ounce **apricot brandy**

1 ounce **freshly squeezed grapefruit juice**

2 **lemon twists** for garnish

1. Fill a cocktail shaker halfway full with ice cubes. Add the vodka, brandy, and grapefruit juice. Shake well.

2. Strain into 2 cocktail glasses. Squeeze a lemon twist over each glass, and then drop it in, blissfully. Serve with a proposal (If that's your pleasure, of course. I don't want to force you into anything).

Six Bad-Boy Bachelor Party Beverages

Hey, hey, it's a wild weekend (or at least a wild Saturday night) when the fellas come together to say goodbye to the single years of one of their own. Before spending every dollar bill on, say, a poker game, put a few aside to ensure that the almost-blushing-groom doesn't end up sipping sarsaparilla. Instead, have him slamming one of these (in no particular order).

1. Italian Valium (page 363)
2. Fireball (page 359)
3. Retreat from Moscow (page 130)
4. Little Red Teddy (page 365)
5. Widow's Kiss (page 238)
6. Corpse Reviver (page 206; this may be served the next morning)

Bustier

At least it's not the bra-burner, the clasp-unclasper, or the Double D. There may be a smidge of old-timey charm in calling **(in a throaty, come-hither voice)** to your dinner companion in the next room, "Can you come in here and help me with my Bustier?" If not that, then "Please, bring yourself over to stir my Bustier" might get things started. It'll provide a laugh, let's hope, if nothing else, and break that ice. The drink itself *is* a little icy—more suited to summertime *al fresco* dining than serious candlelit affairs. **Serves 2**

Ice cubes

4 ounces **fresh pineapple juice**

2 ounces **apricot brandy**

1 ounce **Amaretto**

Chilled 7UP or **Sprite**

1 ounce **grenadine**

Maraschino cherries for garnish

1. Fill 2 highball glasses three-quarters full with ice cubes. Add 2 ounces pineapple juice, 1 ounce apricot brandy, and ½ ounce Amaretto to each glass. Stir twice (once for each person).

2. Fill the glasses almost to the top with the 7UP. Stir again.

3. Add ½ ounce grenadine and a cherry to each glass and stir once, just to traipse it around. Really, this should be called "The Red Bustier." Change the name if desired.

A VARIATION: Want to step up the significance of the evening? Drop the 7UP, and shake the brandy, Amaretto, and pineapple juice in a shaker instead of stirring. Strain into 2 cocktail glasses, still adding a cherry to each but dropping the grenadine completely. Call it the Dropped Bustier—but don't tell your mother I told you to.

B.V.D.

This cocktail wasn't stitched originally for Mr. Bradley, Mr. Voorhees, and Mr. Day (who are responsible for the well-known men's underwear line sharing these initials), but simply enough refers to the three ingredients: rum, dry vermouth, and Dubonnet. But that reads R.V.D. Ah, but **the trick lies in the rum**, which in this drink first flew the Bacardi label (to be historically accurate, you can use it still, but it isn't demanded). Think about the countless "want to try my B.V.D.s?" or "let me shake your B.V.D.s" lines that are available when serving this to a paramour. **Serves 2**

Ice cubes

3 ounces **white rum**

2 ounces **dry vermouth**

2 ounces **Dubonnet rouge**

1. Fill a cocktail shaker halfway full with ice cubes. Add the rum, dry vermouth, and Dubonnet. Shake those B.V.D.s.

2. Strain into 2 cocktail glasses. Garnish with nothing at all.

Chocolate Heaven

Chocolate has been considered an aphrodisiac since Aztec gentlemen used it to entice Aztec ladies on chilly Mexican evenings. And since this luscious sweet treat releases the mood raisers phenylethylamine and serotonin, it's a good idea to at least offer a bit of chocolate to **set the romantic stage**. To really ramp up the chocolate power, my advice is to unite it with a bit of orange curaçao, a bit of mint, and a bit of alcohol. Then you probably won't even need the fireplace and bearskin rug. But do have a bit of Barry White on hand—not that I'm doubting this drink's heavy-cuddling generating powers, but Barry's a sure thing. **Serves 2**

Ice cubes

4 ounces **chocolate-flavored vodka**

2 ounces **orange curaçao**

Orange or **chocolate mint sprigs** for garnish

1. Fill a cocktail shaker with ice cubes. Add the vodka and curaçao. Shake well, but without seeming anxious about it.

2. Strain the mix into 2 cocktail glasses. Garnish with a sprig of mint, or at least some mint leaves placed attractively.

A VARIATION: Need even more chocolate? Substitute 1 ounce crème de cacao for 1 ounce of the vodka, and garnish with shaved chocolate along with the mint.

Cupid Cocktail

Isn't it special that Cupid has become a doughy winged boy with a bow? In Greek legend (where he's called Eros), he was the offspring of darkness and night, and in his most famous legend he only fell in love with his eternal lady-friend Psyche because he accidentally pricked himself when he was joyously going to force her to fall in love with a garbage heap. This cocktail hasn't forgotten that the sharp part of any arrow, even one released by a doughy winged greeting-card angel, can still cause a bit of a burn. As this recipe's been around for a while (at least since Harry Craddock's *Savoy Cocktail Book* [reprinted by Trafalgar Square Publishing, 2000]), it seems this **spicy love lesson** is one continually relearned. **Serves 2**

Ice cubes

3 ounces **dry sherry**

2 **large eggs,** preferably organic

1 ounce **Simple Syrup** (page 7)

2 dashes **cayenne pepper**

1. Fill a cocktail shaker halfway full with ice cubes. Add the sherry, eggs, simple syrup, and cayenne pepper. Shake well, with long, bow-drawing motions (preferably in the direction of the one you're wooing).

2. Strain into 2 cocktail glasses. Serve carefully.

✖ **A Warning:** *Make sure your eggs are very fresh, and don't serve this drink to elderly guests or those with compromised immune systems.*

Darling Spell

When singing to this bubbler, whether you sing the Beatles' line "Oh, darling, if you leave me, I'll never make it alone," or get more forceful with Screaming Jay Hawkins's classic "I put a spell on you, because you're mine," makes not a whit of difference. **Drinks enjoy being sung to**, and they don't tend to be too particular about the tune. What does make all the difference is ensuring that the Champagne is chilled, so that any actual darling understands the regard you hold for him or her. The Champagne *must* be chilly for the drink to reach the highest heights. How your actual darling feels about your singing fluctuates, I'm hypothesizing, with the number of Darling Spells that you have served. **Serves 2**

3 ounces **Strega**

Chilled Champagne

2 **lemon twists** for garnish

1. Add 1½ ounces Strega to each of 2 Champagne flutes. Fill the flutes with chilled Champagne.

2. Garnish each glass with a lemon twist and a song.

Flaming Youth

New Orleans is a romantic spot, with the languid sultry afternoons spent strolling hand-in-hand with a favored beau or beauty, surrounded by blooming magnolias and the sweet smell of beignets on the air. It's no wonder that the lovely 1933 *Gourmet Guide to New Orleans*, which is a joy to read (and for which I'm indebted to Jim and Robin, as they gave the book to my wife and me for a wedding present), has a drink called Flaming Youth, which, with its combination of cream and honey, seems **ideal for starry-eyed interludes** underneath the branches on late spring days. **Serves 2**

Ice cubes

4 ounces **gin**

2 ounces **heavy cream**

1 ounce **honey**

1. Fill a cocktail shaker halfway full with ice cubes. Add the gin, heavy cream, and honey. Shake well (impress that significant other with your shaking prowess and the relationship is destined to go in a positive direction).

2. Strain into 2 cocktail glasses and serve.

5 First Date Drink Favorites

Ah, the first date—it was invented for cocktails, or maybe vice versa. That wonderful anticipation combined with a stomach bursting with butterflies (whose wings booze dampens so well), screams out: cocktail. The question becomes: What to have? The following, I think, do the trick nicely.

1 Flirtini (page 66)

2 Slik Stocking (page 270)

3 French Connection (opposite)

4 Jasmine (page 169)

5 Kiss in the Dark (page 261)

French Connection

No, no, this isn't just to be used when you're trying to catch the eye of Gene Hackman. Think of it as a drink making a French connection in a passionate sense (as the French are still somewhat renowned for their romantic movements), and not in the endless car chase sense. I realize that some charming conquests may begin to resemble an endless car chase after a while, but **this smooth sipper** should cut a few miles off the map. If it isn't working as promised, or you're not sure it could possible work, try whispering a choice French phrase first. *Que vous êtes belle ce soir dans ces pantalons serrés—seriez-vous intéressée à un rapprochement français?* might be entertaining. **Serves 2**

Ice cubes	**1.** Fill a mixing glass or cocktail shaker with ice cubes. Add the amaretto and brandy together, hand-in-hand, so to speak. Stir well.
4 ounces **amaretto**	
4 ounces **brandy**	
Lemon twists for garnish (or cherries, for those feeling frisky)	**2.** Fill 2 old-fashioned or similar glasses with ice cubes. Strain the mix into the glasses and garnish each with a lemon twist.

⬆ *A Translation: You look beautiful this evening in those tight jeans—could I interest you in a French connection?*

A VARIATION: In *The Joy of Mixology*, Gary Regan makes this with Grand Marnier instead of amaretto and Cognac instead of brandy. This, I think, isn't a bad version to try at all.

> "The gentleman in his cups **is a gentleman always**, and the man who tells his friend in his cups that he is in love does so because the fact has been very present to himself in his cooler and calmer moments."
>
> ANTHONY TROLLOPE, *He Knew He Was Right*, 1869

Gin Daisy

On those idyllic sunny afternoons, when you and your significant other (or almost significant other, or even just that cutie from the cube down the hall) have packed a plum picnic basket and are heading toward greener pastures, a greener park, or a balcony with a lot of plants on it, plan ahead and bring extra ice and gin and other Daisy ingredients along with the requisite blanket to recline on while thinking thoughts that **might make one blush**, but not too badly. You'll be a hero or heroine, and the afternoon might just be one you tell the grandkids about.

Serves 2

Crushed ice

3 ounces **gin**

1 ounce **freshly squeezed lemon juice**

½ ounce **Simple Syrup** (page 7)

½ ounce **grenadine**

Chilled club soda

Fresh mint sprig or **leaves** for garnish

Orange slices (or lime slices, or both) for garnish

1. Fill 2 highball glasses with crushed ice. Add 1½ ounces gin, ½ ounce lemon juice, ¼ ounce simple syrup, and ¼ ounce grenadine to each glass. Stir twice.

2. Top off each glass with club soda. Stir twice more. Garnish each drink with a sprig or a few leaves of fresh mint and an orange slice.

A VARIATION: No gin available for pretty picnic packing? A Rum Daisy is also a good summertime choice, but go with maraschino syrup (or liqueur) instead of grenadine. Trust me on this.

"Now, I will hold your hand **when it's dark and you're afraid of the boogeyman** and I will tote your gin bottles out after midnight so no one can see but I will not light your cigarette. And that, as they say, is that."

GEORGE (Richard Burton),
in *Who's Afraid of Virginia Woolf?*, 1966

Golden Cadillac

There is a series of sweet drinks (perhaps led by the Alexander, page 18), each of which could serve as **the topper at the end of a candlelit meal** dished up for two people who are celebrating an anniversary, a birthday, or any special occasion. Certainly, multiple drinks could work in this end-of-the-meal position. But if you can choose a Cadillac, then why not add that extra class? **Serves 2**

Ice cubes

2½ ounces **Galliano**

2 ounces **heavy cream**

1½ ounces **crème de cacao**

1. Fill a cocktail shaker halfway full with ice cubes. Add the Galliano, cream, and crème de cacao. Shake well.

2. Strain into 2 cocktail glasses. If you're feeling especially celebratory and high rolling, garnish with a gold ring, gold chain, or golden toothpick.

LIQUEUR SPOTLIGHT
Galliano

Though an Italian liqueur, Galliano has always had an international outlook. It was created by Arturo Vaccari in 1896, for southern Italian pioneers who were traveling to California to try their luck in the gold rush (at least that's what the Galliano lore says). Thinking about these Italians away from home, Arturo combined Italian ingredients with those from other countries, with the end result being a lovely gold-colored mix (the coloring was meant to reflect the travelers' hopes for striking the mother lode). He named the liqueur after a famous Italian military hero, Major Giuseppe Galliano, who defended a small fort with 8,000 soldiers against an army of 80,000 during the first Abyssinian war. Galliano's mellow but layered flavor reflects its long list of ingredients, a list that includes two kinds of anise, lavender, mint, cinnamon, coriander, and vanilla. While worthwhile all on its own, Galliano also mixes well in a large number of cocktails, perhaps highlighted best by the Harvey Wallbanger (page 214).

Golden Lady

Not only a Stevie Wonder song, a movie from 1979, a brand of attractive Italian tights, and a somewhat cheesy pet name for your favorite female companion, the Golden Lady is also an effervescent beverage bursting with citrus highlights. As it features Champagne and a cutesy title, it's a keeper for those early-in-the-relationship dates, where you want to appear at least a dash upmarket, but without any hint of pompousness. Beyond the dating agenda, this also makes **a delightful routine breaker** for a New Year's party that's a little stuck on just bubbly. As a bonus, after a few of these it won't even have to be midnight for the kisses to start. **Serves 2**

Ice cubes

2 ounces **Cognac**

1½ ounces **Cointreau**

1½ ounces **freshly squeezed orange juice**

Chilled Champagne

Orange twists for garnish

1. Fill a cocktail shaker halfway full with ice cubes. Add the Cognac, Cointreau, and orange juice. Shake well.

2. Strain the mix into 2 large cocktail glasses. Top with chilled Champagne, being wary of overflow (due to Champagne's volcanic properties). Garnish each glass with an orange twist.

⬆ **A Note:** *For this precious drink, I would use a sweeter Champagne, such as sec or demi-sec. A Prosecco would shine in the Golden Lady as well.*

"Champagne's funny stuff. I'm used to whiskey. Whiskey is **a slap on the back,** and Champagne's a heavy mist before my eyes."

MACAULAY CONNOR (James Stewart), in *The Philadelphia Story*, 1940

Her Sarong Slipped

In the realm of drinks with slightly off-color names, which is a sizeable realm, there exist drinks sporting bawdy names (Angel's Tit, page 246), and others with names designed to get grins from heaving collegians (Screaming Orgasm, page 347), but there may not be a drink as naughtily coy in name as Her Sarong Slipped. It's the hint of playful flirtation combined with **the allure of the slightly exotic** and loosely attached garment that makes it unforgettable. Oddly, it's an older drink now mostly forgotten. The name matches the actual mix well, too, since it boasts a little sparkle, a little sugar, and a little kick that flutters the senses just enough. My guess is that once you've tasted your first Her Sarong Slipped, you won't forget it. **Serves 2**

Ice cubes

1 ounce **freshly squeezed lemon juice**

3 ounces **brandy**

1 ounce **grenadine**

Chilled Champagne

Strawberry slices for garnish

1. Fill a cocktail shaker halfway full with ice cubes. Add the lemon juice, brandy, and grenadine (in that order, to make certain a happy mixing). Shake briefly.

2. Strain the mix into 2 white wine glasses. Top each with chilled Champagne, and garnish with a strawberry slice, or with a whole strawberry if you're feeling generous. Serve with colorful stir sticks or transparent tiny umbrellas.

Honeymoon

Wait, before you even mention that you won't have time on your honeymoon for making a cocktail containing more than one ingredient, that you'll be busy with more important marital matters, let me interject a few quick words of advice. You and yours need to remember to come up for air and stay hydrated. The Honeymoon cocktail fills both needs (at least somewhat), and as an extra gift ensures that you'll always be able to order **a drink in honor of the occasion** after the occasion's only a memory. **Serves 2**

Ice cubes

3 ounces **applejack**

1 ounce **freshly squeezed lemon juice**

1 ounce **Benedictine**

½ ounce **orange curaçao**

1. Fill a cocktail shaker halfway full with ice cubes. Add the applejack and lemon juice and have your spouse add the Benedictine and curaçao. Shake well (if it takes 4 hands, that's just romantic).

2. Strain into 2 cocktail glasses and serve.

Kiss in the Dark

I don't wish to sound overly sappy, but is there anything as **absolutely moon-in-the-sky enchanting** as that first adolescent kiss, all giggly anticipation and effervescent excitement? As every first-kisser is slightly wobbly in the knees about this kissing thing, and as most first kisses tend to happen once the lights have gone down, it's appropriate that there's a cocktail named Kiss in the Dark. While it won't completely replicate that first-kiss sensation, it will make you warmly nostalgic toward the occasion. **Serves 2**

Ice cubes

2 ounces **gin**

2 ounces **cherry brandy**

2 ounces **dry vermouth**

Maraschino cherries for garnish

1. Fill a cocktail shaker halfway full with ice cubes. Add the gin, cherry brandy, and dry vermouth. Shake well, but tenderly.

2. Strain the mix into 2 cocktail glasses. Garnish each with a cherry (unless it seems too forward).

"When age chills the blood, when our pleasures are past
For years fleet away with the wings of the dove
The dearest remembrance will still be the last,
Our sweetest memorial, the first kiss of love."

GEORGE GORDON, LORD BYRON, *"The First Kiss of Love"*

Lily

Here's **a graceful beverage** that requires a stylish table surrounding it, or stylish art, or if nothing else, stylish shoes, because the Lily, like its namesake flower, is a bit refined, while packing a polished punch. **Serves 2**

Ice cubes

3 ounces **gin**

1 ounce **crème de noyaux**

1 ounce **Lillet blanc**

1 ounce **freshly squeezed lemon juice**

2 **lemon twists** for garnish

1. Fill a cocktail shaker halfway full with ice cubes. Add the gin, crème de noyaux, Lillet, and lemon juice. Shake vigorously, but be poised about it.

2. Strain into 2 cocktail glasses. Garnish each with a lemon twist.

Magnolia Blossom Cocktail

This appealing treat echoes a Southern scene, with rich flowering and somewhat floundering mansions in the background, a ruffled dress and a once elegant suit in the foreground, and people discussing points of ruin and dignified sadness. Remember that scene and bring out a Magnolia Blossom Cocktail when sitting your paramour down to read bits of Faulkner or confess an afternoon dalliance. The Magnolia Blossom won't make the experience happier, but it might make it **a bit smoother going down. Serves 2**

Ice cubes

3 ounces **gin**

1 ounce **freshly squeezed lemon juice**

1 ounce **heavy cream**

½ ounce **grenadine**

1. Fill a cocktail shaker halfway full with ice cubes. Add the gin, lemon juice, heavy cream, and grenadine. Shake well, and quickly.

2. Strain into 2 cocktail glasses. Garnish with a resigned smile.

Maiden's Blush Cocktail

While the blush as a physical phenomenon is usually associated with rosiness on the cheeks, after a few Maiden's Blush Cocktails one may start blushing on other, less public areas. A blush does signal a little risqué phraseology among ears that aren't really so innocent after all, so it could be that the gin punch in this sugary mix only hastens the inevitable. **Serves 2**

Ice cubes

3½ ounces **gin**

1 ounce **orange curaçao**

1 ounce **grenadine**

½ ounce **freshly squeezed lemon juice**

1. Fill a cocktail shaker halfway full with ice cubes. Add the gin, curaçao, grenadine, and lemon juice. Shake in a manner that might make you blush.

2. Strain into 2 cocktail glasses. Serve cold and without hesitation.

A VARIATION: There is, in certain tomes, a Maiden's Blush Cocktail #2. Each serving contains 1½ ounces gin, 1 ounce Pernod, and ½ ounce grenadine (or thereabouts). I suppose there are two versions because not all maidens blush at the same thing, or in the same way. Or, as Harry Craddock says in *The Savoy Cocktail Book* (reprinted by Trafalgar Square Publishing, 2000), there are two, "on the principle that if you first don't succeed, cry, cry again."

A Bouquet of Beverages

If you want to skip presenting the same old bouquet of flowers on your next special occasion, then try serving a bouquet of flower-inspired (or -related) adult beverages. They'll set you apart from the crowd, and look, if not as pretty as a real flower bouquet, at least pretty darn close. And they'll taste quite a bit better, too. Any grouping, or all, of the below makes a lovely arrangement.

1 Lily (opposite)

2 Bird of Paradise (page 374)

3 Sparkling Flower (page 273)

4 Morning Glory (page 121)

5 Magnolia Blossom Cocktail (opposite)

Montmartre Cocktail

Transform a simple evening at home with that singular someone into **a more magical occasion** by serving a plate of creamy cheese and crusty bread, lighting a couple of candles and turning off the lights, putting some violin or piano music on the stereo, and substituting a few Montmartre Cocktails for that tired old Merlot. Next thing you know, you'll both be transported to the north of Paris, and what's more romantic than that? One hint—there's no need to bring up that the Montmartre neighborhood gets its name from the decapitation of a bishop, archdeacon, and priest in 1272. It'll ruin the mood. **Serves 2**

Ice cubes

3 ounces **gin**

1½ ounces **sweet vermouth**

1½ ounces **triple sec**

Maraschino cherries for garnish

1. Fill a cocktail shaker halfway full with ice cubes. Add the gin, sweet vermouth, and triple sec. Shake well.

2. Strain into 2 cocktail glasses. Garnish each with a cherry (or 2, for that matter).

Things Never to Say to a Bartender

No self-respecting cocktail connoisseur wants to become that guy or gal that a bartender dreads seeing walk through the door. Bars and lounges and the like are (or at least should be) communal places, where good feeling and a general joyful exuberance should prevail. Don't ruin it by saying the wrong thing to your bartender (and any of these would be the wrong thing).

1. "Hey, I brought in this groovy CD by this great band. You really should play it. C'mon, play it."

2. "Please make me this extra-confusing specialty Mojito that isn't on the menu."

3. "Give me a glass of wine." (No red or white or varietal is mentioned, and the probability of there being many wine choices is great. As one bartender says of those who do this: "You have revealed yourself to be a moron.")

4. "Your cocktail waitress is hot. Is she single? Can you give me her number?"

5. Worst of all, perhaps: "I know this might be weird, but can you tell me where I can score any [insert drug name here]?"

Night Cap Cocktail

How many relationships, on TV if not in real life, bloomed out of the simple phrase, "Want to come up for a night cap?" It seems so innocent, as if the asker were offering a hat to keep out an evening chill. When in actuality, the asker is thinking, "Come on up and let's us get to our adult business, let's put Al Green on the stereo and follow his advice, let's forget about tomorrow, etc." It's refreshing to bring the dirty thoughts out in the open, and refreshing that there's a drink named Night Cap, ensuring **at least a touch of honesty** lives in the "want to come up . . ." question. A Night Cap might actually be served in those TV shows, after all. Wonder why they never show it? **Serves 2**

Ice cubes

2 ounces **brandy**

2 ounces **orange curaçao**

2 ounces **anisette**

2 **egg yolks,**
  preferably organic

~~~~~~~~~~~~~~~~~~~~~~~~~~~~~

✖ **A Warning:** *Make sure your eggs are very fresh, and do not serve this drink to the elderly or anyone with a compromised immune system.*

1. Fill a cocktail shaker halfway full with ice cubes. Add the brandy, curaçao, anisette, and egg yolks in that order (you don't want to rush things). Shake very well, for at least 25 seconds.

2. Strain into 2 large cocktail glasses. Garnish only with a cutely lecherous look.

A VARIATION: In Patrick Duffy's *Official Mixer's Manual* (Doubleday, 1983), there is a gin version as well as the brandy version; the gin drink being completely different (it features gin, confectioners' sugar, Angostura bitters, lemon peel, and pineapple). When it's late enough for a Night Cap, I tend toward brandy, and the egg addition seems like a good 2 A.M. calculation. But if you only have gin, don't shy away from the other route. It's better than no Night Cap at all.

Paradise Cocktail

If seeing solely the name, you might guess that a Paradise Cocktail equals a saccharine, creamy mess. Lucky for us, the Paradise Cocktail is **a polite balance of citrus** and two friendly alcohols, gin and apricot brandy. Show up with a duo of these and any admirer won't for a minute doubt your drink-making or -selecting acumen. Of course, if you also show up singing Heart's "Almost Paradise," the deal's probably off. **Serves 2**

Ice cubes

3 ounces **gin**

1½ ounces **apricot brandy**

1½ ounces **freshly squeezed orange juice**

1. Fill a cocktail shaker halfway full with ice cubes. Add the gin, apricot brandy, and orange juice. Shake well.

2. Strain into 2 cocktail glasses. Enjoy the amorous accolades.

Pink Lady

At first glance, a drink called Pink Lady seems that it should be, well, pink first and foremost, but then taste like bubble gum. The more modern versions do add a large dollop of heavy cream that's not in the earlier recipes, which gets us more into sugary territory. I, however, enjoy the older recipe best. I also know that not every lady (or gentleman, for that matter) wearing pink is sweet. **This, I think, is a good thing.**
Serves 2

Ice cubes

3 ounces **gin**

1½ ounces **applejack**

1 ounce **grenadine**

2 **egg whites,** preferably organic

❌ *A Warning: Make sure your egg whites are very fresh, and do not serve this to the elderly or anyone with a compromised immune system.*

1. Fill a cocktail shaker halfway full with ice cubes. Add the gin, applejack, grenadine, and egg whites. Shake well.

2. Strain into 2 cocktail glasses. Serve with a pink parasol.

A VARIATION: Want to go the creamier route? Substitute heavy cream for the applejack. Be sure your date doesn't want the stronger cocktail, though. You don't want any confusion on motives.

Pink Princess

I'm not sure if you've ever been to a coronation, but this is what they serve. It's traditional that right after the tiara is angled onto a new princess's head, the first round of Pink Princesses is slung. This isn't to say you can't make these at home; quite the opposite (I can hear your sigh of relief from here). One thing, though—you have to be wearing a dress with at least a four-foot train, and the aforementioned tiara. Seriously. **Serves 2**

Ice cubes

2 ounces **gin**

½ ounce **grenadine**

Chilled Champagne

1. Fill a cocktail shaker halfway full with ice cubes. Add the gin and grenadine. Shake royally.

2. Strain the mix into 2 flutes or tall wine glasses. Top the glasses off with Champagne. Garnish with diamonds, if available.

3 Third Date Drinks

There are slightly flirtatious drinks, and cutesy cocktails, and tall quaffs that hint at rosy futures together. Then there are those mixes that definitely point to a more, shall we say, *heated* evening. These are the third date drinks (or fourth, or fifth, or sixth, etc., depending on individual date agendas)—those served best with a little slow music on the stereo and the lights turned low. Whether a bearskin rug and a fireplace appear depends on personal preference.

1 Her Sarong Slipped (page 260)

2 Soul Kiss (page 271)

3 Between the Sheets (page 325)

Pousse Café

This classic French drink (the name literally means "pushes coffee," pointing to its original position as an after-dinner drink) has been carefully poured for more than a century. It's old enough that drinks made in the same style are usually referred to as being in the Pousse Café family, if not called straight-up Pousse variations. The style mentioned is obtained by layering the liquors and liqueurs and mixers, as opposed to shaking, or stirring, or combining them in any way. The idea is stratification, so that when a Pousse Café is served it is evident how many different ingredients there are, and what color. To make the perfect Pousse, you must have a very steady, slow hand, and it doesn't hurt to pour the liquids over the back of a spoon to ensure that the ingredients flow delicately into the glass. Also, you need to have a good idea of the specific gravities of the various alcohols (or a recipe that knows them for you) and mixers in relation to water. The idea (who knew science would be so helpful at the bar?) is that you want the ingredients that are layered next to each other to have a fairly large difference in specific gravities, because this difference helps to keep them from mixing. The box to the side should help you get started.

Of course, now you're asking why you would want to construct a drink so complicated during or after a romantic dinner for two. Am I insane? Dinners for two already, conceivably, could consist of nerves pureed with pressure. Why add this scientific rigamarole? First, made right, a Pousse Café tastes delightful, as one flavor mixes and then overcomes another, slowly (it's a sipper). Second, if made right, a Pousse Café looks incredibly cool. My guess is that gutsy home bartenders have been making after-dinner Pousse Cafés all these years for this very reason. And there's no reason to stop now.

The Pousse Café recipe here borrows from the recipe in the classic *Stork Club Bar Book* (reprinted by New Day Publishing, 2003) by Lucius Beebe, early twentieth-century author and bon vivant, but alters one or two of the ingredients for color scheme reasons. **Serves 2**

¼ ounce **grenadine**

¼ ounce **orange curaçao**

¼ ounce **dark crème de cacao**

¼ ounce **yellow Chartreuse**

¼ ounce **crème de noyaux**

¼ ounce **brandy**

1. Add half of each of the ingredients, gradually, carefully, smoothly, and in the order listed above, to 2 tall cordial glasses or other tallish thin glasses. Pour each ingredient over a small spoon if necessary to maintain separation.

A VARIATION: As mentioned, there are more Pousse variations than one can count, many with specific names. Don't fear a little experimentation. One specific version that must be mentioned comes first from Jerry Thomas's 1862 *Bar-Tender's Guide*, and it's the recipe for Pousse l'Amour. (If I'm reading it right, that means "pushes love." Take it for what you will.) The Pousse l'Amour is even more complicated than the normal Pousse. First you add maraschino liqueur, and then float an egg yolk on top of it, without disturbing the maraschino. Then you surround the yolk with vanilla cordial (later recipes I've seen use Benedictine), still not mixing anything. It's topped off with a bit of brandy. As Mr. Thomas says, "It requires a steady hand."

Sorting the Specific Gravities

A proper Pousse Café really relies on science. Each liquor (and liquid) has a different specific gravity, and layering ones with varied specific gravities on top of one another helps to keep them from mixing, thereby maintaining that Pousse integrity. Here is a list that goes from highest to lowest, which you can reference when putting together your layered masterpieces.

Liquid or liquor name	Specific gravity	Liquid or liquor name	Specific gravity
Grenadine	1.18	Frangelico	1.08
Crème de cassis	1.18	Orange curaçao	1.08
Anisette	1.17	Campari	1.06
Crème de noyaux	1.16	Apricot brandy	1.06
Dark crème de cacao	1.15	Blackberry brandy	1.06
Kahlúa	1.15	Cherry brandy	1.06
Crème de banane	1.14	Yellow Chartreuse	1.06
White crème de cacao	1.14	Midori	1.05
Maraschino liqueur	1.14	Benedictine	1.04
Parfait amour	1.13	Brandy	1.04
Crème de menthe	1.12	Cointreau	1.04
Blue curaçao	1.11	Kümmel	1.04
Galliano	1.11	Peach liqueur	1.04
Amaretto	1.10	Sloe gin	1.04
Blackberry liqueur	1.10	Green Chartreuse	1.01
Apricot liqueur	1.09	Water	1.00
Tia Maria	1.09	Tuaca	0.98
Triple sec	1.09	Southern Comfort	0.97
Drambuie	1.08	Kirch	0.94

Silk Stocking

Even if neither of the interested parties is actually wearing silk stockings—what a shame that would be—the cocktail version of the legwear might still swing the scales to the sexy side. Smooth in its own right while maintaining a touch of refinement and the ability to cause swoons, the Silk Stocking is **ideal for a romantic rendezvous.** Just don't leave the candles burning when the drinks are done. **Serves 2**

Ice cubes

3 ounces **white tequila**

3 ounces **crème de cacao**

2 ounces **heavy cream**

Ground cinnamon
for garnish

1. Fill a cocktail shaker halfway full with ice cubes. Add the tequila, crème de cacao, and heavy cream. Shake smoothly, but well.

2. Strain into 2 cocktail glasses. Garnish each drink with a little cinnamon.

⬆ **A Note:** If it's Valentine's Day, garnish with heart-shaped cinnamon red hots.

LIQUEUR SPOTLIGHT
Maraschino Liqueur

First and foremost (because this is a common, and regrettable, misconception), maraschino liqueur is not a syrupy sweet concoction, and is not just the juice from a bottle of maraschino cherries. If you're looking for cherry syrup, then pick that up, or combine some of the liquid from the maraschino cherries with some simple syrup. Maraschino liqueur is drier and made from the fruits and pits of Marasca cherries, which are distilled much like a fruit brandy, before having a bit of cane sugar syrup added—after which it's aged and filtered (sometimes the sugaring comes after the aging process). This process and the addition of the pits provide a layered flavor, which hints of both cherries and almonds. There are a number of brands of maraschino liqueurs available. One of the most famous is Luxardo, which is known both for its clear taste and for the liqueur's patented round green glass bottle that boasts a hand-fitted straw wraparound. Luxardo's maraschino liqueur is aged for two years in Finnish ash vats (wood from the ash tree doesn't affect the coloring) after being distilled, but before being diluted and mixed with cane syrup.

Soul Kiss

Not quite the tongue-extending, breathless, sometimes messy experience that we modern smoochers might consider, the Soul Kiss is instead a fairly refined combination of vermouths, Dubonnet (really a vermouth family member itself), and orange juice. How, then, does the drink garner its back-seat name? My guess (and this is only a guess), is that the Italians and French were (and perhaps still are) known for their deep devotion to the kissing and lovemaking arts, so to speak, when this one was first stirred. Hence, a drink that relied on both Italian and French vermouths leads to **a kiss using one's whole soul**. Or, maybe, the bartender making the first Soul Kiss wanted to impress its recipient. **Serves 2**

Ice cubes

2 ounces **dry** (or French) **vermouth**

2 ounces **sweet** (or Italian) **vermouth**

1 ounce **Dubonnet rouge**

1 ounce **freshly squeezed orange juice**

1. Fill a cocktail shaker or mixing glass halfway full with ice cubes. Add the dry vermouth, sweet vermouth, Dubonnet, and orange juice. Stir well and soulfully.

2. Strain into 2 cocktail glasses and serve.

A VARIATION: There's a Soul Kiss #2, if the #1 is too vermouthy, or if you want to bump up the strength a bit. Just substitute rye for the sweet vermouth and add an orange slice garnish.

⬆ *A Note: When speaking of the Soul Kiss in his book* The Fine Art of Mixing Drinks, *David Embury says, "What a placid unemotional soul the guy that named this drink must have had." Maybe you shouldn't use this one for your come-ons after all.*

Sparkling Flower

More for **those sunny afternoons** when you and yours are lounging around in white loafers or comfortable slip-ons than for romantic late nights, the Sparkling Flower is a white wine spritzer that uses edible flowers to enchanting effect. For a really tasty version, be sure your white wine isn't too dry (look for floral or fruity wines) and that your edible flowers are actually okay to eat. You can be sure by getting them at a gourmet store, where they won't have been treated with any chemicals. Picking them at random from the backyard, while somewhat picturesque, could lead to an afternoon visit to the hospital. And that's not enchanting in the least. **Serves 2**

8 ounces **chilled fruity white wine**

7 ounces **chilled club soda**

½ cup **edible flowers,** such as mini carnations or chrysanthemums, lilac florets, or violets

1. Add 4 ounces wine to two 8-ounce flutes or other comparable tall thin glasses.

2. Add 3½ ounces club soda to each glass. Add ¼ cup flowers to each glass. With a long thin, metal spoon, stir gently.

A VARIATION: In case edible flowers aren't readily available, or if you want to keep things from getting stagnant after serving Sparkling Flowers Sunday after Sunday, you can also use fruit to make a standout spritzer. Try using a few frozen raspberries or frozen strawberries (frozen also helps keep everything chilly). Remember the old saying: Variety in drinks is the spice of life.

"Wine is **sunlight**, held together by water."

GALILEO

Sweet Dreams

Perhaps this cocktail should be reserved for those more advanced couples who are used to wishing each other goodnight from the distance of mere inches. Perhaps the newbie couple, or even the wannabe couple, should stick to drinks that don't imply, in their names, **a cozy waking up** together. Just a suggestion, naturally, and don't think you have to take my advice. As the Sweet Dreams contains Kahlúa, a coffee liqueur, it could be that there won't be any dreaming immediately after drinking it anyway. Perhaps the sweet dreams alluded to are actually daydreams. You decide. **Serves 2**

Ice cubes

3 ounces **Cognac**

2 ounces **Kahlúa**

1 ounce **heavy cream**

1. Fill a cocktail shaker halfway full with ice cubes. Add the Cognac, Kahlúa, and heavy cream. Shake well, in a rock-a-bye motion.

2. Strain the mix into 2 cocktail glasses. Garnish with pajamas.

A VARIATION: This isn't so much a variation as a completely different cocktail, but I've also seen a Sweet Dreams recipe containing equal parts rum, gin, and apricot brandy, with 2 dashes pineapple juice, shaken and strained. It might be dandy, but it doesn't seem as dreamy as the above.

Six Sweetheart Bachelorette Party Sippers

Sure, sure, the modern-day bachelorette may not have a prewedding girls' night consisting solely of flowers and cooing about how blissful married life is bound to be—in fact, the bachelorette party might become even wackier than the traditional bachelor blowout. But that's no reason the bouncy bride should have to swill bar slops; instead, ensure that she's treated right with one of these.

1. Lemon Drop (page 341)
2. Princess (page 396)
3. Bridal Path (page 250)
4. Bustier (page 251)
5. Kiss in the Dark (page 261)
6. Stomach Reviver Cocktail (page 234; this may be needed at breakfast)

Sweetie-Pie

Oh, snookums, do you need a widdle drinky-poo? Is bubbly-boo a thirsty sugar-plum pooky? How about this, baby-talking boys and girls (especially those who talk lovey-dovey talk on cell phones when sitting next to me on the bus)? I'll give you the following Sweetie Pie recipe and you'll **promise to sip it silently**. Now that would be sweet.

Serves 2

Ice cubes

3 ounces **gin**

1½ ounces **sweet vermouth**

1½ ounces **maraschino liqueur**

1 ounce **Simple Syrup** (page 7)

2 **maraschino cherries** for garnish

1. Fill a cocktail shaker halfway full with ice cubes. Add the gin, sweet vermouth, maraschino liqueur, and simple syrup. Shake well, puddin'.

2. Add a cherry to each of 2 cocktail glasses. Strain the mix into the glasses. Serve with a little sugar (the sweet-talking sugar, not the granulated kind).

Swinger

Want to impress in a late-'60s style without resorting to flowery Austin Powers–type outfits? Want to slide out an appropriate cocktail for **a night of groovy rump-shaking** as those funky beats blare? Want to wear flared pants and not feel embarrassed? This swinging and bubbling blastoff is the answer for both the first and second questions. As far as the third question goes, I don't think it's going to help until the third glass goes down. **Serves 2**

Ice cubes

2 ounces **gin**

1 ounce **dry vermouth**

1 ounce **Grand Marnier**

Chilled **Champagne**

1. Fill a cocktail shaker halfway full with ice cubes. Add the gin, dry vermouth, and Grand Marnier. Shake well.

2. Strain the mix into 2 flutes. Top with chilled Champagne. Garnish with a brightly colored ascot.

Tin Apple Wedding

Ah, weddings. Aren't they (almost always) lovely, with all the tin decorations, and the apples everywhere? Wait, what's that? All weddings don't have a theme of tin and apples anymore? Where have I been, you ask? **Drinking too many of these** cocktails, I suppose. **Serves 2**

Ice cubes

2 ounces **brandy**

2 ounces **Apfelkorn**

2 ounces **sweet vermouth**

2 dashes **orange bitters**

1. Fill a cocktail shaker halfway full with ice cubes. Add the brandy, Apfelkorn, sweet vermouth, and orange bitters. Shake to the wedding march.

2. Strain into 2 cocktail glasses or glass slippers. Toast the bride and groom.

⬆ *A Note: Apfelkorn is a wheat-based spirit blended with apples, and it has a crisp flavor. Be careful about substituting something syrupy like apple schnapps here, as it will alter the flavor, and perhaps the marriage itself.*

Five Assignation-Worthy Hotel Bars

Looking to meet up for a secret rendezvous or a not-so-secret tryst with that special someone? Or do you just want to have a little get-together and cocktails in a special spot, and then maybe sleep it off in a nice hotel room afterward? These hotel bars won't let you down.

1. **The Roux Bamboo Lounge**, The Sundy House, Delray Beach, Florida
2. **CityBar**, Lenox Hotel, Boston, Massachusetts
3. **Pyramid Bar**, The Fairmont, Dallas, Texas
4. **Redwood Room**, Clift Hotel, San Francisco, California
5. **Columbus Bar**, Columbus Monaco Hotel, Monte Carlo, Monaco

Zoom

An engaging delight that doesn't seem to parallel the ambulatory nature of its designation, this cocktail **does require strenuous shaking**, however, which may have led to the Zoom moniker, as arms must be zoomed to get the correct breakdown of the honey. The honey is crucial as an ingredient. (And it may be used as a sobriquet for whomever you're serving a Zoom to—the Zoom being a drink most reliably served between two, and especially between two feeling amorous. It's the honey, honey, that does start a mood.) **Serves 2**

Ice cubes

4 ounces **brandy**

1½ ounces **heavy cream**

1 ounce **clover honey**

⌁⌁⌁⌁⌁⌁⌁⌁⌁⌁⌁⌁⌁⌁⌁⌁⌁⌁⌁⌁

⬆ *A Note: If the honey isn't dissolving easily, you might try heating it a touch, or thinning it with a small bit of hot water.*

1. Fill a cocktail shaker halfway full with ice cubes. Add the brandy, heavy cream, and honey. Shake exceptionally vigorously for at least 20 seconds.

2. Strain the sweet mix into 2 cocktail glasses. Garnish with fluttering eyelids and a smoky look.

A VARIATION: You can also go Zooming using dark rum, bourbon, or Cognac.

Pacifying a Crowd

Wait, shhh, listen for a minute. Can you hear it? The muted rumbling coming from outside the front door, a step beyond the gate into the yard, only feet away from the back deck?

It's getting louder, and sounds now more like a growl, now more like a roar, now more like a boisterous chant underlined by the stomping of many footsteps. Can you make it out? Louder now, I can hear it: "drinks, drinks, drinks."

What to do when a whole delegation of friends or relatives or neighbors shows up for the party, and you want to be able to serve them a tasty beverage but not spend every minute huddled over the bar or countertop slinging drinks together? Add to this the fact that you want to have delicious drinks (no one wants to have the rep of the party-thrower who serves nasty concoctions), and soon it's not the thunderous noises making you shudder. Fear not, brave explorer into the realm of host or hostess. Pacifying a Crowd has enough punches, cups, and crowd-sized cocktails to set any jam-packed celebration stomping.

Logically, thirst-quenchers scaled to larger levels need a little special care and prep, so don't plan on rushing in too quickly. First off, for many of these recipes, a punch bowl is essential, and not only for the fact that any superior gathering gains cachet when a sparkling crystal (or faux crystal, even) bowl brimming with booze shines. A sturdy, large punch bowl also makes it easier for folks to serve themselves, makes it simpler to merge a mess of drinks for many and have them in a central location, and obviously goes well with those cute little punch cups.

When busting out the punch bowl (said bowls, by the way, are available at most kitchen stores online and off, and aren't as expensive as you might surmise), consider, always, using an ice ring. They're easy to make, and look exquisite, especially when fruit has been added to the ring. Here are the ring rules: Fill a ring mold with about

½ inch of water. Then arrange whatever fruit you're using on top, and freeze until solid. Carefully add more water, until the level nears the mold's top. Freeze again. To unmold, place the frozen ring on a hot towel to loosen it, and then invert it onto a plate until the ice slips out. Voilà!

Now, if the mold trick is too time-consuming, a block of ice fits well into a punch bowl, and chunks of ice also look nice. Always remember the fruit and you'll have half the battle won no matter what genre of ice you use. The other half is won solely by remembering that these generous gatherings, no matter how hectic they might seem, are supposed to be fun—which means you must always reserve a large punch glass for yourself, and don't forget to keep it full.

10 Strong

Here's a model choice for days when the posse is gearing up for a strenuous activity (walking to the bar on a languid afternoon, for example) and needs a swift burst of liquid energy to get the muscles moving, the jaws jabbering, and the gears turning. The 10 Strong is for 10 people, naturally, but it could be served in heftier portions to a smaller group, provided the group could live up to the "strong" moniker. **Serves 10**

Ice cubes

15 ounces **vodka**

7½ ounces **Hpnotiq**

7½ ounces **freshly squeezed orange juice**

5 ounces **freshly squeezed lime juice**

Chilled club soda

10 **lime slices** for garnish

1. Fill a large pitcher three-quarters full with ice cubes. Add the vodka, Hpnotiq, orange juice, and lime juice. Stir 10 times.

2. Fill the pitcher almost to the rim with club soda. Stir again.

3. Pour the mix equally into 10 goblets or regular wine glasses, if it comes to that. Garnish each glass with a lime slice.

American Punch

Let's give a toast to impressive gathering places from the tip of Maine to California's toe, from way out on Orcas Island, Washington, to deep in the heart of the Florida Keys, to the backyards with barbecues blazing, the living rooms with coffee tables pushed back to create room for twisting and Twister, the always popular tiled kitchens with fridges bursting and counters littered with salty snacks, and, of course, the bars in basements, back rooms, and even gracious garages. **Let's give a toast** to every space that provides the room for toasting. And let's make the toast with American Punch. **Serves 10 to 15, depending on mood (theirs, not yours)**

Block of ice (or cracked ice if the block-ice seller is on vacation)

One 750-milliliter bottle **bourbon**

10 ounces **orange curaçao**

8 ounces **Simple Syrup** (page 7)

5 ounces **freshly squeezed lemon juice**

One 750-milliliter bottle **Champagne**

One 2-liter bottle **ginger ale**

1. Add the ice to a punch bowl (if using cracked ice, fill to above the halfway point). Bring on the bourbon, curaçao, simple syrup, and lemon juice. Using a long spoon, stir 50 times (1 for each state).

2. Add the Champagne, then the ginger ale. Stir briefly. Serve in punch glasses or wine glasses, as long as they sparkle.

Four for the Fourth

Show a little pride, a little reverence for our forefathers and foremothers, and demonstrate a little summer-holiday spirit by serving the right mixes at your July 4th celebration. Don't, I beg of you, overindulge and then shoot off fireworks. There's nothing celebratory about a firecracker-related injury.

1. Morning Glory (page 121; perhaps the glory is the reflected glow from revolutionary victories?)
2. American Champagne Cocktail (page 370; perhaps the finest "American"-monikered cocktail)
3. American Punch (above; perhaps the finest "American"-monikered punch)
4. The Abilene (page 410; perhaps the actual center of the continental USA is Abilene—if not, it's darn close)

Arctic Punch

Brrrr, this one's chilly. I sense it's the missing alcohol that keeps it so shivery. But it's **a superior idea** to always have an enjoyable swig for the kids, drivers, and non-drinkers. That idea isn't a twenty-first century one, either. On the contrary, this very recipe is an expanded version of one found in the "Punches—Non-Alcoholic" section of Jacques Straub's slim (though packed with potent recipes) volume titled *Drinks*, which was printed in 1914. **Serves 10**

Block of ice (or, if you must, cracked ice)

One 2-liter bottle **chilled ginger ale**

1 quart **iced tea** (you want a strong tea here—maybe an iced tea made from Earl Grey)

10 ounces **freshly squeezed lime juice**

7½ ounces **raspberry syrup**

Fresh raspberries for garnish

Fresh mint sprigs for garnish

1. Add the ice to a punch bowl (filling it about halfway if using cracked ice). Add the ginger ale, iced tea, lime juice, and raspberry syrup. Stir in the 1914 style (rapidly—no one wasted time in 1914).

2. Serve in punch cups, garnishing each cup with a few fresh raspberries and a sprig of mint.

A NON-VIRGIN VARIATION: Want to make the Arctic saucier? Add 7½ ounces gin to the punch, if your punch bowl can take it.

⬆ *A Note: Substituting other garnishes is fine, if neither raspberries nor mint is in season. Be sure that cups appear festive and that the fruit is fresh. Remember, as Mr. Straub says, "No mixed drink is perfect unless ingredients used are perfect."*

Artillery Punch

This punch is ideal for Fourth of July celebrations after fireworks have been lit, or served before the explosions to folks not taking part in any lighting of fireworks. The reason for the distance from banging, flaming, and incendiary devices while drinking the Artillery Punch is simple: It **packs quite a detonating nature** of its own. There's no need to multiply the dangers. **Serves 10 to 15**

Cracked ice

One 750-milliliter bottle **dry red wine**

One 750-milliliter bottle **bourbon**

One 750-milliliter bottle **brandy**

7½ ounces **freshly squeezed lemon juice**

5 ounces **Simple Syrup** (page 7)

10 dashes **Peychaud's bitters**

Lemon slices for garnish

1. Fill a punch bowl halfway full with cracked ice. Add the wine, bourbon, brandy, lemon juice, simple syrup, and bitters. Stir in a whizzing motion (like those firecrackers that spin in a blazing circle) for a good 20 seconds.

2. Serve in wine glasses or punch glasses. Garnish each glass with a lemon slice.

🔺 *A Note: I like the Peychaud's bitters here, because it helps soften the sharp edges. If you have other bitters, don't shy away from experimenting. It's better to experiment on the punch than to try and make your own fireworks.*

Bacardi Cocktail

The BC (or Bacardi Cocktail) has been a staple since bubbles were introduced into water, or thereabouts. It's such a classic that I'm sure it's odd to some to see it in the Pacifying a Crowd chapter. On the other hand, it's easy to make and tasty; **a crowd-pleaser** that won't leave you struggling to juggle drink construction with conversation during the midst of a busy early Sunday evening shindig—and you don't want to be juggling in this situation, because you might spill onto the white evening wear I'm sure you're decked out in. With the simple BC, there's no real spillage worry to be had, so relax and enjoy. **Serves 6**

Ice cubes

9 ounces **white Bacardi rum**

4½ ounces **freshly squeezed lime juice**

3 ounces **grenadine**

1. Fill a large cocktail shaker halfway full with ice cubes. Add the rum, lime juice, and grenadine. Shake well.

2. Strain the mix into 6 cocktail glasses. Serve knowing that you're sipping a bit of history with each glass.

🔺 *A Note: Is 6 a crowd? That depends on the room. But with a friend who's willing to shake a bit, and an extra shaker, this can easily be made for a bigger crowd.*

Baccio Punch

Taste is a funny thing. Everyone's taste slightly or vastly differs, which is why I cannot underline this enough—you can't please every guest 100 percent of the time. What you *can* do is **control the odds somewhat in your favor** (but not as much as Vegas casinos control the odds in their favor). This especially becomes true when serving something with grapefruit juice, as that particular juice tends to pull people strongly into either the "love it" or the "hate it" camp. If you're serving Baccio Punch, be sure beforehand that at least a quorum of guests falls into the "love it" camp. **Serves 10**

Block of ice or a passel of **cracked ice**

10 ounces **gin**

10 ounces **freshly squeezed grapefruit juice**

5 ounces **anisette**

5 ounces **Simple Syrup** (page 7)

15 to 20 **lemon slices**

1 liter **chilled club soda**

One 750-milliliter bottle **chilled Champagne**

1. Add the block of ice to a large punch bowl, or fill the punch bowl three-quarters full with cracked ice.

2. Add the gin, grapefruit juice, anisette, simple syrup, and lemon slices. Stir once for each person partaking.

3. Add the club soda and Champagne, concurrently. Stir 5 more times. Serve in punch cups or small wine glasses.

Cure the Long Meeting Blues with These 3 Throw-Downs

If you've never had to sit through one of a kind that seems endless, where much of nothing is talked about and nothing much is done, where counting the light bulbs in the room is more exciting than the person droning on, and on, and on, then you should count your blessings. If you haven't had the dubious pleasure of one of these meetings, then turn the page. Everyone else, know that swiftly slurping one of the following drives away that post-meeting depression darn quickly.

1 Tidal Wave (page 194)

2 Adios Amigo (page 322)

3 Brainstorm (page 328)

Black and Tan

Here's where the **beer lovers get theirs**. Not that this book doesn't have other beer-based recipes (see Summer Beer, page 403), but the almost back-to-back Black and Tan and Black Velvet (page 288) let the beer boys and girls pour the barley pop for pals in sizeable numbers. The benefit of the Black and Tan is this: While it takes a second or two to guarantee proper construction, it's not that tricky to make a number of these in a row, lined up on the home bar. When through, the drink's presentation is attractive enough that a round of applause just might be in order.

Serves 9

Six 12-ounce bottles **cold pale ale** or **lager beer** (Bass Pale Ale is ideal)

Six 12-ounce bottles **cold stout** (Guinness is the classic here)

⬆ **A Note:** *If pint glasses aren't at hand, feel free to use smaller receptacles, as long as you pour equal amounts of the two types of beer, and never let them combine when pouring.*

1. Pour the pale ale equally into 9 pint glasses (8 ounces per glass).

2. Slowly (pouring over a spoon if need be to slow the descent of the beer) pour the stout over the ale in each glass, being sure that they don't blend together. Stratification is the watchword here.

Blackberry Cup

Getting back to nature is lovely in theory. As the cup in question uses a number of natural items, and benefits from a bundle of nature as garnish, it should help us celebrate the forest beyond the last dirt road. So I say, pack this along on the next camping trip. **Everyone ends up happier**, singing the praises of the scenery and the drink.

Serves 8

Crushed ice

16 ounces **white rum**

12 ounces **freshly squeezed lime juice**

12 ounces **blackberry syrup**

Fresh mint sprigs for garnish

Lime and **lemon slices** for garnish

Maraschino or **fresh cherries** for garnish

1. Fill a large pitcher halfway full with crushed ice. Add the rum, lime juice, and blackberry syrup. Stir well.

2. Fill 8 goblets or other sturdy glasses with crushed ice. Using a thin stick, long spoon, or tent peg to keep the ice from leaving the pitcher, pour the mix equally into the goblets.

3. Garnish each with a mint sprig, a lime and lemon slice, and a cherry.

A VARIATION: Blackberry not enticing you to sing the beauty of the forest and such? Substitute strawberry or raspberry syrup.

Black Velvet

While a bit more tux and tails and small black dresses than its second cousin the Black and Tan (page 287), the Black Velvet also employs stout for **a deep, rich, thick point**. Here, stout's united with Champagne, with a result comfortably supplied both during a late Sunday football game alongside nachos and pizza and during a black-tie affair after a meal of Tournedos Rossini.

Much like the Black and Tan, the stout in the Black Velvet should be cold for every drop to go down smoothly. This is, I realize, anathema to many beer drinkers, but if induced into that first sip, I feel they'll come around quickly. **Serves 8**

Four 12-ounce bottles **cold stout** or other **dark beer**

48 ounces **chilled Champagne**

1. Add 6 ounces of stout to each of eight 12-ounce beer mugs or other 12-ounce glasses.

2. With a steady hand and wearing shiny shoes, add 6 ounces of Champagne to each glass. Stir each glass once, slowly.

A VARIATION: Substitute 2 ounces of hard cider for the 6 ounces of Champagne in each glass and you'll have a Black Velveteen.

If You Can Only Have One Drink Before Dinner, Have One of These Three

There are those expansive (and expensive) meals that, as they approach, lead a potential eater to restraint. What if the stomach only takes so much, and no more, and then the food bill comes and only part of the plate is cleaned, due to cocktail overindulgence before dinner? A shame, truly (and going against renowned drinker H.L. Mencken's thought that, "most of the trouble from so-called overeating comes from under-drinking."). But if a situation arises where you're worried about getting overstuffed, and therefore are partaking solely of one predinner cocktail, stick to these tried-and-true favorites.

1. Negroni (page 123)
2. The Old Fashioned (page 37)
3. Dubonnet Cocktail (page 104)

Bourbon-Tea Punch

This introduces right off the bat two beverages usually thought of as separate entities. Thanks to Fred Thompson's dandy book *Iced Tea* (The Harvard Common Press, 2002) one of the best views of tea's chilly side, **the word is out about bourbon and tea**, and the word is that, combined, they create a swell charmer—a welcome addition to a backyard picnic or pig roast. **Serves 24**

2 cups **water**

3 **tea bags** (see Second Note)

24 ounces **bourbon**

16 ounces **freshly squeezed orange juice**

8 ounces **Grand Marnier**

8 ounces **freshly squeezed lemon juice**

1 cup **sugar**

Block of ice (or cracked ice—but don't tell Mr. Thompson)

One 2-liter bottle **chilled club soda**

Lemon slices for garnish (optional)

1. Add the water to a small saucepan. Bring it to a boil, then turn off the heat and add the tea bags, leaving them in the water for 15 minutes.

2. Remove the bags and add the tea to a large heatproof pitcher.

3. Add the bourbon, orange juice, Grand Marnier, lemon juice, and sugar to the pitcher. Stir well, until the sugar has dissolved. Set the pitcher in the refrigerator to cool.

4. Add the block of ice to a punch bowl. Pour in the chilled tea mix. Add the club soda and stir well.

5. Serve in punch glasses or other small, attractive glassware. If the glasses look bare, garnish each with a lemon slice.

⬆ *A Note: Mr. Thompson sees this recipe as serving 24 in punch form. His friends are more refined than mine, though. If serving and thinking that more than one glass might be consumed by each person, don't be ashamed if you make this recipe for only 10.*

⬆ *A Second Note: Go with a regular tea blend here, such as Earl Grey, unless you're feeling experimental.*

Bring the House Down

When the ol' office space is bringing you down from the heights of cube heaven to the bottom of the communal kitchen, and the only outlet for this feeling seems to be springing into your boss's office with a beaker of hot coffee poised to throw in his or her face, and when your office- or cube- or hallway-mate has been gritting his or her teeth loud enough to crack glass—stop! Work should never boil over to this degree. Equalize the job equilibrium for you and those close co-workers by **shifting into party mode** with a pitcher of this.

Serves 6

12 ounces **dark rum**

12 ounces **freshly squeezed orange juice**

1½ ounces **cream of coconut**

Ice cubes

Chilled 7UP or **Sprite**

Orange slices for garnish

1. Add the rum, orange juice, and cream of coconut to a large pitcher. Using a slotted spoon, stir well, rapidly, and voraciously, for a good 2 minutes. You have to work to break up the cream of coconut to make it play nice.

2. Fill 6 highball glasses halfway full with ice cubes. Pour the mix from the pitcher equally among the 6 glasses.

3. Top each glass off with 7UP and garnish with an orange slice. Strongly encourage each partaker to squeeze the orange over the glass. That burst of fresh OJ on top brings the world together.

6
Barnyard Favorites

Whether sitting on a picket fence watching your crops grow as the sun sinks down or perching on a rocking chair on the porch of a dude ranch you'll only be at for a week, don't relax without the proper barnyard beverage. For one thing, you'll feel a bit closer to all the livestock, and for another thing, you'll be a hit among the other farmhands after introducing them to these drinks.

1 Horse's Neck (page 304)

2 Milk Punch (page 307)

3 Golden Goose (page 360)

4 Farmer (page 164)

5 Dog's Nose (page 209)

6 Horsefeather (page 387)

Caribbean

Can't make the trip to the Caribbean, forced instead to watch shows about St. Croix on public television? Flip off those flip-flops, flip on serious shoes, borrow a pick-up, fill the back up with sand (from the local sand shop), unload in the driveway, **flip the flip-flops back on** (as well as proper beach wear), pour up this punch, phone up some like-minded friends, and bring the Caribbean home. **Serves 10**

1 **lime,** cut into wedges

5 ounces **Simple Syrup** (page 7)

Cracked ice

One 750-milliliter bottle **dark rum**

5 ounces **freshly squeezed lemon juice**

5 ounces **freshly squeezed lime juice**

5 ounces **fresh pineapple juice**

1 **pineapple,** peeled and cut into chunks (use the juice, if possible, for the required pineapple juice above)

One 2-liter bottle **chilled ginger ale**

1. Add the lime wedges and simple syrup to a cocktail shaker or large mixing glass. Using a muddler or wooden spoon, muddle well.

2. Pour the lime-syrup mixture into a punch bowl. Fill the bowl halfway with cracked ice. Add the rum, lemon juice, lime juice, pineapple juice, and pineapple chunks. Stir well.

3. Add the ginger ale. Stir well again. Ladle into small wine glasses or other glasses.

Champagne Americana

I say, Bubbles, what garden variety of tonic do you suggest we serve to the rabble descending on the south lawn this Saturday for the annual rose show and dachshund display? What's that, you say? It's not a rabble? Instead, attendees' attire of white jackets, white skirts, white shoes, white scarves, and spats demonstrates the desire for **stronger stuff than grammy's old-timey lemon icee recipe**? You suggest the Champagne Americana for future dachshund displays, as well as any spring folly? I suppose you know best, Bubbles dear. Let me grab the bourbon. **Serves 8**

3½ teaspoons **sugar**

8 dashes **Angostura bitters**

8 ounces **bourbon**

Ice cubes

One 750-milliliter bottle **chilled Champagne**

Lemon twists for garnish

1. Add the sugar and bitters to a mixing glass or cocktail shaker. Stir briefly.

2. Add the bourbon to the glass. Stir well, for at least 1 minute.

3. Fill 8 wine glasses with ice cubes. Strain the bourbon mix equally into the glasses.

4. Top each glass off with Champagne. Garnish each with a lemon twist.

Champagne Punch

There are, I would venture to estimate, as many variations on Champagne Punch as there are punch makers (which, according to the last census, was 3,456,987). Even *you* have the liberty to adjust the below recipe to taste and call it your very own. Remember that every punch lacks a, well, punch, if it isn't ladled from a sparkling crystal, or faux-crystal, punch bowl. This rule is tripled whenever Champagne is involved, as the big bubbly C **looks lovely in a classy twinkling bowl**, with fruit bobbing on the surface and a sizeable block of ice drifting in the center. The Champagne Punch below bumps any block party (even if it's at a block of apartments) from mundane to glamorous with a single dip of the ladle (as long as it's followed by further dipping, of course, unless it's a very large ladle). **Serves 10**

Ice (in block form if possible; if not, large chunks)

6 ounces **freshly squeezed orange juice**

4 ounces **Simple Syrup** (page 7)

2 ounces **freshly squeezed lime juice**

2 ounces **freshly squeezed lemon juice**

6 ounces **white rum**

6 ounces **dark rum**

One 750-milliliter bottle **chilled Champagne**

Orange, lime, and **lemon slices** for garnish

1. Add the ice to a large punch bowl. If using chunks (as opposed to a large block of ice), fill the bowl just under halfway.

2. Add the orange juice, simple syrup, lime juice, and lemon juice. With a large spoon or ladle, stir 10 times.

3. Add the light and dark rums. Stir 10 more times.

4. Add the Champagne, but not too quickly. Enjoy the moment. Add a goodly amount of orange, lime, and lemon slices. Stir, but only once.

5. Ladle into punch glasses or festive goblets. Try to ensure that every guest gets a slice of fruit and a smile.

Chickadee Punch

Chick-a-dee-dee-dee, chick-a-dee-dee-dee. **That's the crowd clamoring for more** Chickadee Punch, in the voice of the bird it's named in honor of (I don't say named for, because I fail to see the parallel between this sweet and fruity punch and the tiny bird, though after a few cups guests may twitter around a bit). My first sighting of this punch was via mid–twentieth century punch master Trader Vic, who listed out punches like some folks list birds they've seen. **Serves 10 to 15**

Block of ice (or cracked ice, if you must)

15 ounces **freshly squeezed orange juice**

10 ounces **sloe gin**

7½ ounces **dark rum**

5 ounces **maraschino liqueur**

5 ounces **freshly squeezed lemon juice**

5 ounces **Simple Syrup** (page 7)

One 2-liter bottle **chilled club soda**

Orange slices for garnish

Maraschino cherries for garnish

1. Add the block of ice to a punch bowl (or fill the bowl three-quarters full with cracked ice). Add the orange juice, sloe gin, rum, maraschino liqueur, lemon juice, and simple syrup. Stir well (at the speed a chickadee's wings flutter, if that doesn't cause spillage).

2. Add the club soda. Stir again, but only a few times. Serve in punch cups (if you have them) or wine glasses, garnishing each vessel with an orange slice and a cherry.

⬆ **A Note:** *For those keeping track, 213 cherries have been used in the book up until now.*

Customizing Isn't a Crime

Many feel that a definitive answer is always the way to go (especially when it's their answer), even in matters of taste. This sentiment cuts across many genres of art and criticism. I, myself, have at one time or another thought that very same thing. But with cocktail recipes, even those right here in this book, I think a little customization to fit personal taste isn't a bad route. Here's the deal: People's tastes are different, in both big and subtle ways. If you try any drink and absolutely can't stand it, you should pick another recipe entirely, but if you try a drink and think, "Well, I like it, but would like a touch more lemon tang even better," you shouldn't give up on the drink completely. Instead, add a touch more fresh lemon juice and be happy.

Christmas Punch

In days of yore, people spent winter hours seated near the fire debating whose holiday punch reached the top rung of the long ladder of festive beverages. This is how the great Hatfield/McCoy holiday feud of 1857 began, which lasted for many, many Decembers—sad Decembers, I have to mention, as the feud meant no one was getting to **ladle a friendly cup** from the neighbor's punch bowl. Perhaps this contributed to the lack of neighborly punch sharing we have today. Well, I say "bah, humbug" on the ending of this merry ritual and demand that my neighbors whip up their grandparents' (or great-great-grandparents') holiday punch, to re-instill the idea that at any time one should be able to stop in, say "Season's greetings," and be drinking punch within minutes. I'll be serving the below recipe, of which the orange wards off colds, the brandy warms the stomach and soul, and the Champagne matches the season's joyful nature. **Serves 10**

Ice (in block form if possible; if not, large chunks)

4 ounces **Cointreau**

4 ounces **brandy**

2 **oranges,** cut into wedges

Two 750-milliliter bottles **chilled Champagne**

1. Add the ice to a large punch bowl. If using chunks, fill the bowl just under halfway.

2. Add the Cointreau and brandy. Using a trusted ladle or long spoon, stir briefly.

3. Add the orange wedges, and then pour in the Champagne. Stir 12 times, and let sit for a minute, so that the ingredients can get acquainted in the manner of the times.

A VARIATION: If wanting to up the holiday stakes even more, add 1 cup frozen cranberries to the above recipe.

Cider Cup

It's different enough from its brother-in-law (they share the same name, but not much else), the Blackberry Cup (page 287), that to only list the Cider Cup as a variant of said in-law encourages a lack of confidence in this beauty. And, as it's being served to a number of revelers here, showing **any lack of confidence could be deadly**. Never let revelers see weakness—they'll take over, no matter how good the drink. And never drink this while standing on two feet. For good luck, you must drink while standing on one foot. (No, I'm not insane. See the quote below.)

Serves 8

Cracked ice

8 ounces **brandy**

6 ounces **Cointreau**

4 ounces **Simple Syrup** (page 7)

1 quart **apple cider**

16 ounces **chilled club soda**

Apple slices for garnish

Maraschino cherries for garnish

1. Fill a pitcher three-quarters full with cracked ice. Add the brandy, Cointreau, and simple syrup. Stir with confidence.

2. Add the apple cider. Stir once. Add the club soda and stir twice.

3. Pour the mixture into 8 goblets, getting some ice into each goblet. Garnish each with an apple slice and a cherry. If those garnishes aren't to your liking, do as Harry Craddock, author of *The Savoy Cocktail Book* (reprinted by Trafalgar Square Publishing, 2000), suggests and "decorate with slices of fruit in season."

"The tallest girl, standing on one foot upon a seat, with her lap full of cakes, **a cup of brandy in her right hand** and a piece of elm-bark or linden-bark in her left, prayed to the god Waizganthos that the flax might grow as high as she was standing. Then, after draining the cup, she had it refilled, and poured the brandy on the ground as an offering to Waizganthos, and threw down the cakes for his attendant sprites. If she remained steady on one foot throughout the ceremony, it was an omen that the flax crop would be good; but if she let her foot down, it was feared that the crop might fail."

SIR JAMES GEORGE FRAZER, *The Golden Bough*, 1922

Crowd Control

There are moments in any soirée when the host or hostess requests nothing more than to regain a soupçon of control of the situation—without resorting to a high-powered hose. Whisk together **this pitcher of goodness**, and breaking out the bullhorn won't be necessary. Mastery of any circumstances will fall right into your hands.

Serves 8

Handful of **fresh mint leaves**

10 to 12 **lemon slices**

Ice cubes

12 ounces **vodka**

8 ounces **limoncello**

Chilled club soda

1. Add the mint leaves and lemon slices to a large pitcher. Using a long muddler or wooden spoon, muddle the mint and lemon together.

2. Fill the pitcher with ice cubes. Add the vodka and limoncello. Stir well.

3. Top off the pitcher with the club soda. Stir again, flexing a bit if anyone in the crowd looks antsy.

4. Pour into 8 wine glasses or goblets, getting some ice into each glass and sharing equally to avoid trouble later in the evening.

Random Excuses for a Party

Honestly, I don't believe there must be a great or even good excuse for a party. The party is, in itself, the excuse for its own existence (if that's not getting too deep). If you are one of those who has to have a preexisting occasion to throw a wingding, I would hate for you not to have one. Here, then, are some reasons to have parties on particular dates, or near particular dates (the latter gives needed leeway).

1. February 6, birthday of Babe Ruth: Have a big one for the Bambino.

2. March 13, anniversary of the discovery of Pluto: Get Pluto'd (which isn't a recognized euphemism for being a tad bit tipsy, but which should be).

3. July 14, Bastille Day: Raise a toast to taking down monarchies (have it be a Champagne-based drink for authenticity).

4. September 4, anniversary of the first electric power station: Blended drinks for everyone.

5. November 10, the day Kentucky outlawed dueling: Celebrate all the bourbon distillers not done in due to duels.

6. February 4, my birthday: I'll let you pick up the tab.

Don't Just Stand There

A fantastic fall frolic favorite, the Don't Just Stand There should be served when the leaves are turning. It makes for **a fine addition to hay rides** or square dances, as well as more citified ballroom bacchanals, group Go Fish games, last-gasp picnics, and quilting parties (see quote below). Have a couple of ripe apples on hand though, because someone's going to want to start bobbing.

The Don't Just Stand There shines at well-populated proceedings. With this in mind, I've set down the recipe for ten folks. It could work for less, but they'd have to be a hearty crew. **Serves 10**

Ice cubes

One 750-milliliter bottle nonalcoholic **sparkling apple cider**

One 750-milliliter bottle **applejack**

Apple slices for garnish (optional)

1. Fill a large pitcher with ice cubes.

2. Add the cider and applejack to the pitcher. Stir well with a large wooden spoon.

3. Pour into highball glasses until everyone looks happy. Garnish each deserving glass with an apple slice.

"Here is the recipe that made Aunt Dinah's quilting parties **such a success**."

ROBERT S. ALLISON, JR., referring to the Don't Just Stand There, from Crosby Gaige's *Cocktail Guide and Ladies Companion*, 1941

Excellent Eggnog

Warning: this holiday favorite is often misguidedly made ahead, resulting in a less-than-celebratory concoction. It could challenge preconceptions and change winter celebration menus forever, once people start realizing that eggnog is excellent, attractive, and tastes great. Best of all, when made well, taking the necessary time, **the crowd goes wild** after the first cup. I can hear their screams of joy from here. **Serves 8**

8 **large eggs,** preferably organic

2¼ cups **superfine sugar**

8 ounces **brandy**

8 ounces **rum**

4 ounces **bourbon**

1 quart **milk**

Freshly grated nutmeg for garnish

✕ A Warning: *As this recipe uses raw eggs, don't serve it to the elderly or anyone with a compromised immune system. And always, always, use fresh eggs.*

1. Separate the egg yolks from the egg whites, setting the whites aside for a moment.

2. In a large mixing bowl, beat the yolks with a hand mixer until completely combined. Add the sugar and beat until it reaches a creamy consistency.

3. Add the brandy, rum, and bourbon, and then the milk, beating well.

4. In a medium-size mixing bowl, beat the egg whites with a hand mixer until soft peaks form (be sure before beating the whites that you have cleaned and thoroughly dried the beaters).

5. Fold the egg whites into the yolk-sugar-alcohol mixture. Refrigerate the mix until well chilled (at least 3 hours). You may also refrigerate it overnight if desired.

6. Stir to recombine as needed. Serve the eggnog in mugs, topping each serving with some nutmeg.

⬆ A Note: *For a fun party game, take a vote as to who thinks "eggnog" derives from the English word "noggin" (a small glass with an upright handle) versus a combination of "egg" and "grog." All those on the side with the fewest votes make the next batch.*

Fish House Punch

A punch whose history aligns to the history of the United States (in that it has been around since at least the era of the Revolutionary War, according to trustworthy accounts), Fish House Punch originally was caught at the Schuylkill Fishing Company in Philadelphia, Pennsylvania (or the Fish House Club), which was a club of fishermen who also cooked, ate, and drank. If serving Fish House Punch, perhaps accompany it with a fishy dish caught that morning (at least caught at the local fish market—you and I can **keep that secret**). **Serves 10**

Block of ice (or cracked ice, if the fish have taken the blocks)

One 750-milliliter bottle **dark rum**

15 ounces **Cognac**

7½ ounces **peach brandy**

7½ ounces **freshly squeezed lemon juice**

7½ ounces **Simple Syrup** (page 7)

1. Add the ice to a punch bowl (fill it about three-quarters full if using cracked ice). Add the rum, Cognac, peach brandy, lemon juice, and simple syrup. Stir 10 times, and let sit for 10 minutes while you catch that last fish.

2. Stir again. Serve in punch cups or wine glasses.

Golden Dawn Punch

Consuming copious amount of Golden Dawn Punch does not automatically place the drinker as a member of the Hermetic Order of the Golden Dawn, founded in 1888 by doctor and master mason William Wynn Westcott, a group that eventually became the tops of the occult ladder at the nineteenth century's close (a time when occult groups were as popular as entertainment news programs are today). **Let the party start** without any weird vibes. **Serves 8**

Block of ice (or, if unavailable, conjure up cracked ice)

16 ounces **apricot brandy**

16 ounces **freshly squeezed orange juice**

8 ounces **freshly squeezed lime juice**

8 ounces **Simple Syrup** (page 7)

One 2-liter bottle **chilled club soda**

Fresh apricot slices for garnish

1. Add the block of ice to a punch bowl (or fill the bowl halfway with cracked ice). Add the apricot brandy, orange juice, lime juice, and simple syrup. Swirl the liquids contentedly around the ice for 5 minutes.

2. Add the club soda. Swirl for 3 more minutes. Serve in small cups garnished with apricot slices, to bring a melodious air to the room.

A VIRGIN VARIATION: Want to take the punch out of the Golden Dawn Punch? Remove the apricot brandy and the simple syrup and replace them with 24 ounces apricot syrup, which is available at most gourmet stores.

Grog

Gather round the mizzenmast, and let me spill for you sorry lot the story of Grog. Though the lineage of Grog dates to Vice-Admiral William Penn, who began using rum as a ration for the Navy after capturing Jamaica in 1655, the true grogfather was Vice-Admiral Edward Vernon, known for treating sailors a notch better than most, and known by sailors as "Old Grog" due to a black coat he preferred that was constructed of a silk, mohair, and wool fabric called grogam. Vice-Admiral Vernon, on August 21, 1740, ordered that the rum rations should be mixed with water to cut back on onboard drunken carousing—and lime and sugar were added to the mix to make it not quite as nauseating (it wasn't the finest rum). With this Grog knowledge, it should be obvious that this is the ideal drink for any parties where **the attire of choice is sailor suits**, or any party where sea shanties are sung, planks are walked, and jaunty hats are worn. **Serves 10**

1¼ quarts **water**

10 **cinnamon sticks**

15 ounces **rum**

7½ ounces **Simple Syrup** (page 7)

7½ ounces **freshly squeezed lime juice**

1. Add the water and cinnamon sticks to a large, nonreactive saucepan. Heat over medium heat for 5 minutes.

2. Add the rum, simple syrup, and lime juice to the saucepan. Continue heating for 10 to 15 minutes, or until the mixture is good and hot—but not boiling.

3. Ladle the steaming Grog into 10 mugs, making sure that each mug gets a cinnamon stick.

Harvest Bowl

Harvest celebrations have been going on since humankind moved from being hunter-gatherers to planter-pickers. There's no reason that **this ancient tradition**—even if you aren't harvesting anything you planted and haven't even been near a vegetable field or fruit orchard—shouldn't be kept alive and kicking by partying it up in late summer and early fall. **Serves 10 to 15**

Block of ice (if no block is available, cracked ice can be harvested)

15 ounces **apple cider**

7½ ounces **vodka**

5 ounces **orange curaçao**

1 **apple,** sliced, for garnish

1 **lemon,** sliced, for garnish

One 750-milliliter bottle **sparkling apple juice**

One 750-milliliter bottle **chilled Champagne**

1. Add the block of ice to a large punch bowl (if using cracked ice, fill the bowl halfway).

2. Add the cider, vodka, curaçao, and apple and lemon slices. Using a long spoon, swirl the ingredients around the ice.

3. Pour in the sparkling apple juice and Champagne—in that order, and being aware that if poured too rapidly, the bubbly nature of both could cause overflow. Again using a long spoon, swirl multiple times around the ice block. Ladle into wine glasses, goblets, or the glassware of your choice, getting a piece of fruit in each glass.

Hey Honey Punch

Hey honey, pick me up one of those finger sandwiches when circumventing the crowded kitchen, could you? Hey honey, what's that reveler's name, I've forgotten, could you go ask? Hey honey, would you slip me a napkin from the den, and grab me a handful of peanuts, too? Hey honey, you don't mind saving me a place in the bathroom line do you? When the requests overwhelm, inhale a deep breath, remember those enjoyable features of your honey, fill another mug with Hey Honey Punch, and realize you've made the right choice after all.

Serves 12 honeys

¼ cup **water**

¼ cup **light-colored honey**

9 ounces **fresh pineapple juice**

6 ounces **freshly squeezed orange juice**

3 ounces **freshly squeezed lemon juice**

Block of ice or **cracked ice**

12 ounces **vodka**

6 ounces **orange curaçao**

Two 2-liter bottles **chilled ginger ale**

Orange slices for garnish

Maraschino cherries for garnish

1. Bring the water to a boil in the microwave. Pour into a sturdy pitcher and add the honey, pineapple juice, orange juice, and lemon juice. Stir vigorously. Chill in the refrigerator.

2. Add the block of ice to a large punch bowl (or fill it about halfway with cracked ice). Pour in the juice-honey mixture, as well as the vodka and curaçao. Stir smoothly with a large spoon or ladle.

3. Pour the ginger ale in slowly. Add a goodly amount of orange slices and cherries. Stir slowly until all is mixed. Ladle into pretty mugs or wine glasses, trying to get an orange slice and a cherry into the glasses of everyone you like.

Horse's Neck

Animal lovers, have no fear. This recipe in no manner entails actually using the neck of a horse, not even using the mane as a stirring device. No horses will be harmed in the making of this drink. It's an ideal beverage **for those equestrian parties** that entice both drinking and horse riding, as it's possible to serve the more adult version to experienced riders and the virgin version to tenderfoot nonriders. **Serves 8**

Ice cubes

16 ounces **Kentucky bourbon**

One 2-liter bottle **ginger ale**

16 dashes **Angostura bitters**

8 long **lemon spirals** for garnish

1. Fill 8 large highball glasses halfway full with ice cubes.

2. Add the bourbon first to each glass, and then the ginger ale (bourbon first for respect purposes).

3. Add 2 good shakes of Angostura bitters to each glass. Stir well.

4. Drape a lemon spiral over the edge of each glass, in a manner reminiscent of a horse's mane.

A VIRGIN VARIATION: Simple enough: Remove the bourbon from the above recipe.

Huckle-My-Butt

Even if this wasn't a historic English drink (sometimes called Huckle-My-Buff), **I wouldn't hesitate** to introduce the Huckle-My-Butt. It's called Huckle-My-Butt, for Dickens's sake. You'd never forgive me if I forgot to enter it into this tome. **Serves 6**

2 **large eggs,** preferably organic

18 ounces **lager-style beer**

6 ounces **brandy**

3 ounces **Simple Syrup** (page 7)

½ teaspoon **ground cinnamon**

½ teaspoon **freshly grated nutmeg**

¼ teaspoon **whole cloves**

1. Beat the eggs together in a small bowl. The yolks should be completely indistinguishable from the whites.

2. Add the beer, brandy, and simple syrup to a large pitcher. Stir. Add the cinnamon, nutmeg, cloves, and beaten eggs. Stir well, until all is combined.

3. Pour into 6 mugs. Huckle profusely.

⬆ *A Note: If freshly ground cinnamon and nutmeg are available, they help tremendously with the huckling. And speaking of spices, watch out for those cloves. Don't drink them by accident.*

✖ *A Warning: The raw eggs used in this recipe mean that it shouldn't be served to those with compromised immune systems or to the elderly. And, please, use fresh eggs.*

Signature Drinks, Part I

You're about to send out the invites for your next happy hoedown (or wonderful wingding, or bubbling box-social, etc.), and want to pick out a signature drink or two to serve at the occasion, to make your life as host that much simpler. But how do you decide on just one or two of the many possible options? When I'm facing this same quandary, I think over a few things.

First, how many people are expected? If it's a large crowd and you don't feel like shaking drinks all night, consider a punch that you can serve in a punch bowl. If it's more intimate, and you want each individual guest to feel special, then you'll probably want to shake something up.

Second, what genre of party are you planning? Is it a fancier affair (in which case you'll want a fancier drink, one with Champagne perhaps, or one that has an elegant garnish), a shorts and swimsuits around the pool party (in which case a pitcher of blended drinks might be perfect), or a picnic in the backyard where jeans and T-shirts will be worn (in which case you might lean toward a highball that has a bit of bite to it)?

Also, when thinking about your signature drinks, consider the time of year. If it's winter, or chilly, perhaps a warm drink (or at least a warming drink) is in order. In late spring, something that uses some fresh mint works well. At the height of summer, look for something crisp and not too sweet.

Finally, you want to remember if any of your guests have a particular allegiance or allergy to certain base liquors. If a high percentage of the crowd isn't going to appreciate a gin-based cocktail, then remember that—if you happen to love gin and can't imagine a party without it, then consider two signature drinks. It's no fun to have the highlight of your celebration be unloved.

For more on signature drinks, see page 324.

Limoncello

A true *nettare degli dei*, and worthy of all modern Junos and Jupiters, with a golden hue that seemingly emanates from any glass it's poured into, Limoncello chilled and sipped **turns a mere mortal day into memorable hours**. Not to get too poetic, but when famous fourteenth-century Italian poet Petrarch said, "To be able to say how much you love is to love but little," he may have been referencing this Italian liqueur, because those who really love it (and I'm one) know that it's better to serve Limoncello than to talk about it—it's impossible to say how much we love it, anyway. **Serves at least 10, and probably more**

14 **lemons**

1 liter **grain alcohol**

24 ounces **Simple Syrup** (page 7)

⬆ **A Note:** *Look for grain alcohol in your local liquor mart. As it isn't available in some states, it is possible to make this recipe with vodka, instead. I'm not sure you'll reach the same celestial plane, but it's better than no Limoncello at all.*

1. Peel the lemons, making sure to get as little of the white pith as possible. Add the peels to a large glass container, one that has a lid that fits tight and stays secure. Use the peeled lemons to juice for other drinks.

2. Add the grain alcohol to the glass container with the lemon peel. Put the lid on the container, and put it in a secluded, cool, shady spot (the basement, perhaps). Let it sit for 2 weeks.

3. After 2 weeks, add the simple syrup and stir briefly. Reseal and put the container back into the same safe, dark, cool spot (being sure to keep it away from sun and prying eyes).

4. After another 2 weeks, carefully strain the Limoncello through double layers of cheesecloth carefully into a pitcher or other large container that's easily poured from.

5. Using 2 new sheets of cheesecloth, strain the Limoncello into bottles or jars that have tight-fitting lids. Store it in the freezer, drinking it once it's reached a chilled demeanor.

Milk Punch
My kingdom for anyone who can make me a mighty Milk Punch, one that mirrors the grand milk punches of yore, when **every dainty tavern and smoky den of iniquity** boasted of their milk punch, made from a mother's recipe handed down generation to generation. Okay, if not my kingdom, how about $5? The below recipe should start the Milk Punch juices flowing, while you work on developing a new one that also meets the above requirements, and which would make your great-great-great-great-great grandparents proud as well. **Serves 8**

Ice cubes

24 ounces **bourbon**

24 ounces **milk** (use the percentage you're used to, but don't use skim)

4 ounces **Simple Syrup** (page 7)

2 ounces **dark rum**

Freshly grated nutmeg for garnish

1. Fill a large pitcher halfway full with ice cubes. Add the bourbon, milk, simple syrup, and rum. Stir voraciously.

2. Fill 8 large highball glasses halfway full with ice cubes. Using a spoon to ensure that no ice leaves the pitcher, pour the Milk Punch equally among the glasses.

3. Add a thin sprinkling of nutmeg to each glass. Serve with a Cockney accent.

A VEGAN VARIATION: The Milk Punch isn't exactly the same when made with soy milk, but neither is it a poor experience (the soy milk actually adds nice body). If trying this option, use plain soy milk; the flavored kind detracts from the other flavors in this drink.

Making Your Own: The Joys of Liqueur-Creating

The making of liqueurs at home rewards on multiple levels: it's fun, it can save you money, it provides a nice platform for gentle bragging to friends when drinking said liqueurs, and it lets you use your imagination in a way that ties into your cocktail love (as the liqueurs can be used in cocktails after they're made). The one downside is that you have to always wait a bit to taste the finished project. As the Limoncello recipe (opposite) demonstrates, letting the ingredients get acquainted for a couple of weeks is key. When experimenting, feel free to use that recipe as a guide, switching the base liquor from Everclear to vodka as desired, and replacing the lemon with other fruits and spices. Some tasty ideas are oranges, cherries, cinnamon sticks, vanilla beans, and coffee beans.

Monsoon

The rainy season has some alluring features: sharing umbrellas, for example, or having a good excuse for not cutting the lawn, or **for staying in on the couch** and watching silly movies all afternoon. There's also jumping in puddles, huddling in bars, the comforting noise the rain makes on the roof (for the first day, at least). Add this drink to the list—provided you don't start singing "Riding the Storm Out" after the second batch is brought out. **Serves 10**

Cracked ice

15 ounces **white rum**

10 ounces **freshly squeezed lime juice**

10 ounces **fresh pineapple juice**

10 ounces **Simple Syrup** (page 7)

7½ ounces **dark rum**

5 ounces **Hpnotiq**

1. Fill a punch bowl halfway full with cracked ice. Add the white rum, lime juice, pineapple juice, simple syrup, dark rum, and Hpnotiq. Stir well.

2. Ladle the Monsoon into 10 punch cups or other attractive, sturdy glasses.

⬆ *A Note: No Hpnotiq (a Cognac, vodka, and fruit juice blend from France)? Try this with Alizé instead.*

The-More-the-Merrier

Isn't it the truth? Even when the front room's **bouncing from the bass beats**, the kitchen's overflowing like a punch bowl with people, the line to the bathroom makes a major airport security line seem short, and the porch is packed with smokers and hand-holders, one more friend showing up at the front door for the party is still a good thing—as long as there's more More-the-Merrier fixings. **Serves 10 hearty folks**

Block of ice (or cracked ice, if it comes to that)

One 750-milliliter bottle **lemon-** or **citron-flavored vodka**

15 ounces **freshly squeezed lemon juice**

10 ounces **Simple Syrup** (page 7)

5 ounces **bourbon**

One 2-liter bottle **chilled club soda**

Lemon slices for garnish

1. Add the block of ice to a punch bowl (or fill it up halfway with cracked ice). Add the vodka, and swirl once around the ice.

2. Add the lemon juice, simple syrup, and bourbon. Swirl well.

3. Add the club soda. Swirl well again (you're getting so good at it). Serve in goblets or glasses, making sure each glass gets a lemon slice garnish.

Native

Let no arguments start while drinking the Native. Also, let no one drinking the Native participate in any games of physical skill—it's strong enough that doing so would be a prescription for injury. And I don't want to see any doctors' bills. **Serves 8**

Ice cubes

8 ounces **white rum**

8 ounces **dark rum**

4 ounces **sweet vermouth**

4 ounces **blue curaçao**

4 ounces **freshly squeezed orange juice**

2 ounces **freshly squeezed lime juice**

2 ounces **Simple Syrup** (page 7)

Crushed ice

Orange slices for garnish

Maraschino cherries for garnish

1. Fill a large pitcher halfway full with ice cubes. Add the white and dark rums, sweet vermouth, curaçao, orange juice, lime juice, and simple syrup. With a long spoon, stir well.

2. Fill 8 large goblets with crushed ice (if you don't have crushed ice at hand, cracked ice can be used, but the effect won't be quite the same).

3. Using a spoon to ensure that no ice escapes, pour the mix from the pitcher into the goblets. Garnish each with an orange slice and a cherry.

Peach Bowl

It's simple to make, alluring to look at, and a crowd-pleaser, but don't be tempted to change the name of this one. Patrick Gavin Duffy—it was his *Bartender's Guide* (Pocket Books, 1970) from which I first nabbed the recipe—might rise up from his grave. While having a zombie Mr. Duffy behind the bar sounds good, in the long run it'll just be messy. And a messy bar isn't needed, especially when serving **a centerpiece drink** like the Peach Bowl. **Serves 8**

8 ripe, well-washed, fairly small, unskinned **peaches**

Two 750-milliliter bottles **chilled Champagne**

Thin **peach slices** for garnish (optional)

1. Make 4 slices with a sharp knife on 2 sides of each peach—the cuts don't need to be too deep, but they need to be clean cuts.

2. Place 1 peach into each of 8 wide-mouthed goblets.

3. Fill the goblets with the Champagne and garnish each with a single peach slice, if desired.

↥ *A Note: If these bowls don't have enough fruit flavor for you or your guests' tastes, add ½ ounce chilled peach schnapps to each goblet before adding the Champagne.*

A VARIATION: No peaches available? Give strawberries a whirl in this recipe, using 3 or 4 strawberries per goblet (depending on the size of the strawberries).

Five Rules for Successful Winter Holiday Parties

1. Serve drinks that are "warmers." Either by serving drinks that are hot in temperature or cocktails that have that warming fortitude (they put a touch of fire in the belly), you help to ensure that guests coming in from the cold won't stay cold. Of course, if you're throwing a holiday party in the Bahamas, you'll want to cool things down, so serve chillier items in that case.

2. Serve drinks that match the festive nature of the season. I'm a firm believer in having "dressier" holiday gatherings—it's so rare that we see pals in snazzy duds, sparkling and shiny. Be sure beverages have something to match the festive attire, whether it's a sweet garnish or just an extra bit of flair.

3. Plan on just serving one or two signature drinks. If you underline your party with one or two signature drinks (even mentioning the drinks on the invites or e-mails about the seasonal soirée), it will stand out from the rest, not just for that evening, but in your guests' memories. And isn't having memorable parties what it's all about? Indeed.

4. Proper prior planning prevents poor performance. I received this bit of advice in a fortune cookie, and it hasn't steered me wrong. Proper prior planning translates two ways. First, be sure that even if you have more guests than expected (someone always has a friend in town during the holidays), you have enough of the crucial ingredients for your signature drinks. Nothing brings a celebration to its knees like running out of drinks. Second, be sure to prepare garnishes like twists, fruit slices, etc. early so that you don't spend the whole night at the bar chopping.

5. Have the number of a local taxi company on hand. Something about holiday parties often leads to one or two overly merry merrymakers. And that's all right—as long as they don't drive home. Nothing stops the revelry faster than an accident. With this in mind, also be sure to have a festive nonalcoholic beverage option for any designated drivers in the house, such as Virgin Steaming Spiked Cider (page 459).

Pineapple Punch

I believe it's because of the awkward, tough, and prickly skin, but people shy away from using fresh pineapples. This is a crying shame. Hand me the Kleenex. Okay, now, get over those fears. Fresh pineapple is **worth the effort**, especially when making Pineapple Punch, which goes hand in hand with an upscale Hawaiian barbecue. Garnish every glass with a tiny lei around the stem. **Serves 10**

1 whole **pineapple,** skinned and cut into chunks

10 ounces **Simple Syrup** (page 7)

Cracked ice

15 ounces **fresh pineapple juice**

5 ounces **white rum**

One 750-milliliter bottle **chilled Champagne**

1. Add the pineapple chunks and simple syrup to a punch bowl. Using a muddler or wooden spoon, muddle well, but don't break the bowl.

2. Fill the bowl halfway with cracked ice. Add the pineapple juice and rum. Stir well.

3. Add the Champagne. Stir a bit more. Ladle into wine glasses.

⊙ *A Note: Need to get more garnish going? Try adding a pineapple chunk speared with a cocktail umbrella to each drink.*

Planter's Punch

In every bar on every beach in every tourist trap, it's likely that a Planter's Punch is served, and as likely that half the recipes differ from the ones served on the beach two miles up the coast. There are two certainties that Planter's Punch always boasts: rum and pineapple juice. The former tends to be plentiful, which is why most folks forget about the other ingredients. With the possibilities available, and the potential for the item being "planted" being you, make this in a big batch; call six friends; set out six lawn chairs facing the ranch, yard, deck, big corner window, or pool; make sure cups are brimming; and then discuss the merits of other Planter's Punch recipes. **Serves 6**

Ice cubes

12 ounces **dark rum**

12 ounces **freshly squeezed orange juice**

12 ounces **fresh pineapple juice**

3 ounces **freshly squeezed lime juice**

3 ounces **Simple Syrup** (page 7)

1½ ounces **freshly squeezed lemon juice**

6 dashes **Angostura bitters**

Pineapple chunks for garnish

Orange slices for garnish

1. Fill a large pitcher halfway full with ice cubes. Add all of the ingredients except for the pineapple chunks and orange slices. Stir well with a long spoon, or a very clean arm.

2. Fill 6 goblets three-quarters full with ice. Pour the punch into the goblets. Garnish each with a few pineapple chunks and an orange slice, either speared or floated on top.

A VARIATION: If you must fiddle with the recipe, try adding a little grapefruit juice, which brings a tang. Or try the above recipe sans bitters and lemon juice. You could also add 2 ounces of club soda to each goblet after the punch is furnished, but I don't see the fun in that.

Power to the People

This isn't, I'll admit, quite as insurgent a beverage as the name might imply. Not to say that a popular movement couldn't be **fueled by this people-pleaser**, but it might better suit those favoring inaction (such as lying in a hammock) over action. The multiple "p's" lead us to the main ingredient, though, which is Prosecco, the sweetish Italian sparkling wine. **Serves 8**

2 **peaches,** peeled, pitted, and sliced

2 **apricots,** peeled, pitted, and sliced

4 ounces **Simple Syrup** (page 7)

Ice cubes

8 ounces **brandy**

4 ounces **freshly squeezed orange juice**

One 750-milliliter bottle **Prosecco**

8 **orange slices** for garnish

1. Add the peaches, apricots, and simple syrup to a large pitcher. Using a muddler or long wooden spoon, muddle the fruit and syrup well.

2. Fill the pitcher halfway full with ice cubes. Add the brandy and orange juice. Stir.

3. Add the Prosecco and orange slices. Stir well. Serve in wine glasses, trying to get an orange slice in each glass.

Four Corners, Four Bars

Travel from the deep southeast to the hilly northwest, from way back northeast to the southwest's heat. Crisscross this large United States of America and you'll discover worthwhile bars, lounges, taverns, watering holes, pubs, and dives at almost every stop. While traversing to each of the continental corners, try out these particular stops, each with its own character, when your whistle needs wetting.

1. **Pappy and Harriet's**, Pioneertown, California. With live music, cool spirits, and spicy barbecue, what more is needed?

2. **Bal-Mar**, Seattle, Washington. This lounge has a hip but cozy atmosphere and a menu that features classic cocktails alongside refreshingly new mixes.

3. **Chamber Lounge**, Miami, Florida. This dark throwback (re: solid and serious cocktails) hotel basement bar doesn't have the encumbrance of a hotel, as the hotel closed years ago.

4. **Lompoc Cafe and Pub**, Bar Harbor, Maine. This pub boasts a garden, a bocce court, a bar where beers and cocktails cohabitate, and an open-air dining area that keeps the heat on.

Sangria

Much like Pancho Villa, Sangria is "hated by thousands and loved by millions." I believe this touch-and-go feeling about Sangria is caused solely by the muck served at many restaurants, often out of a bottle and sometimes having been in the fridge since the late 1800s, or the time of the above-mentioned hero of the Mexican revolution. **Take control of destiny** by consuming Sangria only when constructed using your own hands. **Serves 6**

1 **orange,** cut into wheels

1 **lime,** cut into wheels

1 **lemon,** cut into wheels

6 ounces **Simple Syrup** (page 7)

4 ounces **freshly squeezed orange juice**

2 ounces **freshly squeezed lime juice**

One 750-milliliter bottle **dry red wine**

6 ounces **brandy**

Ice cubes

Additional **fresh fruit** for garnishing as desired

1. Place the orange, lime, and lemon wheels in a large glass pitcher, along with the simple syrup. Muddle well with a large muddler or wooden spoon.

2. Add the orange juice and lime juice and muddle a little more.

3. Add the red wine and brandy and stir well for 15 seconds. Place the pitcher carefully in the refrigerator for at least 2 hours and up to 36 hours.

4. Add ice cubes until the pitcher is full. Give the mix a couple of good stirs. Pour into 6 stemmed wine glasses and garnish with fresh fruit. *Viva la revolución!*

A VARIATION: White Sangria is also an attractive option. Substitute one 750-milliliter bottle dry white wine for the red, 3 ounces white grape juice for the lime juice, and 1 apple for the lime in the above recipe.

Scorpion

The Scorpion as jumbo-drink-sloshed-by-happy-groups-in-tiki-bars is so omnipresent in most imbibers' bubbly brains that they forget about its diminutive deadly namesake, that member of the arachnid family that trolls deserts waiting to sting any uncovered ankle. If you happen to get stung, **have a full punch bowl** of Scorpions to soak your foot in. If, after making them, you and your nearest and dearest must drink the punch, so be it. One should never drink a Scorpion alone. It's much too dangerous. **Serves 10**

Ice in block form
(or large ice chunks)

One 750-milliliter bottle **dark rum**

2 ounces **gin**

2 ounces **brandy**

2 ounces **freshly squeezed orange juice**

2 ounces **freshly squeezed lemon juice**

2 ounces **orgeat syrup**

1 cup **fresh mint leaves**

Orange slices for garnish

1. Add the ice to a large punch bowl. If using ice chunks, as opposed to a block, fill the bowl about halfway.

2. Add everything else but the orange slices to the punch bowl. Stir well with a large spoon or Bowie knife (it is a Scorpion, after all). Let sit for at least 10 minutes to allow the flavors to blend.

3. Serve in goblets, garnishing each with an orange slice. Or just get straws for everyone at the party and start sucking right out of the punch bowl. If you do the latter, throw the orange slices into the bowl.

⬆ *A Note: The recipe in Trader Vic's* Bartender's Guide *(the 1947 version), suggests that gardenias be used as garnish. Why not? Just make sure they're unsprayed.*

⬆ *A Second Note: This is built for 10, but it could be served to fewer guests, if they're exceptionally hardy explorers. Also, it could be stretched to more guests, if they're arachnophobic.*

Skipper's Punch

Feeling as if a soirée is stuck in the dingy? Unveil the Skipper's Punch. **Sensing a celebration** has swerved into slow waters? Unleash the Skipper's Punch. Understanding a wing-ding is sandbagged by whining wind? Untie the Skipper's Punch. Some landlubber reaching for your glass of punch? I believe you know what to do. **Serves 10**

Block of ice (or ice cracked off an iceberg)

10 ounces **gin**

7½ ounces **freshly squeezed lemon juice**

5 ounces **grenadine**

5 ounces **Simple Syrup** (page 7)

One 750-milliliter bottle **chilled Champagne**

1 **lemon,** cut into slices

10 more **lemon slices** for garnish

10 **maraschino cherries** for garnish

1. Add the block of ice to a punch bowl (or fill the bowl halfway with cracked ice). Add the gin, lemon juice, grenadine, and simple syrup. Mix well.

2. Add the Champagne and the lemon that's been sliced. Stir briefly.

3. Ladle into punch glasses or small wine glasses. Garnish each glass with a lemon slice and a cherry.

🔼 **A Note:** *The grenadine and simple syrup can be a tad sweet. If you find that to be the case, cut them both down to 2½ ounces. But remember, it gets cold at sea, and the sugar provides insulation.*

Strawberry Punch

The strawberry is such a lovely, modest fruit, taking its chances down low on the ground. If not already apparent, let me trumpet how strawberries make exceedingly attractive garnishes, and how they bring out the best in Champagne, a sparkler almost perfect on its own. Is it possible to **take perfection and double it** to make perfection squared? Instead of pondering these odd mathematics, try a bowl of this punch—the answer is contained in the cup. **Serves 10 to 12**

One 10-ounce package **frozen strawberries**

1 **lemon,** cut into slices

Cracked ice

4 ounces **Simple Syrup** (page 7)

Two 20-ounce cans **pineapple chunks,** drained, or 1 whole fresh pineapple, peeled and cut into chunks

One 750-milliliter bottle **chilled white wine** (a Sauternes would work well)

Two 750-milliliter bottles **chilled Champagne**

1. Add the strawberries and lemon slices to a punch bowl. Let sit until the strawberries have defrosted most of the way.

2. Add enough cracked ice to fill the bowl halfway. Add the simple syrup and pineapple chunks. Mix the fruit into the ice.

3. Add the wine and Champagne. Stir well. Serve in wine goblets.

🔼 *A Note: Want to up the elegant meter? Add a fresh strawberry slice as a garnish to each glass.*

Tonga Punch

One must wear the appropriate skirt when consuming Tonga Punch (a punch originally made **internationally famous** via Trader Vic, whose version I have adapted here) and not be afraid to be obviously enjoying the brightly colored clothing, either. As everyone around should sport a similar skirt (or at least a skirt of some kind), and as Tonga is known as the friendly island, the ankle-baring attire won't generate any awkward looks from other revelers (unless you have one too many mugs of punch and end up standing on your head). **Serves 12**

Cracked ice

One 750-milliliter bottle **white rum**

8 ounces **freshly squeezed lemon juice**

6 ounces **brandy**

6 ounces **orange curaçao**

6 ounces **freshly squeezed orange juice**

6 ounces **passionfruit syrup**

3 ounces **grenadine**

1. Fill a punch bowl three-quarters full with cracked ice. Add the rum, lemon juice, brandy, curaçao, orange juice, passionfruit syrup, and grenadine. Stir ferociously, while avoiding spillage.

2. Serve in punch cups or other small sturdy glasses, or feather the punch bowl with 12 long straws and have guests start slurping.

4 Drinks to Have When Winning Money

In this context, I believe winning money equals both big amounts (such as the lottery), and smaller amounts (be it through gambling, trivia, or a footrace to the shuffleboard table). Don't undercut the winningness with any old drink. The gesture of buying a properly rich drink doubles, in a way, that winning feeling you worked so hard (or sorta hard) to get in the first place.

1 Millionaire (page 119)

2 Cape Cod (page 378)

3 Million Dollar Cocktail (page 393)

4 Golden Goose (page 360)

Collegiate Classics

It's 7:30 A.M. and, when rolling over to gaze tiredly at the clock, you realize that your anthropology final starts in 15 minutes, and if you don't make it (and it's in a building all the way across campus, and your roommate borrowed your car and never returned last night, and where are your shoes?), if you miss this final, you'll fail the class and have to retake it next year. And now you're halfway there but you forgot your belt and your pants keep slipping and you can't remember where your belt could be, and then the building is right in front of you, you're in the front door and down the hall and think there are minutes still to spare, but then the door's locked, and a note taped to it reads, "I guess you should have spent last night preparing for this test instead of wearing a giant sombrero."

Then, with a shudder, you wake up and realize it was a dream, and that you would never have let school get in the way of your socializing. There are many paths of study that a burgeoning professional must take before succumbing to the inevitable 9 to 5, and one of those paths is the study of the amusingly named (sometimes, between us, stupidly named) concoctions that university bars, taverns, saloons, and lounges, as well as house parties, deck parties, lake parties, and dorm parties, come up with to ensure that they stand out in any student's eyes.

These drinks, from the Purple Python to the Purple Panties, aren't always poured purely for knockout value (though that's often a component), and often taste surprisingly good, with a focus on a refreshing nature and an amusing personality. The Collegiate Classics in this chapter take us back with their youthful verve and utter disregard for any worry about decorum in name (Duck Fart, anyone?), with one eye always on attitude and the other always on great flavor.

As those days spent avoiding hallowed lecture halls are also spent trying to attract any and all students to your orbit, you'll find the obligatory innuendo drinks, both the more subtle (such as the Between the Sheets) and the complete come-ons (such as the Screaming Orgasm and the Quickie). Remember, college is made for exuberance, and everyone should Hop, Skip, and Go Naked without thinking too much about the consequences. So you shouldn't flip the pages of this chapter's text too quickly, looking only for the prehighlighted sections, even if We Have to Be at Work by 10 A.M. There will always be a make-up test if you happen to oversleep after spending too much time studying these Collegiate Classics.

Adios Amigo

There comes a time in every collegiate career when one has to **don an extra-extra-large hat**, for your own amusement or for someone else's. It could be of the 20-gallon variety, a straw boater sized for a giant, a fantastic fez with a 40-inch diameter, a plenty large pillbox, a tremendous toque, or a very big Balibuntl made from the Buri plant. All are fine hats. But if your enormous hat happens to be a serious sombrero, then I suggest you accompany it with an Adios Amigo.

Ice cubes

1 ounce **white rum**

¾ ounce **freshly squeezed lime juice**

½ ounce **dry vermouth**

½ ounce **brandy**

½ ounce **gin**

Lime slice for garnish

1. Fill a cocktail shaker halfway full with ice cubes. Add the rum, lime juice, vermouth, brandy, and gin. Shake heartily, but without losing your hat.

2. Strain the mix into a cocktail glass. Garnish with the lime slice and a tip of the hat.

Amaretto Sour

If the old and distinguished sour family were to send its many members to college, then the Amaretto Sour would be **the one that stuck around**, taking a couple of courses a semester, making pals of the local bartenders, maybe turning into quite a pool player, but never leaving town. Not that this sour shouldn't be given a modest respect. It has taken every obscure philosophy class offered, and when made well still reveals its honorable lineage.

Ice cubes

2 ounces **amaretto**

1 ounce **freshly squeezed lemon juice**

Orange twist for garnish

Maraschino cherry for garnish (optional)

1. Fill a cocktail shaker halfway full with ice cubes. Add the amaretto and lemon juice. Shake for 10 seconds and ponder what it's all about.

2. Strain into a cocktail glass. Garnish with the orange twist. Add the cherry if you think it'll impress that singular someone.

⬆ **A Note:** Amaretto is an almond-flavored liqueur. This drink goes south fast if a cheap and sickly sweet amaretto is used. Amaretto di Saronno, from Saronno, Italy, is a good choice.

✚ **A Tip:** When ordering this drink out in the world, you'll often see a bartender reach for the premade sour mix. Don't let this happen to you. If fresh juice isn't used, this drink isn't even worth it.

Four Fine Small-City Bars

Paeans to the tiny town tavern and stories about blustery big-city lounges abound, but rarely are the praises sung of the best watering holes in those middling-size burgs, locales too big to be called towns and too small to be cities. But don't let the lack of literature on these spots (at least so far) fool you. If passing through any of the following four small cities/big towns, you'll be sad if you don't stop at these fine, fine watering holes.

1. **Auntie Mae's Parlor**, Manhattan, Kansas. This is perhaps the best underground bar in the Midwest.
2. **Al & Vic's,** Missoula, Montana. Shoot pool, buy the locals a round, and read the literate graffiti in the bathrooms.
3. **The Corner Bar**, Kalamazoo, Michigan. Come inside out of the cold and warm up with strong snifters and spicy nachos.
4. **The Chapter House**, Ithaca, New York. With hearty cocktails, a hundred kinds of beer, free popcorn, and weird bands, life is right.

Signature Drinks, Part II

Picking out a signature drink to serve at a particular party (see page 305) may not be too hard. Picking out a personal signature drink, though, is a very, well, personal matter. If you've always wanted to pick out one signature drink for yourself, one that's always the highlight of your home bar, or one you're always known for ordering when out, one that you favor above all others, then first consider a couple of key points. First, naturally, it must be a drink that you both love the taste of and love making. After all, you'll probably be having it a lot and making it a lot, as friends begin to pick up on the fact that you and this signature beverage go hand-in-hand. This means that while you can (and probably should) consider the name of the drink when deciding on it, you shouldn't consider it as the only factor. In addition, be careful about picking something that is incredibly difficult to make, because you might get tired of slinging something together that's overly complicated, and also because if you're ordering it out a lot you don't want to have every bartender in town irritated with you.

After reading through all the recipes in this book, and other books talked about in this book, if you decide you want to create your own signature drink, my first bit of advice is: Be careful. Randomly combining ingredients, while potentially fun, is potentially dangerous (not in the combustible way, but in the "that-tastes-awful" way). The best way to start is to take a recipe you like and begin by making small substitutions. Change the orange juice to cranberry juice, or try a half ounce of green Chartreuse instead of crème de noyaux. Be very delicate with your substitutions, though—there's no need to waste liquor. After altering an ingredient, test the new version, and then adjust accordingly. Then perhaps alter another ingredient (though be careful when altering the base liquor if it has one, because while gin to vodka isn't so far of a reach, changing gin to whiskey, etc., will radically mutate most drinks). Once you've found that perfect variation on a theme, then you get to come up with a name. I'll leave that up to you.

Between the Sheets

There are numerous and sundry cocktails ordered by 20-somethings based solely on the fact that it's entertaining to say their names to a bartender. Usually those giggly cocktails taste worse than kerosene, but the Between the Sheets is **a well-balanced affair**—really a *ménage à trois*, to follow the metaphor, since three different boozes co-exist happily.

Ice cubes

¾ ounce **white rum**

¾ ounce **brandy**

¾ ounce **Cointreau**

½ ounce **freshly squeezed lemon juice**

¼ ounce **Simple Syrup** (page 7)

Lemon twist for garnish

1. Fill a cocktail shaker halfway full with ice cubes. Add the rum, brandy, Cointreau, lemon juice, and simple syrup. Shake vigorously, with bedroom eyes.

2. Strain into a cocktail glass. Squeeze the lemon twist over the top, and then drape it languidly over the edge of the glass. Smooth, aren't you?

Blue Hawaiian

Ideal for pouring on an early spring day that demands you **skip out early from your obligations**, this drink mingles well with the sun's rays after a long winter of gray indoor life. If you're enjoying that sunny day off with a cuddly companion, then I suggest learning the lyrics to Elvis Presley's song "Blue Hawaii." You can sing while shaking the cocktail shaker.

2 ounces **fresh pineapple juice**

1½ ounces **white rum**

1 ounce **blue curaçao**

Pineapple chunks for garnish

1. Fill a cocktail shaker halfway full with ice cubes. Add the pineapple juice, rum, and curaçao. Shake while hula dancing.

2. Strain into a large cocktail glass. Garnish with the pineapple chunks speared on a small plastic bar sword or toothpick.

⬆ *A Note: Some add ½ ounce cream of coconut to this drink, but I think it makes it slightly too sweet.*

➕ *A Tip: If you're cocktail-glass deficient, or have only very small cocktail glasses, you might serve this over ice in a highball glass. It might even be amusing to top it off with a touch of club soda, if you're into that kind of bubbliness.*

Boilermaker

A serious drink for serious students, the Boilermaker is enough of an institution that Purdue University has it as a mascot. Not only useful when the alma mater has gone down by 24 in the fourth and you just want to forget the whole game, the Boilermaker is in addition **a heroic bonding drink**. Once you have a Boilermaker with someone, chances are you won't forget that person. The rest of the evening is another matter altogether.

15 ounces **draft beer** (on the lighter side)

One 1- to 1½-ounce shot **blended whiskey**

1. Fill a pint glass almost to the top with the beer.

2. Drop the shot glass of whiskey into the beer. Drink in 1 swipe. Then breathe deeply.

⬆ *A Note: Some folks have been known to just drink the whiskey straight, and then drink the beer. This isn't a Boilermaker at all, and don't believe it if you hear someone say it is.*

⬆ *Another Note: If you can't think of a good reason to drink a Boilermaker, do it to celebrate the International Brotherhood of Boilermakers, Iron Ship Builders, Blacksmiths, Forgers, and Helpers. Bottom's up.*

✖ *A Warning: This drink does have a shot glass within the pint glass. Be careful when drinking so that the shot glass doesn't hit you in the teeth.*

Brainstorm

This restorative beverage isn't the lightning bolt or light bulb flashing over your head when you remember the answer to question 36 on the bio-chem final (or when a question put to you at an office meeting reminds you of the bio-chem final). The Brainstorm is just the opposite. It's **a mix to be savored** after the test or meeting is done, once you've laid down the pencil and breathed a sigh of relief.

Ice cubes

2 ounces **Irish whiskey**

1 ounce **sweet vermouth**

¼ ounce **Benedictine**

Orange twist for garnish

1. Fill a cocktail shaker halfway full with ice cubes. Add the whiskey, vermouth, and Benedictine. Shake well.

2. Strain the mix into a cocktail glass. Squeeze the orange twist over the glass, and then drop it in.

Brass Monkey

This pleasant gulp has **a plethora of potential** moniker histories. "Brass Monkey" could come from C.A. Abbe's 1857 book *Before the Mast*, in which he says the weather would "freeze the tail off a brass monkey." Then again, "brass monkey" might refer to a cannon ball storage rack. To the Beastie Boys, it's "that funky monkey" malt liquor, and in the United Kingdom it's an underwear company. No one knows which sources, if any, were responsible for the name of this concoction. This means that after one or two, you should come up with some definitions of your own.

Ice cubes

1½ ounces **vodka**

1½ ounces **white rum**

1½ ounces **freshly squeezed orange juice**

Orange slice for garnish

1. Fill a cocktail shaker halfway full with ice cubes. Add the vodka, rum, and orange juice. Shake well.

2. Strain into a cocktail glass. Garnish with the orange slice.

"The little feller, now, is **smart's a whip**, an' could talk the tail off a brass monkey."

KATE DOUGLAS WIGGIN, *The Story of Waitstill Baxter*, 1913

Cement Mixer

Ugh, this drink's abhorrent—but then again, so are 7:30 A.M. classes, and I had to live through both taking them and teaching them. **Am I stronger for it?** Well, maybe. Will you be stronger for drinking a Cement Mixer? Only by testing it can you know for sure.

1½ ounces **chilled Bailey's Irish Cream**

½ ounce **freshly squeezed lime juice**

1. Fill a large shot glass with the Bailey's. Delicately float the lime juice on top, pouring it slowly over a spoon if necessary.

2. Drink, but don't slam it like you might another shot. Let it sit in the mouth for about 10 seconds before gulping it down.

❌ *A Warning: The "cement" part of this drink happens when the lime juice and Bailey's start to combine and the juice starts to congeal the liqueur. Fairly quickly, it becomes cottage-cheesy in consistency, and then gets even thicker. Drink it before it gets too thick, or spit it out. You've been warned.*

Take a Poem Out for a Drink

There's nothing wrong, ever, with exercising your poetic side. If you've poo-poo'd poems in the past, try the following on for poetic size. All, old and newer, relate in some way to the subject of drinks, bars, and those who enjoy them (which is also the subject of many fun Friday nights).

1. **"Song to Celia,"** by Ben Jonson (1616): "Drink to me, only with thine eyes / And I will pledge with mine."

2. **"The Tavern,"** by E.A. Robinson (1921): "The Tavern has a story, but no man / Can tell us what it is."

3. **"Milltown Union Bar,"** by Richard Hugo (1973): "You could love here, not the lovely goat / in plexiglass nor the elk shot / in the middle of a joke, but honest drunks."

4. **"Praying Drunk,"** by Andrew Hudgins (1991): "Our Father who art in heaven, I am drunk. / Again."

5. **"Dirty Blues,"** by Rodney Jones (1996): "This young living legend leaning / Over the sink of the washroom / Of the Maple Leaf Tavern."

Commodore

This is not your typical collegiate favorite (as it has a bit too much bite and not enough sweet overload, and doesn't feature a kooky name), but it is **a drink for serious study** nonetheless. As described to me by bartender Jeremy Holt, this is a Crown Royal (or rye or Canadian-blended whisky) gimlet with a good dash of Peychaud's bitters. Also, it is not related at all to the Frozen Commodore on page 417. It might be fun, though, to run a test on both at a party and see which is the favorite. Write a five-page paper on the experiment and mail it to me.

Ice cubes

2¼ ounces **Crown Royal (or rye** or **Canadian whisky)**

¾ ounce **freshly squeezed lime juice**

¼ ounce **Simple Syrup** (page 7)

2 dashes **Peychaud's bitters**

1. Fill a mixing glass or cocktail shaker halfway full with ice cubes. Add the Crown Royal, lime juice, simple syrup, and bitters. Stir well.

2. Fill an old-fashioned or similar-sized glass with ice cubes. Strain the mix into the glass.

⬆ *A Note: You could also serve this straight up by straining it into a cocktail glass.*

➕ *A Tip: You'll sometimes see this, like a gimlet, made with lime syrup—avoid it in both instances.*

➕ *Another Tip: If you want your Commodore without any sweetness, omit the simple syrup.*

Cuba Libre

What should be a well-built drink celebrating the period between Cuba's Ten Years' War in 1878 and the beginning of Cuba's struggle for independence in February 1895 has instead turned into a way of sounding sophisticated when ordering a rum and Coke. Often, there's not even lime juice involved, though it is the most crucial ingredient. So I say—bring back the revolution. **Insist on fresh lime juice** and enough of it. *Viva Cuba Libre!*

Ice cubes

2 ounces **white rum**

1½ ounces **freshly squeezed lime juice**

Chilled Coca-Cola

Lime wedge for garnish

1. Fill a highball glass three-quarters full with ice cubes.

2. Add the rum and lime juice and stir once.

3. Top the glass off with the cola, and then stir 3 times, once for each ingredient. Garnish with the lime wedge.

5 Drinks I Couldn't Get Myself to Try

Hey, I'm as bold as the next barfly. There have been, however, mixes suggested to me that I couldn't bring myself to sample. Everyone has to have limits, and these five alcoholic apparitions held no appeal for me. Maybe others are willing to take that plunge—more power to them.

1 Smurf Piss

2 1-900-FUK-MEUP

3 Liquid Cocaine

4 Irish Car Bomb

5 Urine Sample

Duck Fart

I'm not sure where exactly this mix got its chuckle-inducing name. Could it be somehow related to the baseball slang term for a blooper hit in that amorphous zone between infield and outfield? I'm not sure how, except that the drink itself is sort of a blooper, and does have three specific layers, and baseball is a game of threes . . . hey, it **can at least shout at making sense**. Speaking of shouting, this shooter tends to be shouted out by so many tipsy college drinkers that I thought it deserved to be in class with other collegiate favorites, though it's cousin to many drinks in the Shooting the Moon chapter (page 353) and to the classier Pousse Café (page 268).

Ice cubes

½ ounce **Crown Royal**

½ ounce **Kahlúa**

½ ounce **Bailey's Irish Cream**

1. Fill a cocktail shaker halfway full with ice cubes. Add the Crown Royal and shake well. Strain the chilled Crown Royal into a 1½-ounce (or larger) shot glass.

2. Pour the Kahlúa over the back of a small spoon onto the Crown (using the spoon to slow the descent of the Kahlúa into the glass). You want there to be layers, and don't want the liquors to mix together.

3. Pour the Bailey's over the back of a small spoon onto the Kahlúa. Drink slowly or quickly, depending on mood or time in the evening.

⬆ **A Note:** *Created in 1939 to honor the visit of England's King George VI and his wife, Queen Elizabeth, to Canada, Crown Royal is a Canadian blended whisky made using the pristine (or so I've heard) waters of Lake Winnipeg in Gimli, Manitoba.*

Final Final

The sense of relief after that last period or pen stroke is down on paper is as palatable as the first bite of an outstanding meal. Whether it turns out as perfectly as expected isn't the point—the first bite is always amazing. This is how I remember that final final ending, as summer (or winter break) had arrived and I could just unwind. To **celebrate that closing test** of the semester or quarter, I propose the following.

2 **lime wedges**

½ ounce **Simple Syrup** (page 7)

Ice cubes

1½ ounces **vodka**

1½ ounces **white rum**

1 ounce **triple sec**

1 ounce **fresh pineapple juice**

½ ounce **freshly squeezed lime juice**

Chilled Sprite or **7UP**

1. Add 1 lime wedge and the simple syrup to a Collins or similar-sized glass. Muddle well with a muddler, wooden spoon, or novelty pencil.

2. Fill the glass with ice cubes. Add the vodka, rum, triple sec, and pineapple and lime juices. Stir once for every A you plan on receiving.

3. Top off the glass with chilled Sprite. Stir carefully again for every A you deserve. Now put your feet up, pat yourself on the back, and cool out.

4 Drinks to Serve the In-Laws

There are meals, dangerous meals, where you're either meeting the in-laws for the first time, cooking for the in-laws for the first time, or letting the in-laws know they're going to be in-laws (meaning, you're filling them in on the wedding plans). Serving up the completely wrong balance of base liquor and mixer could blow the whole scene before the salad course is even served (see Four Drinks Not to Serve the In-Laws, page 343, if that's your goal). Or, serve the right mix and have the mantle of favorite son-in-law or daughter-in-law bestowed on you in a matter of minutes.

1 Listen to Your Elders (page 171)

2 Florida Special (page 416)

3 Your Favorite Aunt (page 240)

4 Godfather (page 212)

Freddy Fudpucker

The kids are alright. Even though they **get a giggling kick** out of ordering drinks that sound close to naughty words, they're all right. Truth be told, between me and you (keeping it at a whisper), I get the giggles a bit myself when ordering drinks that sound close to naughty words, too.

Ice cubes

4 ounces **freshly squeezed orange juice**

2 ounces **silver tequila**

¾ ounce **Galliano**

Orange slice for garnish

1. Fill a highball glass three-quarters full with ice cubes. Add the orange juice and tequila. Stir well with a long spoon and a grin.

2. Carefully float the Galliano on top of the tequila-orange juice combo, pouring it over the back of a spoon if necessary.

3. Slip the orange slice onto the rim as a garnish, without vexing the Galliano.

Fuzzy Navel

This cuddly named peach specialty seems to be one of the first cocktails people try—my own introduction to it came earlier than I intend to admit in writing. But don't regulate it to just memories of yesteryear—it's a bit too tasty for that. Instead, next time you're entertaining old school chums, agitate up a bunch of Fuzzy Navels and **watch the nostalgia start to flow** like peach schnapps.

Ice cubes

2 ounces **peach schnapps**

2 ounces **freshly squeezed orange juice**

1 ounce **vodka** (if you can find peach-flavored vodka, grab it)

Peach or **orange slice** for garnish

1. Fill a cocktail shaker three-quarters full with ice cubes. Add the peach schnapps, orange juice, and vodka. Shake well.

2. Fill a highball glass with ice. Strain the mix into the glass. Garnish with the peach or orange slice.

Go Team!

Let me assure you that this one is worth the perceived dip it might make in one's student loan or weekly food-shopping budget. It was concocted by one of Chicago's finest booze slingers, Joel Meister (who cut his bar-teeth in a college town), at the Rodan (a bar on Milwaukee Avenue), and you can trust that any team with **this cool tall drink** in view will go, go, and go some more.

2 **lime wedges**

5 to 8 **fresh mint leaves**

½ ounce **Simple Syrup** (page 7)

Ice cubes

1 ounce **Stolichnaya Vanil vodka**

1 ounce **Stolichnaya Ohranj vodka**

½ ounce **Midori melon liqueur**

Chilled soda water

1. Add the lime wedges, mint, and simple syrup to a Collins glass. Using a muddler or wooden spoon, muddle well.

2. Fill the glass three-quarters full with ice cubes. Add the vanilla and orange vodkas and the Midori melon liqueur. Stir well.

3. Top off the glass with chilled club soda. Stir one more time, while cheering.

⬆ *A Note: Joel is such an honorable bartender that he said I could only re-use this recipe here if I mentioned that Dan-O, a bartender at Chicago's Skylark (on Halstead), suggested adding the Midori. Here's a cheer to both of these members of the bartending family.*

Hop, Skip, and Go Naked

My memory may be faulty, but I don't recall students at my particular university needing a drink for this activity. The recipe is sometimes constructed as a punch; however, I feel that if you're going to **get the old groove on** with a drink called Hop, Skip, and Go Naked, you shouldn't have to do it in a group.

Ice cubes

1 ounce **vodka**

1 ounce **white rum**

1 ounce **apricot brandy**

½ ounce **freshly squeezed lime juice**

½ ounce **grenadine**

1. Fill a cocktail shaker halfway full with ice cubes. Add everything, including your shirt (no, no, leave that on, at least while making the drink). Shake well. Skip if you must.

2. Strain the mix into a cocktail glass. Garnish with your now-removed shirt.

⬆ *A Note: There are at least as many versions of this drink as there are mascots of U.S. universities. If this one doesn't quite match the one you grew fond of, feel free to rename it appropriately.*

Hurricane

A New Orleans tradition (as well as a reliable choice at the Hibachi Hut in Manhattan, Kansas, which has no hibachis and where I pretended to work during my own tender collegiate years), this drink rapidly **livens up an evening.** It's tropical and, when made right, not overly sugary. If you have actual Hurricane glasses, then use them—but if not, don't let that stop you.

Ice cubes

1 ounce **freshly squeezed lime juice**

1 ounce **fresh pineapple juice**

1 ounce **passionfruit syrup**

½ ounce **grenadine**

3 ounces **white rum**

1 ounce **dark rum**

Orange slice for garnish

1. Fill a Hurricane glass or other wavy 8- to 12-ounce glass about three-quarters full with ice cubes.

2. Add the lime and pineapple juices, passionfruit syrup, and grenadine. With a large wooden spoon (or other spoon), stir 3 times longitudinally.

3. Add the white and dark rums. Stir the mix a second time, latitudinally.

4. Garnish with the orange slice and a little umbrella.

⬆ *A Note: Passionfruit syrup can be hard to find. If you absolutely can't track it down, substitute 1 ounce Simple Syrup (page 7).*

A VIRGIN VARIATION: If you have designated drivers or nondrinkers or note-takers at the party, a drink featuring just the juices, grenadine, and syrup is awfully nice, and it will let them take part in the tropical feel of the event.

Jungle Juice

Oh, your head's going to hurt, and perhaps internal organs, too, and **the tongue might possibly turn purple** or grow some sort of fuzz, but how can an upstanding youthful scholar turn down a potion called Jungle Juice? Experimentation is part of learning.

Ice cubes

1½ ounces **orange-flavored vodka**

1 ounce **amaretto**

1 ounce **peach schnapps**

1 ounce **cranberry juice cocktail**

½ ounce **freshly squeezed lime juice**

½ ounce **freshly squeezed orange juice**

½ ounce **fresh pineapple juice**

Orange slice for garnish

1. Fill a Collins glass or a large goblet three-quarters full with ice cubes. Add all of the ingredients except for the orange slice. Stir well.

2. Garnish with the orange slice.

⬆ *A Note: Questions about why this isn't in punch form, or why it isn't exactly as you might have made it in some distant locale? See Hop, Skip, and Go Naked (opposite) for the answer.*

Kamikaze

In the interest of academia, let me first say that *kamikaze* can be defined in Japanese as "divine wind," and that the word came into usage as the name of a typhoon that, legends say, rose up to aid Japanese threatened by a Mongol invasion in the latter 1200s. Now that I have that out of the way, let me also say that the Kamikaze, due to its element of danger combined with its typical high percentage of booze, is **tops on campuses worldwide**. It's a shame that the ingestion of Kamis (as they are affectionately called) tends toward shot form. Making the drink over ice is much nicer.

Ice cubes

2½ ounces **vodka**

¾ ounce **triple sec** or **Cointreau**

¾ ounce **freshly squeezed lime juice**

Lime wedge for garnish

1. Fill an old-fashioned or a similar-sized glass with ice cubes (almost to the top).

2. Add the vodka, triple sec, and lime juice to the glass. Stir well.

3. Squeeze the lime wedge over the top of the glass and then drop it in. Watch out for the splash.

⬆ *A Note: While your basic triple sec is dandy for the Kami, I think that using Cointreau takes the drink to higher heights.*

A VARIATION: Want a classier Kamikaze? Add the ice and ingredients to your handy cocktail shaker, shake away, and strain into a cocktail glass before garnishing.

Kick-Off

I'm completely for traditional tailgating. But as the ancient saying goes, "One must be supple like the willow to not break like the ankle," or something along those lines. (I always slept through my Ancient Sayings 101 class. It started at 8 A.M.) This means that even the most traditional, die-hard tailgater must ensure that his or her tailgate continues to remain the place to huddle before heading inside the stadium for the big game. Let me suggest adding the Kick-Off next year to keep yours **the most hopping parking spot** in the lot. Sure, it's a little more trouble than tapping a keg, and has a few more ingredients than a bottle of Boone's Farm, but the additional points on your tailgating reputation outweigh any trouble.

Ice cubes

1½ ounces **gin**

½ ounce **dry vermouth**

½ ounce **Benedictine**

½ ounce **Simple Syrup** (page 7)

2 dashes **Angostura bitters**

Lemon twist for garnish

1. Fill a cocktail shaker halfway full with ice cubes. Add the gin, dry vermouth, Benedictine, simple syrup, and Angostura bitters. Shake well (if you need to shake in a Hail Mary–style passing motion, be sure a tight grip remains so the Kick-Off doesn't end up on the pavement).

2. Strain into a cocktail glass. Squeeze the lemon twist over the glass and then drop it in like the ball dropping through the uprights with no time left on the clock.

Three Hot Cocktail-Pizza Combos

Usually the refrain is "pizza and beer, pizza and beer." It's not a poor pairing, but with the amazing pie options available, why not try a more dynamic duo? Like one of these:

1. Slap on the Hawaiian shorts and go tropical with the Beach Bum (page 153) and a pineapple and caramelized onion pizza.
2. Bring home the windy city with a Chicago (page 101) and a deep-dish pizza packing pounds of pepperoni.
3. Try a Soledan (page 402) and a pie topped with Italian sausage, roasted garlic, and extra mozzarella. Now that's Italian.

Lemon Drop

Sometimes served as a shot (see page 364), which I call a Lemon Dropper to differentiate, the Lemon Drop has become **as popular as a spring schedule** that has no classes starting before noon. The popularity stems from the drink's combination of tangy and sweet combined with the kick from the vodka base. I don't deny that it's a ripe combo. I do deny that the shot form is always the way to go, though. Serve it up in a cocktail glass and show a little panache. It's never too soon.

Ice cubes

1½ ounces **citrus-flavored vodka**

½ ounce **Cointreau**

½ ounce **freshly squeezed lemon juice**

½ ounce **Simple Syrup** (page 7)

Lemon slice for garnish

1. Fill a cocktail shaker halfway full with ice cubes. Add the vodka, Cointreau, lemon juice, and simple syrup. Shake it up.

2. Strain into a cocktail glass. Garnish with the lemon slice.

⬆ *A Fancy Note: If you have a desire to add a sugary skirt to your Lemon Drop, here's the ticket. Before making the drink, add a bit of sugar to a small plate or saucer. Then, using a lemon wedge or slice, coat the outside rim of the glass with juice (but don't get sloppy). Then, carefully, rotate that outside rim through the sugar, working to get it only on the outside of the glass.*

⬆ *A Note: There are oodles of slight variations on this drink (including one where the sugar quotient must be obtained by licking it off someone's neck). Most don't have the Cointreau, but I find it a welcome addition to the party. If you don't, just ask it to leave and add another ½ ounce vodka in its place.*

Long Island Iced Tea

A pet of collegians on spring breaks, study breaks, coffee breaks, half-time breaks, date breaks, and beer breaks, the Long Island Iced Tea is **revered for its severe jolt** and the fact that, oddly enough, it tastes like iced tea. My advice? Don't waste time brooding over the actuality of drinking five different liquors at once. And don't forget that one Long Island is nice, two is okay, and three tends to start unhappy problems.

Ice cubes

¾ ounce **vodka**

¾ ounce **silver tequila**

¾ ounce **white rum**

¾ ounce **gin**

¾ ounce **triple sec**

¾ ounce **Coca-Cola**

½ ounce **freshly squeezed lemon juice**

Lemon slices for garnish

1. Fill a large glass or goblet three-quarters full with ice cubes. Add the vodka, tequila, rum, and gin. Then add the triple sec, as it's a bit of a loner. Stir once.

2. Add the Coca-Cola and lemon juice. Stir briefly. Garnish with the lemon slices.

A VARIATION: Long Island not quite healthy enough for you? Try a Long Beach Iced Tea instead. Just substitute cranberry juice cocktail for the Coca-Cola.

Purple Panties

I'm not saying that Prince pours this one at his Minneapolis mansion, but he should, because the record *Purple Rain* makes an ideal accompaniment when swilling these and because, well, Prince is crazy for the color purple. For you, I suggest that no matter your age, you ensure beforehand that you have a copy of *Purple Rain* (or the even finer *1999*) on pause, so that it can begin blaring instantly after the first Purple Panties is unveiled. If you must **wear a raspberry beret** or dance dirty until the neighbors protest, I won't tell a soul.

Ice cubes

2 ounces **vodka**

1 ounce **purple grape juice**

¾ ounce **triple sec**

¾ ounce **fresh pineapple juice**

Chilled club soda

Lime slice for garnish

1. Fill a Collins glass or other fairly large glass three-quarters full with ice cubes. Add the vodka, grape juice, triple sec, and pineapple juice. Stir once for every member of Prince's band.

2. Top off the glass with club soda. Stir well (choosing to stir to the beat of "Let's Go Crazy" or "I Would Die 4 U" is a personal choice).

3. Squeeze the lime slice over the drink and then drop it in.

4 Drinks Not to Serve the In-Laws

If the goal at a particular meal or cocktail hour is to impress new in-laws, old in-laws, or almost in-laws, then check out Four Drinks to Serve the In-Laws on page 335. If, on the other hand, you know things are going to go south with the in-laws (so to speak), and you want to speed up the process, serve one of the following.

1 Monkey Brain (page 221)

2 Cement Mixer (page 329)

3 Vodka Slippery Knob (page 196)

4 Duck Fart (page 333)

Purple Python

This little pretty shouldn't lead to hazardous crushing, but should instead **initiate very sociable squeezing**. With that thought, serve it the next time you play Twister—it's always a good idea to match drink to occasion.

Ice cubes

1½ ounces **vodka**

1 ounce **Chambord**

1 ounce **sloe gin**

Lemon twist for garnish

1. Fill a cocktail shaker halfway full with ice cubes. Add the vodka, Chambord, and sloe gin. Shake well, avoiding—for the moment—any hugs.

2. Strain the embraceable mixture into a cocktail glass. Squeeze the lemon twist over the glass and, sadly, release it into the drink.

⊕ A Note: No Chambord? Crème de cassis is an attractive substitution.

Pussy Foot

There are bright mornings when even the most strenuous merrymaker must take a break. For those mornings, or evenings, when a cleverly named alcoholic beverage just induces shuddering, **don't be ashamed** to be called, and to sip, a Pussy Foot. Everyone needs to replenish at some point, so as not to burn out too brightly, too quickly.

Ice cubes

1½ ounces **fresh pineapple juice**

1½ ounces **freshly squeezed orange juice**

1½ ounces **white grape juice**

½ ounce **grenadine**

Lime wedge for garnish

1. Fill a highball glass three-quarters full with ice cubes. Add the pineapple, orange, and white grape juices. Stir well.

2. Add the grenadine. Stir twice, but not so the grenadine gets completely mixed into the juices. You still want it to look fun. Garnish with the lime wedge.

A NON-VIRGIN VARIATION: Want a Pussy Foot with pop? Reduce the juices to 1 ounce each, and add 1½ ounces vodka.

Quickie

There have been no studies done to determine whether this pulse-pounder or the Sloe Comfortable Screw (page 348) operates better as a pick-up assistant—which means **that field of study is still open**, for undecided PhDs.

Ice cubes

1½ ounces **bourbon**

1 ounce **white rum**

¾ ounces **triple sec**

Maraschino cherry for garnish

1. Fill a cocktail shaker halfway full with ice cubes. Add the bourbon, rum, and triple sec. Shake well (if it has to be shaken quickly, at least shake with vigor).

2. Strain into a cocktail glass. Garnish with the cherry and a phone number.

Salty Dog

This is not a swearing sailor (though after a few of these **any bright-eyed youth might become one**), but an old favorite at college bars and parties where attendees end up attired like sailors. Meaning, stripped down in the sun with no more than bikinis, shorts, and tennis shoes for clothing. While revitalizing these situations, the Salty D does feature grapefruit juice in a big way, so be sure that all salty revelers are grapefruit fans, and be sure to be stoked up.

Kosher salt

2 **lime wedges**

Ice cubes

2 ounces **gin**

4 ounces **freshly squeezed grapefruit juice**

1. Pour a small layer of kosher salt onto a small plate or saucer. Take a highball glass, and wet the outside of the rim with 1 of the lime wedges. Holding the glass firmly, rotate the rim through the salt. You want to be sure that salt gets on only the outside of the rim (you don't want the salt to get in the actual drink).

2. Fill the glass three-quarters full with ice cubes. Add the gin. Add the grapefruit juice. (It's best to let them enter separately. You know how sailors fight.)

3. Squeeze the second lime wedge over the drink and then drop it in. Stir well.

A VARIATION: I tend toward serving this over ice, because the warm weather situations it's best served at lend themselves to having ice in the drink. But this can be shaken and strained into a cocktail glass instead. Just don't forget to dip the cocktail glass in salt first.

Screaming Orgasm

This memorably named tipple was **destined to be a phenomenon**—not only suggestive in title, but also a smidgen sweet, a bit naughty, and slightly flirty. Combine those points and you have a sure-fire on-campus (or off-campus) darling. I like my Screaming Orgasms (well, there's no other way to say it) served shaken and strained into a cocktail glass, and not as the shot sometimes served at the bar. It seems a tad more tasteful, and lends itself to sipping rather than slamming. One might as well enjoy the moment.

Ice cubes

1½ ounces **vodka** (if you can get chocolate-flavored vodka, use it)

1½ ounces **Bailey's Irish Cream**

½ ounce **Kahlúa**

Small chocolate heart for garnish (optional)

1. Fill a cocktail shaker halfway full with ice cubes. Add the vodka, Bailey's, and Kahlúa. Shake well.

2. Strain into a cocktail glass. If you want to be smooth (and not seem like a last-call Lothario), garnish with the chocolate heart.

A VARIATION: If you drop the vodka, this is just an Orgasm.

Don't Fear the Scale

Walking into the bathroom and stepping on a scale to make the annual (or every five years, in my case) pilgrimage to check on the old poundage is a scary thing. Scaling up one of the recipes in this book (or down, if that's the case) shouldn't be as scary. But scaling drinks can get tricky. A safe rule to follow is that when it's the first time you are scaling a particular drink, go in steps, meaning, double the base liquor but maybe only go 1¾ up on the secondary ingredients. Don't be afraid of tasting once, then adding a little more of a secondary ingredient, then tasting again before serving to the general public. Go especially slowly with powerful spices, such as cloves or cinnamon, as they can easily overpower a drink.

Sloe Comfortable Screw

Whether running relentless on the pick-up (and ordering these back-to-back with Screaming Orgasms, page 347, for a date) or just desiring **a robust pick-me-up** after an extended evening, the Sloe Comfortable Screw fits the bill. A Screwdriver successor, whether it was built to beef up its progenitor or to fill the "funny and loosely sexy" requirement for a bar special board has been lost to the annals of history. Whichever the case may be, the Sloe Comfortable Screw is now propped up and popular at parties from the University of Maine to the University of Southern Cal.

Ice cubes

3 ounces **freshly squeezed orange juice**

1 ounce **vodka**

1 ounce **Southern Comfort**

1 ounce **sloe gin**

Orange slice for garnish

1. Fill a highball glass three-quarters full with ice cubes. Add the orange juice, vodka, Southern Comfort, and sloe gin. Stir well (while promising that you'll still respect the drink in the morning, of course).

2. Garnish with the orange slice.

A VARIATION: Lending itself to numerous variants is one of this drink's charms. If you want to make a Sloe Comfortable Screw Up Against a Wall, reduce the vodka, Southern Comfort, and sloe gin to ¾ ounce each, and add ¾ ounce Galliano. Want to get even nuttier with your Screw? Try a Sloe Comfortable Screw Up Against a Wall Mexican Style. Just take the vodka, Southern Comfort, sloe gin, and Galliano down to ½ ounce each, and add ½ ounce silver tequila and an extra ½ ounce orange juice.

Summer Vacation →

For those hot breaks between schooling, or for those days when summer school isn't in session, or **for those bright sunset evenings** when there's no class waiting in the morning, or for those January Saturdays when the big break seems achingly far away, this thirst-quenching sipper settles in politely when one's sprawled over a lawn chair, bare feet in the air, without a care.

Ice cubes

1 ounce **silver tequila**

1 ounce **yellow Chartreuse**

4 ounces **freshly squeezed orange juice**

Orange slice for garnish

1. Fill a highball glass three-quarters full with ice cubes. Add the tequila and Chartreuse. Stir once (but don't sweat it).

2. Add the orange juice. Stir twice more. Garnish with the orange slice and sunshine.

We Have to Be at Work by 10 A. M.

Not only a sunrise special, this cocktail boasts the lengthy pleasure of having the longest name in this book. That can be a downside when ordering it in a bar (plus the fact that the bartender might need instruction in construction techniques), so **keep it in-house**. It arose from the shelf one summer when my roommate and I had to be at work by (you could guess this part) 10 A.M. most days, and yet spent too much time out too late doing charity work, organizing neighborhood watches, training for marathons, and swilling an inordinate amount of liquor.

Ice cubes

1 ounce **vodka**

1 ounce **freshly squeezed orange juice**

1 **large egg,** preferably organic

3 dashes **Angostura bitters**

1. Fill a cocktail shaker halfway full with ice cubes. Add the vodka, orange juice, egg, and Angostura bitters. Shake well.

2. Strain into a cocktail glass—or straight into your mouth if in a rush. There's no time for garnishing or you'll be late.

⬆ *A Note: I'm not advocating actually slamming down one of these before heading off to the job (especially if you're operating any machinery, or, for that matter, driving to work). But if a pick-you-up is absolutely necessary, it fits the initial bill.*

✖ *A Warning: Since this does contain a raw egg, do not serve it to the elderly or anyone with a compromised immune system, and make sure your eggs are very fresh.*

White Russian

It seems odd, in a way, that this merger (which dates back a ways) has taken hold in campus-oriented alcohol consumption. For one, its name isn't at a high level of silliness. For two, having "Russian" in its title conjures up terrifying visions of poli-sci or history classes, and no serious student wants to be reminded of studies when bellying up to the bar or **chatting up a charmer** at a backyard blowout. The trick is the cream, I think. It adds that sweetness that less experienced cocktail palates crave, while still allowing for a more adult-sounding and adult-looking glass-ful in the hand, which then equals a sort-of sophisticated aura.

Ice cubes

2 ounces **vodka**

1½ ounces **Kahlúa**

1 ounce **heavy cream**

1. Fill an old-fashioned or a similar-sized glass with ice cubes. Add the vodka, Kahlúa, and cream (in that order, to avoid strife between the players).

2. Stir well.

A VARIATION: If the creamy nature doesn't appeal to you (or if you're dieting to drop those freshman 15), leave out the cream. You'll be having a Black Russian.

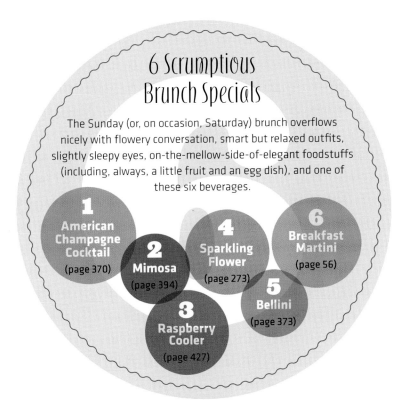

6 Scrumptious Brunch Specials

The Sunday (or, on occasion, Saturday) brunch overflows nicely with flowery conversation, smart but relaxed outfits, slightly sleepy eyes, on-the-mellow-side-of-elegant foodstuffs (including, always, a little fruit and an egg dish), and one of these six beverages.

1 American Champagne Cocktail (page 370)

2 Mimosa (page 394)

3 Raspberry Cooler (page 427)

4 Sparkling Flower (page 273)

5 Bellini (page 373)

6 Breakfast Martini (page 56)

Shooting the Moon

Bang! Bang! Bang! The sounds aren't the harsh fire of a pistol (thankfully), but the echo of shot glasses smacking onto the bar after a round has been promptly consumed. Usually these bangs are heard in earsplitting bars frequented by the young and want-to-seem young who are more interested in the results of rapid alcohol intake than in sipping an enjoyable drink that truly tastes delicious.

This isn't to say that a shot can't taste dandy—many do. It's only that the majority of those ordering shots don't have taste at the forefront of their minds. They have getting woozy from the booze-y on the mind instead. This leads to many claims that shots usually taste slightly of airplane fuel (or what someone would guess airplane fuel might taste like, most people not having actually consumed any). This may not be a revelation. Most of you have probably consumed shots like this.

Why, then, I hear you asking, include this chapter at all? Good question. My simple answer? There are times when you or your guests might want or need a quick intake, and as to provide aid in a variety of social situations is one of the goals of this book, a section such as Shooting the Moon is needed. There are shots that rise to the occasion—that tickle rather than curl the tongue as they pass by, and that sing to any drinker's soul (and taste buds).

I give you two parting shots. First, the consumption of shots should always be a communal affair. There is nothing so cheerless as a single shot drinker, attempting to rally by shooting one of the following recipes alone. Therefore, all the drinks in this chapter are made to serve two. Second, all this talk about shots in no way refers to drinks made of one individual liquor, served up neat (sometimes when ordering these, especially in the Old West, they'll be delivered in shot glasses), and served to be sipped. Sipping a single shot of singularly good whiskey, Scotch, rum, etc. is a pleasure, and should be treated as such.

Alabama Slammer

Is it a tongue-rolling term for a Southern state prison, or slang for the signature move of a pro wrestler from Birmingham? With shots, **it's often best not to know.** Just tilt your head back, close those peepers, and drink. **Serves 2**

Ice cubes

1½ ounces **Southern Comfort**

1 ounce **amaretto**

1 ounce **sloe gin**

1 ounce **freshly squeezed orange juice**

1. Fill a cocktail shaker halfway full with ice cubes. Add the Southern Comfort, amaretto, sloe gin, and orange juice. Shake well.

2. Strain into 2 large shot glasses. Drink immediately.

Anaconda

I like to think this is named to commemorate the Jon Voight cinematic classic of the same name—this shot **will wrap you up and start squeezing.** If that's not the case, let's all work together to change the public's perception of this shot. Mr. Voight deserves his own drink, and I don't see any liquid versions of *Midnight Cowboy* out there. **Serves 2**

Ice cubes

1½ ounces **whiskey** (the suggested model here is Jack Daniels, but feel free to experiment)

1½ ounces **white sambuca**

1. Fill a cocktail shaker halfway full with ice cubes. Add the whiskey and sambuca. Shake well.

2. Strain into 2 shot glasses. Consume quickly, before the snakes have time to get much of a grip.

⬆ *A Note: An anise-flavored liqueur, sambuca boasts the addition of witch elder as well as the traditional mysterious and unknown herbs and spices. The white variety is what tends to be served, as it's slightly mellower on the licorice-tasting scale than the black variety.*

Seven Party Packages

Worried about when to throw your next wingding,
what to have as the signature drink, what to serve for snacks,
and what to spin on the CD player? Fear no more.
The following party suggestions cover the bases for you.

1. **Hang Loose Hawaiian Hoedown.**
Date: Any time when the temperature's over 85 degrees.
Signature drink: Lava Flow (page 422) or Blue Hawaiian (page 325).
Snacks: Grilled pineapple and pork (or pepper) kebabs.
Music: Don Ho, *Greatest Hits*.

2. **St. Urho's Day Soirée.**
Date: March 16. Signature drink: Grasshopper (page 418);
St. Urho drove a swarm of grasshoppers out of Finland).
Snacks: Grasshopper pie. Music: Lordi, the Finnish metal band,
which won the Eurovision song contest in 2006.

3. **Halloween Spooktacular.** Date: October 31 or thereabouts.
Signature drink: Steaming spiced cider or Blood and Sand (page 204).
Snacks: Pumpkin risotto cakes or stuffed tomatoes (which look just
bloody enough). Music: Andrew Gold, *Halloween Howls*.

4. **Croquet Celebration.** Date: Late spring or early fall.
Signature drink: Go Team! (page 336). Snacks: Mini sandwiches and
cheese straws. Music: Duke Ellington, *Masterpieces: 1926–1949*.

5. **Poppin' Poker Party.** Date: Anytime after the sun goes down.
Signature drink: Set Up (page 231). Snacks: Speared shrimp
and mini frittatas. Music: Tom Waits, *Small Change*.

6. **Get Down Groundhog Day.** Date: February 2.
Signature drink: Spiked Hot Chocolate (page 457).
Snacks: Cheddar cheese, sliced summer sausage, pretzels.
Music: Frankie Yankovic, *Songs of the Polka King, Vol. 1*.

7. **Cantamaggio** (an Italian party celebrating spring).
Date: Any day between April 15 and April 30.
Signature drink: Soledan (page 402).
Snacks: Basil and tomato bruschetta, mushroom crostini.
Music: Dean Martin, *Italian Love Songs*.

B52

A collegiate and youthful darling due to its pleasing and painless demeanor, the B52 resembles the large bomber it's named after in color only. Most shots really deserve a whole raft of people partaking in them at once for the shot to earn its keep, but the B52's cuddly character turns it into **a prime target** for shots done by just two. The date shot, I suppose it could be called. You do run the risk of being completely embarrassed if ordering a shot on a date (many find shots tedious at best), so wait until after a few nonshot drinks have been put to bed.

Many shot aficionados demand that their B52s be layered. I, in dissent, think that any mix designed solely to be tossed swiftly down the gullet, with no hesitation to admire craftsmanship, no moment of admiration for aesthetic—in short, most shots—doesn't honestly deserve that much time spent making it. **Serves 2**

Ice cubes

1 ounce **Kahlúa**

1 ounce **Bailey's Irish Cream**

1 ounce **Grand Marnier**

1. Fill a cocktail shaker halfway full with ice cubes. Add the Kahlúa, Bailey's, and Grand Marnier. Shake while making a noise like an airplane.

2. Strain into 2 shot glasses. What are you waiting for? Drink it.

Buttery Nipple

Ah, butter: It's not only **perfect for cooking and baking**, but it also lends itself readily to the giggly name of this sweet treat. There isn't any actual butter in this shot, but without the idea of butter it loses a little of its entertainment value. If suggesting this measure (I'm thinking along the lines of, "How'd you like to share a Buttery Nipple, sweetheart?") to a reveler who doesn't already know of it, you may end up slapped. Remember, though, that often great rewards come only with great risks. **Serves 2**

Ice cubes

1½ ounces **Bailey's Irish Cream**

1½ ounces **butterscotch schnapps**

1. Fill a cocktail shaker halfway full with ice cubes. Add the Bailey's and butterscotch schnapps. Shake excessively.

2. Strain into 2 shot glasses. Consume while thinking naughty thoughts. Well, you are already—you might as well continue.

A VARIATION: If you tag-team the butterscotch schnapps with sambuca instead of Bailey's, you'll have a Slippery Nipple. It seems, on a purely factual level, that a Buttery Nipple would by definition also *be* slippery. But this is not the case, as they taste quite different.

Three Rad Reprints

As many classic cocktail books are difficult (to say the least) and expensive to track down, it's a toast-worthy affair when a publisher decides to reprint a classic. Here are three fine examples of this occurrence.

1. *173 Pre-Prohibition Cocktails* (first published in 1917 as *The Ideal Bartender*, expanded and reissued in 2001 by Howling Moon Press), by Tom Bullock. "Potations so good they scandalized a president," is all the publicity this books needs.
2. *The Old Waldorf-Astoria Bar Book* (first published in 1935, reprinted in 2003 by New Day Publishing), by Albert Stevens Crockett. Five hundred recipes for "cocktails and mixed drinks served at the World's Most Famous Brass Rail."
3. *The Stork Club Bar Book* (first published in 1946, reprinted in 2003 by New Day Publishing), by Lucius Beebe. Morning, noon, and night, bon vivant Beebe and a host of New Yorkers partook at the Stork.

Depth Charge

Look out below! A variation on the renowned, if not refined, Boilermaker (page 326), the Depth Charge differs in the fact that tequila is usually used (as opposed to whiskey), and in the fact that sometimes when you order one, a tall fruity drink much closer in essence to the Long Island Iced Tea (page 342) shows up. I say to make a DC stand out and be its own poison, always construct it with tequila and a Mexican lager-style beer, such as Corona or Sol; a little lime juice adds extra buzz, too.

Serves 2

Two 12-ounce bottles **lager-style Mexican beer**

Two 1½-ounce shots **white tequila**

2 **lime wedges**

1. Fill 2 pint glasses almost to the top with the beer.

2. Drop a shot glass of tequila into each beer. Squeeze a lime wedge over each drink, then discard it to the waters. Caution those swimming beneath, then drink all at once.

❌ *A Warning: This drink does have a shot glass within the pint glass. Be careful when drinking so that the shot glass doesn't hit you in the teeth.*

Fireball

While liquor intake in any style shouldn't be painful, sometimes one needs a liquid wake-up call, a slight something that induces the head to tilt up swiftly and start paying attention to *what's going on* (as the song says). It could be that you aren't the one needing this spicy attention-getter, but one of your friends. Don't warn them—just give them the shot and grin. If they're nutty enough to accept a shot without question, they may deserve it. **Serves 2**

Ice cubes

1½ ounces **cinnamon schnapps**

1½ ounces **white rum**

4 dashes **Tabasco sauce** or **other Louisiana-style hot sauce**

1. Fill a cocktail shaker halfway full with ice cubes. Add the cinnamon schnapps, rum, and hot sauce. Shake well.

2. Strain into 2 shot glasses. Serve with a glass of milk.

Flaming Dr Pepper

Oh my gawd, it's the Flaming Dr Pepper, **come to take over the city.** Who could possibly save us from his evil intentions, dousing him and saving babies and sweet puppies alike? Who has the courage and slight stupidity needed for this battle? Friend, I feel you are this superhero. You don't even need tights. A sturdy liver and a high tolerance win this battle and once again make the world safe for us less heroic drinkers. **Serves 2**

3 ounces **amaretto**

1 ounce **151-proof rum**

American-style lager beer

➡ **A Note:** This is, in theory, supposed to taste like Dr Pepper.

❌ **A Warning:** This drink does have a shot glass within the double old-fashioned glass. Be careful when drinking so that the shot glass doesn't hit you in the teeth.

1. Add 1½ ounces amaretto to each of 2 shot glasses. Carefully, using a spoon or just your own ultra-sure hand, float ½ ounce of rum on top of the amaretto in each glass.

2. Place each shot glass into another, slightly taller glass (a double old-fashioned should work—you want a pretty wide mouth).

3. Carefully, using a long match, or, if you have one, a crème brûlée torch or long lighter, light the rum on fire. Stand back.

4. Fill each glass with beer, but only to the level of the top of the shot glass. Blow out the flame. Drink everything rapidly.

Golden Goose

There was a man who had three sons, the youngest of whom was called Dummling, and who was despised, mocked, and sneered at on every occasion. Then Dummling picked up some high-end vodka and schnapps full of pure gold, mixed them together, served it to everyone in the room, and was instantly proclaimed **the beau of the ball.** The moral? Good drinks, even in shot form, equal at least a passing popularity, and much more quickly, too, than kissing up to some little gray-haired man in the forest (that doesn't sound safe at all). **Serves 2**

Ice cubes

1½ ounces **Goldschlager cinnamon schnapps**

1½ ounces **Grey Goose vodka** or **other top-shelf vodka** (but then you won't be able to call it a Golden Goose)

1. Fill a cocktail shaker halfway full with ice cubes. Add the cinnamon schnapps and vodka. Shake well.

2. Strain into 2 shot glasses. Toast the Brothers Grimm. Consume rapidly.

Italian Valium

This particular small socker was first developed for public consumption in Auntie Mae's Parlor, a Manhattan, Kansas, bar that is about 90 percent underground. It takes a bar slightly removed from daylight to unveil an amaretto and Crown Royal mix to the public (that's "Italian" for the amaretto and "Valium" for the Crown), and to birth the **kind of deranged genius** that Jeff Denney, owner and lead bar hack at Mae's, possesses. I suggest you visit, but do it before the snow hits or you might never leave town. **Serves 2**

Ice cubes

2 ounces **amaretto**

2 ounces **Crown Royal**

1. Fill a cocktail shaker halfway full with ice cubes. Pour the amaretto and Crown Royal into the shaker at once. Shake well.

2. Strain the mix straight into 2 shot glasses (feel no need to drain it through a plastic tube). Drink before the chill rescinds.

⬆ **A Note:** *Never, ever, drink an I.V. alone. For that matter, never drink it with less than a pal whom you trust (even with your wallet).*

Jell-O Shots ←

It could be there aren't enough drinks combining food and alcohol. Or, it could be there are too many (even if the Jell-O Shot were the only one). I'll leave that discussion to the trained debaters. The addition of gelatin to drinks does go back a long way. But there's still something, well, yucky about the practice, even when the end result tastes good.

There are many, many recipes for Jell-O Shots. Just imagine how many flavors of Jell-O there are and the mind gets befuddled. The recipe below is a basic starting point, using vodka for its malleability and lime Jell-O because I like lime, but **jump off into the extreme** reaches of Jell-O if you're that kind of high diver. It's also scaled up for serving a bunch of jiggly fanatics, because it's simpler and more fun that way. **Serves 8 to 10**

One 6-ounce box **lime Jell-O**

2 packets **unflavored gelatin**

1¼ cups **boiling water**

1½ cups **vodka** or **rum,** or even **tequila**

1. Combine the Jell-O and unflavored gelatin in a large bowl.

2. Add the boiling water and stir to combine and dissolve the gelatin. After just a minute, add the vodka (you don't want the water to meet the vodka in a full boil). Stir again, and let the mixture cool for 2 minutes.

3. Pour everything into an 8-inch square baking pan or ice cube trays. Refrigerate or freeze until solid enough to cut, at least 1 hour. Serve squared up on toothpicks or in shot glasses, or just hand out spoons to everyone standing around the pan.

Lemon Dropper

This is a favorite of sophisticated shot slammers, due to its layers of flavors. Okay, I can't lie, there are no sophisticated shot slammers, and the Lemon Dropper is **loved for the same reasons** as other shots: It doesn't taste gawd awful and it goes down quickly. Many, many people call this a straight Lemon Drop, but I like my Lemon Drop in strained form in a cocktail glass (page 341), and so add the extra "per" to this shot form. Both versions have their plusses, and are appropriate in different situations. **Serves 2**

Sugar

1 **lemon slice**

Ice cubes

2 ounces **citrus-flavored vodka**

1½ ounces **freshly squeezed lemon juice**

½ ounce **Simple Syrup** (page 7)

1. Spread the sugar on a small plate. Run the lemon slice around the edge of 2 shot glasses. Carefully rotate the outside of each shot glass rim through the sugar. You want to coat the outer edge of the glass with sugar, but avoid getting excess sugar in the glass.

2. Fill a cocktail shaker halfway full with ice cubes. Add the vodka, lemon juice, and simple syrup. Shake in an old-timey manner (remembering that those old-timers shook the heck out of a drink).

3. Strain the mix into the shot glasses and serve.

Little Red Teddy

Ah, the seductive Little Red Teddy. Wear this on cold winter nights when wanting to heat things up in front of the fire and on the bearskin rug. Wait, wait, wait. For a moment I thought I was writing copy for one of those catalogs that come in an almost translucent cover when sent through the mail. Forget all that nonsense. Serve this sweetheart shot in one gulp **when your sweet tooth is in need** of a little action, or when wanting to drink dessert, or when needing to entrance a passel of pals who like nothing better than eating chocolate by the barrel. **Serves 2**

Ice cubes

1½ ounces **vodka**

1½ ounces **white crème de cacao**

1 ounce **grenadine**

1. Fill a cocktail shaker halfway full with ice cubes. Add the vodka, crème de cacao, and grenadine. Shake your booty, and the cocktail shaker, well.

2. Strain into 2 shot glasses. Drink before anyone gets embarrassed.

3 Drinks to Buy for Someone Annoying at the Bar

While most think of buying drinks to impress a fellow bar patron, there are those trying times when you'd rather have that fellow bar patron scoot away. You can always resort to throwing a cold beverage (or a hot one) on a persistent person, but I hate to see booze wasted. Instead, set him or her up with one of these and turn your back. The offender should get the hint.

1
Brain Hemorrhage
(page 204)

2
Rattlesnake Cocktail
(page 226)

3
Widow's Kiss
(page 238)

Mugshot →

Don't serve this at a movie party where you're going to watch a flick featuring **the latest celebrity-to-be busted** for some sort of wrongdoing. That would just be tasteless. Do serve this shot, which meets its line-up responsibilities by being vaguely dodgy, when you're safe at home watching a celebrity shenanigans TV show. The Mugshot sets the mood for that secret pleasure nicely. **Serves 2**

Ice cubes
1½ ounces **vodka**
1 ounce **blue curaçao**
1 ounce **cranberry juice cocktail**

1. Fill a cocktail shaker with ice cubes. Add the vodka, curaçao, and cranberry juice. Shake in a fleeing-the-law manner.

2. Strain into 2 shot glasses. Drink before the line-up photographer's flash expires.

Silver Bullet

"Even a man who is pure at heart, and says his prayers by night, may become a wolf when the wolfbane blooms, and the autumn moon is bright." And if this man (or woman, as the case may be) can't be stopped, by any method or regular shot, then **serve him up this hefty mix**, and watch him drop into a fix. But if you serve him bathtub gin, he'll raise up a legendary din, tear your favorite shaker to shards, and pass out flat in the front yard. That's what the gypsy legend says. **Serves 2**

Ice cubes
2½ ounces **gin**
1½ ounces **Scotch**
Lemon twist for garnish

1. Fill a cocktail shaker halfway full with ice cubes. Add the gin and Scotch. Shake as if Lon Chaney, Jr., himself were after you under a full moon.

2. Strain into 2 shot glasses. Twist the lemon twist over each glass, and then drape it over the edge. Be sure that the drinker of said bullet doesn't let the twist hit him in the eye when shooting.

Cool It Down

The song says that "there ain't no cure for the summertime blues,"and while the singer may not have been referring just to the high temperatures that often accompany summer, which make even moving around outdoors draining, never mind hosting a rollicking revelry for a posse of pals, at least part of the sentiment of the lyric points to how the heat can take much of the fun from those bright blue summer days. If only there were a cure.

Friends, I'm here to tell you, your high-temperature prayers have been answered, and the answers are bubbling over with refreshment and respite from that ol' sun beating down. Right here in the chapter known as Cool It Down exist the antidotes for those days when the mercury has met the top of the thermometer, when even opening the door to the boiling outdoors seems to induce a sweat. These elevated and breezy liquid remedies instantly change beat-down attitudes, change a stuck-in-hot-mud afternoon into a lusciously icy and legendary day, and change a wholly downtrodden affair into a happening hula party.

From the Beachcomber's and the Sweet Press's sandaled and cut-off joys to the more upscale white-skirt and cuffed trouser pleasures of the Castello Special and the Kir Royale, the bright minglings in Cool It Down live up to their billing, as all are designed to take the edge off a sweltering day. No matter what style of soirée you're hosting, there's a cocktail here that will have your guests opening up and sighing a sweet sigh of contentment.

Therefore, don't allow yourself to be mugged by muggy weather or stifled by too much sun. Enjoy the outdoors even if the temperature's toasting the three-digit mark by taking a Horsefeather to your hammock or a Summer Beer to your swimming hole. Want to pretend that, while enjoying this scorching weather, you're on an extended vacation? Make your traveling companion a Suissesse, a Soledan, or a French 75, and take the imaginary trip while keeping yourself as chill as an ice cube.

There's no need to sweat it out—not when you can Cool It Down. The pages aren't too heavy to turn, and the instructions here have an eye on simplicity. And if it ever gets too much, let the Eden transport you back into a paradise. There are no summertime blues—or any-other-time blues—this chapter can't cure.

American Champagne Cocktail

This tall drink of patriotism first came to me via Jeremy Holt, a fine bartender and publisher of *The Husky Boy*, a revered small 'zine devoted to eats and drinks. The ACC (American Champagne Cocktail) combines what may seem at first glance to be disparate items: Champagne and bourbon. If that gives an initial shudder, shake it off. These two were made to tango, as the bubbly combines with the bourbon's smoke smoothly, instead of being overpowered by it. As it also brings orange juice into the picture, this drink is ideal for breakfasts, brunches, and more intimate late-afternoon soirées.

Ice cube (optional)

4 ounces **chilled Champagne**

1½ ounces **freshly squeezed orange juice**

1 ounce **bourbon**

Orange slice for garnish

1. Add one cube of ice to a Champagne flute. (If both your Champagne and orange juice are chilled, feel free to omit the ice.)

2. Add the Champagne to the flute, then the orange juice. Stir to mix.

3. Float the bourbon on top of the other ingredients, pouring it slowly over the back of a spoon if necessary. Garnish with the orange slice.

➕ **A Tip:** *I'd use a polite mid-priced Champagne for this drink. There's no need to spend all your drinking dollars on a high-priced bubbly that's being mixed.*

Arizona

Hold on to those hats (worn as defense against that bright hot ball in the Arizona sky) and listen up. This here alcoholic combination is what brings the ghosts of Clark Gable and Carole Lombard back to the Oatman Hotel, the ghosts of countless miners back to Choride, and the ghost of Big-Nose Kate back to Tombstone. Sadly, none of these ghosts is able to **slurp up this potent potable**, so I suggest you have an extra for them.

Ice cubes

2½ ounces **vodka**

1 ounce **Midori melon liqueur**

½ ounce **freshly squeezed lime juice**

Chilled 7UP or **Sprite**

Lime slice for garnish

1. Fill a highball glass three-quarters full with ice cubes. Add the vodka, Midori, and lime juice. Stir like the dickens with a rattlesnake, whip, or long spoon.

2. Fill the glass up with 7UP. Stir again, and again, and once again. Garnish with the lime slice.

Bay Breeze

Some days, when the thermometer's riding near triple digits and the wind won't move more than the lightest leaf, you shouldn't work too hard—even at making a cooling drink. But then again, you don't want to be drinkless, either. Those days, I suggest taking the simple route toward making your own breeze, a Bay Breeze. It's **easier than swinging palm fronds** around to get the wind progressing, and the end result is more effective and tastes better.

Ice cubes

2 ounces **white rum**

2 ounces **cranberry juice cocktail**

1½ ounces **fresh pineapple juice**

Pineapple chunks for garnish (optional)

1. Fill a highball glass up to the rim with ice cubes. Add the rum, cranberry juice, and pineapple juice. Stir, but gently, without straining yourself or working up even a drop of sweat.

2. Garnish with the pineapple chunks on a toothpick or tiny umbrella—if you don't mind the extra work.

➕ *A Tip: No matter how much you get the urge (and after a couple of these, the urge will come), avoid singing "Sitting on the Dock of the Bay."*

Beachcomber Cocktail

I'm not saying one must actually be on a beach to enjoy this particularly refreshing cocktail, or even be **hanging around the wading pool** with pals dressed in brightly foliaged shorts. But if you aren't at least wearing slightly dogged sandals and contemplating the idea of bringing in 40 pounds of sand for the back porch, watch out—the cocktail gods don't look kindly on that kind of behavior.

Ice cubes

2 ounces **white rum**

½ ounce **Cointreau**

½ ounce **freshly squeezed lime juice**

¼ ounce **maraschino liqueur**

Lime slice for garnish

1. Fill a cocktail shaker halfway full with ice cubes. Add the rum, Cointreau, lime juice, and maraschino liqueur. Shake well, with a hula-hooping motion.

2. Strain the mix into a cocktail glass. Garnish with the lime slice.

Six Summer Cocktail Requirements

1. They must be refreshing in some way.
2. They must also be slightly sultry in some way.
3. They must be fun but fit the occasion's spirit, whether it's a flip-flops and cut-offs gang or a lawn party.
4. They must represent the season's personality, which is a reflection of when we were in school and had summers off—this is why we're so attuned (hey, it's instinct) to parties in the summer.
5. They must be relatively uncomplicated, meaning you don't want to spend the summer worrying over 86 hard-to-find ingredients, memorizing a ton of crucial drink creation steps that involve shaker gymnastics and complex hand movements, or wasting any of that sweet summertime sweating making the drinks, instead of enjoying the drinks.
6. They must taste great.

Bellini

It's rare that a drink is named after any artist—even though artists have been known to have a drink, or 10. Of those few artist-named drinks, the Bellini is the most illustrious, by **a bubbly landslide**, even if 96.8 percent of folks sipping Bellinis don't realize the name descends from the fifteenth-century Italian painter Giovanni Bellini. The name and the original recipe for this luscious drink are creations of Giuseppe Cipriani, who mixed Bellini number one in 1948 at Harry's Bar in Venice. The legend (or, in Italian, *la leggenda*) goes that Giuseppe thought the coloring of the drink echoed a "pink glow" that the artist's paintings boasted.

The secret to the Bellini is two-headed, and while the drink seems undemanding, without paying attention to both parts of the secret a lacking libation ensues. First, this should be made with white peaches (which are especially good around Venice, if you're in that neighborhood). If white peaches aren't available, then at least get ones that aren't bruised and that have unblemished skin. Second, Prosecco—a sweet Italian sparkling wine—and not the drier Champagne, is required.

Ice cubes

1 **white peach** (or as close as you can get), pitted

¼ ounce **freshly squeezed lemon juice**

4 ounces **chilled Prosecco**

1. Add 1 or 2 ice cubes, the flesh and skin of the peach, and the lemon juice to a blender. Puree the mix until you have a fairly smooth, even, consistency.

2. Add 2 ounces of the peach puree to a Champagne flute. Slowly, while stirring, add the Prosecco. You must add the Prosecco slowly, integrating it into the peach puree throughout, or else a peach puree sludge gathers at the bottom of the glass. That won't look good at all.

⊕ *A Note: Really, though there's only a little, the lemon juice ensures that the peach puree reaches and keeps the desired coloring and taste. I'm indebted to champion cocktailian Gary Regan for this knowledge. Please thank him for me next time you see him.*

⊕ *Another Note: If you don't feel like making your own peach puree, you can order white peach puree (and many other puree varieties) from Perfect Purée of Napa, California (www.perfectpuree.com).*

Bird of Paradise

Summer sometimes gets a bad rap. Many go from air-conditioned car to air-conditioned indoors in a heat-avoidance crouching run. This leads not only to missing many outdoor party chances (and chances to delve into a wide range of hot-weather alcoholic specialties), but also to missing hot-weather foliage hits, like giant growing vegetable gardens, herbs galore, and flowers **bursting with colors and exquisite scents**. These big blooms lead not only to a better appreciation of the season and a reason to stick around outside, but also to dandy drink names. While I'm not positive that the Bird of Paradise was named after the flower sharing its heavenly autograph, I would think the flower would make an exceptional garnish for the drink, and know for a fact that the drink is ideal for garden parties (though it might outshine the garden).

Ice cubes

2 ounces **gin**

1 ounce **heavy cream**

1 ounce **freshly squeezed lime juice**

Crushed ice

1 ounce **loganberry liqueur**

Chilled club soda

1. Fill a cocktail shaker halfway full with ice cubes. Add the gin, cream, and lime juice. Shake well.

2. Fill a goblet three-quarters full with crushed ice. Strain the mix over the ice and stir once.

3. Add the loganberry liqueur and stir. Add the club soda and stir.

⬆ **A Note:** *A great loganberry liqueur is available from the Clear Creek Distillery (www.clearcreekdistillery.com). If you can't track down loganberry liqueur, try using a blackberry or raspberry liqueur.*

BLC

Vegetarians, don't fret, and carnivores, don't salivate (well, salivate if you must, but not for the reason you're thinking)—no pork products are used in the making of **this chilly refreshment**. But the BLC *does* get bloody. Wait, wait, don't call the SPCA—it's just blood orange juice.

Ice cubes

2 ounces **Cointreau**

1 ounce **freshly squeezed blood orange juice**

½ ounce **freshly squeezed lemon juice**

Chilled ginger ale

Lemon slice for garnish

1. Fill a highball glass three-quarters full with ice cubes. Add the Cointreau, blood orange juice, and lemon juice.

2. Top the glass off with chilled ginger ale and a mischievous smile. Stir well and garnish with the lemon slice.

Blue Lagoon Cocktail

We need to get something straight. Loving this cocktail doesn't mean that you: still harbor a crush on Brooke Shields due to seeing a movie that happens to share this cocktail's name during your formative years; still remember Christopher Atkins due to seeing a movie that happens to share this cocktail's name during your formative years; have been known to wear an animal skin bikini or Speedo and **run around the backyard** trying to spear birds off of trees. Now that we have that worked out, start shaking.

Ice cubes

2 ounces **vodka**

1 ounce **blue curaçao**

¼ ounce **freshly squeezed lemon juice**

Lemon twist for garnish

1. Fill a cocktail shaker halfway full with ice cubes. Add the vodka, curaçao, and lemon juice. Shake for at least the duration of a Brooke Shields's Calvin Klein commercial.

2. Strain the mix into a cocktail glass. Squeeze the lemon twist over the top of the drink, and then drape it over the side of the glass like a grass skirt.

Bubbly Blue Moon

There are nights, important nights, romantically inclined nights, when the idea is both to cool it down and to keep the heat on. The Bubbly Blue Moon **facilitates those romantic feelings** without dampening the lovey-dovey stuff. It even lends a helping hand, generating starry-eyed "moon" talk, such as, "Isn't the moon enchanting tonight?" and "Let's dance as we sip these divine moons." Ah, I love a happy ending.

Ice cubes

2 ounces **gin**

1 ounce **parfait amour**

Chilled club soda

Lemon twist for garnish

1. Fill a highball glass three-quarters full with ice cubes. Add the gin and the parfait amour.

2. Top the glass off with club soda. Squeeze the lemon twist over the drink and then drop it in with a yearning look. Stir twice.

A VARIATION: This is a treat without bubbles, too, and easy to make. Just shake the gin and parfait amour with ice, then strain into a cocktail glass.

LIQUEUR SPOTLIGHT
Parfait Amour

"My parfait amour, lovely as a summer's day . . . my parfait amour, pretty little liqueur that I adore, you're the liqueur my heart beats for." I believe that Stevie Wonder probably forgives my alteration of his lyrics, because his song's about love, and parfait amour is a liqueur that many used to think was a French love potion (the name means "perfect love"). Maybe it is. It's also a slightly sweet, violet-flavored brew, sometimes (depending on the brand) with hints of orange and/or vanilla and lavender. Elegant and completely equal to its amorous name, it has been a fixture within seductive cocktails for generations. Though there's no exact story on its background, it became popular in the later nineteenth and first half of the twentieth centuries, mostly as a favorite among the ladies of the time, due to its sweet nature (or, at least, that's supposedly the reason). It has fallen a bit to the back of the bar, but is thankfully still available in many liquor stores, usually under the Marie Brizard brand. Thanks, Marie.

Cape Cod

Vodka and cranberry juice were meant to be a team, like peanut butter and jelly or Peaches and Herb. While there may be drinks better known, the Cape Cod has a **highball elegance** that allows you and yours to wear white tennis shoes and no socks while consuming and not feel ashamed.

Ice cubes

2 ounces **vodka**

2 ounces **chilled cranberry juice cocktail**

¼ ounce **freshly squeezed lime juice**

Chilled club soda

Lime wedge for garnish

1. Fill a highball glass three-quarters full with ice cubes. Add the vodka, cranberry juice, and lime juice. Stir once.

2. Fill the glass almost to the top with club soda. Stir again.

3. Squeeze the lime wedge over the glass, and then drop it in. Stir twice. It's like dancing, isn't it?

⬆ **A Note:** *Sometimes you hear this drink called the Cape Codder, often by people from Massachusetts, so I think this must be a perfectly acceptable variant name.*

➕ **A Tip:** *Be sure that your cranberry juice and club soda are cold. This way, you preserve the ice and the integrity of the drink.*

Castello Special

There's no demanding of those craving this bubbly beauty that they scale the closest castle wall to get one. All that castle-storming might cause too much commotion, which would delay the enjoyment. Think this over: Instead of breaking in, why not **walk the moat and ring the bell**? I'll bet the inhabitants of any castle would be happy to share this cooling treat with invaders.

Ice cubes

1½ ounces **limoncello**

¾ ounce **freshly squeezed blood orange juice**

½ ounce **Simple Syrup** (page 7)

Chilled club soda

Blood orange slice for garnish

1. Fill a highball glass three-quarters full with ice cubes. Add the limoncello, blood orange juice, and simple syrup. Stir twice with a thin spoon, stir stick, or very tiny ladder.

2. Top the glass off with club soda. Stir again, at least 5 more times around. Garnish with the blood orange slice.

A VARIATION: If no blood oranges are available, use regular orange juice and orange slices. It completely changes the drink's character, naturally, but won't make a poor drink. Maybe retitle it the Tower Special, as it won't be a complete castle.

Champagne Cobbler

The cobbler family of drinks traces its heritage to when people really knew how to sweat (none of this air-conditioning for the original cobbler-lovers). Rest assured, though, that even if you've been known to partake of climate control, you'll still enjoy an icy Champagne Cobbler once it's settled in the palm—which will also be icy before too long, no matter what the temperature.

Crushed ice

1½ ounces **Simple Syrup** (page 7)

5 to 6 ounces **chilled Champagne**

Orange twist for garnish

Mint leaves for garnish

1. Fill a goblet three-quarters full with crushed ice. Add the simple syrup and Champagne, in that order.

2. Squeeze the orange twist over the glass, and then drop it in languidly. Stir well, until the outside of the goblet begins to get frosty. Garnish with the mint leaves and serve with a straw.

A VARIATION: The cobbler family isn't limited to Champagne. You can also compose gin, whiskey, rum, applejack, or brandy cobblers. When going another liquor route, feel free to play around with the formula a little bit, adding maraschino liqueur instead of (or going halves with) simple syrup when using gin, or substituting Cointreau for the simple syrup when using whiskey. Just be sure to add the syrup or sweeter liquor to the glass first, and then the base alcohol. You also may want to use a lemon twist instead of orange. And if you're feeling really old school, try a sherry cobbler.

"This drink {the sherry cobbler} is without doubt the most popular beverage in this country, with ladies as well as with gentlemen. It is **a very refreshing drink** for old and young."

HARRY JOHNSON, circa 1880 (quote taken from David A. Embury's *The Fine Art of Mixing Drinks*)

Dragonfly

It's possible to actually see this drink flying around when it becomes uncomfortably hot. Like a mirage, it's there in the distance, **waiting for a thirsty soul** to slide right in. Unlike a mirage, the Dragonfly is available, easy to sling together, and thirst quenching.

Ice cubes

2½ ounces **gin**

Chilled ginger ale

Lime wedge for garnish

1. Fill a highball glass three-quarters full with ice cubes. Add the gin, with reverence. Add the ginger ale until you're slightly fearful of spillage.

2. Squeeze the lime wedge over the drink, and then drop it in smoothly. Stir 5 times with a buzzing sound.

Eden →

Whether thought of religiously, metaphorically, or as the finest party ever thrown, Eden sounds like a pretty dandy spot. It deserves a signature drink, and luckily the Eden fills the bill. A fruity mix (but not forbidden fruit, so don't fret) that **has a plentiful kick** combined with just a bit of bubbles, it gets any Adam or Eve into a meditative state of mind.

Ice cubes

2 ounces **white rum**

1 ounce **Campari**

1 ounce **fresh pineapple juice**

1 ounce **freshly squeezed orange juice**

Prosecco or **other slightly sweet sparkling wine**

Orange slice for garnish

1. Fill a highball glass three-quarters full with ice cubes. Add the rum, Campari, pineapple juice, and orange juice, naming each as they're added. Stir 6 times.

2. Top with Prosecco. Stir a seventh time. Garnish with the orange slice. Then sit back and enjoy what you've created.

⊕ *A Note: After one of these, you'll feel as if any old backyard is a garden of paradise. After two, you might just want to put on a fig leaf. Warn the neighbors in advance (or invite them over to have a few Edens).*

French 75

When having what the French refer to as *le summer partee*, **this cross-continental classic** is the classy drink to serve. It's cool, employs a judicious amount of Champagne, and facilitates guests' talk of Impressionism and avant garde cinema. Whether this is a good thing is still under debate.

Ice cubes

½ ounce **freshly squeezed lemon juice**

½ ounce **Simple Syrup** (page 7)

1 ounce **gin**

Chilled Champagne

Lemon and **orange slices** for garnish

Maraschino cherry for garnish

1. Add 1 or 2 ice cubes to a flute glass. Add the lemon juice, simple syrup, and gin, in that order.

2. Top off the flute with Champagne and the lemon slice, orange slice, and cherry. Feel free to coordinate the garnishes with a toothpick (but don't forget that cherry). Serve each drink with a red straw or umbrella.

A VARIATION: If a French 75 seems just a little light, and not quite mature enough for you, move on up to a French 76 by substituting brandy for gin.

*↻ **A Note:** The French 75 can be, and is, made in a number of styles. Sometime, when it's so hot that even Notre Dame Cathedral starts to melt, I like to make this in a highball glass with a little extra ice.*

"Champagne, if you are seeking the truth, is **better than a lie detector**."

GRAHAM GREENE, *Travels with My Aunt*, 1969

Garibaldi

From what I can ascertain, this drink is named after Giuseppe Garibaldi, a French-born Italian patriot who helped propel the unification of Italy in 1861 while commanding his "red-shirt" army. The lesson learned from that sentence? When on an extended summer campaign, whether you're playing Risk, capture-the-flag, or just making the campaign from one watering hole to the next, the Garibaldi is **the drink you'll want in the canteen.**

Ice cubes

5 ounces **freshly squeezed orange juice**

2 ounces **Campari**

Tiny **Italian flag** for garnish (if possible)

1. Fill a highball glass three-quarters full with ice cubes. Add the orange juice and Campari.

2. Stir until the Campari and juice have been unified. Garnish with the tiny Italian flag.

➕ **A Tip:** *Don't really fill a canteen with Garibaldis. There's no need to involve the local constable in any drink revolution.*

Four Fantastic Places to Get Friendly with a French 75

The French 75 (opposite), at one point almost lost to the annals of bar history, made a comeback—not a monumental comeback, but a solid rising back into the eye of the discerning public. This bubbler is best with the right atmosphere, though—it should match the drink's class. Much like these spots:

1. The Benson Hotel, Portland, Oregon. Listen to jazz and chuckle happily when they bring out the Champagne in its own bottle on the side.

2. French 75 Bistro, Burbank, California. It shares the name and knows the history, and they serve the bubbly up right, too.

3. Round Robin Bar, Washington, D.C. Sip smoothly while catching up on political intrigue. You'll probably need at least two drinks.

4. Anywhere, Villefranche-sur-Mer on the French Riviera. Five miles east of Nice, you can make your own French 75 and enjoy the view and lack of tourists.

Gin Fizz

The fizz family (whose venerable patriarch I consider the more complex and complicated Ramos Fizz, page 129) is long, consists of many branches, and sadly isn't on the speed dial of many modern-day drink dialers. This is an early-morning shame—the fizz family prides itself on being developed to **ease the pain of party people** who played too late the night before. Fizzes are first-rate hangover helpers, or at least that was the belief in the fizz heyday. The Gin Fizz is the most basic of the bunch.

Ice cubes

1½ ounces **gin**

1 ounce **Simple Syrup**
(page 7)

½ ounce **freshly squeezed lemon juice**

Chilled club soda

Lemon slice for garnish

1. Fill a cocktail shaker halfway full with ice cubes. Add the gin, simple syrup, and lemon juice. Shake well.

2. Fill a highball glass three-quarters full with ice cubes. Strain the mix into the glass.

3. Top off the glass with club soda. Garnish with the lemon slice.

A VARIATION: Add the white of an egg to the shaker along with the gin, syrup, and lemon juice and you have a Silver Fizz.

A SECOND VARIATION: Add the yolk of an egg to the shaker along with the gin, syrup, and lemon juice and you have a Golden Fizz.

A THIRD VARIATION: Add a whole egg to the shaker along with the gin, syrup, and lemon juice and you have a Royal Fizz. And breakfast.

Great Green Freezer

A lovely-to-look-at-and-taste green delight, the GGF (for short) does take a bit of work, perhaps stipulating a step more in construction than many mixes made to take the edge off of a sultry sweaty afternoon. I'm not saying it's not worth it, because it is. You'll have to start up the blender, though, and deal with a honeydew melon—you've now been officially warned.

Ice cubes

1 cup **chopped honeydew melon**

½ ounce **Simple Syrup** (page 7)

1½ ounces **vodka**

1 ounce **Midori melon liqueur**

Chilled club soda

1. Add ½ cup ice cubes, the honeydew, and simple syrup to a blender. Blend until smooth. Pour into a highball glass.

2. Add the vodka and Midori melon liqueur to the glass. Stir thrice.

3. Fill the glass almost to the top with chilled club soda. Stir well. Taste. If not chilly enough, add 2 more ice cubes.

Greyhound

This late-July, early-August archetype may induce rounding up neighborhood dogs to have them race around the backyard. For safety's sake, be sure the dogs are given lots of water breaks and lots of those beefy treats dogs love. For your personal safety, make sure neither gin nor grapefruit juice runs low. People get plumb parched around running dogs.

Ice cubes

2½ ounces **vodka**

Freshly squeezed grapefruit juice

1. Fill a highball glass three-quarters full with ice cubes. Add the vodka.

2. Add the grapefruit juice to ¼ inch from the glass's rim. Stir well, as if you were a wooden hare being chased by greyhounds.

⬆ *A Note: This is one of the few drinks without a garnish, but if you really need one, add a cherry. Because everyone loves a cherry.*

Harvard Cooler

There are, or have been, numerous and various drinks falling under the moniker of "cooler," with connecting features being a "school's out" nature, club soda, ice, and a tall glass (though the wars raged between those pledging a cooler in a highball glass and those pledging it in a Collins glass have been harrowing). A lemon twist, lemon juice, and some form of sweetener may also **make the grade**. My thought with a cooler is to aim high and head straight for the Ivy League.

Ice cubes

1½ ounces **applejack**

½ ounce **Simple Syrup** (page 7)

½ ounce **freshly squeezed lemon juice**

Chilled club soda

Lemon twist for garnish

1. Fill a cocktail shaker halfway full with ice cubes. Add the applejack, simple syrup, and lemon juice. Shake well.

2. Fill a highball glass three-quarters full with ice cubes. Strain the shaken mix into the glass.

3. Add club soda to the glass, to the level where the tassel would hang if the drink were going through graduation. Garnish with the lemon twist (allow classmates to squeeze the twist over the drink if they'd like). Serve with a long straw or stirring stick and suggest they give it a whirl.

Horsefeather

There's always a particular late spring day when summer is pawing outside the picket fence, snorting a little bit, and **waiting to bust down the gate** and come storming in with the heat and sun that rides on summer's back. On that spring day, I suggest shaking any remaining dust off the cut-offs, polishing up the patio furniture's aluminum, and calling all sun-loving pals over to toast a spring that's been and a summer that's almost arrived with a whole passel of Horsefeathers. As it fits so well in either season, it's only right to use this long drink to celebrate both.

Ice cubes

3 ounces **Kentucky bourbon** (I find Maker's Mark ideal in this situation)

Chilled ginger ale

2 dashes **Angostura bitters**

1. Fill a highball glass three-quarters full with ice cubes. Add, smoothly and leisurely—steady now—the bourbon.

2. Top off the glass with ginger ale. Add the Angostura bitters. Stir well.

A VARIATION: Some folks out on the real or imagined plains find the Horsefeather needs a little something to make it the ideal companion for sunset watching. If you fit this bill, use a zester to take a long strip off a lemon. Before adding the ice in step 1 above, drape your lemon spiral onto the glass's edge—then proceed. The drink will have magically changed to a Horse's Neck (page 304) or, on some traditional farms, A Horse's Neck with a Kick.

"Alcohol is like love. **The first kiss is magic**, the second is intimate, the third is routine. After that you take the girl's clothes off."

RAYMOND CHANDLER, *The Long Goodbye*, 1954

Italian 75

Though borrowing a name from its European neighbor, the French 75 (page 382), the Italian 75 deserves its own place (much like the French Riviera and the Italian Riviera each getting its own section in touring guides). This drink originates (at least for me) at Seattle's Café Lago restaurant in the Montlake neighborhood. Sitting at their big front windows, sipping an Italian 75 while waiting for luscious lasagna–there are much worse ways to savor June-in-Seattle's long daylight hours.

Ice cubes

1 ounce **gin**

½ ounce **pear grappa**

½ ounce **freshly squeezed lemon juice**

½ ounce **Simple Syrup** (page 7)

Chilled Prosecco

Lemon twist for garnish

1. Fill a cocktail shaker halfway full with ice cubes. Add the gin, grappa, lemon juice, and simple syrup. Shake as if you were standing in line for the Uffizi Gallery in Florence, and could only get to the front by demonstrating prodigious shaking ability.

2. Strain the mix into a flute glass. Top it off with chilled Prosecco, and garnish with the lemon twist.

⬆ *A Note: Many people fear the grappa. I, my-own-courageous-self, for years wouldn't order or buy it. This could have to do with the fact that the first glass I ever had brought to mind warm gasoline. I finally rediscovered my nerve and tried a second glass. It was delightful. Firm and serious, but still complex (as well as soothing after a large meal), grappa comes in many different varieties, so overcome the fear and take the grappa plunge.*

Kir Royale

The Kir Royale is **fit for a king and queen**, or at least a recently deposed monarch who has a line on his country's oil reserves and who is in a room overflowing with tuxes and glittering gowns, usually a casino in Monte Carlo. If you can't travel to any place so mythically glamorous, don't let that stop this drink from being poured—invite some friends over in tux T-shirts and spangled tank tops and start betting over hands of gin rummy. Eventually, the atmosphere equals out, and the Kir Royales taste as fine.

1 ounce **framboise**

Chilled Champagne

Lemon twist for garnish

⬆ **A Note:** Framboise is a raspberry-flavored brandy. If it's not readily available, try Chambord (a black raspberry–flavored liqueur) or crème de cassis, a mouth-watering black currant–flavored liqueur often used in the Kir Royale. (It could well be that old Felix Kir himself used crème de cassis, as it originates, like he, from the Burgundy region of France.)

1. Add the framboise to a flute glass. Fill the flute with Champagne.

2. Garnish the glass with the lemon twist and a devil-may-care grin, so that anyone watching knows you'll push all-in at a moment's notice.

A VARIATION: If you use a dry white wine instead of Champagne, you're drinking a Kir. Both were named after Canon Felix Kir, mayor of Dijon, France, from 1945 to 1968.

✚ **A Tip:** If you're spotlighting the Kir Royale at a casino night, preslice a bowl of lemon twists for the second and third rounds.

The Fresh Fruit Factor: Ignore at Your Peril

If it isn't enough that the word "fresh" signifies not only how long it's been since a fruit or vegetable was picked (thereby corresponding to its readiness to be chowed), then the fact that the word also signifies an inventive, hip, and original style should tell you that fresh is a good thing. The high percentage of drinks in this book that use fresh fruit juice or fresh fruit as a garnish lets you in on the fact that the fruit is important for good beverages (both of the alcoholic and nonalcoholic variety). Using less-than-fresh fruit and fruit juice, then, following our fresh equation, equals substandard drinks. Said drinks then turn you from Gallant to Goofus as a host or hostess.

Lime Rickey

There is nothing not to love about a Lime Rickey. Sounds good and is somewhat enigmatic in front of a lady or gentleman you're trying to impress? Indeed. **Can be drunk while wearing a fedora** or other classy-sounding hat? Indubitably. Uses fruit juice and so is, at some very odd level, healthy? Definitely. Could have been invented near the tail end of the nineteenth century for a mysterious colonel who later became a lime importer? Certainly. A swell sip on a blistering day? Check, check, and mate.

¾ ounce **freshly squeezed lime juice** (save the lime after squeezing)

Ice cubes

1½ ounces **gin**

Chilled club soda

Lime wedge for garnish

1. Drop the lime half (which the juice was squeezed from) into a highball glass, and then fill the glass three-quarters full with ice cubes.

2. Add the gin and lime juice. Top with club soda. Stir, but not too much. Garnish with the lime wedge, and serve with a stirring device, preferably a long thin spoon.

A VARIATION: Try almost any liquor, including applejack, bourbon, rum, Scotch, sloe gin, or vodka. It's that simple.

A VIRGIN VARIATION: A Virgin Rickey also helps out on a hot summer's 24 hours. Instead of gin, add 1 ounce Simple Syrup (page 7) and a shake of Angostura bitters to each glass.

Limoni

Picture this: You're outside of the massive and mighty *duomo* of Milan, sitting at a café and observing the scads of tourists and locals alike as they flitter between the cathedral and the Galleria and gelato stands. What's this? The heat reflecting off the bricks, marble, and pavement starts to intrude onto this idyllic scene? **Give a friendly come-hither smile** to that pleasant *signora* or *signore* at the counter and request this lemon libation. Ahhh, that's better.

1½ ounces **gin**

2 tablespoons **lemon gelato**

Chilled club soda

Lemon slice for garnish

1. Add the gin and lemon gelato to a chilled highball glass.

2. Fill the glass with chilled club soda. Stir lightly with a long elegant spoon. Garnish with the lemon slice and serve with a straw.

⬆ *A Note: No gelato available on your block (where's a kid with a gelato stand when you need one)? Subbing in lemon sherbet won't bring the dream completely alive, but it at least gets it started.*

When to Buy a Round

For many, the easy answer is "any time a round's been bought for you." However, always being the one buying the second round develops a cheap rep that no one wants to wear over any period of time. If a kick-start in your round-buying is needed, begin by using the following as excuses for opening that wallet (pretend they're real if necessary). Soon, it'll become second nature.

1. I just had a baby, let me pick up the first round.
2. My boss left the company, the first round's on me.
3. When walking in, that cute guy/girl winked at me. I'll get the first round so I can get another wink.
4. I finally won first prize in a beauty contest, and standing the first round lets me show off.
5. I found a twenty on the sidewalk, and demand to use it to secure the first round with these lucky gains.

Million Dollar Cocktail

This cocktail can in no way make you a millionaire—but it might make you feel like a million bucks in the middle of July (for all those millionaires reading, this cocktail might make you feel like two million bucks). So it's time to **break out the Bentley**, the diamond-encrusted swizzle stick, the platinum shaker, and the silver dollar ice cubes. Or you can just take pleasure in pretending with pals that a million is yours to blow on glitzy, ritzy, slightly ditzy bar equipment. I suggest at one point in the big bank-book evening lighting a candy cigar with $100 of Monopoly money.

Ice cubes

2 ounces **gin**

1 ounce **sweet vermouth**

½ ounce **fresh pineapple juice**

¼ ounce **grenadine**

1 **egg white,** preferably organic

1. Fill a diamond-encrusted cocktail shaker halfway full with ice cubes. Twirl your pinky ring.

2. Add the gin, sweet vermouth, pineapple juice, grenadine, and, carefully, the egg white. Shake well, for at least 20 seconds. Or, have the butler do it.

3. Strain into a crystal cocktail glass. Garnish with a golden smile.

❌ *A Warning: Using eggs in cocktails isn't a bad thing, and at one time it seemed as natural as using booze. But drinks and cocktails with raw eggs shouldn't be served to guests who are elderly or have compromised immune systems. And always be sure the eggs are very fresh.*

Mimosa

While it's a fact that many serious partakers of the morning libation swear by the Bloody Mary (page 21), many others swear by the Mimosa as a lighter and friendlier breakfast or brunch accompaniment. Even if the night before ended at 4 A.M. with the couch spinning clockwise and the ceiling counter-clockwise, a Mimosa brings a sunshiny outlook to the day, and helps a little in replenishing any missing vitamin C. The fact that it's an easy drink to make for one or many is a beautiful bonus for those feeling a bit tired.

2 ounces **freshly squeezed orange juice**

Chilled Champagne

Orange slice for garnish

1. Add the orange juice to a flute glass. Fil each glass with Champagne.

2. Garnish with the orange slice and, if feeling up to it, a bouncy rendition of "Here Comes the Sun."

⬆ *A Note: My Mimosa tends to be a little lighter on the OJ than the traditional ratio (if tracking the drink back to its Paris-in-the-1920s origins). Some may even be so bold as to say that the above recipe is closer to a Buck's Fizz—a Champagne and orange juice combo created in London a few years before the Mimosa was created in Paris. They may even be right. But during their long spiel I've already finished my first Mimosa. I think it's evident who wins in that scenario.*

Nostromo

Avast, ye mateys! Lash the mizzenmast! Unfurl the sails! Wheel the wheel aft! Swab the bow! Batten down the jib! Button up the boom vang! Reel in the rudder! Jury-rig the jib sheet! All hands on deck (even if it's the backyard deck)! All glasses brimming with Nostromos!

Ice cubes

3 ounces **freshly squeezed orange juice**

2 ounces **white rum**

Chilled club soda (orange-flavored, if available)

Orange slice for garnish

1. Fill a Collins glass three-quarters full with ice cubes. Add the orange juice and rum.

2. Top it off with the club soda. Stir well, but without causing any squalls. Garnish with the orange slice.

⬆ *A Note: Nostromo is a sad sailor novel from Joseph Conrad, the Italian word for boatswain, and a handy excuse for throwing a boat-oriented shindig.*

Peach Nehi

A light throwback to a less complicated time (or, at least, so my grandmother would have me believe), this drink depends on very modern ingredients. Even though the list is a dash in-depth, it's worth the complex combinations. If feeling fancy, garnishing the Nehi with an actual fresh peach slice provides that **extra-decorative extravagance** to match the sentiment.

Ice cubes

¾ ounce **vodka**

¾ ounce **peach schnapps**

¾ ounce **DeKuyper Pucker Cheri-Beri**

½ ounce **freshly squeezed lime juice**

½ ounce **fresh pineapple juice**

Chilled **7UP** or **Sprite**

Peach slice for garnish (optional)

1. Fill a cocktail shaker halfway full with ice cubes. Add the vodka, peach schnapps, Cheri-Beri, lime juice, and pineapple juice. Shake well.

2. Fill a highball glass halfway full with ice cubes. Strain the mix into the glass.

3. Top off with 7UP. Stir once, in a rocking-chair motion. Garnish, if you're feeling it, with the peach slice.

⬆ **A Note:** *DeKuyper's Pucker Cheri-Beri is a sweet cherry schnapps. Sure, you might seem a bit teen-queen when buying it. But keep that chin up.*

Pimm's Cup

The Pimm's Cup started me on a life of cocktails. It was the United Kingdom, I was 14, for some reason my parents thought it was okay for me to have an alcoholic drink since we were overseas, the Pimm's Cup was served, and I fell in love for the first time with its spring-time taste. Ah, **the intercontinental romance**.

Ice cubes

2 ounces **Pimm's No. 1 Cup**

Chilled **ginger ale**

Cucumber slice for garnish

1. Fill a large Collins glass three-quarters full with ice cubes. Add the Pimm's No. 1 Cup.

2. Top the glass off with ginger ale. Garnish with the cucumber slice.

A VARIATION: You might see a Pimm's Cup made with 7UP, and it's not bad—though neither, in my humble opinion, will it set the proverbial world on fire. You might also, if you are very lucky in this life, have at the Napoleon House in New Orleans a Pimm's Cup made with fresh lemonade.

⬆ **A Note:** *Pimm's is a readily available, gin-based, slightly fruity liqueur made using a top-secret recipe.*

Princess

A royally delicious, refreshing quaff, the Princess was created and named by Natalie Fuller, who not only served me a whole treasure trove of drinks at venerable Auntie Mae's Parlor in Manhattan, Kansas, when she slung the sauce there from 1995 to 1996, but who also became my wife a few years later. Having one of your favorite bartenders around the house is only one of the benefits of being married. Another one is that she brought her Princess drink recipe with her. This mix is sure to be **the sparkling crown** to any noble summer's day, with its combination of limoncello, fresh raspberries, and mighty majesticness.

Ice cubes

1½ ounces **limoncello**

Chilled club soda

5 or 6 **fresh raspberries**

➕ **A Tip:** *This tasty treat is also a hit with other small members of the berry family, such as blueberries. But they need to be fresh and ripe, so that they burst a bit when they're stirred and add just a faint touch of juice to the mix.*

1. Fill a Collins glass three-quarters full with ice cubes. Add the limoncello, humming any coronation march you choose.

2. Fill the glass to about ½ inch from the top with the club soda. Add the fresh raspberries. Stir slowly, but with purpose. Don't be afraid (actually you're encouraged) to bust up the raspberries a little. You want to stir until this is well combined. Serve with a stirrer, long-necked spoon, or diamond ring.

Purple Cow →

Usually, it's Pink Elephants flouncing around the alcohol-tinged landscape (or, at least, the perceived landscape), busting out their elephantine dance in the haze of a mighty bender. Purple Cows, however, may **make a move in the zoo-yard** if enough of these are consumed without a break.

Ice cubes

4 ounces **fresh lemonade**

2 ounces **vodka**

2 ounces **purple grape juice**

⬆ **A Note:** *Mooing after the third Purple Cow is mandatory.*

1. Fill a highball glass three-quarters full with ice cubes. Add the lemonade, vodka, and grape juice. Stir well with a long stick of wheat, or a spoon.

Shandy Gaff

This is an **old dear thirst quencher** that has a quite a history; most of those who knew it in its early days had a few too many Shandy Gaffs and forgot to write anything down. What is known is that Dickens probably quaffed Shandy Gaffs, that beer has always been a central element of the formula, and that the name fluctuates between "Shandy" and "Shandy Gaff" depending on how many breaths are taken between drink orders. Add a little Shandy personality to a tailgate party or Super Bowl shindig and listen to the accolades fly.

12-ounce bottle **amber ale**

Chilled ginger ale

1. Pour the beer into a 24-ounce beer glass, avoiding creating any foam.

2. Fill each glass up with the ginger ale. Stir once, but without much flexing.

⬆ **A Note:** *If you don't have 24-ounce beer glasses (what some call "big girl" glasses), feel free to use a pint glass, keeping the mix at half ginger ale and half beer. You won't use a full bottle of beer for each drink, but I'll bet you'll discover a place for the leftovers.*

A VARIATION: If the amber-style ale seems a little lightweight for the fight, try using a Guinness or other stout beer, keeping the ratio of 1 to 1 with the ginger ale. You'll be drinking a Guinness Shandy and loving it.

A SECOND VARIATION: Sometimes, you see a shandy made with lemonade instead of ginger ale. It's not my favorite, but on a hot day, I'd be grateful to have one.

Negotiating the Waters: Four Drinks

Is putting in a diminutive raft before a run of whitewater, rapids, holes, drop-offs, haystacks, and laterals not exactly a dream date? Yet, the river looks darn pretty, and inviting. As does the ocean, right before that surfboard is paddled out beyond the point of no return. What to do? Instead of risking life, limb, and hairstyle, try tackling one of these river- or ocean-oriented mixes while merely looking at actual water.

1. Volga (page 236)
2. Blue Lagoon Cocktail (page 376)
3. White Water (page 406)
4. Tidal Wave (page 194)

Singapore Sling

This is a gem, both in taste and in nomenclature, but personally one I'd be tempted to shy away from during the hot months, lest **eyes pop out of sockets**. The problem is that everyone (from here back to Raffles Hotel bartender Ngiam Tong Boon's first 1915 recipe) makes a Singapore Sling slightly differently—or really differently—sometimes too sweet, sometimes too dry, and sometimes without any fruit juice, which might just take it completely out of the Sling family tree. But if balanced right, all the intrigue and weighing of mystical formulas equals a pretty swell potion.

Ice cubes

1½ ounces **gin**

½ ounce **cherry brandy**

¼ ounce **Benedictine**

¼ ounce **freshly squeezed lime juice**

Chilled club soda

Lime twist for garnish

1. Fill a cocktail shaker halfway full with ice cubes. Add the gin, cherry brandy, Benedictine, and lime juice, in that order. Shake well, while furrowing your eyebrows at the futility of it all.

2. Fill a highball glass three-quarters full with ice cubes. Strain the mix into the glass. Top with chilled club soda. Squeeze the lime twist over the glass, and then drop it in. You may also drape a tiny flowered silk scarf around the bottom of the glass if desired.

⬆ **A Note:** The cherry brandy used here should be of the sweet-toothed variety. Cherry Heering works well.

Slow Poke

Hey you! Yeah, you! Catch up, you're lagging behind! Hurry, you'll be late! Put some quick in it; you're going too slow! Getting tired of hearing all these commands to rush rush rush your way through the world? **Show disdain for speeding through life** by sitting back with a tall Slow Poke. And let the world come to you.

Ice cubes

1½ ounces **sloe gin**

¾ ounce **freshly squeezed lemon juice**

2 dashes **Angostura bitters**

Chilled club soda

Orange slice for garnish

Maraschino cherry for garnish

1. Fill a highball glass three-quarters full with ice cubes. Add the sloe gin, lemon juice, and Angostura bitters. Stir briefly.

2. Fill the glass up with the club soda. Stir well, but at an even pace. Garnish with the orange slice around the rim and the cherry dropped in the glass. Thumb your nose at those silly folks hurrying past.

Snow Ball

This tall and icy mix-up has survived many summers (at least since 1899, as I've seen it mentioned in *Applegreen's Bar Book*, which has a copyright from that year) and still hasn't faded in its ability to **cool things down** when the temperature cuddles close to triple or near-triple digits (much as a snowball that's been left in the freezer still has a chilly effect when brought out and thrown in July).

Ice cubes

2 ounces **brandy**

1 ounce **Simple Syrup** (page 7)

1 **large egg,** preferably organic

Chilled ginger ale

1. Fill a cocktail shaker halfway full with ice cubes. Add the brandy, simple syrup, and egg. Shake exceedingly well, even if you start to sweat. That egg needs to be fully mixed in.

2. Fill a Collins or other similar-sized glass with ice cubes. Strain the mixture into the glass.

3. Top off the glass with chilled ginger ale (be careful not to let the fizz run over).

✖ *A Warning: As this contains raw eggs, it shouldn't be served to those with compromised immune systems or the elderly.*

Soledan

I discovered **this bella bibita** in a small Italian drink book titled *Cocktail: Classici & Esotici* (Giunti Gruppo, 2002), which I was lucky enough to wander across while wandering in Florence. I think it's credited to Roberto Bruzzesi, and I believe it's referencing the sun, but between you and me, I drink Italian much better than I speak it. No matter. A few of these'll have you thinking in Italian, if not pronouncing anything that well.

Ice cubes

1 ounce **vodka**

½ ounce **Aperol**

¼ ounce **Midori melon liqueur**

Chilled Prosecco

Lemon twist

1. Fill a good-sized goblet halfway full with ice cubes. Add the vodka, Aperol, and Midori melon liqueur. Stir carefully, as if kicking an overtime penalty shot (in soccer, that is).

2. Fill the glass the rest of the way with the Prosecco. Squeeze the lemon twist over the top of the glass and then toss it into the mix.

➕ *A Tip: Be careful with the liqueurs—you don't want this one to get overly* dolce.

LIQUEUR SPOTLIGHT
Aperol

Aperol traces its lineage back to 1919, in Padua, Italy, where the Barbieri Brothers unveiled it at the Padua Exposition as a light alcoholic alternative to the heavier aperitifs on the market. It has a low alcohol content of 11 percent—as well as a very fresh taste and a pretty orange hue. This delicate and appetizing combination has made Aperol hugely popular in Italy, especially since the end of World War II, both on its own as an apéritif and also mixed with club soda, sparkling wines such as Prosecco, fruit juices, and other liquors. After many years of unavailability in the United States, it is now being imported. This means the long Aperol wait is over for those residing in the United States (which also means for many fans that they won't have to lug bottles of Aperol back after each Italian trip), and that it's now easy to enjoy the recipe's (a secret recipe, naturally) combination of 30 herbs and spices, an ingredient list that includes bitter and sweet oranges, gentian, and rhubarb.

Suissesse

Anyone saying the name of this frosty stunner quickly 10 times in a row deserves an extra cherry (which is easy enough on the host, since the only garnish here is ice). It's a bit Swiss, a bit French, and a bit catty. All those "s" sounds are just **likely to lead to whispers** in corners at dusk.

Ice cubes

1½ ounces **Pernod**

½ ounce **anisette**

Chilled club soda

1. Fill a cocktail shaker halfway full with ice cubes. Add the Pernod and the anisette. Shake vigorously, as if the whispers were about you, until the shaker gets uncomfortably chilly.

2. Fill a highball glass three-quarters full with ice cubes. Strain the mix over the ice. Top with chilled club soda and absolutely nothing else. Not another word.

Summer Beer

I originally quaffed this at the Rock-a-Belly Bar and Deli. The 'Belly had a back brick deck, which got to about 110°F in summer. As easily imagined, the ultra-refreshing Summer Beer was **essential to deck survival.**

Ice cubes

9 ounces **fresh lemonade**

One 12-ounce bottle **beer** (go with a nice American brew in this one)

1½ ounces **vodka**

Lemon slice for garnish

✖ *A Warning: I feel compelled to mention that after the second round of Summer Beers, you should be prepared for renditions of "summer" songs, but with "Summer Beer" inserted. For example, "the summer wind, came floating in" from Frank Sinatra's beloved "Summer Wind" becomes "the summer beer, came floating in" and Seals and Crofts's "Summer Breeze" changes to "summer beer, makes me feel fine."*

1. Add a good-sized handful of ice cubes to a 24-ounce "big girl" beer glass. Make sure you've washed your hands first. Add 8 ounces of the lemonade to the glass.

2. Slowly, carefully, achingly, add the bottle of beer to the glass.

3. If you added the beer too quickly, wipe off the counter.

4. Once the beer has settled a bit, add the vodka. Then top it off with the remaining ounce of lemonade. Stir once, with a mighty long spoon. Squeeze the lemon slice over the top, and drop it in.

Sun

Here's to the sun, mother of us (no sun equals no life) and bringer of warmth and occasional sunburns. *El sol*, Astron (that's the name of our sun, for those who are not astronomy buffs), **the hot center of it.** So important is that mass of incandescent gas that there are not only Sunshine Cocktails #s 1 and 2 (page 136), but also this luscious number. Like the cosmic object it is named after, this solar drink packs a punch. In the drink's case it's a gin punch, as opposed to an ultraviolet radiation punch. Taken in moderation, this Sun provides an ideal drinker's tan. On the flipside, when taken too liberally, it might leave a hangover that peels the skin off the following day.

Ice cubes

2½ ounces **gin**

1 ounce **orange curaçao**

¼ ounce **maraschino liqueur**

3 ounces **fresh pineapple juice**

Dash of **Angostura bitters**

Lime wedge for garnish

1. Fill a cocktail shaker halfway full with ice cubes. Add the gin, curaçao, and maraschino liqueur. Shake well, in an orbital motion.

2. Fill a large goblet (if you don't have a large goblet, a highball glass doubles as one) three-quarters full with ice cubes. Strain the mix from the shaker into the glass.

3. Add the pineapple juice to the glass and stir well. Add the Angostura bitters and stir once. Squeeze the lime wedge over the glass and drop it in.

Sweet Press

Ah, simplicity. A perfectly fitting pair of sneakers, a radio with an extension cord that extends to the shady reaches of the backyard, a DJ playing those sweet summertime hits and dismissing commercial breaks, 5 or 10 good friends, **long-lasting sunshine**, and a whole tray of Sweet Presses. You may end up having better days in life, but who's counting?

Ice cubes

2 ounces **gin**

2 ounces **club soda**

2 ounces **7UP** or **Sprite**

Lime wedge for garnish

1. Fill a highball glass halfway full with ice cubes. Add the gin.

2. Add the club soda and 7UP simultaneously, so neither feels slighted. Stir rapidly with a bar spoon or other long spoon. Garnish with the lime wedge.

A VARIATION: Vodka also works well in this easy-going fave. And adding a little fresh orange mint or lemon mint rocks.

Tequila Woo Woo

For long, late August days, when the boiling of the brain has become almost too much to bear, when even speaking coherently has become too much of a strain, pour up a Tequila Woo Woo for any- and everyone stumbling around the yard. After the first sip or two, they'll (and you'll) be **running in circles joyously**, screaming "woo woo, woo woo" like insane—but happy—trains, with all the earlier hot suffering forgotten.

Ice cubes

2 ounces **silver tequila**

½ ounce **peach schnapps**

Chilled cranberry juice cocktail

1. Fill a highball glass three-quarters full with ice cubes. Add the tequila and peach schnapps.

2. Fill the glass to almost over the top with cranberry juice. Stir—but smoothly, and without generating any extra heat.

⬆ **A Note:** *I first found this in Mardee Haidin Regan's* The Bartender's Best Friend *(John Wiley & Sons, 2003), a drink-packed tome that's a joy to read and is indispensable to anyone who wants to dispense drinks and get paid for it.*

Vermouth Cassis

This cool combo's name alone implies the wearing of a white suit coat or a white skirt with slight hints of gold thread twinkling throughout the fabric. I imagine it's the cassis, but it could be the vermouth. Either way, **be sure to wear proper attire** or the drink itself might shake its wet head. And also be sure not to spill when making—there's no need to mar those fancy outfits.

Ice cubes

1½ ounces **dry vermouth**

1 ounce **crème de cassis**

Chilled club soda

1. Fill a highball glass just about halfway full with ice. Add the vermouth and the crème de cassis.

2. Fill the glass with club soda. Stir well. Garnish with a slight French accent.

⬆ **A Note:** *Crème de cassis is a French liqueur made from black currants. If you have extra, it also makes a mean Kir Royale (page 390).*

Waldorf Cocktail

It is, on occasion, necessary to rise up to the heat not with a delicate and light voice, attempting to wheedle out of the intensity, but by being a bit of the heavy yourself, recognizing that, while not above the sun, you can **act snooty and tough and get away with it.** For these occasions when wearing a bowtie and shorts and sipping strapping drinks with disregard for the relentless rays beating down, I suggest a Waldorf Cocktail. From the old-money Rockefellian slant of the name to the considerable dose of bourbon it balances on, this one will show who's boss of whom.

Ice cubes

2 ounces **bourbon**

1 ounce **Pernod**

1 ounce **sweet vermouth**

3 dashes **Angostura bitters**

1. Fill a cocktail shaker halfway full with ice cubes and halfway full with attitude. Add the bourbon, Pernod, sweet vermouth, and Angostura bitters. Shake well.

2. Strain the mix into a cocktail glass.

A VARIATION: If you must make this more attuned to a "summertime" vibe, I suggest garnishing it with a single sprig of fresh mint.

⬆ *A Note: While it's fun to have a stiff cocktail like this in the late spring and summer repertoire, don't think for a second that the Waldorf wouldn't make a friendly addition to any cold-weather holiday situation.*

White Water →

For those summer vacation days spent riding the rapids all day long, when the wetsuit feels like it's about to slide off your tired body, take one of these to add back lost pounds and **revive that beat-down physique.** Take two if deciding to give up the X-Games attitude for the night to recline in the deck chair.

Ice cubes

2 ounces **white rum**

½ ounce **vanilla-flavored vodka**

Chilled club soda

Lime wedge for garnish

1. Fill a highball glass three-quarters full with ice cubes. Add the rum and vodka, and stir once with a bar spoon as if the spoon were a kayak going over Niagara.

2. Once the kayak/spoon has come to a rest, top the glass off with club soda. Garnish with the lime wedge.

The Blender's Whirr

Give it up, y'all, for technology.
Thanks to the modern marvel of a
blender, the recipes in The Blender's
Whirr are easily assembled. While
this tool has been touched on in this
book's introduction, let's go over the
basics again here, for those who skipped straight to this chapter
without pausing to even browse the intro, those who can't wait
another minute for a frosty alcoholic beverage—a delicacy of ice
and juice and liquor (a Florida Special, perhaps?), or a luscious
indulgence of cream and fine spirits (a Grasshopper, maybe?)—those
already wearing flip-flops and swimsuits, who've already lathered
on tanning solution, who are all-but-ready to recline poolside with a
glacial delight, but who need to know more about the blender before
rushing out to pick one up and plug one in.

You'll want to make sure, first off, that it's sturdy and isn't going
to slip around the counter a lot. Some blenders have nonslip feet, or
plastic protectors that reduce slippage, and this is a fine feature. I
think that a 40-ounce blender jar is necessary, and getting a 48-ounce
model makes constructing some of the heftier recipes listed here a
simpler task, and a task less likely to cause chaos with a spill on the
counter. Having a slight lip on the blender jar is nice for pouring the
results into multiple glasses quickly, but only if the lid seals tightly
upon it—a tight seal is key for keeping spillage to a minimum. For
speeds, a pulse feature is a plus, and having the ability to start on
a slow speed and finish at full throttle is a positive, as you may have
to ramp up when blending serious ice. Stainless-steel blades are a
must. Finally, make sure all the pieces come apart easily for cleaning
purposes. You'll thank me tomorrow when the blender still hasn't
been cleaned from today's throw-down.

Okay, you've taken advantage of the twentieth-century advance-
ments in kitchen gear and have the blender set up, plugged in, and
ready to whirr. What are you waiting on? Start blending up a frigid

delight that matches the mood of you and your guests. (Since blender drinks are such festive affairs, the drinks in this chapter all serve more than one person.) Wait, I have one last suggestion. Don't drink that first blended wonder too fast, or you'll succumb to the dreaded brain freeze. And that's actually not cool.

Abilene

Quarters to the Greyhound Hall of Fame, birthplace of ol' shiny, Dwight D. Eisenhower, home of Kuntz's Drive-In and its array of deep-fried delicacies, halfway to Salina, and a hop, skip, and a jump from Hays—Abilene, Kansas, is not the birthplace of this drink. However, if materializing in Abilene in the middle of August, under the implacable Kansas sun, **this thirst-quencher transforms** the visit and goes tremendously well with the fried cheese balls from Kuntz's. **Serves 4**

4 cups **cracked ice**

3 ounces **white rum**

2 ounces **peach liqueur**

2 ounces **freshly squeezed orange juice**

4 **orange slices** for garnish

1. Add the ice, rum, peach liqueur, and orange juice to a blender. Blend well.

2. Pour into 4 large highball glasses or other decent-sized receptacles (the fashion in this part of Kansas is the plastic glass, but I'd shy away from that). Garnish each glass with an orange slice.

Banana Bliss →

I can't resist, I just can't. With apologies to our simian relatives, I must say that this icy beauty is tasty enough that **you'll go ape over it.** You'll lope around the room, scratching under armpits, simulating picking lice from scalp lines (or really picking them—I'm not one to judge), squeezing, and ooh ooh ooh-ing. Now, gorillas, monkeys, and orangutans, please forgive me. **Serves 2**

2 **large, ripe bananas**

2 cups **crushed ice**

3 ounces **dark rum**

2 ounces **crème de banane**

2 ounces **fresh pineapple juice**

1. Peel the bananas and cut them into slices.

2. Add the bananas, ice, rum, crème de banane, and pineapple juice to a blender (preferably one with a good lid, unless you want to lick the drink off the wall, in which case all bets are off). Blend well.

3. Pour into 2 good-sized goblets, while wearing a Tarzan costume or a gorilla costume. One of the two is a must.

Bath Cure

I'm not positive what ailment the Bath Cure's design defeats. It could be the sickness one develops after working 40 hours within a cubicle the size of an airplane pet carrier. It could be the infection one gets after sitting on a crowded bus next to the gentleman who can't stop sniffling while he talks animatedly to his French poodle on a cell phone. **Don't rush to the doctor** in these situations, friends—the Bath Cure is what you need. **Serves 2**

2 cups **cracked ice**

3 ounces **dark rum**

3 ounces **white rum**

3 ounces **brandy**

1 ounce **fresh pineapple juice**

1 ounce **freshly squeezed orange juice**

½ ounce **freshly squeezed lemon juice**

½ ounce **freshly squeezed lime juice**

½ ounce **grenadine**

2 **maraschino cherries** for garnish

1. Add the cracked ice, dark rum, white rum, brandy, the juices, and grenadine to a large blender. Blend well, and feel your health begin to return. Your cheeks look rosier already.

2. Pour into 2 very large goblets or margarita glasses. Garnish each glass with a cherry.

✖ *A Warning: Though this one will cure what ails, more than two might induce a little illness the following day. Remember: Only you can make the final decision on home remedies.*

Blueberry Icy

Sometimes there's nothing more satisfactory than a shiver—coming from an undersized scare, a light touch on the topside of the elbow, or from **swilling a really chilly drink**. The Blueberry Icy provides the latter variety. Though sometimes a drink licked off an elbow's outer curve can be agreeable, it is a bit sticky, just in case you were thinking of experimenting. **Serves 2**

2 cups **crushed ice**

1 cup **fresh blueberries**

3 ounces **vodka**

1½ ounces **Simple Syrup** (page 7)

1. Add all of the ingredients, except for 6 of the blueberries, to a blender. Blend well.

2. Serve in chilled old-fashioned glasses or other chilled receptacles of approximately the same size. Garnish each drink with 3 unblended blueberries.

➕ *A Tip: Fresh blueberries make this drink a charmer. Before resorting to frozen, check out local farmers' markets and local farms.*

Bright Ape

Everyone thinks a drink with "ape" in the title demands an introduction that either references King Kong, says *ooh-ooh, ooh-ooh* while scratching under the arms and bungling around the room, or talks about how the name derives from apricot. Well, let me tell you, pal, this intro does none of those. **Serves 4**

4 cups **crushed ice**

8 ounces **white rum**

8 ounces **apricot nectar**

4 ounces **freshly squeezed lime juice**

3 ounces **Simple Syrup** (page 7)

1. Add the ice, rum, apricot nectar, lime juice, and simple syrup to a blender. Blend well.

2. Pour the mixture into 4 sturdy wine goblets, of a kind that can stand up to being handled while one swings from tree to tree using only vines.

⊕ **A Note:** Apricot nectar is available in many gourmet stores, as well as most larger grocery stores.

The Animal Kingdom: A Drinker's Zoo

Show a deep-rooted love for our untamed friends at the next house hoedown by settling on an animal-drink theme. (To get even deeper into the love of the wild, have a costume party with an "animals-only" rule to go along with the drinks. But be careful—those animal costumes can bring out the beast in folks.) These mammal mixes are for human consumption only. It's nice to revere the animals, but there's no need to share.

1. Bright Ape (above)
2. Brass Monkey (page 328)
3. White Lion (page 236)
4. Scorpion (page 316)
5. Tiger Milk (page 235)

Crème de Menthe Frappé

I worked in a Tex-Mex restaurant called the Texas Star, and once the air conditioning broke down and died during the middle of our Saturday night rush. Did I mention it was late August in the middle of Kansas, and that this particular restaurant instantly rose to the high temperature mark for the United States on every TV meteorologist's map? It was, and it did. In case you were there, I promise I didn't sweat in the food. But that's only because I and my fellow co-worker Katie Campbell devised the ultimate cooldown, which was slamming a kissing cousin to this Crème de Menthe Frappé in the walk-in refrigerator every time the heat became too much to bear.

The only significant difference between our ultimate cooldown and this lovely minty version is the use of the blender (we had no time for blenders). The utilization of the blender is also divergent from the classic "frappé" recipe. My thought is that we should take advantage of technology. And who wants to be worn down frappé-ing when a quick flip of the blender switch does the trick? **Serves 2**

1½ cups **crushed ice**

5 ounces **white crème de menthe** (green works, too)

2 **fresh mint sprigs** for garnish

1. Add the crushed ice and the crème de menthe to a blender. Hit the pulse button twice. If there isn't a pulse button, run the blender on medium speed for 2 seconds.

2. Pour the mix into 2 cocktail glasses or small wine glasses. Garnish each with a mint sprig and serve with a delicate straw.

A VARIATION: This easy frappé can also be prepared with Pernod instead of crème de menthe. I doubt you'll have complaints.

Expedition

I advocate going on this particular jungle crusade with a full contingent of steadfast companions—those trustworthy in the stickiest of situations, who won't leave your side even if you refuse to get up out of the deck chair on the back porch when the sun goes down and the temperature drops. Because the Expedition is the type of drink that **cools down and warms up**, it's ideal for dangerous party excursions that start midday but might not end until deep into the dark heart of night. Be brave, and keep those cohorts close, and you'll be rewarded generously. And if you end up with a hangover, well, no intrepid explorer wants to have that adventure alone. **Serves 2**

2 cups **cracked ice**

3 ounces **white rum**

3 ounces **dark rum**

2 ounces **fresh pineapple juice**

2 ounces **freshly squeezed orange juice**

1 ounce **cinnamon schnapps**

2 **maraschino cherries** for garnish

1. Add the ice, white rum, dark rum, pineapple juice, orange juice, and cinnamon schnapps to a blender. Blend well, but keep it quiet.

2. Pour into 2 goblets. Garnish each with a cherry.

Florida Special

This individual must be blended until it reaches a frothy consistency that resembles the whitecaps off Miami Beach. It chills the teeth, **brings a tang to the tongue**, and forms the ideal companion for meandering walks on the sand beneath the setting sun. If a romantic companion for those meandering walks already resides, I propose making two Florida Specials before even beginning to amble. That way, there won't be any disagreements over who holds the glass. **Serves 2**

2 cups **cracked ice**

4 ounces **white rum**

2 ounces **freshly squeezed grapefruit juice**

1 ounce **freshly squeezed lime juice**

1 ounce **Simple Syrup** (page 7)

2 **maraschino cherries** for garnish

1. Add the ice, rum, grapefruit juice, lime juice, and simple syrup to a blender. Blend well, while humming the TV theme to *Miami Vice* and dreaming of white suit coats.

2. Pour the mix into 2 cocktail glasses. Garnish each with a cherry (or 2, if you're feeling frisky).

Frozen Commodore

No, this isn't a short booze-fueled retelling of a commanding sailor trapped in ice for 50 years and then thawed out to face a world he doesn't understand (though, now that I think about it, that might be a nice yarn to spin while drinking Frozen Commodores). This *is* a mighty refreshing and faintly sweet treat, with just enough tangy undercurrents to keep it from being saccharine—one that's good drinking for girls and boys of every rank. Unlike its nonfrozen namesake (page 330) in almost every way, the Frozen Commodore uses the blender to rally the troops. Not surprisingly, the rum helps, too. **Serves 2**

2 cups **crushed ice**

3 ounces **white rum**

1 ounce **freshly squeezed lemon juice**

½ ounce **Chambord**

½ ounce **Simple Syrup** (page 7)

½ ounce **grenadine**

1. Add all of the ingredients to a blender, saluting each as it's poured in. Blend well.

2. Pour into 2 large cocktail glasses. If you don't have large enough cocktail glasses, pour into good-sized goblets. If you don't have good-sized goblets, aim straight for the closest open mouth.

"My cat has taken to mulled port and rum punch. **Poor old dear!** He is all the better for it."

CARL VAN VECHTEN, *The Tiger in the House*, 1920

Grasshopper

A renowned blender beverage, particularly in dusty restaurants in sweltering Midwestern towns where residents appreciate both sugar and cooling mechanisms, Grasshoppers originally were shaken, not blended, but I think blending rotates them from drawing room standby to **poolside triumph**. If fresh mint is on hand, a sprig here goes a decent way toward establishing your credentials as a reliable host.

Serves 2

2 cups **cracked ice**

3 ounces **green crème de menthe**

3 ounces **crème de cacao**

2 ounces **heavy cream**

2 **fresh mint sprigs** for garnish

1. Add the ice, crème de menthe, crème de cacao, and heavy cream to a blender. Blend on high for about 3 seconds—it shouldn't be too slushy.

2. Pour the mix into 2 chilled cocktail glasses. Garnish each with fresh mint.

A VARIATION: If you'd like to make this sans blender, just add the ice to a cocktail shaker, shake up the ingredients, and strain the mixture into a cocktail glass.

➕ *A Tip: While making Grasshoppers, say the ingredients out loud. And remember, the crème de cacao is pronounced "crème de ka-kow!" with serious emphasis on the ultimate syllable.*

Hollywood Parade

It's possible that one might never manage **the red-carpet stroll** into a movie premiere, awards ceremony, or high-profile trial as the gigantic HOLLYWOOD letters loom over the left shoulder and the photographers unleash a barrage of bulbs. But that doesn't mean you shouldn't have a celebrity happening. Start with mysteriously large shades worn in the middle of the afternoon, a gown that sets you back big bucks, or a small amount of ludicrous behavior. Or forget that and drag the TV outside, whip up some Hollywood Parades, and watch the beautiful people's escapades from a safe distance. **Serves 2**

2 cups **vanilla ice cream**

3 ounces **white rum**

2 ounces **freshly squeezed orange juice**

Chilled ginger ale

1. Add the ice cream, rum, and orange juice to a blender. Blend well, but not so well that the ice cream turns to liquid.

2. Pour the mix into 2 Collins glasses or other similar-sized vessels. Top each glass with chilled ginger ale.

A VIRGIN VARIATION: Omit the rum and add another 1 ounce orange juice. This makes a nice drink for the kiddies or for abstaining adults.

Island Coffee

I scored this tiki temptation from a deck of drinks (now that's a card game I can play—forget this Texas hold 'em stuff) created by the tikiest drinker dudes around, Shag and Adam Rocke. It's **a feet-in-the-sand pleaser** that can collect you up, put you in a grass skirt, and then tip you down under the palm tree—and do all three almost simultaneously. **Serves 2**

2 cups **cracked ice**

4 ounces **chilled brewed coffee**

2 ounces **dark rum**

2 ounces **Kahlúa**

1 ounce **heavy cream**

Whipped cream

½ ounce **coffee liqueur**

1. Add the ice, coffee, rum, Kahlúa, and heavy cream to a blender. Blend well.

2. Pour the mix into 2 chilled goblets. Top each with whipped cream, and carefully drizzle the coffee liqueur over the whipped cream.

Lava Flow

This generously sized cocktail in no way wants to invoke a hoard of Pompeian spirits or rekindle the long-dormant Vesuvius, which in 79 A.D. turned Pompeii from ancient town into modern tourist attraction. Think of it, instead, as a more delicate homage to all those who aren't scared to settle near those ominous mountains (such as Mount Rainier looming over Seattle), a tropical mix that **cools instead of burns**, one that leaves smiles instead of deep furrows in the earth. Serve them up by the trayful fresh and cold on March 25, which, in 1984, was the last day the world's largest volcano, Mauna Loa in Hawaii, erupted. I think if enough are consumed, it might just keep it from erupting again (that may not actually be true—but it'll be an enjoyable test). **Serves 2**

Crushed ice

2 **small, ripe bananas,** cut into rounds

4 ounces **fresh pineapple juice**

4 ounces **cream of coconut**

4 ounces **coconut-flavored rum**

4 ounces **frozen strawberries**

~~~~~~~~~~~~~~~~~~~~~~~

⬆ **A Note:** *Cream of coconut is a thick liquid made of coconut (naturally) and sugar and probably a few additives thrown in for good measure. There are a number of different brands, and it's readily available in most grocery stores.*

1. Add ½ cup crushed ice, the bananas, pineapple juice, and cream of coconut to a blender. Blend well.

2. Fill a cocktail shaker a quarter of the way full with crushed ice. Add the rum and strawberries. Shake rapidly, as if you were about to erupt.

3. Pour the rum-strawberry mix into 2 Hurricane glasses or other tall, thin, curvy glasses.

4. Slowly and carefully, without stirring, pour half the banana mixture into the middle of each glass. The desired effect involves the rum-strawberry combo crawling up the sides of the glass, inducing the desired "lava" appearance.

Limbo

Jack be limbo, Jack be quick, Jack blend up the Limbo drink, all around the limbo sink. Hey, let's do the limbo rock: Limbo lower now, Limbo lower now, how empty can your glass get? Limbo lower now, Limbo lower now, here's the trick now don't forget: First you spread your Limbo feet, then you tilt that Limbo glass, **tastes like a tropical treat**, just don't fall on your Limbo . . . well, I think you get the picture. **Serves 2**

2 cups **cracked ice**

1 cup **peeled** and **cubed papaya**

1 cup **coconut milk**

4 ounces **dark rum**

1. Add the ice, papaya, coconut milk, and rum to a blender that's plugged in nowhere near that limbo pole. Blend well.

2. Pour into 2 large goblets or any glasses that won't spill as you're ambling under that limbo pole.

⬆ *A Note: Don't get coconut milk and cream of coconut confused—they're completely different animals.*

3 Drinks Demanding Big Bass

Don't think of swerving these up unless funky blaring bass (perhaps Parliament Funkadelic) oozes out of the speakers. I'd also be sure there's some space for dancing. No one's going to sit after finishing one of the following, especially if the bass is booming.

1 Soul Kiss (page 271)

2 Cherry Bomb (page 157)

3 Crowd Control (page 297)

MP This luscious looper won't turn you in for going AWOL, but it might sneak up from behind and **knock you gently on the noggin.** It's the large dollop of rum, partially hidden by the Caribbean combination of pineapple and fresh mint, that'll do the knocking. Hey, don't be dragged down by those thoughts, though. Shore leave doesn't last forever, and if you spend your time worried about what *could* happen, where does that leave you? **Serves 2**

2 cups **cracked ice**

2 cups **fresh pineapple chunks**

5 ounces **dark rum**

3 ounces **Simple Syrup** (page 7)

2 tablespoons chopped **fresh mint leaves**

1 ounce **white crème de menthe**

2 **fresh mint sprigs** for garnish

1. Add the ice, pineapple, rum, simple syrup, mint leaves, and crème de menthe to a blender. Blend well.

2. Pour into 2 good-sized glasses, preferably with sturdy handles—it's always pleasant to have something to hold onto. Garnish each with a mint sprig.

⬆ *A Note: As this features both fresh pineapple and fresh mint blended up, having some toothpicks on hand for post-drinking is a good plan.*

Pooh-Poohing Plastic?

Now, there's no necessity to begin glassware class warfare, but it's a plain fact that swilling out of plastic cups lacks savoir faire, and that plastic imparts a slight ickiness to drinks that glass doesn't. With that caveat, remember that serving out of plastic cups is still much better than not serving at all. And sometimes, especially with bigger groups celebrating outdoors, plastic becomes an economic as well as a practical requirement—so don't stick that nose in the air. You don't have to resort to flimsier supermarket plastic cups unless you want to; you can pick up attractive, sturdy, and reasonably priced melamine or other hard plastic cups at most housewares stores.

Mudslide

Whoa, watch out. Despite its name, this isn't for drinking while standing at the top of a very dirty hill during a rainstorm. On the contrary, it's an ideal treat for days when your arms start to roast the minute you mosey outside. On those days, dial up the party posse, rope up a couple of Mudslides, and **be happy imagining the nastier weather** that this drink is named for. **Serves 4**

4 cups **cracked ice**

4 ounces **vodka** (if you have chocolate-flavored vodka, use that)

4 ounces **Kahlúa**

4 ounces **Bailey's Irish Cream**

1. Add the ice, vodka, Kahlúa, and Bailey's to a blender. Blend well.

2. Pour into 4 goblets carved from stone or any good-sized goblets. Hold on tightly and swig before everything starts to melt.

A VARIATION: Mudslides are often made as shaken drinks. If you are craving this style of slide, add the ice to a cocktail shaker instead of a blender, shake the ingredients together, and strain the drinks into cocktail glasses.

Paradiso

Sure, Dante's *Divine Comedy* is extensive and pretty darn depressing, but it's worth reading—because the paradiso comes at the end. Some wearing suit coats with patches on elbows might argue that the paradiso of Dante isn't exactly the same as this blended beauty. But I say that both have **a bit of sweetness** in them, along with a bit of a kick, too. There's no need to just take my word for it: Blend up a Paradiso, start on Canto 1 of Dante's *Paradiso*, and you'll see. **Serves 2**

2 cups **cracked ice**

4 ounces **dark rum**

4 ounces **heavy cream**

2 ounces **freshly squeezed orange juice**

2 **orange slices** for garnish

1. Add the ice, rum, heavy cream, and orange juice to a blender. Blend well.

2. Pour the mix into 2 large cocktail glasses or large goblets. Garnish each with an orange slice.

Piña Colada

The Piña Colada (called just "Piña" after finishing the first) is **an island favorite** that goes landlocked quickly if the sugary components aren't kept in check. The main sweet culprit to watch for is the sticky cream of coconut, which can ruin both the drink and the countertop. Be wary and pour with a feathery and controlled touch. And while I'm giving instructions, never drink a Piña (see, I told you) alone. It goes down best when indulged in with a couple of companions trusted enough to help with the pouring. **Serves 2**

2 cups **crushed ice**

8 ounces **fresh pineapple juice**

3 ounces **cream of coconut,** such as Coco Lopez

2 ounces **white rum**

2 ounces **dark rum**

2 ounces **heavy cream**

2 **pineapple wedges** for garnish

2 **maraschino cherries** for garnish

1. Add the ice, pineapple juice, cream of coconut, white rum, dark rum, and heavy cream to a large blender. Blend well.

2. Pour the mix into two 12-ounce poco grande glasses. If you don't have poco grande glasses—these being a 12- to 13-ounce stemmed glass with a wave-and-half bowl—then serve this up in large goblets. But you'll have to serve with a tear in your eye.

3. Garnish each with a pineapple wedge and a cherry. If you must, garnish with only one or the other. But again, serve with the tear referred to in step 2.

⟳ *A Note: It's possible to make a Piña with just white rum, instead of the half-and-half white and dark rum combo. But it won't have the same effect. You'll only feel like you're in Miami, and not on an actual island.*

A VARIATION: If the thought of any drink with both cream of coconut and heavy cream induces you to put a cardiologist on speed dial, feel free to substitute soy milk for the cream.

A VIRGIN VARIATION: To make a virgin Piña, leave out the rum and use an extra 2 ounces pineapple juice.

Raspberry Cooler

Unlike the Harvard Cooler (page 386), no battles have ever been waged over the glass this cooler should be served in, or waged over any drink elements. **It's so mellow** it doesn't even belong in that contentious cooler family; so mellow, that when consuming a Raspberry Cooler, the theme song is, "summertime, and the livin' is easy." **Serves 2**

2 cups **cracked ice**

1 cup **fresh raspberries**

2 ounces **vodka**

1 ounce **Chambord**

Chilled club soda

1. Add the ice, all but 6 of the fresh raspberries, vodka, and Chambord to a blender. Blend well.

2. Pour the mix into 2 Collins glasses or other 12- to 14-ounce glasses. Top each glass off with the chilled club soda. Stir once. Garnish each drink with 3 of the reserved raspberries.

⬆ **A Note:** *If you'd like to spear the raspberries onto a toothpick or small cocktail sword before floating them on top, that's a personal decision. Only you know whether this is safe. My friends would end up impaled.*

✖ **A Warning:** *Don't, please don't, make the mistake of adding club soda to the blender. No one wants a party with that kind of explosive nature.*

Five Bowling Alley Bars

Bowling and drinking go together like ice and a blender—as long as you don't overdo it and end up nursing a sore arm the next morning from throwing too hard too late in the evening. Stop and aim for strikes at any of these spots and you'll have fun and enjoy the cold beverages.

1. Holler House, Milwaukee, Wisconsin
2. Buster's South Park Lanes, Owatonna, Minnesota
3. Mid-City Lanes Rock 'n' Bowl, New Orleans, Louisiana
4. Forward Lanes, Pittsburgh, Pennsylvania
5. Gibby's Lanes, New Richmond, Wisconsin

Roman

Friends, drunkards, countrymen (and countrywomen)—lend me your empty glasses. I'll load them with a frosty amalgamation that, from what I can establish, may be unrelated to Rome in every way, except for the fact that after two or three, guests will want to **don togas and wear vines** around their noggins. *Et tu*, indeed. **Serves 2**

2 cups **cracked ice**

3 ounces **white rum**

2 ounces **Cognac**

1½ ounces **freshly squeezed lemon juice**

1 ounce **raspberry syrup**

2 **lemon slices** for garnish

1. Add the ice, rum, Cognac, lemon juice, and raspberry syrup to a blender. Blend well.

2. Pour the mix into 2 goblets, preferably with bas-reliefs of Caesar on the side. Garnish each with a lemon slice.

➕ *A Tip: If you don't happen to have any raspberry syrup handy, mash up a few fresh or frozen unsweetened raspberries in ½ ounce Simple Syrup (page 7).*

Rum Runner

This rum companion is the epitome of days when you don't want to get the boat out of dry dock, but continue to entertain pirate-esque fantasies, complete with eye patch, brightly colored scarves, doubloons, and a parrot perched on the shoulder (don't let the parrot poach too much of the potion, though). If boatless, have those pirate fantasies on the edge of a pool instead, with one leg over a particularly sturdy floatie. No pool? Head straight for the bathtub, where **the rubber ducky is ripe** for boarding. **Serves 2**

2 cups **cracked ice**

4 ounces **white rum**

2 ounces **blackberry brandy**

2 ounces **banana liqueur**

1 ounce **freshly squeezed lime juice**

½ ounce **grenadine**

2 **lime wedges** for garnish

1. Add the ice, rum, blackberry brandy, banana liqueur, lime juice, and grenadine to a blender. Blend well, mateys.

2. Pour the mix into 2 large goblets. Garnish each with a lime wedge. Say "argh" as if you belong on the Seven Seas.

Going Global: 10 International Bars

Are you desiring to get out of the same old bar rut and expand the scope of the lounges and pubs that you're attending? Why not hop on a jet and start hitting up some international hotspots? This list will take you on a cocktailing tour that you'll be talking about for years.

1. Soho's Omotesando, Tokyo, Japan
2. Tretter's Bar, Prague, Czech Republic
3. Voile Rouge, St. Tropez, France
4. Duke's Bar, London, England
5. Gado Gado Kafe & Beach Club, Seminyak, Bali
6. Caffè Giacosa, Florence, Italy
7. Lletraferit, Barcelona, Spain
8. La Mina Terraza, Havana, Cuba
9. The Octagon Bar, Dublin, Ireland
10. Absolut Icebar, Jukkasjärvi, Sweden

Strawberry Frozen Margarita

I place this more lighthearted cousin to the venerated and slightly distinguished straight Margarita (page 32) at least two branches away on the tequila family tree. Thereby, it deserves a separate mention. Unlike the shaken original, this baby is blended. Also unlike its progenitor, it's sweet on the tongue. The Strawberry Marg gets away with cutting off half its name and no one blinks. Finally, as opposed to the toothier straight Margarita, this model is relished mainly by folks in tiny bikinis and brassy shorts. **Serves 2**

2 cups **crushed ice**

4 ounces **white tequila**

2 ounces **triple sec**

1 ounce **strawberry syrup**

1 ounce **freshly squeezed lime juice**

8 **fresh strawberries**

2 **lime wedges** for garnish

1. Add the ice, tequila, triple sec, strawberry syrup, lime juice, and 6 of the strawberries to a blender. Blend well, until everything's chill, dude.

2. Pour the mix into 2 considerable margarita glasses or goblets. Garnish each with 1 of the remaining strawberries and a lime wedge.

A VIRGIN VARIATION: Need something for the driver, or for little sis? Remove the tequila and triple sec, boost the strawberry syrup and lime juice to 2 ounces apiece, and add 2 ounces orange juice.

Magic Movie Drinking Scenes

Many cinematic moments revolve around bars and the consumption of cocktails, tracing back to the early days of the movies. Some moments are more delicate in their depictions of drinking, and some kick the roof off (or roll into the curb). Following are a few transcendent scenes, ones worthy of seeking out and watching if you haven't seen them already. But don't watch them without a drink of your own, or you'll just get thirsty.

1. *Jaws:* Chief Brody, Quint, and Hooper on the boat, sharing manly drinking and scar stories while waiting to catch a really big shark.

2. *Raiders of the Lost Ark:* Not one, but two, great drinking contests, between Miriam and a large Nepalese man and between Miriam and Belloq.

3. *Philadelphia Story:* Macaulay Connor (Jimmy Stewart) and Tracy Lord (Katharine Hepburn) in the garden the night before her wedding, drinking.

4. *Casablanca:* Ilsa, Victor, Captain Renault, and Rick, and, of course, "of all the gin joints, in all the towns, in all the world . . . ."

5. *It's a Wonderful Life:* "I'll have a mulled wine . . .," says Clarence. "Listen, you, we sell hard liquor for people who want to get drunk," replies bartender Nick.

6. *The Thin Man:* The first scene showing Nick Charles (William Powell) is, perhaps, my favorite drinking scene of all. The camera threads its way through a sea of couples dancing in a ballroom, hesitating a bit on this couple, then that couple, then moving on. As the camera gets closer to the bar, it begins to focus in on a gentleman at the bar, telling the bartender, "The important thing is the rhythm! Always have rhythm in your shaking. Now a Manhattan you shake to fox-trot time, a Bronx to two-step time, a dry Martini you always shake to waltz time." The gentleman talking is Nick, married to Nora Charles (Myrna Loy). The couple (along with their dog, Asta—well, the dog doesn't drink) cocktail their way through a series of movies and mysteries.

Taboo

You must whisper when making the drink called Taboo. For some, its refreshingly icy combination is almost unmentionable. Is it the combination of rum and three different fruit juices? Is it the slight touch of simple syrup, or the slightly off-key addition of a full pineapple slice for garnish? In my mind, the Taboo revitalizes one nicely during the late summer, especially when playing checkers or cards on a picnic table that's not too far from the beach house or the beach itself. But for others, its forbidden nature underlines the need to **keep voices at a low pitch** when blending up a batch of this beverage. **Serves 4**

4 cups **cracked ice**

8 ounces **dark rum**

3 ounces **Simple Syrup** (page 7)

2 ounces **fresh pineapple juice**

2 ounces **cranberry juice cocktail**

2 ounces **freshly squeezed lemon juice**

4 **pineapple slices** for garnish

1. Add the ice, rum, simple syrup, pineapple juice, cranberry juice, and lemon juice to a blender. Blend well, always looking over your shoulder to make sure no one is watching. Remember, this drink is Taboo.

2. Pour the mix into 4 well-built goblets and garnish each with a pineapple slice. If no slices are available, or if there is a pineapple shortage, garnish with a pineapple chunk and a murmur.

Topper

According to Esquire's 1957 *Art of Mixing Drinks*, this delectable comes from the friendly north, specifically the Winston Theater Grill in Toronto, Ontario. It is, if I may be so bold, the most elegant blender drink I've ever come across, which makes it **a surefire hit** at any white-coat-and-flowery-skirt lawn party, where the talk centers around gi-normous works of art, Beemers, the latest celebrity snafu, the gawd-awful humidity, and other hip spelling atrocities. **Serves 2**

2 cups **vanilla ice cream**

2 ounces **Cognac**

1 ounce **crème de menthe**

2 **fresh mint sprigs** for garnish

1. Add the ice cream, Cognac, and crème de menthe to a blender. Blend briefly, enough to mingle everything well, but not so much that the drink completely liquefies.

2. Pour into 2 Champagne flutes or other elegant glasses. Garnish each with a mint sprig.

Turning Up the Heat

In the movies, it's always a beach party, it seems, or a pool party, or some sort of bikinis-and-flowered-shorts party where the music's cranked and the pleasurable drinks are flowing and every attendee smiles and laughs and the whole scene just makes you want to be there. Rarely do you see the same exuberance indoors or outdoors during the cold winter or fall days and nights (with the exception of the rare and short holiday party scene)—unless you're watching a dramatization of a Jane Austen novel, where every ball happens inside under majestic chandeliers. Oh, the barrenness of the chillier months, where all swank merrymaking slows to a dull crawl. What is a good spirit to do?

Follow the guidelines of the next few pages and start Turning Up the Heat. The reason, I've decided, that there aren't more modern cold-weather parties (where have the hay rides gone, the bonfires, the well-dressed evening affairs?) is that too many of the absolutely scrumptious hot drinks have been forgotten, or at least aren't much in popular usage. Sure, you can get a Spiked Hot Chocolate in some restaurants that have their wits about them, but where is the singing of the Hot Brick song, or the slinging of the legendary Tom & Jerry?

Don't let festive natures be brought down by Old Man Winter (or any other weather-related cliché). Heat up the room and the bellies of your guests, add a hardy glow to the faces in the room, and start a few new trends: Steaming Spiked Cider at every October celebration, Negus at November events, and don't let a December pass without Wassailing. The warmers in Turning Up the Heat insert that extra sizzle wherever they're served, and thaw out frozen bones, ensuring that everybody partaking forgets, for a while, about ferocious snow or ice that's threatening outside (of course, make sure that guests don't forget about it so much that they decide to drive in it after too many of these temperate favorites).

Turning Up the Heat lets you show off your hotness (with Hot Scotch, the Hot Night Cap, Hot Toddies, and more), whether serving a crowd of frosted pals or wanting to warm up with a singular someone (in this case, maybe a Late Date is in order). Remember, though, that the recipes contained in this chapter tend to use the stove in some way. Using the stove demands a little extra care, as nothing ruins a party like a third-degree burn on you or a guest. Follow simple safety rules and your reputation as the cold-weather host or hostess will grow to great heights as surely as a snowman will melt in June.

Apple Steamer

Fall isn't seen, in some areas, as an optimal drinking season (except by those who think every season is optimal). This fall (or next fall, depending on when you are reading this), turn the tables on this trend with some fall frolics. The best way to do this may be by getting to work on an Apple Steamer, which **warms up any night** when the temperature's starting to drop. As a bonus, you get to say "Apple Steamer" a lot, which is just plain fun.

1 **smallish, firm apple,** cored

1½ ounces **rum**

1 ounce **cinnamon schnapps**

½ ounce **Simple Syrup** (page 7)

½ ounce **water**

1. Preheat the oven to 450°F.

2. Place the apple on a nonreactive cookie sheet or in an ovensafe casserole. Bake for 15 minutes.

3. Add the rum, cinnamon schnapps, simple syrup, and water to a small saucepan. Heat over medium heat for 10 minutes, stirring occasionally.

4. Using tongs or a large spoon, transfer the hot apple to a wide-mouthed mug.

5. Pour the warm rum mixture over the apple. Let sit for 2 or 3 minutes to cool slightly. Drink carefully. Serve with a spoon to eat the apple if your guests are in need of a snack.

A Note: To avoid trouble later on in the constructing process, test to be sure the apple fits in the mug. It would be a shame to get to step 4 and have to halt the whole process.

A Second Note: This is somewhat of a labor-intensive process. Why not up the enjoyment ante by making more than one at a time? That way you and yours can sip together.

A Tip: As there are multiple hot pieces of cookware used here, remember that oven mitts are your friends and overindulgence is not.

Black Stripe

Molasses in a drink? The thought of it **might cause many to turn tail and run**. Don't be one of those, because you'll end up branded with the yellow stripe of the coward (to sound like a best-selling novel of the early twentieth century) instead of being branded (only internally, of course) with the better-tasting Black Stripe.

2½ ounces **dark rum**

1 teaspoon **molasses**

4 ounces **water**

Lemon twist for garnish

1. Add the rum and molasses to a sturdy mug. Stir to combine these 2 distant relatives.

2. In a small saucepan, heat the water to boiling, and then pour it into the mug.

3. Squeeze the lemon twist over the mug, then let it dive in. Stir well, and serve with a warning: it's hot, after all.

Blue Blazer

A bartending firecracker to be lit only by experienced hands, the Blue Blazer is almost more of a fiery novelty than a tasty treat. With that said, it's also a drink first made by one of the originators of this cocktail addiction we find ourselves still happily a part of. I'm speaking here of The Professor, Jerry Thomas. But the Blue Blazer, while warming and while a kick (when done right and looking like **a handheld flame-thrower**), isn't for everyone. It's mostly Scotch and hot water, and it's mixed by lighting the mixture and then tossing it between two mugs, preferably silver mugs. Fire and booze is always a dangerous combo, and adding in the throwing part means that if doing this at home, you may want to try it outside. As The Professor said in his 1862 *Bar-Tender's Guide*, "The novice in mixing this beverage should be careful not to scald himself. To become proficient in throwing the liquid from one mug to the other, it will be necessary for some time to practise [sic] with cold water."

3 ounces **boiling water**

3 ounces **Scotch**

½ ounce **Simple Syrup** (page 7)

Lemon twist for garnish

1. Combine the boiling water, Scotch, and simple syrup in 1 silver-plated mug (or other mug or vessel that is somewhat insulated).

2. Using a long match, carefully light the mixture on fire. Toss it 4 or 5 times from the mug it's in into another similar-sized and insulated mug. Do this carefully, as the flames will continue to burn as you toss.

3. Carefully pour the mixture into a double old-fashioned glass or other wide-bodied 8-ounce glass. A little room is necessary at the top to deal with the heat and flames. If there are still any remaining flames at this point, carefully blow them out. Garnish with the lemon twist.

Café Brûlot

Here's another one for those sideshow-lovers in the reading audience, or for those who can't get enough of Def Leppard's album *Pyromania*. Okay, it could be that the only thing this classic beverage has in common with the 1980s metal band is a mutual gravitation toward fire, but I feel that if you're **lighting the kitchen up,** a little 1980s metal might be in order. Musical jokes aside, Café Brûlot is supposed to be made in a silver bowl. I don't have any silver bowls to loan out, so I'm saying, right here and now, that any pretty vessel can be used to mix the Cognac and spices, as long as the vessel is heatproof. I think a smallish, low-sided, nonreactive saucepan might work and not look too poorly. **Serves 5**

5 ounces **Cognac**

1½ tablespoons **sugar**

4 **orange twists**

4 **lemon twists**

3 **cinnamon sticks**

½ teaspoon **whole cloves**

4 ounces **fresh hot coffee**

1. Add the Cognac, 1 tablespoon of the sugar, the orange and lemon twists, cinnamon sticks, and cloves to a silver bowl (or another heatproof device that can hold the ingredients).

2. Scoop a bit of the Cognac up in a large metal ladle and add the remaining ½ tablespoon sugar to the ladle. Using a long match, carefully light the ladle contents on fire.

3. Without letting the flame go out, pour the Cognac in the ladle back into the silver bowl. Carefully scoop up and pour back the mixture several times to blend it, making sure the fire never goes out.

4. Slowly add the coffee, again making sure the flame doesn't ever go out.

5. Once all the coffee has been added, stir gently until the flames subside. Ladle the mixture into 5 espresso cups. Serve with a modest nod, knowing that you've put on quite a show.

French Chocolate

This is for bitterly cold days when the snow outside has topped the four- or five-foot mark, making the sidewalk and roads impenetrable. Ack! At least there's chocolate to help calm those battered nerves until the sun comes back.

1 ounce **bittersweet chocolate**

1 tablespoon **sugar**

¼ cup **water**

1 cup **milk**

1½ ounces **dark rum**

1. Grate or finely chop the chocolate and place it in the top of a double boiler. Add the sugar and the water. Heat over low heat for 15 minutes, or until the chocolate melts.

2. Meanwhile, in a small saucepan, heat the milk until almost boiling. Add the milk and the rum to the melted chocolate mixture, stir briefly, and pour into a mug.

Glogg

A traditional wine-based cozy staple in the cold northern climes of Sweden and Norway, usually mugged up during Advent (that being the six weeks leading up to Christmas), Glogg traces its warm origin to the 1800s. This lengthy tradition means that when filling the Glogg glasses at winter shindigs (sometimes called win-digs), one must wear clogs, three-quarter–length colorful trousers, and a smile, and be ready to dance at the drop of a hat. The first two requirements ensure the guests' enjoyment; the last two ensure your enjoyment. **Serves 8**

20 ounces **dry red wine**

8 ounces **port**

8 ounces **brandy**

4 ounces **Simple Syrup** (page 7)

16 **whole cloves**

2 teaspoons **cardamom pods**

4 **cinnamon sticks,** broken in half

16 **raisins**

16 **whole unsalted almonds**

1. Add the wine, port, brandy, simple syrup, cloves, cardamom pods, and cinnamon sticks to a large saucepan. Heat well over medium-high heat until steam is rising in full off the pan, but do not allow it to boil.

2. Place 2 raisins and 2 almonds in the bottom of each of 8 large, sturdy mugs or Irish coffee glasses. Pour the wine mixture into the mugs. Drink carefully.

⬆ *A Note: Go with nothing more costly than a medium-priced red wine here, as its taste will be well modified by the other ingredients.*

⬆ *Another Note: Do not, I repeat, do not, forget the raisins and almonds. They are traditional, and there's no call to be insulting a whole region.*

Gloria

Whether sharing an elegant French herb omelet at brunch with Gloria Gaynor (of "Last Night" disco fame), Gloria Estefan (of "Music of My Heart" fame), or Gena Rowlands (who played the title character in the 1980 movie *Gloria*), don't forget to order a round of these classy coffees after the meal is done, and watch the spotlight (and the cheers) aim in your direction.

2 ounces **Cognac**

4 ounces **fresh hot coffee** (I suggest a dark French roast)

1. Add the Cognac to a coffee mug. Add the hot coffee. Stir slightly with a silver spoon and serve warm.

Glühwein

A German holiday-season favorite, the name of this spiced red wine affair translates into "glow wine," from what I've picked up during my German holiday party years. While the drink doesn't actually "glow" in the normal, luminous sense, those consuming it can count on getting the internal glow that makes the winter lose a lot in the formidable department. **Serves 8 to 10**

1 cup **water**

¾ cup **sugar**

2 **cinnamon sticks**

5 ounces **freshly squeezed orange juice**

1 teaspoon **orange zest**

8 **whole cloves**

One 750-milliliter bottle **red wine** (a hearty red works best)

8 to 10 **orange slices** for garnish

1. Add the water, sugar, and cinnamon sticks to a medium-size saucepan. Heat until just boiling, then reduce to a simmer.

2. Add the orange juice, zest, and cloves to the simmering water mixture. Simmer for 30 minutes.

3. Strain the mixture over another pot and discard the cloves and cinnamon. Add the wine to the liquid. Heat over medium heat until everything is toasty, but not boiling.

4. Add 1 orange slice apiece to the bottom of 8 to 10 sturdy goblets. Pour an equal amount of the Glühwein into each glass. *Prost! Zum Wohl!*

Hot Apple Pie

Why not, I ask, go all the way and have actual hot apple pie (à la mode, no matter how far the temperature's dipped) with a Hot Apple Pie? Are you afraid of confusing yourself, or the cute waiter or waitress at the corner bar who's managed to dress rather skimpily, even with the frosty weather? Let me tell you, if making them at home you'll thank yourself, and if you're ordering them, tip a lot and **any confusion mysteriously vanishes**—as rapidly as the dual pies, I'm guessing.

5 ounces **apple cider**

1½ ounces **Tuaca**

1 **cinnamon stick**

Freshly grated nutmeg

Whipped cream (optional)

1. Add the cider to a saucepan. Heat over high heat until on the edge of boiling.

2. Pour the Tuaca into a heat-resistant mug (or, if you have one constructed of thick glass, a large goblet. If using the goblet, run under warm water first to avoid breakage).

3. Add the cinnamon stick to the mug. Pour the apple cider into the mug. Stir briefly.

4. Top with grated nutmeg. If you can't live without it (and why should you?), top also with whipped cream and serve with a spoon.

LIQUEUR SPOTLIGHT

Tuaca

Supposedly created during the Renaissance (when many dandy works of art and literature were created) by Lorenzo de Medici, the wild politician and magnificent patron of artists, Tuaca is an Italian liqueur that flows with citrus and vanilla overtones. It mixes well in tall drinks when combined with ginger ale or other bubbly beverages, and also in more elegant cocktails when shaken with a base liquor. It goes nicely, in addition, in warm drinks such as the Hot Apple Pie (above).

Tuaca became a hit with American servicemen (so the story goes) stationed in Italy during World War II, servicemen who then demanded (politely, I'm hoping) that it be imported to the United States. Beginning in the 1950s, it was. And this is a beautiful thing, as it allows a little bit of Italy to be easily brought into any afternoon.

Hot Brick

Doesn't it seem like there should be an easily chantable, catchy song to go with a drink called Hot Brick? Something like, "Hot Brick, can't get enough, Hot Brick, of **that sweet hot stuff**, Hot Brick, warms me from the inside out, Hot Brick, makes me want to scream and shout!" See, first-class beverages not only make any lackluster afternoon an event, but they also inspire fresh artistic heights. Try out a few Hot Bricks with the beautiful people and see how many verses get added to the above anthem. Remember, we split the profits.

2 ounces **bourbon**

1 ounce **Simple Syrup** (page 7)

½ teaspoon **unsalted butter**

¼ teaspoon **ground cinnamon**

3½ ounces **water**

1. Add the bourbon, simple syrup, butter, and cinnamon to a thick-walled goblet (that has been slightly preheated by running it under warm water) or to a sturdy mug.

2. Heat the water to almost boiling in a small saucepan or in the microwave. When good and hot, pour the water into the goblet over the other ingredients. Stir quickly and serve steaming.

"If you are any good they call you **a 'brick,'** so both ends of this name express the truth."

W.C. WHITFIELD, *Here's How: Mixed Drinks*, 1941

Hot Buttered Rum

The practice of warming a mug of rum and water, a mug of rum with a little spicing, a mug of rum with lemon peel, a mug of rum and cider, a mug of rum and a turkey leg, a mug of rum and a greatcoat, a mug of rum and a quarter bale of straw, a mug of rum and two shoes with holes in the heels, or solely a mug of rum has occurred since rum first made its way into the world—or into English taverns and stories. None of this means that one should heat rum together with any old item. Instead, try the combo below on the next winter's night. It's **more than story-worthy.**

2 ounces **dark rum**

½ ounce **Simple Syrup** (page 7)

3 ounces **apple cider**

2 teaspoons **salted butter**

3 ounces **water**

Cinnamon stick for garnish

Freshly grated nutmeg for garnish

1. Add the rum and simple syrup to a large mug. Then add the cider. (You must add the cider second. It's an olde English tradition.)

2. Add the butter to the mug. Heat the water to boiling in the microwave and add to the mug.

3. Garnish with the cinnamon stick (also use the stick to stir) and a touch of freshly grated nutmeg.

Make Winter Holiday Planning Pleasurable: Serve Festive Mixes

Pulling those hairs out before even stepping into a sparkling ball gown shouldn't happen—planning a holiday party isn't that hard. Start by deciding on the ideal drink for warming up each guest. Wait, make it even easier. Decide on one from the below list and the decision is already made. Now, relax and go stand under the mistletoe.

1. **Steaming Spiked Cider** (page 459)
2. **Spiked Hot Chocolate** (page 457)
3. **Wassail** (page 462)
4. **Mulled Wine** (page 454)
5. **Gloria** (page 442)

Hot CP

World cranberry growers, rejoice. Your hold on the cocktail category (said hold being established by the popularity of the Cosmo, page 159) now expands into hot drinks, thanks to the Hot CP. Print this recipe on every bottle of juice between October 1 and February 28 (that should cover most cold-weather occasions) and you're bound to **increase juice market share.** Don't forget who brought this to your attention, though. I expect a kickback. **Serves 4**

6 ounces **white rum**

4 ounces **cranberry juice cocktail**

4 ounces **water**

3 ounces **Simple Syrup** (page 7)

2 ounces **fresh pineapple juice**

½ teaspoon **ground cinnamon**

½ teaspoon **ground cloves**

4 **cinnamon sticks**

¼ teaspoon **freshly grated nutmeg**

1. Add the rum, cranberry juice, water, simple syrup, pineapple juice, cinnamon, and cloves to a medium-size saucepan. Heat over medium-high heat until hot but not boiling.

2. Add a cinnamon stick to each of 4 mugs. Pour the hot mix equally into the mugs.

3. Sprinkle a hint of nutmeg on top of each mug. Serve with a warning: It's hot.

Hot Night Cap

Is the Night Cap Cocktail (page 265) not sounding quite steamy enough for a post-date invitation up to the pad? Try laying down the Hot Night Cap as **the line** *du jour* when waiting out those awkward moments between date proper and after-date activities. You'll either get slapped or be headed for one of those nights that live in memory like an electric blanket.

1½ ounces **Drambuie**

½ ounce **white crème de cacao**

3½ ounces **milk**

Grated bittersweet chocolate for garnish (optional, but it's sure tasty)

1. Add the Drambuie and crème de cacao to a sturdy mug.

2. Heat the milk gently in a small saucepan or in the microwave. Top the mug with the heated milk. Garnish with the grated chocolate.

⬆ *A Note: Be sensitive here to the heating of the milk. You don't want it to get scalded. With that in mind, heat it to hot, but don't let it boil.*

Hot Scotch

Good golly, is absolutely nothing sacred when our toesies chill? Will any poor bottle left lounging solo in the liquor cabinet be sacrificed for a few minutes of creature comfort? Yes, and gladly, someone said in (I think) January of 1937—or maybe it was '34? Either way, that January brought about the need to dust off the family recipe for Hot Scotch, said recipe having been **passed from warmth-loving generation to warmth-loving generation.** Use it wisely.

2 ounces **Scotch**

¾ ounce **Simple Syrup** (page 7)

Lemon twist for garnish

3 ounces **water**

1. Add the Scotch and simple syrup to an old-fashioned glass (or a glass that wishes it were an old-fashioned glass) that has been cozy with hot water and then dried.

2. Wring the lemon twist over the Scotch and syrup pairing and drop it in the glass.

3. Heat the water to boiling in the microwave and pour over the mixture. Let cool somewhat and dive in.

Hot Toddy

The Hot Toddy traces its roots back, basically, as far as the beginnings of fire and booze and the common cold, though which came first, history is quiet about. I choose to believe the theory of happy accident, with an ancient drinker (let's call him Ed) stumbling around the cave cursing his lack of luck in a primordial language. See, he had contracted a cold on the very eve of the whopping annual spring festival, and therefore wouldn't be taking part, instead relegated to heating water for his accursed aunt's Saturday night bath. Suddenly, Ed tripped on a rock the size of a horse, dropped his clay vessel of fermented liquid into the water he was heating, and also dunked his own head, swallowing much of the mixture in the process. When he shook the water off, not only was his cold a remote memory, but Ed was also **raring for the spring festival** and all the merriment and revelry he could fit into the skin of a bear.

2½ ounces **water**

1½ ounces **brandy**

½ ounce **Simple Syrup**
(page 7)

1. Heat the water in a small saucepan or in the microwave until almost boiling.

2. Add the brandy to an old-fashioned glass (if it's been prewarmed and has thick walls) or a mug. Add the simple syrup and stir once.

3. Pour the hot water over the brandy-syrup mixture. Stir once more.

A VARIATION: I tend to love a lemon peel in many drinks, but here I like to keep it clean. If you need the citrus, feel free to add it.

Drinking Songs for All Occasions

It's reassuring that there are songs in every key and every genre and for the many varied tastes found any time a group of folks are gathered together—and even more reassuring that there are songs about drinking (at least partially) in every key and every genre. Whether it's a softer sound, harder rock, rap, country, blues, or a combination of any and most of the above that's desired for accompanying a cocktail with friends, there's a song out there for you. And just to prove my point:

1. **"Have a Drink on Me,"** by AC/DC
2. **"Gin and Juice,"** by Snoop Dogg
3. **"Escape,"** by Rupert Holmes
4. **"Jockey Full of Bourbon,"** by Tom Waits
5. **"One Bourbon, One Scotch, One Beer,"** by John Lee Hooker
6. **"White Lightning,"** by George Jones

Hot Whiskey Punch

There are nights, bitter nights, when **the temperature has descended**. Nights when going outside without a thick hat that has earmuffs is a dangerous choice. Nights like these are designed for Hot Whiskey Punch. **Serves 5 to 10, depending on the temperature**

1 pint **whiskey**

10 ounces **brandy**

4 ounces **freshly squeezed lemon juice**

Peel of 1 **lemon,** chopped into 4 pieces

1 cup **sugar**

1 quart **water**

1. Add the whiskey, brandy, lemon juice, and lemon peel to a large, heatproof punch bowl. Mix slightly.

2. Add the sugar and water to a medium-size saucepan. Heat until boiling, stirring occasionally. Boil until the sugar is completely dissolved.

3. Pour the boiling water into the punch bowl, over the bourbon mixture. Stir well and ladle into mugs.

Seven More Obscure Facts to Bring Up at the Bar

For even more to jaw upon, see pages 70 and 169.

1. In old England, a whistle was baked into the rim or handle of ceramic cups used by pub patrons. When they wanted a refill, they used the whistle to get service. So when people went drinking, they would "wet their whistle."

2. The shallow Champagne glass originated with Marie Antoinette. Legend has it that it was first formed from wax molds made of her breasts.

3. Tequila is thought to be the first distilled liquor in the Americas. The Aztecs were known to have drunk it before Cortez landed.

4. To "mind your p's and q's" refers to English drinks being served in pints and quarts. In past times, bartenders would advise customers to mind their pints and quarts when they were becoming unmanageable.

5. No drinkable alcohol can be over 190 proof (95 percent alcohol), because at any higher proof, the beverage draws moisture from the air and self-dilutes.

6. At one point in the 1700s, there were 30 rum distillers around Boston and Rhode Island, and approximately 600,000 gallons of rum were being exported annually. There are no rum distillers there today.

7. British troops fighting against the Spanish in Holland during the Dutch War of Independence in the late sixteenth century were introduced to a juniper-flavored spirit, which, when they drank it, provided them with what was soon called "Dutch courage." The juniper-flavored spirit was soon called "gin."

Hot Wine Punch

I've always thought a professional wrestler (called The Urbanite, perhaps, and wearing a tuxedo, or at least a tuxedo T-shirt) should have **a signature move** called the "Hot Wine Punch." Now, if this ever happens, I get royalties, which I will use up mixing more Hot Wine Punch.

Seriously, mixes of warm wine such as this (and Mulled Wine, page 454, its near neighbor) are a fantastic way to use those bottles of wine that have been hanging out on top of the fridge for a year. **Serves 6**

2 cups **water**

5 ounces **Simple Syrup** (page 7)

5 **cinnamon sticks**

Peel of 1 **lemon,** chopped into 1-inch pieces

One 750-milliliter bottle **Cabernet Sauvignon** or **other full-bodied red wine**

1. In a medium-size saucepan, add the water, simple syrup, cinnamon sticks, and lemon peel. Heat until it reaches a rolling boil.

2. Add the wine to the saucepan and heat until warm (it shouldn't take long). Do not let the mixture reboil.

3. Ladle the mixture equally into 6 mugs.

Irish Coffee

There are mornings when the sidewalk is invariably covered by a sheen of slippery ice, when the body itself feels more like an ice cube than a human. On those mornings, take control in the manner of Brian Boru, the last king to rule a united Ireland, and **rev up at least the internal heater** with an Irish Coffee. It may not speed the window's defrosting, but the wait will matter a lot less.

1½ ounces **Irish whiskey**

½ ounce **Simple Syrup** (page 7)

6 ounces **fresh hot coffee**

Whipped cream (optional)

1. Add the whiskey and simple syrup to a mug.

2. Fill the mug with the hot coffee. If that something extra is desired, top with whipped cream.

⬆ **A Note:** *For some, even the simple syrup is too much sweetness early in the day. Leave it out if that describes your morning persona.*

⬆ **Another Note:** *You may use your choice of coffee here, but make it something with bite, such as a Colombian Supremo blend.*

Late Date

I'm not concluding that anyone needs help with their dates—but it never hurts to add a small flame to an evening, and neither does it hurt to spice up matters with cinnamon. The boiling water **adds a hot touch**, too (don't physically touch it, though). These reasons are why a Late Date slips smoothly into late dates (like slipping into something more comfortable, without having to utter such a cliché phrase during the actual date).

Orange wheel

Lemon wheel

2 ounces **Drambuie**

½ ounce **cinnamon schnapps**

3½ ounces **water**

1. Add the orange wheel and lemon wheel to a sturdy mug. Using a muddler or wooden spoon, gently muddle the wheels (but not so hard as to break a sweat).

2. Add the Drambuie and cinnamon schnapps to the mug.

3. In a small saucepan or in the microwave, heat the water until boiling. Pour into the mug. Stir twice. Drink, but carefully.

"They indulged in **no lamentations**, but sturdily produced the schnapps and sandwiches without which no Dane is easily to be tempted out of sight of his home."

JACOB A. RIIS, *The Making of an American*, 1901

Mulled Wine

If you devote too much time to mulling the ingredients over, or spinning a globe in an attempt to find the Isle of Mull in Scotland, the Mulled Wine itself will get cold, losing the property that led you toward wanting it in the first place. Keep the ingredients of Mulled Wine simple: cloves, cinnamon, lemon, sugar, and wine. That way, **the mind is free** to devote itself to more important things. **Serves 6**

One 750-milliliter bottle **dry red wine** (claret is fashionable)

4 **cinnamon sticks,** broken in half

8 to 10 **whole cloves**

2 ounces **Simple Syrup** (page 7)

4 **lemon twists**

3 ounces **brandy**

1. Add the wine to a medium-size saucepan. Add the cinnamon, cloves, simple syrup, and lemon twists. Heat over medium heat for 10 minutes, but do not allow to come to a boil.

2. Add the brandy to the wine and friends. Heat for 5 minutes at least, again refusing the impulse to let it boil. If you'd like to heat it longer, or if it doesn't seem well warmed, leave it on the stovetop for a few more minutes. Carefully ladle into 6 mugs.

🔼 *A Note: The key here is—to underline—keeping the heat high enough to get the mix steaming, but low enough never to boil.*

A VARIATION: I've seen Mulled Wine with a touch of fresh nutmeg grated over the top when serving. I take mine without; however, I see the virtue in nutmeg and never refuse a mug of Mulled Wine with nutmeg when offered one.

Negus

Negus dates as far back as basic brandy and water, plain punch, ales and stouts, and that demon rum. In his *The Fine Art of Mixing Drinks*, David Embury says the drink traces its origin to a Colonel Francis Negus from the time of Queen Anne (the late 1700s). By the time of Charles Dickens's first novel, *The Pickwick Papers*, in 1876, Negus must have been popular, as it's taken by more than one character (or at least it was popular with Dickens). With these facts in mind, **bring out a tray of custard cups** brimming with Negus during the next Dickens caroling party, or the next time a pal shows up wearing a velvet skirt, blouse, and capelet, or a long black cape and top hat. **Serves 8**

One 750-milliliter bottle **tawny port**

1½ quarts **water**

½ cup **sugar**

5 **lemon twists**

2 ounces **freshly squeezed lemon juice**

Freshly grated nutmeg for garnish

1. Pour the port into a large saucepan or a large heatproof bowl.

2. Add the water, sugar, lemon twists, and lemon juice to a large saucepan. Heat over high heat until the sugar has dissolved and the water is boiling.

3. Pour the boiling water mixture into the port. Stir once and serve immediately, ladling into 8 mugs. Top each much with a dusting of grated nutmeg.

"There was another thing that Paul observed. Mr. Feeder, after **imbibing several custard-cups** of Negus, began to enjoy himself."

CHARLES DICKENS, *Dombey and Son*, 1848

Purl

If you think of Charles Dickens only as an author one might read in school, then you really should take another look. Dickens's best works (when I say "best" I mean pretty much every book) stand the test of time, and still boast characters that seem real and storylines that retain their relevance. His novels also are brimming with an array of interesting pubs and friendly (and not-so-friendly) drinkers. These are the launching subject for Cedric Dickens's (Charles's great-grandson) book *Drinking with Dickens* (Hippocrene Books, 1983), a jolly read that picks drinks from the Dickens canon and surrounds them with recipes, quotations, and good times—Cedric's love of the London pubs is evident in every line. A number of the recipes are warmers, and a number of them use porter or ale as a base, such as this recipe for Purl, which uses both, as well as a **dollop of gin for moral measure**. Serve Purl for yourself when reading Dickens, or for a whole posse of Dickens-ites when watching one of the excellent BBC television versions of the novels.

6 ounces **porter**

6 ounces **ale** (a pale ale works)

½ teaspoon **freshly grated ginger**

1 ounce **gin**

½ teaspoon **freshly grated nutmeg**

1. Add the porter, ale, and ginger to a small saucepan. Heat over medium heat until warm but not boiling.

2. Carefully pour the porter-ale mixture into a pint glass that has been slightly warmed (by running it under warm water).

3. Add the gin. Stir once with a spoon. Sprinkle the grated nutmeg over the top.

Spiked Hot Chocolate

This is an easy-listening kind of a mug for those fireside chats couples have when lounging around on a bearskin rug in silk (or flannel, if in the mountains) pajamas as the flames crackle nicely in the background. Simple to make, simple to consume, and **simply delish**, the only difficulty is if there are only enough fixings for an odd number of mugs—that's when the strength of a relationship really shows itself. **Serves 2**

2 cups **milk**

2-ounce chunk **unsweetened chocolate**

¼ cup **sugar**

2 ounces **Frangelico**

1. Add the milk to a medium-size saucepan. Heat on medium heat until warm but not boiling.

2. Grate the chocolate or chop it finely and add it to the milk. Add the sugar. Cook over medium heat for 15 minutes, or until the chocolate has melted and the sugar has dissolved.

3. Add the Frangelico equally to 2 large mugs. Pour the chocolate mix equally into the mugs and stir.

⬆ *A Note: Frangelico is a hazelnut liqueur from Italy. If the hazelnut flavor doesn't do it for you, try this one with Bailey's Irish Cream instead.*

⬆ ***Another Note:*** *If you want to up the decadence level, and have any whipped cream on hand, I think you'll know where to squirt it.*

Drink Like Dickens

If not the top English-language novel writer of all time, Charles Dickens at least rests in the top five. While Dickens's books are fabulous reads (don't you forget it), it's also pretty cool that Dickens loved his pubs and pub dwellers, and it seems clear that he would have been awfully enjoyable to hang out with in said pubs, or on his stoop, or around his fire. Sadly (at least not until time-travel becomes a reality), this hanging with CD isn't possible. It is possible to sip some of the same drinks he did, though, starting with these.

1 Grog (page 301)

2 Negus (page 455)

3 Hot Buttered Rum (page 445)

4 Purl (opposite)

Taking the Party Online

Isn't this electronic age a kick? It makes it really easy to connect with other cocktail lovers from distant parts, as well as drink lovers and drinkers of all shapes and sizes. If you haven't visited the following sites, then I suggest you do (but if you're having an Old Fashioned while surfing in this new fashion, be careful not to spill on the keyboard. It's damaging).

1. Ardent Spirits, at www.ardentspirits.com.
Here you will find the Web site of Gary and Mardee Haidin Regan, two of the world's foremost cocktailians, spirit experts, and bar consultants. You'll find lots of info, well-tested recipes, and a link to sign up for their snazzy e-mail newsletter.

2. DrinkBoy, at www.drinkboy.com.
This site has articles on issues that drinkers obviously appreciate (such as "A Proper Chill"), as well as fresh and classic recipes. There are also links to the DrinkBoy message boards, where cocktail fanatics come to discuss the finer points of bitters and other worthy topics.

3. The Museum of the American Cocktail, at www.museumoftheamericancocktail.org. The museum is "a nonprofit organization dedicated to providing education in mixology and preserving the rich history of the American Cocktail." Amen. The site fills you in on the main museum, as well as dates for traveling exhibits and more.

4. King Cocktail, at www.kingcocktail.com.
Meet King Cocktail himself, Dale DeGroff; look up hot cocktail recipes; and learn about the Beverage Alcohol Resource (BAR), a partnership of leading spirits and cocktails authorities.

5. Modern Drunkard Magazine, at moderndrunkardmagazine.com.
This is pretty boozy stuff, and packed with barfly information and articles (like "Soused Cinema" and "The Booze and I"). It also has a free e-mail newsletter (which doesn't show up with a drink and a five-day beard, as you might expect).

Steaming Spiked Cider

When I was a wee laddie, we lived in a large house on top of a large hill, the ideal house for huge Halloween parties, with a different spooky tableau set up in each of the house's many rooms. We invited numerous friends and neighbors to this big house every Halloween, and my parents would always have hot apple cider as the beverage of choice, an alcoholic version for parents and a virgin variation for kids. The house blossomed with that unmistakable cider aroma, and now whenever I smell apple cider brewing, I think of late fall and winter parties. So, naturally, when starting to throw holiday parties of my own, I worked to remake the recipe I remembered from when I was a kid. **Serves 10**

4 quarts **fresh apple cider**

20 ounces **cinnamon schnapps**

16 ounces **white rum**

1 teaspoon **whole cloves**

¼ teaspoon **freshly grated nutmeg**

10 **cinnamon sticks**

10 **apple slices** for garnish

1. Add the cider to a large nonreactive saucepan. Heat over medium heat for 5 to 10 minutes.

2. Add the cinnamon schnapps, rum, cloves, nutmeg, and cinnamon sticks. Simmer for 15 minutes, but do not let the mixture boil.

3. Once thoroughly warm, ladle the mixture into heatproof mugs, making sure that each mug gets a cinnamon stick. Garnish each mug with an apple slice.

A VIRGIN VARIATION: Remove the rum and schnapps, and add an additional ¼ cup cider and 1 ounce cinnamon extract (available in most gourmet and specialty shops).

⬆ *A Note: Here are three things to remember: 1) Be careful with the cloves when changing the quantity (meaning, too many cloves can take over the flavor); 2) Use apple cider (which is good and cloudy), not apple juice; 3) Boiling boils off some of the alcohol. If the mixture happens to boil, or if you leave it on the stovetop for an extended period, add more rum as needed.*

Thomas & Jeremiah

A lesser-known variation of its older brother the Tom & Jerry (opposite), the Thomas & Jeremiah may have the more nose-in-the-air name, but it's **a steamer for the people**, using the old favorite hot cider united with rum to birth a potent mix. It's potent enough that in the *Here's How: Mixed Drinks* guide, it says after the recipe, "and pleasant dreams, perhaps" beside a picture of a Thomas & Jeremiah devotee sprawled under a table. The lesson? Be sure every table in the vicinity is tall enough before pouring even one of these.

2 teaspoons **light** or **dark brown sugar**

1 **lime wedge**

1½ ounces **white rum**

6 ounces **apple cider**

1. Add the brown sugar and lime wedge to a slightly warmed highball or other tall glass. Using a muddler or wooden spoon, muddle well.

2. Add the rum to the glass and muddle a bit more.

3. Using a small nonreactive saucepan, heat the cider on the stove over medium heat, until it's warm but not boiling.

4. Pour the cider into the glass. Stir 3 times. Serve with a napkin to assure the drinking hand doesn't get too hot.

The Worst Bar Pick-Up Lines

If a laugh is needed at the local watering hole, then roll out one of these gawd-awful lines. Oh, when I say "roll out," I mean as a joke among friends. Never actually try to use one of these (or, at least, don't say you picked them up from me).

1. "Can I see the tag of your shirt?" (look at tag) "Just as I thought, it says 'made in heaven.'"
2. "You must be tired, because you've been running through my mind all night."
3. Line giver: "Can I borrow a quarter?" Reply (one would hope): "Why?" "I want to call my mother and let her know I just met the girl of my dreams."
4. "Do you have a map? I need one because I'm getting lost in your eyes."
5. "I've heard this bar is a meat market. If that's the case, you must be the prime rib."

Tom & Jerry

Another hot drink pointing back toward Jerry Thomas (see the Blue Blazer, page 437, too) and the end of the eighteenth century, the Tom & Jerry has nothing to do with the cat and mouse cartoon (though they may have been named for this drink) and everything to do with the Tom & Jerry mug. A drink can truly be called famous when it has its own style of glassware sharing its name. The T&J mug is short, squat, and silver, and in an ideal world has a rim curling outward and tucking itself back into the sides. It is the ideal mug, I might venture to say, for a mix topped by boiling water or milk (I go for the milk) and containing rum and brandy as well as an egg. It's **a good breakfast beverage** before going ice-skating or snow-person making, but don't take more than a couple unless face down in the snow is the activity of choice.

1 large **egg,** preferably organic, separated

¾ ounce **dark rum**

1 teaspoon **sugar**

¼ teaspoon **ground allspice**

¾ ounce **brandy**

2½ ounces **milk**

Freshly grated nutmeg for garnish

❌ *A Warning: Always use very fresh eggs, and do not serve this drink to the elderly or anyone with a compromised immune system.*

1. In a small bowl, mix the yolk of the egg with the rum, sugar, and allspice. Mix a tad more (just to get the right consistency).

2. In another small bowl, preferably using a handheld blender, whip the white of the egg until it holds stiff peaks. Blend it and the brandy into the yolk mixture.

3. Pour the whole mixture into a Tom & Jerry mug, or any old mug or punch glass that sparkles under the right light and that has been heated via a hot water rinse (don't forget the heating of the mug—it's key).

4. In a small saucepan, heat the milk until it just boils—no longer. Pour it into the mug and stir to mix. Sprinkle a bit of fresh nutmeg over the glass.

Wassail

"Here we come a-wassailing, among the leaves so green; here we come a-wand'ring, so fair to be seen. Love and joy come to you, and to your wassail, too, and God bless you, and send you a happy New Year, and God send you a happy New Year." Now, I don't know what "wassailing" means, but **pour enough of this holiday hit** and you and anyone you know can easily fake it—before you have too much Wassail and start "a-wand'ring," that is. **Serves 8 to 10**

2 quarts **lager-style beer**

5 ounces **Simple Syrup** (page 7)

3 ounces **freshly squeezed lemon juice**

1 teaspoon **freshly grated nutmeg**

1 teaspoon **freshly grated ginger**

1 quart **dark rum**

Apple slices for garnish

Lemon slices for garnish

1. Add the beer, simple syrup, lemon juice, nutmeg, and ginger to a medium-size nonreactive saucepan. Heat the mix over medium-high heat until it is hot, 8 to 10 minutes. Do not let it come to a boil.

2. Add the rum to the saucepan and stir well.

3. Add the apple and lemon slices to a heatproof punch bowl or Wassail bowl (shop for these at the Wassail Store). Pour the hot mixture into the punch bowl. Stir 3 times.

4. Ladle into as many mugs as there are people in the room (provided they've promised to go "a-wassailing").

⊙ *A Note: Always wondered what "wassail" means? It means "be in a good health," and it's proper to say around the New Year.*

Measurement Equivalents

Please note that all conversions are approximate.

Liquid Conversions

U.S.	Imperial	Metric
1 tsp		5 ml
1 tbs	½ fl oz	15 ml
2 tbs	1 fl oz	30 ml
3 tbs	1½ fl oz	45 ml
¼ cup	2 fl oz	60 ml
⅓ cup	2½ fl oz	75 ml
⅓ cup + 1 tbs	3 fl oz	90 ml
⅓ cup + 2 tbs	3½ fl oz	100 ml
½ cup	4 fl oz	120 ml
⅔ cup	5 fl oz	150 ml
¾ cup	6 fl oz	180 ml
¾ cup + 2 tbs	7 fl oz	200 ml
1 cup	8 fl oz	240 ml
1 cup + 2 tbs	9 fl oz	275 ml
1¼ cups	10 fl oz	300 ml
1⅓ cups	11 fl oz	325 ml
1½ cups	12 fl oz	350 ml
1⅔ cups	13 fl oz	375 ml
1¾ cups	14 fl oz	400 ml
1¾ cups + 2 tbs	15 fl oz	450 ml
2 cups (1 pint)	16 fl oz	475 ml
2½ cups	20 fl oz	600 ml
3 cups	24 fl oz	720 ml
4 cups (1 quart)	32 fl oz	945 ml
		(1,000 ml is 1 liter)

Weight Conversions

U.S./U.K.	Metric
½ oz	14 g
1 oz	28 g
1½ oz	43 g
2 oz	57 g
2½ oz	71 g
3 oz	85 g
3½ oz	100 g
4 oz	113 g
5 oz	142 g
6 oz	170 g
7 oz	200 g
8 oz	227 g
9 oz	255 g
10 oz	284 g
11 oz	312 g
12 oz	340 g
13 oz	368 g
14 oz	400 g
15 oz	425 g
1 lb	454 g

Oven Temperature Conversions

°F	Gas Mark	°C
250	½	120
275	1	140
300	2	150
325	3	165
350	4	180
375	5	190
400	6	200
425	7	220
450	8	230
475	9	240
500	10	260
550	Broil	290

Index
of Drinks by Primary Liquor

Note: *Italicized* page references indicate photographs.

General Index

Notes: *Italicized* page references indicate photographs.
Liquor entries include recipes where liquor is a secondary ingredient. See page 465 for Index of Drinks by Primary Liquor.